COLD WAR, COOL MEDIUM

TELEVISION, McCARTHYISM, AND AMERICAN CULTURE

Film and Culture
A series of Columbia University Press
Edited by John Belton

THOMAS DOHERTY

COLD WAR, COOL MEDIUM

TELEVISION, McCARTHYISM, AND AMERICAN CULTURE

COLUMBIA UNIVERSITY PRESS   NEW YORK

Columbia University Press
Publishers Since 1893
New York Chichester, West Sussex

Library of Congress Cataloging-in-Publication Data
Doherty, Thomas Patrick.
    Cold War, cool medium : television, McCarthyism, and American culture /
Thomas Doherty.
        p.   cm.—(Film and culture)
    Includes bibliographical references and index.
    ISBN 0–231–12952–1 (acid-free paper)
    1. Television and politics—United States—History.   2. Television broadcasting of
news—United States—History.   3. McCarthy, Joseph, 1908–1957.   4. Anti-communist
movements—United States—History.   5. United States—Politics and government—
1945–1953.   6. United States—Politics and government—1953–1961.   7. United States—
Social life and customs—1945–1970.   8. Cold War—Social aspects—United States.
I. Title.   II. Series.

PN1992.6.D64 2003
791.45'658—dc21

                                                                            2003051501

∞

Columbia University Press books are printed on permanent and durable acid-free paper.

Printed in the United States of America

c 10 9 8 7 6 5 4 3 2 1

CONTENTS

PREFACE AND ACKNOWLEDGMENTS

Sen. Joseph R. McCarthy, who died in 1957, lives as a metaphor. No time-bound demagogue, he has long since metamorphosed into a Cold War totem and universal bogeyman, nearly as vivid in the present as he was in the past. Television—a site for his ascent, the stage for his downfall—continues to keep his image vital and alive.

Viewed through a gauze of memory and motives, newsreel clips and video snippets, McCarthy and the era named after him are hot combat zones in a fierce Kulturkampf over Cold War America. The man and his "-ism" have launched a multitude of memoirs, biographies, critical studies, and documentaries, many as ideologically driven as their subject. The historian who presumes to lob another volume onto the pile needs a clear rationale; the reader deserves a frank confession of allegiances.

The outlook for this study of the phenomenon known as McCarthyism is televisual. Rather than a retrospective glance backward via interpretative scholarship, I have viewed the period dating roughly from the late 1940s to the mid-1950s through the lens of television programming and the contemporary commentary about the embryonic medium. Save for a few necessary flash forwards, the window into this chamber of the American past has been the television screen.

Unfortunately, the extant materials are easier read about than looked at. All historians are bedeviled by problems of access and imagination, but researchers into the early days of television have special reason to whine. Until the advent of magnetic videotape in 1956, television came live or on film. Networks treated the heritage haphazardly, and the official repositories of the federal government were oblivious to its future significance. Counterintuitive as it seems, the 35mm film used by the newsreels to chronicle the pretelevision history of the 1920s, the 1930s, and the 1940s is sharper, clearer, and more readily retrievable than the live telecasts of the 1950s. Caught in the interregnum between film and videotape, the passage exists in a kind of moving-image lacuna.

Whenever possible I have watched the original telecasts, but much enticing material is just plain gone, never recorded, vanished into the ether. In these instances, I have relied on transcripts of the shows, trade press accounts, and newspaper reports. Among the pioneering commentators on the medium, I found Jack Gould of the *New York Times*, John Crosby of the *New York Herald Tribune*, Marya Mannes of the *Reporter*, and Dan Jenkins of the *Hollywood Reporter* especially reliable and astute (meaning that I tended to agree with them).

The archival gaps in the television record are magnified by a problem of perception. Since its official coming out party at the New York World's Fair in 1939, television has undergone a series of tectonic changes, audiovisual revolutions akin to the leap from silent film to sound cinema or from theatrical motion pictures to home television. The difference in the programming and technology of television in the 1950s and television in the 1960s and 1970s (during the era of Three Network Hegemony) and in the 1980s and 1990s (during the Age of Cable) is a gulf that the single word *television* cannot adequately straddle.

However, that one word is used to describe the full life span of the medium, a linguistic holdover that is not only imprecise but deceptive. Yet to invent a neologism—paleo-video, classical television, IKE-TV—seems unduly cute. "Television" will do, with the caution that television then was a different medium than television later, or now, and broadcast over a different cultural atmosphere.

Within that atmosphere, the question of political allegiance weighed heavily—the answer, or the refusal to answer, shaping or stunting a life. Today, the stakes are not nearly so high, but few cultural historians who venture onto the field emerge unscathed from the polemical firefights that swirl around McCarthyism. Thus, though the pages that follow are in the end more about the medium than the man and the ism—a portrait of television and American culture at a pivotal moment in the history of each—to answer that question once asked under duress and subpoena seems a necessary gesture of self-identification rather than self-incrimination. So, like the Cold War liberal, that now nearly extinct creature, I believe it is not mutually exclusive to conclude that Soviet communism posed a menace to human freedom and that Joseph R. McCarthy was a scoundrel.

While writing the book, I have exploited the expertise and challenged the patience of a number of friends and colleagues. David Weinstein generously shared his knowledge of the forgotten fourth network, DuMont. Richard Kozsarski and Gary Edgarton permitted me to rework material on the Kefauver crime committee hearings and the Cohn-Schine affair originally written under their aegis for *Film History* and the University Press of Kentucky, respectively. My colleagues in the American Studies Department at Brandeis

University were unfailingly encouraging, especially my fellow travelers in Cold War history, Joyce Antler, Jacob Cohen, and Stephen Whitfield. Jennifer Crewe and Roy Thomas at Columbia University Press guided the manuscript and encouraged the author. Contributing factoids, tapes, and suggestions were Glenn C. Altschuler, Susie Carruthers, John Chambers, Jim Deutsch, Ester Kartiganer, Daniel Leab, James Mandrell, David Marc, Sofia McAllister, Jeffrey Miller, Dane Morrison, Susan Ohmer, David Oshinsky, Michael Schiffer, Jeffrey Shandler, Alexandra Silverberg, and Tom van der Voort.

Of course, a media scholar is always dependent on the kindness of archivists: Madeline Matz, Rosemary Hanes, and Joe Belian at the Motion Picture Division of the Library of Congress; Michael Buening and Jane Klain at the Museum of Television and Radio in New York City; Dan Einstein at the UCLA Film and Television Archives; Michael C. De Mono at Actors' Equity Association; David Lombard at CBS; Rona Tuccillo at Time-Life; Scott Roley and Anita Smith at the Harry S. Truman Library; Beverly Lindy and Susan Naulty at the Richard M. Nixon Library; Rodney A. Ross of the legislative branch of the National Archives; Barbara Hall at the Production Code Administration archives of the Margaret Herrick Library, Trevor James Bond at the Washington State University Libraries, Carolyn Cole at the Los Angeles Public Library, Margaret Appleman at the Martin Luther King Library in Washington, D.C., and Linda Kloss at the Federal Bureau of Investigation. I have also been greatly aided by a necessarily nameless coterie of buffs and collectors operating on the frontiers of American copyright law.

As always, and above all, the last and best name to name belongs to my wife, Sandra.

COLD WAR, COOL MEDIUM

ONE

VIDEO RISING

Before fiber-optic cable and satellite dishes served up a buffet of triple-digit narrowcasting, before videocassette recorders and camcorders put the means of replay and production in the hands of the people, before even the ruthless network troika of NBC, CBS, and ABC acquired dominion over prime-time programming, American television was a different kind of creature comfort. At the halfway mark of the twentieth century, the seedling medium had not yet blossomed into a garden of color, cable, and World Wide Web-bing. Their TV did not look like our TV.

Condemned to a mere handful of channel selections, paleo-televiewers adjusted rooftop antennae to receive clear reception and trudged vast distances across carpeting to rotate dials manually. Drab two-tone images in black and white, fuzzy and flippy, beamed forth from a pitifully small screen. The sets were serious pieces of furniture, mammoth in girth, encased in walnut or mahogany, molded to dominate a living room and displace the upright radio from the family hearth. Once common parlance, even the video lingua franca of the day has all but lapsed into anachronism: "snow," "ghosts," "vertical rollover," "horizontal tear," "airplane flutter," "rabbit ears," "test patterns," "vacuum tubes," "Please stand by, we are experiencing technical difficulties," and—that bracing red alert, perhaps a portent of things to come—THIS IS A TEST OF THE EMERGENCY BROADCASTING SYSTEM.

The half-forgotten phrases and extinct folkways recall the tender years of a millennial force. The shows were mainly live, the programming scarce, and the viewers still somewhat spellbound before a miraculous new communications technology. In the early 1950s, as war raged in Korea and McCarthyism roiled at home, television first mounted its full-scale incursion into American culture. Growing up in parallel waves, the Cold War and the cool medium negotiated a cultural pact that demanded adjustments on both sides of the dial.

The terms of the contract were updated almost on a yearly basis, but eventually one partner gained the upper hand and resolved a vexing point of contention. Of the incalculable ways that television transformed American life—in family and friendships, leisure and literacy, consumer habits and common memories—the expansion of freedom of expression and the embrace of human difference must be counted among its most salutary legacies. During the Cold War, through television, America became a more open and tolerant place.

The conventional wisdom claims otherwise. Not just an aesthetic blight, television is cast as coconspirator in the conformities and repressions of Cold War America. Purveyor of sedative pabulum, facilitator of the blacklist, handmaiden to McCarthyism, the small screen abetted moral cowardice, retarded intellectual growth, and smothered resistance. The dark times and the dumb medium deserved each other.

So dismal a reputation reflects more than critical payback from highbrow tastemakers and wounded liberals. The acute videophobia expresses the resentment of partisans of the sacred word at the rise of the sordid image. Before the primacy of television, democracy in America had always been linked to writing and literacy. For the Enlightened thinkers of the Revolutionary War era, pamphlets and books were invested with an almost divine aura. Comprehended in silence and pondered in tranquility, the founding documents presupposed a well-read, rational citizenry. The Declaration of Independence, *The Federalist Papers*, and the U.S. Constitution were binding contracts, typeset and permanent, set down in black and white, the secular scripture for a modern demos. "*Litera scripta manet*," cautioned the epigrammatic Benjamin Franklin in his *Autobiography*, "the written word remains," and who as author, publisher, and founder of the U.S. Postal Service was as good as his word. It is the motto engraved above the entranceway of the National Archives in Washington, D.C., an agency still more scrupulous about the collection and preservation of pieces of paper than film reels or video cassettes.

Like radio and motion pictures, television rebuked that literate faith. Instantly accessible and immediately apprehensible, it transmitted an alphabet of meaning that required only the senses of sight and sound, not the tedious diligence of book learning. Broadcasting moving images into the home, giving pictures to the radio signals, the hybrid medium grew to be exponentially more powerful and penetrating than its parents. The greatest leap forward in the graphic revolution, television radiated through the life of the present and the memory of the past with a force that dwarfed the impact of the other media. Soon print itself came to seem the hieroglyphics of a lost civilization.

The rise of video was concurrent with a frigid season in the Cold War, a temporal bond that suggests a codependent relationship. Orbiting around television, a cluster of transformations in American culture comes into focus. Economic prosperity and national security, the twin obsessions of the generation forged by the Great Depression and the Second World War, began to share space with freedom of expression and civil rights, the obsessions of the next generations. As prosperity became an expectation not a dream, as the dread of social insecurity faded amid the cornucopia of postwar affluence, the nexus of American culture folded ever inward—to information and expression, to media access and on-screen visibility. Collaborator and catalyst, television acted as a featured player in the action.

Beset from birth by the harsh elements of the Cold War, television came of age oppressed by a "witchhunt atmosphere" and "traumatized by phobias," asserted Erik Barnouw, the indispensable historian of American broadcasting. "It would learn caution, and cowardice." True enough—but it would also utter defiance and encourage resistance. The Cold War and the cool medium worked out an elastic arrangement, sometimes constricting but ultimately expanding the boundaries of free expression and relaxing the credentials for inclusion. Within a few short years, television had become the prized proscenium in American culture, and the stage was open to an array of unsettling opinions and unruly talent.

A Television Genealogy

As conventionally personified, the development of television reenacts the life stages of man: an embryonic term of gestation (1939 to 1945), infant steps (1946 to 1950), adolescent growing pains (1951 to 1960), mature adulthood (1961 to 1980), and then, after being grafted onto coaxial cables and computer networks for home delivery, mutation into an entirely new species (1981 and beyond). Like the illustrations in a worn biology textbook, where the amphibian crawls from the sea and shape-shifts through the millennia into mammal, slouched ape, upright Neanderthal, and finally to business-suited Dad, briefcase in hand, walking purposefully to work, television is forever aborning technologically into a crisper, sleeker, toned-up model. Of course, the Darwinian conceit presumes not only that television has attained a heightened stage of evolutionary development but that it is actually going somewhere. Alas, the final destination of television must remain an open question, but the history of the medium— what it once was and what it once meant—is more readily answered. By rerunning the programs, freezing the frames, and reading between the lines, the viewer discovers a picture of Cold War America that belies the black-and-white clichés in cable syndication and current scholarship.

Unjaded as yet to the miracle of light and sound, Cold War Americans looked upon television not as a lesser order of moving imagery, but as a thrilling new household appliance. The monochromatic, washed-out images seen on surviving kinescopes fail to conjure the initial wonder at the magic show.[1] Spectators weaned on high-definition screens gleaming with computer graphics and rumbling with digital sound are apt to find the pictures slow, static, and stunted. Upon first sight, however, the video vista was not a vast wasteland but a cool oasis beheld with eyes of delight and discovery.

Well, not quite all eyes. "In my frayed estimation, television today is nothing more than agitated decalcomania rampant on the tavern wall and in the family living room," humorist Fred Allen snarled in 1948. "For entertainment, television offers loquacious puppets, stout ladies bending over ovens assembling cucumber ragouts, blurred newsreels, assorted sporting events, antiquated B pictures, and a few entertaining shows." Allen's jaundiced perspective summarized elite opinion on the reviled "boob tube," an attitude in his case fueled also by the flop sweat of an eminent radio star facing obsolescence. Admittedly, Allen's cranky catalogue of scheduled programming rings true. Hollywood had yet to sell any A-picture attractions to its despised rival, and primitive items like *The Adventures of Oky Doky, I Love to Eat, Kukla, Fran, and Ollie*, and *Film Shorts* typified the banal lineup during a paltry few hours of prime-time telecasting. Worth remembering too is the social venue for television spectatorship, as likely in 1948 to be watched in noisy taverns as in private homes.

By the middle of the next decade, television had become a living room fixture, ascendant not only over radio but motion pictures and, so it seemed, all of American culture. The seizure of media mastery occurred with dizzying speed. Envisioned and perfected for the 1939 World's Fair, dormant commercially during the Second World War, television took off as soon as V-J Day sounded the starting gun for the postwar boom in consumer spending. To register the breakneck pace, metaphors of plague and pestilence flowed from the pens of wary journalists. Aerial antennae sprout like noxious weeds from apartment rooftops and suburban homes while video-born catchphrases spread like viruses through the vocabulary of children. A simple statistic suggests the scale of the invasion: in 1949 television was a luxurious indulgence in one out of ten American homes; in 1959, television was essential furniture in nine out of ten American homes.

As early as 1951, guilt-mongering advertisements warned parents that their children would "suffer in school and be shunned by their friends" if the family resisted buying a television set. The prospect of social ostracism was real

---

1. Kinescopes, or "kinnies" to insiders, are 16mm films, shot straight off television monitors, that preserved a tiny fraction of live telecasts before the introduction of videotape recording in 1956.

Motion picture magic in the living room: an advertisement for DuMont Television (1949).

enough. Soon it would be impossible to participate in schoolyard chatter or watercooler banter without the common reference point of the small screen. No longer an exotic new appliance but basic survival gear, television became an artery as vital to the pulse of American life as the refrigerator humming in the kitchen. More necessary: forced to choose between fresh food and home entertainment, a solid majority of Cold War Americans opted to jettison the ice box for that other box.

Though not yet granted the prerogatives it would take as due recognition of its supreme status—unrestricted entry into every nook and cranny of mortal existence—television in the early years of the Cold War was already changing the way the nation did business. In 1954, NBC President Sylvester "Pat" Weaver, the reigning visionary of network programming, declared that television would soon become "the shining center of the home," transmitted in color, recorded on magnetic tape, "with world wide news service, symphony orchestras and opera companies, with telementaries of still undreamed magnitude, with entertainment that in part becomes highly literate, that serves every segment of our population with programming that is valuable and rewarding." If Weaver's forecast of a highbrow prime-time lineup was mere wishful thinking, his vision of the shining centrality of ever higher-tech television in American culture was a dead-on prophecy.

Nowhere was the impact of television felt more keenly than in Hollywood, hometown of the precedent and soon-to-be subordinate moving-image medium. The arrival of television in 1946 coincided with classical Hollywood's last great season, when a weekly audience of 90 million paying spectators flocked to ornate palaces and homey neighborhood theaters. In a few short years, what Hollywood called "free television" (the implication being that anything free could not be worth much) had metastasized to lethal levels. "TV Audience Now Equals Films" blared a frightful headline in the *Hollywood Reporter* in 1950. The forced boosterism of studio sloganeering ("Movies Are Better Than Ever!" protesteth the official motto) echoed like a whistle past the graveyard.

Every week Hollywood tallied up the escalating ratings for television, gaped at the plummeting box office revenues, and noted the causal relation between small-screen highs and big-screen lows. The Friday Night Fights on *The Gillette Cavalcade of Sports* (1948–1960) provided a weekly lesson in connecting the dots. On October 26, 1951, the epochal match between the aging former champion Joe Louis and the gritty challenger Rocky Marciano emptied theaters like a smoke bomb. Television "tossed Joe Louis right into our living room on his back," marveled the television critic Dan Jenkins, a lifelong fan of the Brown Bomber. "If it had to happen, we'd much rather have read about it in the cold impersonal print of Saturday morning's paper. But it did prove that TV has all the impact of one of Marciano's punches." Alarmed motion picture executives contemplated a future where the local Bijou crumbled under the nightly onslaught of living room exhibitions comprised of "big fights, maybe the World Series switched into night-time play, the big football games, or incidents of national interest." Like Joe Louis, Hollywood played the slow, lumbering has-been, down for the count against the scrappy new kid, swift, lean, and hungry.

The turnabout in the media hierarchy foretold and facilitated other shifts. At the start of the new decade, with a suggestive synchronicity, the Cold War and the cool medium collided on the calendar. As simultaneous threats on the international and domestic fronts reached fever pitch, the publication of a thin volume called *Red Channels* took the fight onto a field that sooner or later all future American conflicts would enter.

Red and Other Menaces

On the morning of June 25, 1950, North Korean military forces burst south through a line of latitude on the Korean Peninsula. The Korean War, a three-year conflict fought to a tense stalemate in a remote locale, was the bloody backdrop to a superpower rivalry that was never merely ideological. Korea would later be labeled "the forgotten war," but between 1950–1953 Americans were reminded of it in the most tangible ways: newspaper headlines, radio bulletins, newsreels, television reports, and the delivery of 36,914 notices from the Department of Defense containing regrettable information.

A brutal chapter in the fierce struggle with communism, the Korean War was allegedly an international "police action" by the United Nations, but the United States manned the front lines in the order of battle. Lost to the West in 1949, the People's Republic of China ("Red China" to all but her allies) was perceived as the puppetmaster pulling the North Korean strings while behind Red China was the guiding hand of the Soviet Union. From command central in the Kremlin, the Sino-Soviet alliance gained force and moved forward, a red tide infused with a yellow menace, poised to thrust the dagger of the Korean Peninsula into the heart of Japan and from there move south into Indochina, then west to India and Pakistan, and inexorably eastward across the Pacific. Taught by World War II propaganda films to appreciate the march of totalitarianism on a map, Americans didn't need Hollywood to draw them the big picture. Just as black swastikas had once slithered outward from the heart of Germany to spread over Poland and France, red hammer and sickles bled into Eastern Europe and Asia and seemed poised to cover the world.

Back on native ground, the arrest of the Soviet spies Julius and Ethel Rosenberg confirmed the presence of a homegrown fifth column to the overseas menace. In 1949 the reputedly scientifically backward USSR, ahead of schedule and with shocking suddenness, had ended the U.S. monopoly on atomic weaponry. Top secret information had clearly changed hands, and the Federal Bureau of Investigation (FBI) soon ensnared two of the principle transfer agents.

An international cause celèbre and the most sensational spy case of the Cold War, the arrest, trial, and execution of the Rosenbergs sounded a steady backbeat to the clamor over communist subversion. Again, the lesson from the last war—that the ideological campaign for hearts and minds sustains the frontline combat—took hold for the current war. Punctually enough, the Rosenberg case, which began with the arrest of Julius on July 17, 1950, and crested with the execution of the couple on June 19, 1953, marked time with the outbreak and resolution of the Korean War, which ended with a formal truce signed on July 27, 1953.

Viewed through the tunnel vision of television history, the tandem escalations of the Cold War coincide neatly with another red-letter date. On June 22, 1950, the editors of *Counterattack*, a four-page "newsletter of facts on communism," issued a slim volume with weighty impact: *Red Channels: The Report of Communist Influence in Radio and Television*, a listing of entertainers deemed to be Communist Party members or to have like-minded opinions and associations ("fellow travelers" in the argot of the day). The publication was the work product of three former FBI men organized as an outfit called American Business Consultants: Theodore C. Kirkpatrick, the public voice of the organization; John G. Keegan, the business brains; and Francis J. McNamara, the hands-on editor of *Counterattack*, the main source for *Red Channels*. Vincent Hartnett, another self-motivated anticommunist who later spearheaded a kindred outfit called AWARE, Inc., penned the introduction. By printing so many names between covers, *Red Channels* formalized the previously ad hoc practice of blacklisting in the broadcasting industry.

The introduction to *Red Channels* charged the Soviet Union with an "increasing domination of American broadcasting and television, preparatory to the day when . . . the Communist Party will assume control of this nation as the result of a final upheaval and civil war." In classic Leninist fashion, a vanguard elite sought to harness the tools of mass communication to indoctrinate Americans with "Communist ideology and pro-Soviet interpretation of current events." Admittedly, few entertainers were card-carrying communists, but all too many were useful idiots and reliable dupes. "Our so-called 'intellectual' classes—members of the arts, the sciences, and the professions—have furnished the Communist Party USA with the greatest number of these classifications," the editors lamented. "Red Fascism has exploited scores of radio and TV stars at pro-Soviet rallies, meetings, and conferences."

After the warm-up, *Red Channels* went about the business of enumeration, "an alphabetical index of names," 151 in number, from Larry Adler ("harmonica player") to Lesley Woods ("actress—radio"). The artists listed ranged from lockstep Communist Party hacks, to mainstream liberals, to bewildered innocents; the offenses encompassed everything from blunt avowals of party-line doctrine to innocuous expressions of progressive sentiment. It was one playbill on which actors did not want to see their names printed and their credits listed.

Even as *Red Channels* showed its colors, a specter more haunting than even communism shadowed Cold War America. The atomic bomb and, after 1952, the hydrogen bomb augured an apocalyptic payoff to the superpower face-off. For the first time in human history, the prospect of species annihilation, not just military defeat or cities laid to waste, loomed as a decided possibility. The cultural fallout from the Bomb settled all over American culture, but a series of made-for-television events sent out particularly intense shock waves.

On the morning of February 6, 1951, Los Angeles stations KTLA and KTTV transmitted the first live images of an atomic blast to a select but no doubt attentive local audience. Positioned atop Mount Wilson, some 250 miles from the atomic test site at the Las Vegas Proving Ground, the cameras caught "the flash of eerie white light" from the experimental detonation. In Las Vegas,

Atomic age affluence: viewed from downtown Las Vegas, a nuclear plume looms on the horizon (February 6, 1951).

KTLA reporter Gil Martin delivered play-by-play commentary and interviewed witnesses. The mushroom cloud was clearly visible from atop the hotels and casinos in the desert oasis.

The next year, progress in nuclear science coincided with advances in television technology. At precisely 12:30 P.M. Eastern Standard Time, on April 22, 1952, from the wastelands of Yucca Flat, Nevada, another demonstration of an atomic bomb explosion was telecast live, this time coast to coast. "The home audience heard the call of 'bomb away' and listened to the counting of the seconds and saw a flash that, for a few seconds, blackened TV screens with a dark penumbra around the central point of light that was the blast," reported the trade magazine *Broadcasting/Telecasting*. Viewers squinted to discern a tiny white spot in a wall of pitch black, unaware that the white pinhole centered in the blackness resulted from an optical malfunction: the orthicon tube in the pickup camera had blacked out under the blinding light of the blast. Though the announcer gaped at the "beautiful, tremendous, and angry spectacle," many viewers complained about poor audio quality and erratic reception distorted by geometric swirls and diagonal bars. With characteristic glibness, *Variety* panned the show under the headline "A-Bomb in TV Fluff Fizzles Fission Vision."

On March 17, 1953, the Atomic Energy Commission (AEC) and the Civil Defense Administration staged a more successful television special, again live from Yucca Flat. To simulate the impact of an atomic explosion on an average homestead, a fabricated two-household community dubbed "Doom Town" was constructed, with nuclear family mannequins occupying each abode, standing upright, not sitting around a television set. Pooling their resources, all the major networks telecast the preparations for countdown, the instant of the blast, and the aftermath. The special show was presented as an unsponsored public service program because, explained *Washington Post* television critic Sonia Stein, commercial advertisers "did not feel eager to associate their products with the horrors of war exemplified by atomic bombing."

Viewers watched trucks unloading U.S. Army troops to within 3,500 feet of ground zero. A long shot framed the detonation site, a tall slim tower, eerily illuminated by floodlights. Then the show began. "The tremendous atomic burst over Doom Town in Nevada sent TV screens across the nation into 'wobbles,' and a brief blackout at the instant of the blast," observed a shaken reporter for the wire services. "But then the picture returned and tense watchers at their TV sets got their clearest look yet at what an atomic explosion is." Seconds later, a narrow cloud "like a tall thin mushroom" billowed upward and then changed shape "into something approaching an irregular upside down 'L.'" The newsmen near ground zero—Walter Cronkite for CBS and Morgan Beatty for NBC, at a site seven miles from the tower, and Chet Huntley for ABC, huddled with the GIs less than two miles away—spoke of ground tremors and dust in their eyes. For viewers who missed the live telecast, all the networks scheduled kinescope reruns later that night. Imagine, warned civil defense authorities, if "one of the homes belonged to *you* and *your* family was inside."

Later that year, the detonation of the hydrogen bomb upped the ante by megatons. Though set off at 7:15 A.M. on November 1, 1952, on the island of Eniwetok in the Marshall Islands, the deed was not formally announced to the nation until the afternoon of Sunday, November 16, when AEC chairman Gordon Dean confirmed reports from loose-lipped sailors who had broken the news—and security—in letters home. To render the scale of the holocaust, newspapers played up the local angle, superimposing the H-bomb's blast radius on aerial maps of hometown environs. No heartland was too remote to escape the apocalypse, no suburb promised safe haven from the radioactive thundercloud emanating from the blistering furnace at ground zero.

On that very same Sunday, the CBS news magazine *See It Now*, "a document for television" hosted by the famed broadcaster Edward R. Murrow, jumped on the late-breaking news to ruminate on the arrival of the thermonuclear age. Reporting from Washington, correspondent Bill Downs commented that the occasion "seems to me to be more a day for searching the human soul perhaps than any kind of scientific celebration" and suggested that "perhaps the Atomic Energy Commission would have been wise to have made the announcement *before* today's church services." In grim, sulfuric tones, Downs reported that "we've now designed mankind's most devastating weapon, a weapon that will make Hiroshima and Nagasaki and the Bikini tests and the rest of them look puny by comparison." Groping for points of comparison, he explains that "the experts tell us that the difference between the atomic bomb and the hydrogen bomb is the difference between a 12-gauge shotgun and a 16-inch cannon." He then recites a long list of cities around the globe—New York, Moscow, Peking—that would be utterly obliterated by a blast, though naturally the destruction would not be limited to ground zero. Murrow then quotes Albert Einstein's prediction that "radioactive poisoning of the atmosphere and hence the annihilation of any life on earth has been brought within the range of technical possibility." At the end of the show, the host apologizes not for the message but the medium. Regrettably, "so far there is no film available and there is not likely to be any available of the first hydrogen bomb."

Murrow failed to reckon with the photographic compulsions of the moving picture age. On April 1, 1954, the H-bomb ("for Hydrogen," explained a now-chastened *Variety*, "also for Hell") made its screen debut when film of the blast was finally released to the newsreels and television. Projected on the motion picture screen, in crisp 35mm, the stark black-and-white cloud expanded spectacularly, ominously, roaring upward and outward, engulfing and obliterating an entire island from the face of the earth, a science fiction fantasy in a documentary format. "First Films . . . H-BOMB BLAST" blared the Universal-International Newsreel title card as the awed voice of narrator Ed Herlihy harkened "the second era—the thermonuclear era—of the atomic age." Graphic illustrations helpfully brought home the magnitude of the explosion and the immediacy of the threat. "Now, for dramatic effect, we superimpose [the explosion] on the skyline of New York." As the fireball from the "awful destructive power of the H-bomb" balloons out to scorch the horizon, Herlihy notes that "the heart of the metropolis would be instantaneously transformed into an inferno while shock waves devastated the rest of the city."[2]

---

2. Unwilling to leave motion picture audiences with the aftertaste of annihilation before the unspooling of the featured attraction, the newsreel followed its terrifying ten-minute report on the H-bomb with an upbeat "Hollywood Fashion Holiday," wherein "starlets Mamie Van Doren, Ruth Hampsen and other lovelies model an eye-appealing array of summer styles, ranging from travel suits to swim wear, a lovely picture."

Yet because the theatrical newsreels were already being supplanted by news on television, the force of the H-bomb hit closest to home with the telecast of a 28-minute film entitled *Operation Ivy*, a joint venture of the Department of Defense and the Atomic Energy Commission. A creepy blend of civil defense stiffness and cinematic slickness, *Operation Ivy* tells the story of the first H-bomb explosion, a device nicknamed "Mike." Awaiting detonation from aboard the deck of a U.S. Navy cruiser in the Marshall Islands, actor Reed Hadley, best known as the dauntless police captain on CBS's *Racket Squad* (1951–1953), lights a pipe and promises viewers that "we'll soon see the largest explosion ever set off on the face of the earth—that is, the largest that we know about." The success of the mission is something of a gamble, but after all "the uneasy state of the world puts everything on a gambling basis." The virgin landscapes and the spacious serenity of the Pacific Ocean lend a suitably biblical backdrop for the entry of a satanic force into paradise. As ever, though, the thrill of spectatorship overrides all other considerations. Remote television cameras have been positioned to record the big event. "You have a grandstand seat here to one of the most momentous moments in the history of science," enthuses Hadley, the proud master of ceremonies. "In less than a minute you will see the most powerful explosion ever witnessed by human eyes."

Gesturing screen left, Hadley points out that "the blast will come out of the horizon just about there. And this is the significance of the moment. This is the first full-scale test of a hydrogen device. If the reaction goes, we're in the thermonuclear era." He pauses thoughtfully. "For the sake of all of us, and for the sake of our country, I know that you join me in wishing this expedition well." Time now to don goggles and turn away from the direction of the blast.

Ominous soundtrack music builds to a crescendo during the countdown, and at zero hour a huge billowing fireball fills the screen. In the aftermath, an entire atoll has disappeared from the face of the earth. As in the newsreels, stateside reference points are superimposed on the blast radius. The fireball alone would engulf one quarter of the island of Manhattan. With the Capitol dome in Washington, D.C., as ground zero, a radius of three miles would experience "complete annihilation."

On April 1, 1954, the networks telecast the H-bomb imagery again and again. CBS scooped the competition with a sampling of clips on *The Morning Show*, ABC showed the complete film twice (once in the morning, once in prime time), and NBC telecast it at 8:00 A.M., 7:00 P.M., and 11:15 P.M. Sold commercially at $28 a print and widely distributed in the secondary school system, *Operation Ivy* had a long half-life as an educational tool in science and civics classes, not to mention the nightmares of impressionable baby boomers.

The next month, on May 18, 1954, ABC's *Motorola TV Hour* turned the documentary reality into television melodrama in "Atomic Attack," a live fantasy in prime time depicting the effects of a hydrogen bomb dropped on New York City. With Manhattan vaporized and her husband dead, a Westchester house-wife must cope with social disorder in her neighborhood and radiation sick-ness in her family. Adding an element of unnerving verisimilitude, ABC news-man John Daly delivered actual civil defense instructions over the radio. A somber and stark projection, with no triumphalism and scant hope, "Atomic Attack" spooked viewers and critics alike. "A frightening reminder of what might be in store for us, [but] viewers must have asked themselves the purpose of such a show," complained *Variety*. "It must have alarmed an already alarmed people. All it accomplished was to accent the terror ahead."

Hollywood also caught the Cold War shivers. A new breed of science fic-tion film emerged as transparent allegory for the fears of bombs and spies, an-nihilation from above and subversion on native ground. The lurking terrors surfaced in the blunt, third-person pronoun titling the accusatory *Them!* (1954). "A horror-horde of crawl-and-crush giants clawing out of the earth's deep catacombs," shrieked the ad copy. "Human in their cunning! Monstrous in their endless terror! Kill one—and two take their place!"

McCarthy: Man, Ism, and Television

Propelled high on the atmosphere of external threat, internal insecurities, and nuclear tremors, the figure of Sen. Joseph R. McCarthy (R-Wis.) swirled with cyclone force across newspaper headlines, newsreels, and television screens: McCarthy, the great ogre of Cold War America, who as noun and adjective earned his dictionary entry as part of the language. Of all the verbal bludgeons that propel politically driven debate—Fascism, communism, racism—only "McCarthyism" is indigenous and peculiar to American culture. No other sur-name coinage trips off the tongue so smoothly as a slashing epithet. Little wonder that today Joseph McCarthy seems more "-ism" than man.

Given the titanic figure McCarthy cuts in popular memory, the brevity of his career and the speed of his demise comes as a surprise. The arc of Mc-Carthy's political influence begins with a speech in Wheeling, West Virginia, in February 1950 and concludes definitively with his televised immolation at the Army-McCarthy hearings in June 1954, a stretch of little more than four years as a first-string player. Throughout that interval, he was always a divisive and despised figure, on the defensive as often as on the attack. If he made the weak cringe, he also stiffened the backbone of politicians, journalists, and or-dinary Americans who relished the battle and gave as good as they got.

Born in 1908 in rural Grand Chute, Wisconsin, Joseph Raymond McCarthy came up the hard way and ever after wore his hardscrabble Irish-Catholic roots as a point of pride. Alert, ambitious, and gregarious, he worked his way through law school at Marquette University and by the age of thirty had won election to a circuit judgeship. In 1942, farsighted enough to know that a war record was the ticket to Washington in a postwar era, he resigned his judgeship and enlisted in the U.S. Marines. Elected to the Senate in 1946 under the self-bestowed moniker "Tail Gunner Joe," he floundered at first on the national stage. Though not yet tagged with the condescending diminutive favored by his enemies, "the junior senator from Wisconsin" was then notable mainly, if barely, for his quixotic campaign to rehabilitate the Nazi soldiers who murdered American GIs at Malmédy, undertaken to court favor with his German-American constituency.

On February 9, 1950, McCarthy stumbled into his moment of destiny. During a Lincoln Day dinner speech to a Republican Women's Club in Wheeling, West Virginia, he claimed to possess a list of 205 known communists in the State Department, a number that proved flexible in the days ahead. The accusation caused a sensation. As the organs of mass communications and the publicity-hungry pol fed off each other, the once obscure senator rode the anticommunist wave to national prominence. Unfortunately, McCarthy's career-making talk was neither filmed by the newsreels nor telecast live, a lapse in public relations he was not to repeat.

Within weeks of entering the headlines, the senator also entered the American language. As a proper noun fitted with a suffix, McCarthy became the incarnation of a demonic zeitgeist, a shorthand term for the stifling of free debate and the denial of constitutional rights by the imputation of communist sympathies. Originally too the word was yoked to the manner of the man, a boorish and reckless bluster captured in newsreel clips and television appearances. A constant incantation throughout the Cold War, McCarthyism gained force not only from the dark charisma of the senator but the passions of the moment. In the 1950s, after all, communists, anticommunists, and anti-anticommunists were all deadly serious about communism.

As a matter of etymology at least, the roots of McCarthyism are readily traceable. The editorial cartoonist Herbert Block first used the senator's surname as a term of abuse in the March 29, 1950, edition of the *Washington Post*, when he scrawled "McCarthyism" on a tar pot, the emblem of a smear. The coinage caught on immediately, as if the turbulent anticommunism forming with the new decade were an offshore weather system just waiting to be upgraded to hurricane status and christened. In a televised address on November 16, 1953, former President Harry S. Truman voiced a terse definition:

[McCarthyism] is the corruption of truth, the abandonment of our historical devotion to fair play. It is the abandonment of the due process of law. It is the use of the Big Lie and the unfounded accusation against any citizen in the name of Americanism and security. It is the rise to power of the demagogue who lives on untruth; it is the spread of fear and the destruction of faith in every level of our society.

As if brushing aside a gnat, Truman stressed that he was not referring to the senator himself: "He is only important in that his name has taken on a dictionary meaning in the world."

Also on television, McCarthy responded that Truman's definition "was the same as the *Daily Worker*, word for word, comma for comma. Let them [that is, Truman and the Communist Party newspaper] define it if they care to." The casual deployment of the plural pronoun to link the former president with the communist conspiracy exemplifies the ism, right from the mouth of the master.

Fitting though it is that the man who branded so many should himself become a brand name, McCarthy was hardly a solitary soldier in the domestic war against communism. All the Cold War forces subsumed under his name predated and postdated his tenure: President Truman imposed loyalty oaths on federal employees in March 1947, the FBI had been investigating political malcontents of all stripes since the 1920s, and the House Committee on Un-American Activities launched its first investigations into Hollywood subversion in 1947, well before McCarthy detected 205 communists in the State Department. Today, in the popular mind, McCarthy's preeminent notoriety obscures important distinctions: between executive and legislative branch investigations, between agencies of the federal government and private pressure groups, between investigating and blacklisting, and, not least, between principled liberals and cynical communists.

The linkage of McCarthy with Hollywood and television warrants the most debunking. Though the word *McCarthyism* conjures images of persecuted screenwriters shouted down by gavel-wielding demagogues or blacklisted actors banned from the airwaves by craven network executives, it was not the McCarthy committee but the House Committee on Un-American Activities that subpoenaed Hollywood filmmakers; it was not the McCarthy committee but the McCarran committee that investigated subversive content in motion pictures and television; and it was not McCarthy but a confederation of private organizations and special interest groups that purged television of artists deemed "controversial personalities." McCarthy's focus was mainly intramural, aimed at government not media. The McCarthy committee (officially, the Senate Permanent Subcommittee on Investigations, chaired by McCarthy from 1953 to 1954) is most often confused with the

House Committee on Un-American Activities (inevitably abbreviated as HUAC).[3] Perversely, McCarthy is given too much credit for McCarthyism.

The reason, then and now, is television. McCarthy ranks with a select cadre of prescient politicians—Estes Kefauver, Richard Nixon, Dwight Eisenhower—who possessed a keen eye for the main chance of the new medium. In 1953, as McCarthy was blitzing the airwaves in news shows, press conferences, and televised hearings, he had to deny persistent rumors that he was considering hosting a television series. "Completely phoney," he grinned. "There's nothing to it. I wouldn't have time for it and I have no TV plans." Yet McCarthy always had TV plans—not to play host, but to dominate news shows, to command network air time, and to star as the leading man in his own series of televised hearings.

Viewed through a television lens, however, the many images of Joseph McCarthy send back such mixed signals that the historian may be tempted to twist the antenna or hit the set to bring in a clear picture. On one channel, the senator seems fierce and all-powerful, dominating programming and frightening the populace. Facing McCarthy and the forces he embodied, many Americans quivered with the fear that unfettered opinions had dire consequences, that agents of the state might disrupt their lives on the basis of a casual remark, a signed petition, or membership in a long-forgotten college discussion group. And if a one-way ticket to the Gulag was not in the offing, the prospect of public opprobrium, termination of employment, and the hassle of a lifetime was real enough.

In 1954, a young naval officer teaching at Princeton University wrote a fan letter to Edward R. Murrow. He closed his correspondence by pleading: "Please *destroy* my letter when you're finished reading it. McCarthy could *ruin me* with *one flick* of his ugly wrist since I'm on active duty and a 'professor' at one of those 'leftist dominated universities'!" Obviously the man felt vulnerable, but not too vulnerable to commit his name and letterhead to the U.S. Post Office and to entrust his fate to a broadcaster whom he had never met. The broadcaster, for his part, never complied with the panicky request. Whether through negligence or a sense that the young man was being a tad too melodramatic, the letter went unburnt, the officer unmolested.

---

3. The muddling of Senator McCarthy and HUAC may be a misconception too deeply implanted ever to be expunged. In 1997, even *Variety*, the show business bible, bungled the facts in a commemorative article on the Hollywood blacklist: "It's been 50 years since the House Un-American Activities Committee began looking for communist sympathizers in all fields, but the committee, led by Sen. McCarthy, took a special interest in the high profile film industry."

Man and epithet: displaying a propaganda picture from North Korea, Sen. Joseph R. McCarthy beams at his contribution to the American vernacular (January 30, 1954). (Courtesy Photofest)

Meanwhile, flipping over to another channel, television transmits a program featuring a bolder cast of characters. Telecast from Washington, D.C., and billed as "America's oldest unrehearsed discussion program," NBC's *American Forum of the Air* (1950–1957) was a live news program whose format obliged politicians to answer questions from a studio audience. On December 6, 1953, the guest was Sen. Joseph McCarthy. The members of the audience are not cowering peasants struck dumb before a tyrannical liege, but upright citizens who behave pretty much the way Americans have always behaved in the presence of their elected representatives: respectful but skeptical, the questions polite but probing, sometimes downright hostile.

A pleasant young woman, the picture of ladylike deportment in Eisenhower America, raises her hand. "Senator McCarthy, do you believe a man is innocent until proven guilty in a court of law?" she asks.

"Yes," replies McCarthy.

"Then why do you call men spies, security risks, and communists before they have been proven such?" she demands.

Taken aback, McCarthy mutters that the rules for a congressional inquiry are different from the rules for a criminal proceeding.

Another questioner stands to remark that "there doesn't seem to be any middle course" about the senator. "A lot of people like McCarthy, a lot of people hate McCarthy." Gauging the vox populi, the man reports that when he goes to the movies and sees McCarthy in the newsreels, "sometimes you hear a lot of boos, sometimes you hear a lot of cheers."

Playing against type, an American Legion commander takes issue with McCarthy's recent request that Americans send telegrams to President Eisenhower to protest foreign aid to nations that trade with Red China. Isn't this, he asks belligerently, putting the presidency "on the public auction block?"

The animosity continues unabated. McCarthy gets entangled in testy exchanges with two women. Neither backs down, despite McCarthy's rude interjections. "Pardon me for interrupting a lady," snorts the senator.

Stuart Finley, the nervous moderator of the program, requests questions, not commentary, from the obstreperous studio audience. In a surreal flash forward, a young lawyer in the audience confronts McCarthy with the definition of McCarthyism lately offered by former President Truman. "[Truman] meant that you were a demagogue, that you were unfair, you were guilty of the Big Lie," declares John Sirica, looking straight at McCarthy, just as he would stare down President Richard Nixon during the Watergate scandal twenty years later.

To tune in to the television of Cold War America is to see a portrait more textured and multicolored than the monochrome shades fogging the popular imagination. Dependent for sustenance on the very freedoms that McCarthyism restricted, the medium was preprogrammed for resistance. Of course, the commitment to free expression and open access was self-interested; television needed to fill the air time.

TWO

THE GESTALT OF THE BLACKLIST

"Television's top detective flatfoot show should do some detecting in its own household," advised the *Hollywood Reporter*. "One of its employees is a Lefty actor who worked in the commie movie *Salt of the Earth*." In 1953, when the warning was issued, the elliptical references were clear as crystal to the trade-wise readership of the motion picture daily. Translation: Jack Webb, producer-star of NBC's hit police drama *Dragnet*, had better fire the actor David Wolfe for working on the communist-backed agitprop *Salt of the Earth*, an independent production by blacklisted filmmakers Herbert Biberman, Michael Wilson, and Paul Jarricho.

Dark intimations, murky insinuations, cutesy code-words: the world of the blacklist speaks a special language of double meanings and sideways glances. Even the blunt nomenclature sends back strange echoes across time, a calibration of ideological positioning whose sliding scale once determined honorable dissent from treasonous sentiments: liberal, progressive, New Deal Democrat, Popular Fronter, fellow traveler, Soviet dupe, pinko, dyed-in-the-wool red, and—the apex of aberration—card-carrying communist. Like any foreign tongue, matters of definition divulge only part of the meaning; to enter the linguistic field requires an appreciation of the boundaries of belief, the gestalt of the blacklist.

A boldfaced word in any phrasebook for Cold War America, *blacklisting* is the practice of refusing to hire or terminating from employment an individual whose opinions or associations are deemed politically inconvenient or commercially troublesome. Theoretically, anyone who worked for a living comprised the pool of potential blacklistees, but employees in government, education, and media were most vulnerable and left-wing activists in any line of work most suspected.

Yet history, like life, is not fair. Though the blacklist stained all manner of occupations, the word invariably conjures the plight of motion picture and television artists rather than the purging of military officers, civil service employees, or public school teachers. In popular memory, the media retain near-exclusive rights to the legacy of the blacklist. Ironically, the Hollywood studios and the television networks, the very institutions that implemented the blacklist, would later make certain that their victims received top billing as the featured attractions: inflicting the wound did not keep them from nursing the grievance. The entertainment industry was "scarred by the blacklist," as the operative phrase had it, and the artistic community still trembled with post-traumatic jitters, even workers never exposed to the original scourge.

Obviously, the travails of the famous in glamorous careers seize the spotlight more readily than the troubles of the obscure toiling in quiet desperation, but the prominent profile of motion picture and television personalities in the annals of blacklist victimhood is only partly a consequence of celebrity fixation. The blacklist was written to constrict free expression in private opinion and public screens. Trafficking in both, motion pictures and television were the natural places to enforce the letter of the law.

Doubtless too the blacklist still haunts the entertainment industry because of the uniquely nerve-racking nature of show business employment. A profession built on personal contacts and prejudice, gut instincts and lucky breaks, typecasting and casting couches, it is laden with more job insecurity and performance anxiety than a civil service slot or union job. When the phone stopped ringing, was it because of a lack of talent or surplus of controversy, a personal slight or suspected sedition?

The Blacklist Backstory

Though the shadow of the blacklist hovers over the popular memory of the 1950s, cultural contexts are often forgotten and signature events tend to blur together. Even guided by a detailed flow chart, the lines of influence and points of pressure criss-cross and intertwine. Nonetheless, some factors need to be foregrounded, others to be distinguished from kindred, but still distinct, happenings.

As ever with the postwar era, the big picture backstory to the blacklist is World War II. After four years of screen propaganda, Americans had developed a keen sensitivity to the ideological currents of the popular media. Whether in the grim combat reports of the newsreels, the history lessons of Frank Capra's *Why We Fight* series (1942–1945), or the stirring melodrama of *Casablanca* (1942), *Mrs. Miniver* (1942), and *Since You Went Away* (1944), all items on the wartime motion picture program fit the propaganda bill. Before 1941, audiences tended to see Hollywood in ethical or sociological terms. The local Bijou might weaken the moral fiber of young girls or incite wayward lads to criminality, but it certainly could not undermine political institutions or threaten national security. During the war, moviegoers learned to appreciate cinema for what it was: a powerful delivery system for ideology.

Schooled in celluloid persuasion, postwar Americans looked upon the screen with more sophisticated eyes and discerned bright-lined messages and hidden agenda in even the most escapist motion picture fare. When the Iron Curtain descended in 1946, the contest between East and West, Soviet Communism and American Democracy, found its domestic expression in fierce debates over the subversive influence of the popular media. With the early days of television paralleling precisely the escalating intensity of the Cold War, the wartime lessons were taken to the heart of the new medium.

However, as the precedent and still ascendant source of moving imagery, Hollywood was scrutinized first. In October 1947, the House Committee on Un-American Activities launched nine days of sensational hearings into alleged communist influence in the motion picture industry. Under the kleig lights of five newsreel companies and over the airwaves of four radio (but not television) networks, HUAC staged a political-cultural fandango more akin to a gala premiere at Grauman's Chinese Theater than a somber legislative inquiry. The 1947 pageant featured a star-studded cast of witnesses, fiery face-offs between interlocutors, and an overflow crowd of extras who raucously booed and cheered the players. The hearings were chaired by the intemperate J. Parnell Thomas (R-N.J.), who even in black-and-white newsreel footage looks perpetually red-faced with exasperation. Also playing their assigned roles was a cadre of seven screenwriters, two producers, and one director, all communists, who defied the committee by refusing to answer what in preinflationary currency was dubbed the $64 question: "Are you now, or have you ever been, a member of the Communist Party?"[1]

The Hollywood Ten (then called the Unfriendly Ten, orthodox Hollywood not wanting to claim the heretics as its own) engaged chairman Thomas in a series of rancorous shouting matches. Easily baited and rhetorically bested, Thomas barked at the strident communist screenwriter John

---

1. HUAC subpoenaed nineteen unfriendly witnesses, but called only eleven: the screenwriters Alvah Bessie, Lester Cole, John Howard Lawson, Albert Maltz, Samuel Ornitz, Dalton Trumbo, Ring Lardner Jr., the director Edward Dmytryk, the producer Adrian Scott, and the producer-director Herbert Biberman. The eleventh to testify, the German playwright Bertolt Brecht, dissembled rather than defied the committee. Cited for contempt for refusing to testify under their First (not Fifth) Amendment rights, the Ten went to jail in 1950. In order to raise funds and consciousness, they produced a 15-minute anti-anticommunist short entitled *The Hollywood Ten* (1950), in which the self-proclaimed "casualties of the Cold War" accused HUAC of "legal lynching."

Howard Lawson (THOMAS: "You'll be responsive!" LAWSON: "I'm not on trial here! The committee is on trial!") and huffed at the more congenial party-liners Dalton Trumbo (escorted from the stand by six uniformed guards, he howled: "This is the beginning of an American concentration camp!") and Ring Lardner Jr. (whose laconic response to Thomas's $64 question became the best-remembered line from the hearings: "I could answer it, but if I did, I would hate myself in the morning"). Immortalized by the newsreels, the 1947 hearings bequeathed the iconic images of the Hollywood blacklist and two sturdy metaphors for Washington investigations into the entertainment industry—the "witch hunt" and the "circus."

Seriously rattled by the subpoenas and sermons from a government so lately a congenial partner in propaganda, the motion picture industry adopted two defensive strategies that the television industry later took as models of rapid response: the purging of communist-tainted employees and the production of anticommunist films.

Soon after the Hollywood Ten hearings, on November 25, 1947, executives from the major motion picture studios emerged from a two-day confab at the Waldorf Astoria Hotel in New York and issued what became known as the Waldorf Statement, a document that asserted the determination of Hollywood to stand up to HUAC even as it knuckled under. "We are not going to be swayed by hysteria or intimidation from any source," proclaimed Eric Johnston, president of the Motion Picture Association of America. "Creative work at its best cannot be carried on in an atmosphere of fear. We will guard against this danger, this risk, this fear." Speaking for the swaying moguls, Johnston pledged never to "knowingly employ a communist" and to "take positive action" on "disloyal elements." In a flash, the front office banished the unfriendlies from the studios and erased their credits from the screen.

The negative action endorsed by the Waldorf Statement was coordinated with positive proof of pure intentions. No sooner had Thomas pounded down the final gavel on the 1947 hearings than MGM rushed to reissue *Ninotchka* (1939) and *Comrade X* (1940), two prewar romantic comedies that gently ribbed the Soviet system. As visible evidence of patriotic zeal, the major studios then released a series of anticommunist thrillers with titles like *The Iron Curtain* (1948), *The Red Menace* (1949), and *I Was a Communist for the FBI* (1951). Just as in World War II, when Hollywood had marshaled its forces to fight Nazism, the studios took up the fight against communism: but where the wartime service was a willing enlistment, the Cold War recruitment was conscripted labor.

Between 1948 and 1954, the anticommunist films served as a kind of burnt offering, the celluloid version of the flesh-and-blood sacrifices made to the blacklist. In case anyone missed the point, *Motion Picture Daily* praised the punctual arrival and "happy appropriateness" of *I Was a Communist for the FBI*, noting that "at a time when the House Un-American Activities Committee is exposing communist infiltration in isolated segments of the industry, it shows where the industry as a whole stands on the questions. It will at once dissipate popular impressions that may have been carelessly formed about the industry and at the same time enlighten the filmgoing public on the nature of home grown communism." Although the sops to HUAC flopped at the box office, the high concept was never commercial: the anticommunist films were protection payments in 35mm.

Though the Hollywood Ten hearings jolted Hollywood into anticommunist action, HUAC's madcap production received terrible reviews. From the press gallery and the legislative cloakrooms, the inquiry was widely derided as a circus that brought discredit upon the Congress, an opinion confirmed when the ringmaster was indicted for embezzlement. In a twist of poetic justice that the men he held in contempt might have scripted, J. Parnell Thomas served his prison time at the same federal penitentiary as Ring Lardner Jr. Burned by bad publicity and worse casting, HUAC took an extended hiatus from tussling with professional entertainers, not resuming public hearings into screen subversion until 1951.

By then, the dominant screen media was no longer motion pictures. Though not yet equal in star power and social cache, television was already surpassing the motion picture in pervasiveness and centrality. "The feeling is strong among [HUAC] members that since television is such a powerful medium of propaganda and since it comes directly into the home, TV should get the most thorough going-over," *Variety* reported in 1951. Jack O'Brian, television critic at the *New York Journal-American*, agreed, arguing that video-born subversion demanded the strictest vigilance. "This is lots different than the stage and movies where the lefties gamboled so long, different even from radio," warned O'Brian. "In TV, the actors come right in to our living rooms. In films we weren't forced to go down the street to help line their wallets with swimming pool money." Conjuring a dire scenario, *Broadcasting/Telecasting* warned that "broadcasters must be especially wary of Red infiltration which could, at whatever D-Day the Communists pick, seize radio-TV facilities which would be of greatest value in espionage and fifth column activity."

In 1951, taking the hint, the Internal Security Subcommittee, a unit of the Senate Judiciary Committee popularly known after its chairman, Sen. Patrick McCarran (D-Nev.), expanded the original HUAC purview with hearings on the "Subversive Influence of Radio, Television, and the Entertainment Industry." "Those who are responsible for [television's] development must also accept responsibility for its character and the type of programs it channels into the homes of America," lectured McCarran, who detected "strategically placed to take advantage of television's progress . . . either Communists or very active pro-Communists."

Not to be outflanked by the upper chamber, HUAC followed suit. "Communists will endeavor to infiltrate TV on a large scale because it is rapidly becoming an important entertainment medium in the United States," HUAC warned in its annual report to Congress in 1952, signaling a shift in investigatory emphasis. Thereafter, during separate sets of hearings chaired by John S. Wood (D-Ga.) in 1951–52 and Harold H. Velde (R-Ill.) in 1953–1954, HUAC corralled television performers with the same fervor as motion picture stars.

As a backhanded recognition of how video was rising and film declining, the bicameral investigations confirmed the new state of media affairs. Increasingly, disputes about communism and civil rights focused on things televisual. While in the docket, the medium was schizophrenic: as an institution, more easily scared; as a medium, less easily silenced.

Pressure Groups and Pressure Points

As in the motion picture industry, the blacklisting of directors, writers, and performers in the broadcasting industry was the mission of a broad coalition, a web of alliance comprised of executive branch agencies, legislative committees at both the state and federal levels, private interest groups, patriotic organizations, and activists without portfolio. They applied pressure on, and worked in concert with, fearful and compliant network executives, corporate sponsors, and advertising agencies to curtail the employment opportunities and civil rights of targeted undesirables. However, all parties agreed on a core principle: what was screened on television really mattered.

Or rather *who* was screened on television. The focus of anticommunist activism was almost never the meaning of the text and almost always the presence of the performer. *Red Channels*, the founding document of the television blacklist, enumerated rather than analyzed, tallied up references rather than interpreted messages. Artists were blacklisted; shows were bypassed. The personality was political.

The mania for lists grew out of the postwar impulse for the reassuring ballast of statistical measurement, a proclivity firmly institutionalized in the social sciences then booming in the American university system. The credits of artists were sifted and filed, recorded and researched, written down and logged in. Weighed together and added up, the data pointed to one inescapable conclusion.

So acute was the need for raw data that reports from the godless were taken as gospel. The most authoritative source for the blacklist was not the FBI or

Naming names: the radio-centric cover of *Red Channels*, the founding document of the television blacklist.

HUAC but the *Daily Worker*, the official communist newspaper judged to be "meticulously accurate" by American Business Consultants, the publishers of *Red Channels* and the newsletter *Counterattack*. A favorable review or a tangential mention in its pages tarred the recipient with subversive residue. "That is to say," explained the capitalist guidebook *Sponsor* of its ideological opposite, "the *Daily Worker*, suspect in most circles, becomes the unofficial arbiter of whether or not a sponsor may use a performer on the air."

The *Daily Worker* as vetted by *Red Channels* was not the only source of names. Page after page of lists and publications, notations culled from rumor, supplemented by innuendo, and littered with transcription errors, might also render a personality controversial.

Finding names: Senator McCarthy examines a copy of the *Daily Worker*, the Communist Party newspaper and primary source for anticommunist activists. (National Archives)

Next to American Business Consultants the most vigorous private agent of the blacklist was an organization called AWARE, Inc., formed in 1953 and headed by Vincent Hartnett, the uncredited author of the introduction to *Red Channels*. Like so many of the characters in the front lines of anticommunism, Hartnett was a Catholic-educated former law-enforcement type with a penchant for microfilm research, index cards, and file cabinets. Circulating newsletters and pamphlets with titles such as *Publication No. 12* and *File 13*, Hartnett posed as an efficiency expert in the sociology of subversion, his numerology lending an aura of mathematical precision and statistical certainty to the job.

Of the dozens of national, state, and local patriotic organizations publishing lists of suspect entertainers in their magazines and newsletters, the most dreaded marshaled a membership in uniform. With ranks swollen by ex-GIs, the American Legion, the Veterans of Foreign Wars (VFW), and the Catholic War Veterans concentrated prolonged and withering firepower on media targets considered insufficiently vigilant in the war against communism. The appearance of uniformed veterans on a picket line terrified motion picture exhibitors. The arrival of a single letter of protest on American Legion stationery made sponsors shudder.

Serving as a guerrilla auxiliary to the brand-name patriotic organizations, a circuit of self-appointed guardians acted as one-man anticommunist fronts. The exemplar was Laurence A. Johnson, a supermarket owner from Syracuse, New York, who tormented sponsors by linking their wares to communism. If a company bankrolled a television show featuring a suspect actor, Johnson threatened to post signs on his supermarket shelves accusing the manufacturer of corporate fellow traveling, the marketing equivalent of a skull and cross-bones. "Perhaps we could work out a questionnaire," he suggested in a registered letter to the president of a toothpaste manufacturer, "reading, for example, as follows:

DO YOU WANT ANY PART OF YOUR PURCHASE PRICE
TO BE USED TO HIRE COMMUNIST FRONTERS?

YES [　]　　　　　　　NO [　]

Working in collusion with Hartnett and the American Legion, Johnson exerted an influence along Madison Avenue out of all proportion to the weekly receipts of his supermarket chain.

American Business Consultants, AWARE Inc., the American Legion, and Laurence Johnson were all serious players, well-versed in the tactics of pressuring networks and squeezing sponsors. However, the anticommunist crusade was also served by a claque of authentic whack jobs. Against the rabid screeds of the megalomaniacal Myron C. Fagan, the language and lists in *Red Channels* appear positively level-headed. A tireless pamphleteer, the Dickensian-named zealot published incendiary booklets ablaze with a menacing glare: *Red Treason in Hollywood!*, *Red Treason on Broadway*, and *Reds in Your Living Room*. Fagan also produced short films financed by the VFW (*It Can Happen Here* and *Operation Survival*, both 1951) and mounted didactic theater productions, such as his play *Red Rainbow* (1953), which exposed the United Nations as a Trojan Horse for "Moscow's spies and America's traitors" and accused FDR adviser Harry Hopkins of selling atomic secrets to the USSR. "When TV came along . . . it quickly became apparent that here was a transmission belt that was going to be more effective than films and radio combined," fumed Fagan. "The Red masterminds decided that this medium to the minds of the American people must be ONE-HUNDRED PERCENT controlled."

Absent a listing in the premiere book of the damned or its offshoots, an actor might still run afoul of "private blacklists" kept by network executives, sponsors, and ad agencies, lists drawn from all of the above and supplemented by even more ephemeral word of mouth. "Everyone—ad agencies and net-works—seems to have a little list. Heaven knows how anyone's name gets on these little lists," protested John Crosby, the television critic for the *New York Herald Tribune*. "The most irresponsible charges are enough apparently to get an actor proscribed."

Typically, the sins alleged dated back to the 1930s and fell under the rubric of Popular Front activism. In 1935 the Soviet Comintern had directed the Communist Party USA to cooperate with heretofore deviationist elements, notably socialists and New Deal liberals, to cement a unified front against fascism, a tactical compromise necessitated by the rise of Hitler in Europe. During the Great Depression, a broad coalition of left-wing activists marched alongside the hammer and sickle, some from hard-line conviction, others from the same pragmatism that motivated the communists. They organized rallies, attended benefits, and signed petitions for the causes that galvanized a generation of leftists: the trials of the Scottsboro Boys, the Republican cause in the Spanish Civil War, and the unionization of workers in agriculture and industry, not least the actors, scribes, and craftsmen in the motion picture industry.

For media-savvy agents of revolution, popular entertainers were prize trophies in the work of agitprop, pushed to the front of the line in parades and up to the podium at rallies. Equally serviceable were screenwriters, whose polemical wit emblazoned placards and manifestos, and theater people, whose stagecraft energized street protests and stadium rallies. Recruited from a class of workers whose ideological sophistication was often less finely tuned than their passionate intensity, the well-heeled talent was doted on by the party elite even if the rank and file sneered at their pampered Californian comrades as "the swimming pool reds."

A decade or more later, with the winds of political fashion blowing in another direction, the activism of the 1930s might be made to appear stupid or sinister. Two moments of decision readily divided the independent-minded artist-activist from the lockstep Communist Party–liner. On August 23, 1939, when the Soviet Union entered into a nonaggression pact with Nazi Germany, the interventionist march of the Communist Party USA screeched to a halt and turned on a dime, only to swing about-face again on June 22, 1941, when Nazi Germany invaded the Soviet Union. The artists and intellectuals who executed those precision dance steps, on cue, could rightly be said to have taken choreography lessons from the Soviet Union.

To the editors of *Red Channels* and their ilk, the shadings that distinguished the red-blooded American from the American red were academic. Lumped together were a mélange of hard-core communists, standard-issue FDR liberals, and naive tag-alongs, an assembly that linked the downright Stalinist with the mildly reformist. Working from left to right, the arc of belief traced a slope that was slippery only to the disoriented.

The supreme pariahs were the authentic Communist Party members. In a sense, the card-carrying communists and unrepentant unfriendlies possessed a psychological advantage over other targets: they knew they were blacklisted and they knew why. Dalton Trumbo's famous quip when asked how he knew he was blacklisted ("My agent told me, my wife told me, and my landlord told me") bespeaks the enviable lucidity of a comrade girded for a good fight. Outcasts though they were, the communists enjoyed the consolation of righteous martyrdom and the unwavering support of cells of like-minded true believers. In the depths of Cold War America, few argued that communists deserved the lucrative cushion of employment on American screens. Communists were not controversial; they were beyond the pale.

Spiritual kindred to the card-carrying communist but less certifiable was the fellow traveler. A communist in all but membership, the fellow traveler hewed to the party line without the inconvenience of attending regular meetings or adhering to formal party discipline. He or she tended to belong to communist front groups, a label assigned to activist coalitions conceived and dominated by communists but without official party sponsorship. The fellow traveler maintained the illusion of ideological independence while performing the acts of lapdog loyalty.

A good distance away from either the communist or the fellow traveler stood the liberal. Characteristically a New Deal Democrat with a firm commitment to progressive causes, especially the civil rights campaigns for African Americans, the liberal may once have been aligned, of necessity, with communist front groups, but his own sympathies resided somewhere in the comfort zone between Franklin and Eleanor Roosevelt. The authentic liberal was readily distinguished from the communist or fellow traveler by idiosyncratic deviations from the communist party line, above all on matters of American foreign policy toward the Soviet Union.

A common variant of the Popular Fronter gone awry was the prodigal politico, usually a former communist or fellow traveler who recanted his past and enlisted in the anticommunist crusade. Self-portrayed as an accident of history, the prodigal politico had become unhinged during the hard times of the Great Depression and the heady days of the Popular Front. Sure, he had attended meetings, signed petitions, and marched in parades, maybe even joined the party for a time in the flush of youthful ardor, but always in the spirit of good-hearted progressivism. Later, he learned the true nature of the cause he served and, like a good boy fallen in with bad comrades, redeemed himself with a sincere confession and active penance. "At that time nearly all of us felt menaced by two things: the depression and the ever growing power of Hitler," explained the director Elia Kazan in a statement published in 1952. "The streets were full of unemployed and shaken men. I was taken in by what might be called the Communists' advertising or recruiting technique." To return to the fold in good standing, however, the prodigal politico needed to pay a price for reentry by naming the names of his former comrades.

An extreme version of the prodigal politico was the self-styled dupe. Almost always, the dupe donned a mask of gullibility to deny culpability. Not even entertainers were so guileless as to sign their names and lend their prestige to causes they knew nothing about year after year. Still, better to be thought a dolt than a scoundrel. "I was an innocent dupe, I was a fool," sobbed bandleader Artie Shaw, testifying before HUAC in 1953. The title of actor Edward G. Robinson's apologia, printed in the pages of *American Legion* magazine, sums up the motto of the species: "How the Reds Made a Sucker Out of Me."

Communists, fellow travelers, liberals, prodigal politicos, and dupes had all at least marched in the Popular Front parade. However, a small band of totally innocent bystanders became collateral damage in the blacklist wars, artists whose names through glitches, misprints, and misinformation were hit by unfriendly fire. Ireene Wicker, dubbed "the Singing Lady" of radio and television, was hauled off her children's television program within weeks of the publication of *Red Channels* on the basis of a petition she had allegedly signed in 1945. Wicker, who had just returned from a private audience with Pope Pius XII, claimed never to have heard of the petition. At least three actresses named Madeline Lee—one, the real target of the blacklist, the wife of actor Jack Gilford, and two who just happened to share her name—were all blacklisted. A fourth hapless actress, who merely looked like the real Madeline Lee, was also blacklisted. To allay confusion, the *Hollywood Reporter* published lists of actors whose names sounded like the names of the genuinely blacklistable actors. The unluckily surnamed also took out advertising space in the trade press to ward off potential mix-ups.[2]

Encompassing all of the above save the hard-core communists and committed fellow travelers was the catch-all, catch-22 category known as the "controversial personality," by far the most populous species of blacklistees. The controversial personality was someone involved in the blacklist imbroglio and therefore ipso facto controversial on the basis of involvement in the blacklist imbroglio. "In the radio and television industries, a category of human beings

---

2. The jeopardy attendant to mistaken identity resulted in a blacklist version of a screwball comedy "meet cute." In 1951, a young actress named Nancy Davis was confused with a controversial personality of the same name. Distraught, she approached Ronald Reagan, then president of the Screen Actors Guild, for help in clearing her name.

has been devised known as 'the controversial person,'" explained syndicated columnist George Sokolsky in 1953. "By that is meant an actor, writer, commentator, etc., who has at some time in his life taken a position on a public question which has attracted attention." Infinitely elastic in application and maddeningly circular in reasoning, the designation was not reserved for performers alone. In 1953 *TV Guide* reported that Harry S. Truman was nixed from hosting a documentary interview program because the networks feared the former president of the United States was "too controversial a personality."

In the gestalt of the blacklist, categories shifted and anomalies abounded. An (undeservedly) controversial personality might become a (deservedly) controversial personality by embracing the cause of the controversy. For example, on March 21, 1951, the name of the actor Lionel Stander was uttered by the actor Larry Parks during testimony before HUAC. "Do you know Lionel Stander?" committee counsel Frank S. Tavenner inquired. Parks replied he knew the man, but had no knowledge of his political affiliations. No more was said about Stander either by Parks or the committee—no accusation, no insinuation. Yet Stander's phone stopped ringing. Prior to Parks's testimony, Stander had worked on ten television shows in the previous 100 days. Afterwards, nothing. "I am not now, nor was I ever a member of the Communist Party," Stander declared after Parks's testimony. "I firmly believe in our Constitutional democracy and oppose all forms of totalitarianism, whether fascistic or communistic."

Two years later, on May 6, 1953, when Stander testified before HUAC, a long career hiatus had stiffened his native pugnacity. He angrily denounced HUAC as an "inquisition" and the vituperative exchanges between the actor and the committee forced an adjournment in the hearings. Previously a controversial personality by dint of tangential mention in 1951, Stander became a controversial personality by action in 1953.

Under whatever designation, for talent tainted with the brush of communism or controversy, the fallout was life-altering and the path to vindication tormenting. Once accused, actors might suffer in silence, defy the accusations, or engage in rituals of public recantation or denial ("clearance") either before Congress, in the public press, or at the offices of American Business Consultants or AWARE Inc. "You should see the big act some of them put on in this very office," chortled Francis J. McNamara, editor of *Counterattack*. "It's a panic to hear them!"

Almost anyone who was not a communist in membership or ideology condemned the listing and proclaimed innocence and hatred of communism, under oath and before a congressional committee if need be. The authentic communists tended to stand on their constitutional rights, not denying the charges but refusing to answer by citing their Fifth Amendment protection against self-incrimination. Precious few stood purely on principle: that is, liberals who were not now nor were ever communists but refused to say so.

The wisest course was to mix condemnation of communism with outrage at the charge. In a sworn deposition, ecsdysiast Gypsy Rose Lee denied the accusation ("I am not now and never have been a member of the Communist Party, fellow traveler, sympathizer or any one of the associate brand") and attacked the accusers ("I abhor totalitarians—whether red, brown, black—and their treacherous methods of guilt by smear and without trial. This way may be all right for Russia, but I hope not for us"). ABC president Robert E. Kintner sent along Rose's deposition to protesters with the request, "If you have any evidence to the contrary, please advise me." Rose appeared as scheduled on the radio program *What Makes You Tick* and weathered the storm. In the aftermath, Kintner and ABC won a Peabody award "for their courageous stand in resisting organized pressures, and for their reaffirmation of basic American principles."

A few tried to deflect the charges with humor. Satirist Abe Burrows, a popular panelist on CBS's *This Is Show Business*, joked that although he had attended parties whose hosts had turned out to be communists, he had never joined the Communist Party. But rare was the entertainer who could muster black humor about the blacklist. For every television actor who stood firm, dozens more quaked and complied. They signed loyalty oaths, released sworn affidavits, and composed exculpatory personal statements.

The most demeaning road to clearance, proof positive of reformation, was the ritual of naming names before a congressional committee. To be truly friendly, a subpoenaed witness needed to testify not only to personal malfeasance but to name former comrades in subversion. Though reviled from schoolyard to prison yard, the act of informing was recast as a gesture of self-abnegation both patriotic and penitent, the only sure way to drag the agents of the secret cells of the communist fifth column into the sunlight.

So myriad were the sources of the accusations, so elastic the definition of deviance, and so formidable the hurdles to clearance, that even prodigal politicos who repented their past and testified before HUAC as friendly witnesses were blacklisted as controversial personalities. "Individual [HUAC] members have been disturbed by reports that some cooperative witnesses, who admitted one time communist membership but who have now renounced all Red ties, are still being refused employment in show business," *Variety* reported in 1952. "It is understood that this is particularly true in radio and television." Even naming names might backfire, tossing the namer's name onto the blacklist of the controversial personalities just named.

The stark injustices and the surreal incongruities did not go unprotested. Contrary to subsequent memoirs, films, and television shows, opposition to the blacklist was vociferous during the blacklist era. Before congressional committees, at union meetings, and in pages of the entertainment trade press, the practice was exposed and excoriated. For every blacklist-friendly columnist like Jack O'Brian at the *New York Journal-American* or Hedda Hopper at the *Los Angeles Times* a counterweight like Jack Gould at the *New York Times* or John Crosby at the *New York Herald Tribune* condemned blacklisting. At the *Hollywood Reporter*, Dan Jenkins repeatedly urged a firm stand against "the sly slanderers and mudslingers who in the past have had only to whisper the word 'communist' in connection with a man's name to have him blacklisted by sponsors, agencies and networks alike." The blacklist, John Crosby sagely predicted in 1953, is "one of the things our generation is going to have to answer for to succeeding generations." If dissenting voices went unheeded, they did not go unheard—even on the medium that enforced the blacklist.

The most concentrated counterattack at *Counterattack* and *Red Channels* was Merle Miller's *The Judges and the Judged*, published in 1952 and sponsored by the American Civil Liberties Union (ACLU). Though Miller claimed to be "as coldly analytic as a reporter can be," his prose seethed with indignation. "A large segment of one of this country's largest industries remains panicked, partly by the hysteria of the times, partly by what is, relatively, one of the country's smallest corporations, American Business Consultants, and a handful of supporters," Miller charged. "All of the 151 listees [in *Red Channels*] are stained with the same careless red paint."

Miller's *j'accuse* was prominently reviewed and fulsomely praised. "Exactly as though someone had shouted 'Fire!' in a crowded theater, a handful of men have shouted 'Communism!' at radio and television," lamented the drama critic Walter Kerr in a laudatory notice in the *New York Herald Tribune*. "The stampede has been immediate, uncritical, total; more destructive, as always, than the fire might have been."

On April 10, 1952, television granted Miller a forum for his views excoriating television when DuMont's *Author Meets the Critics* hosted a lively debate about *The Judges and the Judged*. Faye Emerson moderated as Miller and John Crosby lined up against Theodore C. Kirkpatrick, spokesman for *Counterattack*. Miller charged that a "minuscule minority" of self-appointed guardians had ended the careers of a number of good actors, and Crosby called the compliant network executives "men of goodwill and small courage." In response, Kirkpatrick claimed that *Red Channels* was merely a bibliography. He then had to fend off charges of anti-Semitism and racism as well as blacklisting. Throughout the vituperative exchange, Kirkpatrick was not just double but triple-teamed: moderator Emerson addressed Crosby with an affectionate "John" and disdained Kirkpatrick with a chilly "Mr. Kirkpatrick."

The most comprehensive critique of the blacklist from within the industry was an exhaustive three-part series published by the advertising biweekly *Sponsor* in fall 1951. "Are American advertisers being blackmailed? What's behind Red Talent accusations?" asked the magazine. Anticommunist in temper but temperate in tone, the article expressed a consensus outlook about the blacklist: that communists must be kept off the air, of course, but that the situation had gotten out of hand. "The question of what to do with alleged subversives has become the most hush-hush subject along Madison Avenue and Michigan Boulevard," reported the editors. "Normally voluble executives changed into clams. Mention of the epithet 'Red Channels' transmuted usually fearless businessmen from lions into mice." The wall of silence, said *Sponsor*, spoke volumes.

To prevent private vigilante groups from intruding into "what is essentially the business of advertisers and the broadcasting industry alone," *Sponsor* called for the enactment of "a really effective plan for handling accusations and weeding out Communists on a just basis." What the industry needed was sanity—a reliable system for processing accusations and facilitating clearance in order to protect advertisers from "the current hysteria arising from pressure-group attacks on radio and TV." As *Sponsor* saw it, the harassed sponsor was the real victim of the blacklist.

By 1953, the racket had raced beyond Orwell and careened straight into Kafka. Even performers fired due to bad acting and shows canceled due to low ratings "suddenly find themselves lumped with suspect personalities and properties," noted *Variety*. "Confusion now exists over the status of shows that have been [taken] off the air purely for cancellation reasons to affect budgetary cutbacks or change of programs." Better to be thought unbankable than blacklistable.

Institutional Practices

Whereas the response of vulnerable entertainers to the blacklist varied according to ideology and temperament, the reaction of powerful institutions was consistent: networks, sponsors, and advertising agencies buckled in unison. In December 1950, CBS instituted loyalty oaths for its 2,500 regular employees and the next year required performers who appeared on the network "on a one-shot basis" to sign a statement as well. Referring to President Truman's recent declaration of a national emergency over the Korean War, CBS vice president Joseph H. Ream asserted that "the new crisis in our national life" required two courses of action: "first, we must make sure that our broadcasting operations in the public interest are not interrupted by sabotage or violence; second, we must make sure that the full confidence of our listeners and viewers is unimpaired." Extreme as it sounds in retrospect, Ream's nightmarish vision of bands of communist guerrillas roving Manhattan to sabotage CBS transmitters reflects a national temper made feverish by the Korean War and the Rosenberg arrests. "Even in World War II networks did not take such a step," whispered a fearful CBS employee.

The first television-related casualty attributed to *Red Channels* was the actress Jean Muir, then slated to star as the warm-hearted matriarch in NBC's *The Aldrich Family*. A sometime political activist and wife of Henry Jaffe, general counsel for the Television Authority, Muir had been listed for supporting the Spanish Refugee Relief Campaign and sending a cable of congratulations to the Moscow Arts Theater upon its fiftieth anniversary in 1948.

On August 27, 1950, an executive from General Foods, the sponsor of *The Aldrich Family*, appeared at the cast dress rehearsal to announce the cancellation of the show, scheduled to begin its fall season that same evening. He offered no explanation and answered no questions. Later Muir learned she had been fired. In a formal statement from General Foods she learned why: Jean Muir was "a controversial person" whose presence on *The Aldrich Family* might harm the sales of Jell-O. Muir declared that she had been "undeservedly attacked" and that her termination was ironic given her staunch opposition to communism, "which I regard as one of the most vicious influences in the world today." Pleading that she did not want to become "the center of a campaign," Muir loudly answered the $64 question. "I am not and never have been a member of the communist party." No matter: General Foods cared only about Muir's profile not her politics. The company bought out her 18-week contract for $10,000 and hired the noncontroversial Nancy Carroll to play Mrs. Alice Aldrich.

Protests of the Muir firing to network, sponsor, and ad agency were forceful but futile. The normally dulcet singer Rudy Vallee snarled that the firing of Jean Muir "stinks in Technicolor" and warned the publishers of *Red Channels* that if his name were ever listed he would not just sue for libel but "will come to see you with a horsewhip." The ACLU lectured General Foods that "the people of America need freedom as well as food, and a powerful corporation is specially obligated to take some risk to help them keep it," and then tried to prick the company's conscience with a patriotic appeal: "the makers of Jell-O might profit from the publicity identifying their product with the principle which is America's backbone." As more than one wag wisecracked, however, the corporate backbone was also made of Jell-O.

Rather than discouraging blacklisting, the Muir case simply taught television how better to blacklist. The abrupt, dramatic, and widely publicized firing of Jean Muir attracted the very kind of controversy the sponsor sought to avoid by firing Jean Muir. The Muir blacklisting was clunky and amateurish; future blacklistings would be smooth and professional.[3]

To streamline the operation of the blacklist, the television industry devised administrative procedures to assign responsibility and standardize decision-making. A typical case set into motion an orderly three-step process involving three principal players: a producer, a clearance officer, and an anticommunist agitator-*cum*-mediator. A television producer or perhaps a casting director telephoned a network or advertising agency executive (often with a formal title such as "security officer" or "clearance officer") tasked with vetting potential employees. The security officer possessed a list of controversial personalities, perhaps a copy of *Red Channels*, perhaps a private in-house list. After the producer uttered the name of the performer over the phone, the factotum checked the name against the list and red-flagged or green-lighted the performer. The potential employee could then be shelved or hired. Not incidentally, the third corner of the triangle might be the anticommunist agitator, perhaps Vincent Hartnett himself, who for a fee of two to twenty dollars investigated actors and adjudged them fit or unfit for broadcast.

Often performers were unaware of either the background check or the job opportunity. Often too, if performers knew they were under consideration and then rejected, they did not know the blacklistable offense. The lowest level of blacklist hell was reserved for the controversial personalities who didn't know why they were controversial or how to become uncontroversial.

Stripped of ideological trappings, the blacklist operated as a classic protection racket. Just as the racketeer promised the saloon owner security from a threat the racketeer embodied, the blacklister promised relief from a plight inflicted by the blacklister: picket lines, angry letters and telegrams, boycotts of shows and sponsors—in sum, the kind of ugly controversy that led to bad press and costly distractions. Demur and the store windows get smashed.

By the end of 1950, the blacklist had settled into standard operating procedure within the television industry, the cost of doing business. Under the trilateral arrangement, the producer got a cleared cast, the sponsor got a huge audience, and the racketeer got a nice payoff. Whatever the damage done to the career of the blacklisted artist and the quality of television programming, the racket thrived because it paid regular dividends to the principals.

---

3. Not until June 10, 1958, would Jean Muir sneak quietly back on television with a starring role in "The Story of Marsha Gordon" on *NBC Matinee Theatre*, prior to a more publicized return to prime time (on December 15, 1960) on CBS's *The Witness*, a short-lived courtroom drama set in a congressional hearing room.

THREE

CONTROVERSIAL PERSONALITIES

Though the effect of the blacklist was punitive, the rationale was preemptive. From the perspective of the networks, its purpose was less to rid the medium of subversive content than to avoid the uproar over suspect individuals. Rather than forcing the cancellation of scheduled appearances or firing known talent, the blacklist tended to operate off-camera, behind the scenes, by eliminating names from the potential talent pool. Neither networks nor sponsors wanted controversy or a *cause célèbre*; they wanted peace and profits.

Nonetheless, television was too public a medium to keep all its business private. The institutional workings of the blacklist surfaced most visibly when a familiar performer disappeared from the television screen after *Red Channels*-type agitation, when a famous artist tussled with a congressional committee, or when a principled recalcitrant blew the whistle on the racket.

Given the difficulty of proving a negative, the total number of entertainers burned by the blacklist—jobs lost, careers derailed, or energies squandered—is difficult to gauge, but hundreds were listed and investigated and thousands were singed by paranoia. Like the unhappy families in Tolstoy, each blacklist story is unhappy in a different way, but two case histories, at the extreme ends of the experience, may stand for many.

The Goldbergs: The Case of Philip Loeb

"Yoo-hoo, Mrs. Goldberg!" bellows a nasal voice from somewhere offscreen. Harkening to the summons—rather, "taking the yoo-hoo"—a plump, oval-faced matron appears at an apartment house window. She can only be Molly Goldberg, mother hen and ruler of the roost at 1038 East Tremont Avenue in the Bronx, home to the television family, *The Goldbergs*.

The Goldbergs (1949–1955) was a vintage exemplar of the ethnic situation comedy, a trademark genre from the early days of television. Thick with shtick and rife with stereotypes, the ethnic sitcom was part melting-pot melodrama, part situation comedy, and all cornball schmaltz. First on radio, then on Broadway, and finally on television, *The Goldbergs* claimed immigrant kinship to the Italian *Life with Luigi* (1952), the Irish *The Life of Riley* (1949–1958), and the Nordic *Mama* (1949–1956). What made the show exceptional was that it broke the restricted covenants of the airwaves in the tribal allegiance of the dramatis personae: the Goldbergs were Jews.

Running continuously on radio from November 1929 until March 1945, *The Goldbergs* ranked second only to *Amos 'n' Andy* in sheer longevity. Like *Amos 'n' Andy*, *The Goldbergs* trafficked in broad caricature and linguistic patois— not the alleged mangling of syntax by ill-educated blacks but the grafting of Yiddish onto English by Jewish immigrants. Despite being fixtures on the vaudeville stage since the 1890s, loquacious Jewish stereotypes offered a novel listening pleasure with the advent of radio. Due to "radio's fear of offending the racial and religious viewpoints of listeners-in . . . the only laugh material in dialect to slip by without censorship has been blackface talk," *Variety* reported in 1929. "Since broadcast of the Goldbergs' rise in broken lingo, there has been a constant stream of requests for more Hebe comedy."

Though never inspiring the fanatical devotion of Godsen and Correll's blackface duo or warranting the prestige berth of a continuous prime-time broadcast slot, *The Goldbergs* endured year in and year out on the strength of a loyal but limited fan base. Originally titled *The Rise of the Goldbergs*, the opening episodes chronicled the family's move from Hester Street to the Bronx with Park Avenue beckoning as the eventual summit of assimilation. During the Great Depression, however, the series dropped the presumptuous "rise" and veered away from weepy melodrama toward situation comedy. The themes of *The Goldbergs*—the ties that bind an extended family, plucky persistence in the face of adversity, tenacious faith in a better future—struck a special chord in the grim 1930s. Only the most cold-hearted nativist was unwarmed by the open-armed embrace of the American dream by Eastern European Jews, and America's embrace in turn. Even as Hitler ascended to power in Germany, *The Goldbergs* prospered in America, fostering "a certain quiet tolerance in a time of prejudice" as *New York Times* radio critic John K. Hutchins reflected in 1944.

The auteur of *The Goldbergs* was the redoubtable Gertrude Berg, a pioneer multihyphenate who played Molly, wrote the scripts, and produced and packaged the series. A control freak of obsessive dimensions (she once insisted that real eggs be fried on a skillet during a radio broadcast), Berg orchestrated every detail of the franchise that was her life's work. Dubbed the "Baalabosteh of the airwaves," she remains one of the few women in television history to reign on both sides of the camera.

Less a participant observer than a skilled ethnographer, Berg was the antithesis of her Molly persona: a cultured lady with a Park Avenue duplex and a twelve-room house next door to Tallulah Bankhead in Westchester County, social worlds away from the shtetl ambiance of the Lower East Side. Reportedly, she would walk like disguised royalty among the Jews of Delancey Street, "observing firsthand the mores of the people about whom she writes," and "finding incidents she can put into her scripts and keeping her ears attuned to the unique speech." Television fame later curtailed her excursions among the minions. "It is hard, darling," she confided. "Everybody now is getting to know what I look like."

In 1945 the show retired from radio after James R. Waters, the actor who had played Molly's husband Jake since 1929, was stricken with a cerebral hemorrhage mid-broadcast. His death was a melancholy punctuation to the classic radio days of *The Goldbergs*. In the postwar world, the series was a relic, creaking with ethnic arthritis even to its target demographic. Unlike the Bronxed-in Goldbergs, American Jews were moving far away, and not just geographically, from the gemeinschaft of New York City enclaves.

In 1948, when Berg took the franchise to Broadway under the title *Me and Molly*, she catered to a core audience now more likely to drive in from the suburbs than take the subway uptown. "Imagine *Awake and Sing* without the backing of Karl Marx and you have some notion of Mrs. Berg's drama of domesticity in the Bronx in 1919," theater critic Brooks Atkinson commented. Atkinson nailed the show on both counts. Not only was *Me and Molly* a Clifford Odets play without the leftist dogma, but in transporting the Goldbergs back to 1919, Berg acknowledged that the family fit more snugly in a bygone era, among the pushcarts and iceboxes of post–World War I America instead of the supermarkets and Frigidaires of post–World War II America.

Nonetheless, *Me and Molly* proved successful enough to inspire a revival of *The Goldbergs* on the airwaves, though now with a retrospective layer of wistfulness and condescension, a holdover from a more innocent time. On January 17, 1949, *The Goldbergs* debuted on television and that September revived on radio (the shows were not simulcast but broadcast as separate performances at different times with minor script alterations as dictated by the forum). "Television called for no important change in writing or even in acting technique from the radio version," Berg claimed, though she admitted that television technology was more daunting for creator and cast. "Radio was child's play by comparison. We would not be rehearsing twenty-seven hours every week for a half-hour show if it were easy."

In whatever medium, Berg incarnated the homespun, lovable Molly Goldberg, a Yiddische mama who ladled out malapropisms and folk wisdom with the chicken soup simmering perpetually on her stove. Presiding over an extended family in a cramped apartment, Molly was a whirlwind of activity whose battle-ship proportions never slowed down her forty-knot cruising speed. The humor derived from the Yiddish lilt in her voice as she fumbled through the twists and turns of American vernacular. "Give me a swallow the glass," Molly says when thirsty. "It's time to expire," she announces at bedtime.

Tied to Molly's apron strings were two deeply assimilated all-American children, an Old World uncle soaked in borscht, and a husband smart enough to know he was only the titular head of the household. On television, daughter Rosalie (played by an Irish American princess named Arlene McQuade) was a precocious teenager, who, in keeping with the Freudian zeitgeist of the 1950s, grew into a dedicated student of psychoanalysis. "Every word you say to her has eighteen meanings," clucks Molly. "She wants to know all my dreams." Son Sammy (originally Larry Robinson, later Tom Taylor) was a sturdy youth who served offscreen in the army for much of the show's run during the Korean War, just as the radio Sammy had been shipped overseas during World War II. Uncle David (Yiddish stage actor Eli Mintz) was the hangdog hanger-on with little to do save read the newspapers aloud and kvetch about his lowly status in the familial pecking order ("still the also . . . "). Starring as Jake Goldberg, Molly's loving but harried husband, was a well-regarded New York stage actor named Philip Loeb.

When *The Goldbergs* premiered on television, viewers knew the backstory, the lineup, and the accents. "Despite a 17-year reign on radio, *The Goldbergs* as video fare is still alive and kicking," enthused *Variety*. "There's no basic change in the familiar characterizations, but it's as though a new dimension has been added to bring them to life via the new medium." To others, though, the old routine smelled stale on arrival. "While *The Goldbergs* does offer a certain nostalgic appeal to those familiar with the background," conceded the *Hollywood Reporter*, "at best the appeal is a limited one that will appear almost esoteric to most audiences."

For American Jews, of course, the Goldbergs of the Bronx were far less esoteric than the Protestant-Norwegian Hansens of San Francisco on *Mama*. Fortunately for Berg, the New York metropolitan area accounted for a disproportionate number of television-equipped households, thereby allowing the regionally clustered Jewish population to skew the overall ratings. Despite the seemingly narrow demographic niche, *The Goldbergs* ranked among the three most highly rated television shows in the East to Midwest circuit in 1949–1950. It was also the first television show popular enough to inspire a feature film version, released under two titles—first *The Goldbergs*, then *Molly* (1950)—so moviegoers wouldn't think the film was a big-screen version of a television episode they had already seen. "No doubt the picture will prove especially popular in metropolitan areas," speculated *Motion Picture Daily*.

No doubt: but Broadway and Hollywood had been selling Jewish schmaltz to Christian America since before *The Jazz Singer* (1927). Fan letters to *The Goldbergs*, said Berg, always maintained a steady 50–50 average between Jews and non-Jews. Berg loved to tell the story about a Mother Superior who wrote her requesting a synopsis of the last six weeks of programming for her convent. Though loyal listeners, the nuns had given up *The Goldbergs* for Lent, and "now they were wondering what had happened."

Chances are the good sisters had not missed too much. From the Depression thirties to the Cold War fifties, *The Goldbergs* occupied that peculiar time warp inhabited by comic-strip characters and picaresque heroes, where life was static and personality immutable. Son Sammy first began studying for his bar mitzvah on the radio show in 1930 and was still memorizing his Hebrew decades later. "You see, darling," Berg explained. "I don't bring up anything that will bother people. That's very important. Unions, politics, fund-raising, Zionism, socialism, inter-group relations, I don't stress them at all. After all, aren't all such things secondary to daily family living?"

The Goldbergs was an unlikely site for subversive activity, but perhaps the very all-Americanism of the assimilationist conceit—and the nascent suspicion of the American Jew as an alien intruder in Christian America—targeted the show for special scrutiny. In *The Jazz Singer*, when a piano-playing Al Jolson ad-libs to his beloved mother, he jokes about moving her away from the ghetto-like Lower East Side to the bourgeois promised land of the Bronx, among "the Ginsbergs, and the Guttenbergs, and the Goldbergs—oh, a whole lot of 'Bergs.'" After 1950, the suffix of the Jewish surname sent back another echo. Next door to the Goldbergs might reside the Rosenbergs.

Among the 151 names listed in *Red Channels* was that of Philip Loeb, the actor who played Jake Goldberg, Molly's husband. A steady and strong Jewish patriarch, Jake was a serene breadwinner struggling, in his postwar incarnation, not just to make ends meet but to grab the next rung up the ladder: to outfit Rosalie for summer camp, to send Sammy off to a good college, to sustain Molly in her schemes for self-improvement via dance lessons, book clubs, and exercise classes.

Loeb had been an actor, stage manager, and director in New York theater since 1916, the kind of yeoman performer better known around the tightly knit community of New York actors than to the public at large. By all accounts, he was a generous teacher to apprentice actors and a tireless worker for his union, Actors' Equity. He was also a fervent political activist, lending his name and energies to a number of Popular Front causes in the 1930s. As

The all-American Jewish family: Jake (Philip Loeb), Molly (Gertrude Berg), a houseguest (Eberhard Krunschmidt), Rosie (Arlene Mc-Quade), Sammy (Larry Robinson), and Uncle David (Eli Mintz) on the CBS television version of *The Goldbergs* (1949). (Courtesy Photofest)

with many nonmarquee actors who had long labored for scale wages on the stage and screen, Loeb traded the downside of typecasting for the upside of a regular paycheck. With *The Goldbergs*, his ship had docked: a prominent berth on a beloved, long-running show.

Like Loeb, the General Foods Corporation also found *The Goldbergs* a profitable family to be around. The company had sponsored the show on both television and radio since its revival in 1949. In character as Molly, Berg opened and closed each episode extolling the virtues of Sanka instant coffee from her apartment window, where an empty can of Sanka served conspicuously as a plant pot. "When Molly Goldberg leans out the window she almost makes a Sanka Anonymous do a backslide," *Variety* raved, rating her with pitchman par excellence Arthur Godfrey as "easily the two top video hucksters extant." But General Foods, as the blacklisted Jean Muir knew, was especially sensitive to the menu of forbidden items listed in *Red Channels*. Having readily purged a controversial personality playing a gentile matriarch on *The Aldrich Family*, the company showed an ecumenical intolerance for a controversial personality playing a Jewish patriarch on *The Goldbergs*.

To avoid the very public uproar surrounding the firing of Jean Muir, General Foods sought to handle the termination of Philip Loeb quietly. On September 16, 1950, Loeb and Rebecca Brownstein, a lawyer for Actors' Equity, met Berg, her husband, her lawyer, and her agent at Berg's home. Loeb was told that General Foods, through CBS, had informed Berg that if Loeb were not fired in two days, the program would be canceled. Berg offered Loeb $85,000 to buy out the remainder of his five-year contract. (Berg denied that she had ever made the initial offer of $85,000 to Loeb and said that his contract had expired.)

Loeb refused. "I don't want to take the money," he told Berg. "I want to fight it." A distraught Berg backtracked. She embraced Loeb and promised, "I will not fire you. I will stick by you."

Faced with a newly defiant Berg, General Foods backed down and retained the show with Loeb until June 1951 when "for business reasons" it then dropped *The Goldbergs*. The next month, unaware of the internecine controversy, NBC snapped up *The Goldbergs* for "an exclusive long term contract" at the hefty price tag of $350,000. The network planned to debut the show in the upcoming fall season.

Thus far, the intrigue over Loeb had remained in house and out of the press, but the affair went public when Jack O'Brian, television critic at the *New York Journal-American*, revealed that "the real reason *The Goldbergs* disappeared from the Columbia Broadcasting System after a long and luxurious hiatus in that network's pink-tinged boudoir" was that Loeb was "a veteran sponsor of organizations named by Congress or the U.S. Attorney General as Communist fronts." Never discreet about naming names, O'Brian gloated that "the Columbia Broadcasting System may deny it, but won't most of the flagrant *Red Channels* nominees find it necessary to earn their crackers and caviar on other networks next fall? Including Philip Loeb of *The Goldbergs*?"

After O'Brian's exposé, the once hot show was given a "cold shoulder" by ad agencies. Skittish about Loeb, nearly twenty potential sponsors rejected *The Goldbergs*, despite the fact that NBC sales executives crowed about how Sanka coffee sales had risen 57 percent while its logo graced Molly's windowsill on CBS. Suspecting a "silent conspiracy" because of Loeb, NBC delayed the air date of the show.

"Since Sanka's cancellation there have been no lines of sponsors queuing up in front of my door," Loeb told *Sponsor* during the hiatus. "I was not consulted before the show was dropped, even though the sponsor knew I had officially stated I am not and never have been a member of the Communist Party." Loeb declined to take another well-traveled path to penance. "No, I have not dignified the *Red Channels* people by giving them a personal statement. NBC-TV has picked up *The Goldbergs*, and I am hopefully sure that Mrs. Berg will fulfill her contract with me."

However, unable to sell the show with Loeb in the cast, Berg finally capitulated. According to Loeb, she communicated the news to him by telephone. "Philip, I have some bad news for you; I have sold the show without you," she confessed. "I would rather cut off my right arm than do this. Maybe when the situation clears up, I will take you back. I would like to have you back, but I can't sell it with you; therefore I am going to let you go. My lawyer will call on your lawyer today."

Loeb knew what was afoot. "I have been blacklisted on smear premises, shadowy indicated, which are untrue."

On January 11, 1952, the Loeb case was debated at an emotionally charged meeting of Actors' Equity, where a resolution before the membership urged the Television Authority (TvA) to declare *The Goldbergs* "unfair."[1] After listening to his case be debated, Loeb rose to take the floor. "I always wanted to speak at my own funeral," he began laconically. "It is not only my own funeral; it is a divorce. I am losing my entire family. I am not only losing my family, but I will have to watch them in the hands of another man." He continued: "Since this *Red Channels* thing came up, I have never received any calls at all for work, although before that time, not only with *The Goldbergs* and another program, I was called, and for the last six months I am not called at all for radio and television." The membership of Actors' Equity gave Loeb an ovation and voted 180 to 3 to label *The Goldbergs* "unfair" as long as Loeb was barred from the program—an act that, if approved by the TvA, would have forbidden the rest of the cast from performing on the show.

Like the meeting at Actors' Equity, the TvA meeting on Loeb's case was "riotous." The options for the fledgling union were bleak. To back Loeb and label *The Goldbergs* "unfair" would mean the unemployment of the entire cast and the likely end of the show; to refuse to take action would mean that the TvA condoned the blacklist while throwing a loyal union member to the wolves. "Either of two things will happen," Loeb declared. "Those who have made al-

---

1. The Television Authority (TvA) was formed in 1949 to mediate employment disputes in the field of television. On September 20, 1952, TvA merged with the American Federation of Radio Artists (AFRA) to form the umbrella union for performers in the two broadcasting media, the American Federation of Television and Radio Artists (AFTRA).

legations against me may be afraid to make their charges in the light of an open court, or they make them and I'll blast them to pieces."

But it was Loeb who was blasted off the air. A few weeks before the scheduled premiere of *The Goldbergs* on February 4, 1952, NBC announced his dismissal from the show. Left with no choice but to fold his cards, Loeb agreed to a deal, brokered by the TvA, in which Berg paid him $40,000 to sever the two remaining years on his contract. The writer Rex Stout, on behalf of the Author's League of America, called on the Federal Communications Commission (FCC) to hold hearings to investigate Loeb's blacklisting, but the FCC, characteristically, claimed no jurisdiction.

Almost immediately, NBC sold the show to Vitamin Corporation of America, whose officials, at least in public, seemed less nervous about Loeb than either CBS or NBC. "This may sound stupid on my part," said company president Morton Edell, "but at that time I'd never heard of the controversy about Mr. Loeb." Loeb's denial of communist affiliation "has me on edge," Edell admitted. "I feel terrible. If he is a communist I wouldn't want him within a thousand miles of the show. But if he is not, I wish there were some way to find out." When asked whether Vitamin Corporation of America would have sponsored the program with Loeb in the cast, a company spokesman stated, "The question never came up. We bought *The Goldbergs* as a whole. I would have bought it with Mr. Loeb. I believe a man is innocent until he is proved guilty." From *Red Channels* to General Foods to CBS to NBC to Vitamin Corporation of America and back—no one wanted to take responsibility for blacklisting Loeb. "Who is the culprit?" Loeb pleaded. "Who kicked me off the program?"

After the settlement, the three parties to the dispute all issued statements. Loeb was gracious:

> Despite the fact that I believe a grave injustice is being done to myself and others in the entertainment industry by this "blacklisting," I appreciate Mrs. Gertrude Berg's position throughout this situation. I see nothing gained in this particular case by creating a situation which will interfere with the return of *The Goldbergs* or which would deprive other actors of employment on this show or disappoint millions of viewers who have been looking forward eagerly to its return.

Loeb insisted that his agreement to a financial settlement was not an admission that he regarded "the vicious practice of blacklisting as inevitable," merely that he felt compelled to accept an "unsatisfactory" resolution in the interest of all concerned.

TvA released a statement deploring "the unfortunate dilemma which confronted Gertrude Berg and Philip Loeb as individuals" but wished to "commend

Gertrude Berg for her courageous stand during the past one and a half years against blacklisting in broadcasting. We appreciate that her discontinuance of Philip Loeb's services was necessitated by broad pressure beyond her control and does not constitute a reflection on Mr. Loeb."

Abashed, Berg issued a poignant apology:

Philip Loeb has stated categorically that he is not and never has been a Communist. I believe him. No evidence has been presented to the contrary. I believe in the American principle that a person is innocent until proven guilty. In these respects, there is no dispute between Philip Loeb and myself.

The producer-star summed up her dilemma:

I have had to discontinue the services of Philip Loeb because of the failure of anyone to assure employment to persons who are merely controversial as contrasted with those who are Communists. Since going off the air last June [1951], I have fought to make this distinction and continue Mr. Loeb's services. I regret that my efforts have been unavailing since this is a problem which can be solved only by the industry as a body and not me as an individual.[2]

Having jettisoned her costar, Berg needed to find a new screen husband, fast. After some "frantic auditioning" at NBC, Harold J. Stone, then playing in *Stalag 17* on Broadway, was hired to replace Loeb and written into the premiere episode. Yoked to a new costar and a new sponsor, Berg, in character as Molly, now trilled the virtues of Rybutal vitamin capsules to her neighbors across the courtyard window.

After two years of irregular scheduling and middling ratings on NBC, *The Goldbergs* moved to DuMont in 1954 and the new network recruited a new Jake, the actor Robert H. Harris. By 1955, when Molly and the family, now on film and in syndication, packed up the *mezuzah* from their Bronx apartment and fled to the mythical suburb of Haverville, the show also seemed ready to be put out to pasture. "Isn't it possible that the specialized area of Jewish humor-folklore is a thing of the past?" *Variety* speculated. "It's entirely possible that the longrunning *Goldbergs* is the last and final holdout in the field." In one haunting episode, a lonely Molly prowls her well-furnished but sterile

---

2. In what literary scholars would call a "structured absence," Gertrude Berg makes no reference to the Loeb controversy in her 1961 memoir *Molly and Me*.

suburban home, her once-bustling hive now still and empty, the children grown and flown the coop, the nearest neighbor an acre of lawn away, well out of "yoo-hoo" range. Intratextually, with the visual equivalent of three different mates in three years, Molly may have seemed less the faithful Yiddische mama than a husband-swapping *korvah*.

Upwardly mobile though the Goldbergs were, moving in the course of their television life from a small apartment in the Bronx to a spacious home in suburban Haverville, *The Goldbergs* was downwardly mobile on the airwaves, plummeting from prime-time showpiece on CBS (1949–1951), to shifting time slots and haphazard scheduling on NBC (1952–53), to the bargain-basement shelves at DuMont (1954), and finally to the dimestore of filmed syndication (1955). As the Goldbergs rose, *The Goldbergs* sank.

More than anticommunism or anti-Semitism, the shifting demographics of television may best explain the waning fortunes of *The Goldbergs*. Like Milton Berle, whose vaudeville antics on *Texaco Star Theater* made him television's first superstar when a New York City minority owned a majority of television sets, *The Goldbergs* was destined to be ethnically anomalous as television spread across America. "There is some hinterland TV trade and audience opinion that there's too much borscht tinting TV comedians," cautioned *Variety*'s veteran reporter Abel Green in 1951. "The Catskill Mt. resort-trained comics are coming into their own in vaudeo, and while the New York metropolitan area has almost 50% of the 10,000,000 TV sets in U.S. homes today, there is still a sizable audience away from a melting pot metropolis like Gotham." The future of television lay out in the heartland, away from the Judeo-centric regions of the greater New York area. Warning against what he called "Lindy's patois," "dialectic boobytraps," and "nitery asides," Green argued that the wisecracks exchanged at Jewish delicatessens like Lindy's in New York "don't belong on TV." The homespun humor of *The Goldbergs*, Green hastened to protest, was "as frank in [its] idiom as *Mama* is in its Norwegian derivation," but Berg's humor was no less tinted by borscht than Berle's.

If gentile America was thought to require subtitles to comprehend the Lindy's patois of a borscht-flavored sitcom, American Jews sometimes cringed at the Old World caricatures parading on video. "A certain segment of the nation's viewers have found fault with *The Goldbergs*, asserting that the show tends to perpetuate the stereotype of the people about whom Mrs. Berg writes," *TV Guide* noted in 1953, straining for a circumlocution for the ethnicity in question. "But Mrs. Berg treats the characters so sympathetically that the show actually should help, not hinder, the fight against bigotry and intolerance." Perhaps so, but by then even the target ethnicity was deserting the show.

Meanwhile, Philip Loeb was faring materially worse than his former television family. On April 25, 1952, he was called to testify before a closed session of the Senate Internal Security Subcommittee. Like many Popular Front veterans, he attributed his association with radical causes to his "humanitarian leanings," insisting he was neither a communist nor a fellow traveler. Somewhat contradictorily, he testified that he found such investigations commendable but also considered them illegal. Loeb's closed-door testimony was later released, but neither HUAC nor the McCarran committee subpoenaed him at an open hearing, an indication that the actor was pretty much what he claimed to be, a liberal actor with a good heart.

Exiled from the airwaves after his dismissal from *The Goldbergs*, Loeb hustled for theater work. In 1953 he counted himself fortunate to land a part on Broadway and later in the touring company of the hit comedy *Time Out for Ginger*.

Sitting among the theatergoers watching Loeb were agents of the Federal Bureau of Investigation. Though the FBI had kept a file on Loeb since 1940, his *Red Channels*–inspired notoriety earned him a fresh listing in the FBI's "security index" of suspect individuals. Though not known communists, suspect individuals (the FBI's version of "controversial personalities") still warranted surveillance as potential security risks. Confidential FBI informants described Loeb as a "concealed communist" who "has always followed the Communist Party line and continues to do so until this day [June 2, 1951]." The FBI adjudged him "sponsor, member, and supporter of numerous Communist Party front organizations."

For years, the FBI kept tabs on Loeb, its field agents filing reports as he played in the touring company of *Time Out for Ginger* or languished in unemployment around New York. Eventually, Loeb's FBI watcher came to a decision and went out on a limb. "Since there is no definite information concerning [Loeb's] membership in the communist party within the past five years or activity in a front group," he advised in a memorandum dated August 25, 1955, "it is recommended that subject be removed from the Security Index." Five years after his name was published in *Red Channels*, Loeb had, even in the eyes of the FBI, proved he was no threat to national security.

A week later, on September 1, 1955, Loeb checked in to the Hotel Taft in New York and swallowed an overdose of sleeping pills. He left no note. The ailing 61-year-old actor had plenty of reason to be despondent: his beloved wife had died and his mentally disabled son required constant medical care. Of course, he was also worn out and impoverished by then, and, despite a recent upsurge in stage work, the blacklist still denied him the full compensations and consolations of his craft. In a melodramatic twist that Gertrude Berg at her most maudlin would have balked at scripting, Loeb closed his own file unaware that the FBI, if not CBS and NBC, had finally processed his clearance.

I Love Lucy: The Redhead and the Blacklist

The first true coast-to-coast sensation born of television, Lucille Ball was the most beloved and profitable performer of the 1950s, perhaps, adjusted for inflation, in the history of the medium. Unlike Gertrude Berg, a matron from another age, milking the calcifying genre of the ethnic sitcom, tossed from network to network and time slot to time slot, Lucy was a slim product of postwar American prosperity and the queen bee of CBS. Star of the number one–rated show in television from 1952 to 1955, she embodied the named object in *I Love Lucy*, with the antecedent of the pronoun being not just her hyper-temperamental Cuban husband Desi Arnez/Ricky Ricardo but, so it seemed, all America.

In a decade misremembered as all whitebread homogeneity, male dominance, and stately decorum, the first breakout television show was brazenly multicultural, emphatically female-driven, and loopily anarchic: Lucy Ricardo (née MacGillicuddy) and Ricky Ricardo, zany redhead and hot-blooded Latin, cornfed girl and exotic spice, wild woman and straight man. In episode after episode, Lucy's will to power deflated Ricky's faux machismo. No wonder feminist critics have embraced *I Love Lucy* as a concave window into the blinkered options of the 1950s female, the repressed housewife kept under lock and key like a medieval princess chained in a tower by an evil ogre: Lucilleball, Lucilleball, let down your red hair.

Faded and creaky after decades as a syndication evergreen, *I Love Lucy* glowed with the blithe spirit of its vivacious star during its original run. In context, the show was fast, fresh, and cutting edge. Unlike Milton Berle's vintage vaudeo, with the static theatrical stage as proscenium arch and the Catskills as training ground, *I Love Lucy* exuded a crisp ultramodern sensibility, a mobile sitcom shot on film "before a live studio audience." Edited into a concise twenty-four minutes, it made a practical commercial package for staggered time-zone telecasting, summer reruns, and global syndication. Drawing the blueprints for the sitcom genre, producer-star Desi Arnez devised the innovative three-camera setup for filming rehearsals and live performances, the sharper resolution of 35mm celluloid and the smooth intercutting of close-ups and medium shots showcasing the malleable face and agile physicality of his versatile spouse-star. "She is a consummate artist, born for television," gushed Dan Jenkins at the *Hollywood Reporter*. "She combines the facial mobility of Red Skelton, the innate pixie quality of Harpo Marx, and the daffily jointless abandon of the Patchwork Girl of Oz, all rolled in to one."

From its debut on October 15, 1951, *I Love Lucy* was heralded as a zeitgeist avatar. Reaching back for a telling precedent, television critic Jack Gould declared that "not since the heyday of the fifteen minute broadcast of *Amos 'n'*

Hot-blooded Latin and zany redhead: Desi Arnez and Lucille Ball strike an iconic pose in CBS's *I Love Lucy*. (Courtesy Photofest)

Andy, which back in the 1930s brought American home life to a halt every evening, has a program so completely caught the attention of the public."

Naturally, the attention of advertisers followed. In what CBS hailed as the "largest single contract ever signed in television," Philip Morris agreed to a noncancelable contract to sponsor *I Love Lucy* for an unprecedented $8 million. Company president O. Parker McComas bragged to a convention of financial analysts that he considered the deal a bargain.

As you must be aware, this show is the all-time phenomenon of the entertainment business. On a strictly dollars-and-cents basis, it is twice as efficient as the average nighttime television show in conveying our advertising message to the public. It is nearly three times more efficient dollar-wise in reaching adults than *Life* or your own newspapers. Three times more people see every Monday night's *I Love Lucy* show than watched all the major league baseball games last year.

Speaking the advertising lingo of the day, suffixwise, McComas put the $8 million in perspective:

Dollar-wise, although the entire sum sounds huge, it is probably one of, if not the most, efficient advertising buys in the entire country. In addition, we derive many supplementary merchandising and publicity benefits from the show. As you can see, "We Love Lucy."

The *I Love Lucy* phenomenon rocketed to stratospheric heights during the Eisenhower inauguration ceremonies, an event it basically upstaged. In a landmark sacrifice of privacy in the service of publicity, Lucille Ball's real-life pregnancy was shared with Lucy Ricardo. In the December 8, 1952, episode, Lucy needs to break the news of the blessed event to a clueless Ricky. Facing an atypical dilemma—not trying to keep a secret from Ricky but trying to tell him one—Lucy wants to pick just the right moment to break the big news. Though the upstairs neighbors, the Ike and Mamie-like Fred and Ethel Mertz (William Frawley and Vivian Vance), are privy to the secret, Desi is too preoccupied with rehearsals at the Copacabana nightclub to interpret Lucy's frantic hints. Lucy decides to go to the Copa and make an anonymous request for Ricky to sing "We're Having a Baby, My Baby and Me." Ricky croons the tune to likely couples sitting around the bandstand, all of whom shake their heads—not us. Finally, Ricky comes upon Lucy, sitting alone at a table, glowing. He gets it.

At the time, a plotline build around pregnancy was a risqué scenario, for the word *pregnant* had yet to be uttered on the big screen outside the frame of a sex education film. Yet Protestant, Roman Catholic, and Jewish clergy all gave their blessings to the delicate handling of Lucy's delicate condition. "We made no attempt to hide Lucille's condition," declared Desi. "She wore maternity dresses just as she did in real life."

Though the gestation period for the baby was televisually compressed (in the December 8, 1952, episode, Lucille Ball is concealing a pregnancy that will come to term the next month), network scheduling outweighed the mathematics of reproduction. In fact the pregnancy, birth, and infant episodes were filmed over the previous summer, before Lucy's condition became too visible.

Fortunately, Lucy's obstetrical matched her comic timing. IT'S A BOY! shouted banner headlines, publishing the birth announcement: Desiderio Alberto Arnez IV born at 8:00 A.M. on January 19, 1953, at Cedars of Lebanon

Hospital and Ricky Ricardo Jr. born at 9:00 P.M. on January 19, 1953, at CBS. The pre-scripted gender of the child was pure serendipity. "It would be nice to have a boy," Lucy had said. "I'll have one on television anyway." That night an estimated 44 million people "joined Mr. Ricardo in the fathers' waiting room," the show accruing an all-time high Trendex rating of 68.8 for a regular commercial program. Delivering Little Ricky the day before Dwight D. Eisenhower delivered his inaugural address as president of the United States, the fertile Ricardos easily out-Nielsened the menopausal Eisenhowers.

On April 3, 1953, the prince of the first family of television graced the cover of the premiere issue of *TV Guide*. Under the headline "Lucy's $50,000,000 Baby," the article tallied up the ancillary marketing opportunities spawned by Little Ricky's nativity: nursery sets, baby clothes, toys, games, and "a Lucy living room suite modeled on the TV furniture" (a series of tie-ins not open to the childless honeymooners occupying a cold-water flat on CBS's *The Jackie Gleason Show*).

Offscreen too, the couple's success prefigured the cultural ascendancy of the medium they dominated. Desilu, their eponymous production company, thrived. (By 1958, residuals from *I Love Lucy* would finance Desilu's purchase of RKO, a television company supplanting a Hollywood studio.)

The heartwarming success story of Lucille Ball and Desi Arnez—a husband-and-wife shop selling ethnic pluralism, upward mobility, entrepreneurial smarts, and healthy fecundity—reads like a template of Cold War virtues. That the blacklist cast its shadow over the all-American couple suggests just how all-American the blacklist was.

On September 6, 1953, Walter Winchell read a blind item on his Sunday night ABC telecast, *The Walter Winchell Show*, a 15-minute fusillade of show business and political gossip. "While the House Committee on Un-American Activities was holding secret sessions in California, the most popular of all television stars was confronted with her membership in the Communist Party," brayed Winchell. Viewers could do the math: "the most popular of all television stars" plus a female pronoun equaled Lucille Ball.

After Winchell rattled off his coded accusation, the buzz during the next week insinuated the culprit's identity. Though the notion of the zany redhead in cahoots with the reds conjures a madcap sitcom scenario—imagine a teenage Lucy MacGillicuddy muscling her way into a Federal Theatre Project production of *The Cradle Will Rock* with calamitous results—the stakes were high and the drama was dead serious. "Lucille Ball announces in the current *Silver Screen* magazine that she intends to retire in five years," television critic Jack O'Brian snickered. "It may be a lot sooner than Lucille plans."

Hot on the scent, Hedda Hopper, the powerful show business gossip columnist, telephoned Lucy and Desi to get the lowdown. Both denied the

Winchell report. "You tell your readers this, Hedda," insisted Desi, trying out a line he would use often in the next few days, "the only thing that is red about this kid is her hair—and even that is not legitimately red."

Again, a backfire from the once–Popular Front ignited the controversy. In 1936 Lucille Ball, with her mother Mrs. Desiree E. Ball and her brother Fred H. Ball, had all registered their intention with the County Registrar of Voters in Los Angeles County to vote for the Communist Party ticket. That same year, Lucy had also signed a petition sponsoring the candidacy for state assembly of a Communist Party candidate named Emil Freed. Allegedly too she had been nominated to be a delegate at the Central Committee of the Communist Party in California and had hosted communist meetings at her home.

The charges against Lucy were actually a decade old, having originally been aired in 1943 during hearings conducted by a committee of the California legislature, under the chairmanship of state senator Jack Tenney.[3] Lending credibility to the accusation was Lucy's membership in the Committee for the First Amendment, a group of Hollywood stars who had flown to Washington, D.C., in October 1947 to protest the original HUAC hearings. Speaking out in defense of the Hollywood Ten, Lucy had sounded very nonzany. "The way to [defend the Constitution] is not by shutting up the man you disagree with," she declared. "All civil liberties go hand in hand, and when one goes, the others are weakened, just as the collapse of one pillar in a house would endanger the whole structure."

Thus did Lucille Ball come to the attention of congressional investigators. Two days before Winchell's telecast, on September 4, 1953, a HUAC subcommittee consisting of Donald L. Jackson (R-Calif.) and Clyde Doyle (D-Calif.) held executive sessions in Hollywood. Among the witnesses who testified was Lucille Ball, her mother, and her brother. Casting herself midway between prodigal politico and self-styled dupe, Lucy claimed ignorance and naïveté. "I have never been too civic minded and certainly never politically minded in my life," she testified. As Lucy told the story, her eccentric old grandfather, Fred C. Hunt, a lifelong socialist, had implored her mother and her to register as communists and to sign the petition for the communist candidate Emil Freed. To placate the old man, both had done so. Even around the Ball household, her crusty grandfather was forever agitating for the little man and undermining the family's domestic help. "We were never able to keep a maid although we paid the highest prices we could afford," Lucy testified. She denied ever hosting

3. Throughout the 1940s, the Tenney committee served as a kind of state auxiliary to HUAC.

communist meetings at her home and claimed ignorance of her alleged appointment to the Central Committee of the California Communist Party.

Despite her guileless pose, Lucy evinced a shrewd understanding of the calibrations of Popular Front politics. As a staunch FDR-liberal, she admitted
that "we went maybe a little strongly Democratic one year and we got into
trouble doing that. That was when Roosevelt was still alive." FDR "was the
only President I had ever known," she mused, and "in those days [registering
as communist] was not a big, terrible thing to do. It was almost as terrible to
be a Republican in those days." As for her support of the Hollywood Ten in
1947, she asserted, "I was never in sympathy with the Dmytryks.[4] I can't remember any of the other names."

On Friday, September 11, 1953, five days after Winchell telecast his blind
item, the full story of Lucy's HUAC testimony broke in the *Los Angeles Herald
and Express*, which published a photostat copy of the 1936 voter registration
card on which she had signed her intention to vote for the Communist Party
candidate. Confronted by a reporter, a frazzled Desi Arnez snapped, "What
are you going to do—spread it all over the country?"

At 6:00 P.M. that evening, with the story emblazoned above the fold on late-
edition newspapers across the nation and highlighted on radio and television
reports all day, HUAC member Donald Jackson took an unprecedented step.
To refute the "conjecture and rumor with respect to Miss Ball and the extent of
her association and activities on behalf of the Communist Party" and "in light
of the fact that irreparable damage may result to Miss Ball unless the full extent
of the committee's information is disclosed," he called a press conference to
announce that he was satisfied that Lucy "had never had a role in the communist party." He disclosed officially what Winchell and the press had already reported, that Lucy, her mother, and her brother had all testified before HUAC
the previous week. Though Jackson noted that "the investigation is continuing"
and "no case is ever closed," he emphasized that "there is no shred of evidence"
linking Lucy with the Communist Party. HUAC had taken the unusual step of
making a formal public exculpation because "independent sources outside of
the committee" had exposed Miss Ball's record and the committee was anxious
that no injustice be done. "There rests upon the committee an obligation to in-
sure that distortion of available facts be not permitted and that rumor not be
substituted for truth in any case," Jackson declared. "The prominence of Miss
Ball as an outstanding moving picture and television artist is secondary to the
committee's determination to be fair and just in all instances."

---

4. Director Edward Dmytryk was one of the original Hollywood Ten.

Exculpation: Rep. Donald L. Jackson (D-Calif.) (*arrow*) announces that the House Committee on Un-American Activities has "no evidence Miss Ball is or was a member of the communist party" (September 11, 1953). (Courtesy Herald Examiner Collection/Los Angeles Public Library)

By a happy coincidence surpassing even the timing of Little Ricky's birth, the first episode of the new season of *I Love Lucy* was scheduled for filming before a live studio audience of three hundred Lucy-philes at Motion Picture Center Studios that very evening. The emotionally charged atmosphere was chronicled by Dan Jenkins in a special report in *TV Guide*, entitled "The Lucille Ball–Communist Probe Story." Forced to report on a television story that the national guide to television had studiously avoided since its debut issue, Jenkins gave a description of the tense evening that is the only feature article on the blacklist in *TV Guide* during the height of the blacklist era.

"Welcome to the first *I Love Lucy* show," Arnez announced to the studio audience. "We are glad to see you back and we are glad to be back ourselves. But before we go on, I want to talk to you about something serious. Something very serious. You all know what it is. The papers have been full of it all day."

"Lucille is no communist," he insisted. "We both despise the communists and everything they stand for."

"Desi is an emotional Latin," columnist Jenkins pointed out. "His eyes now filled with tears and his voice was shaking. He was angry."

"Lucille is 100 per cent an American," Arnez declared. "She is as American as Barry Baruch and Ike Eisenhower [the emotional Latin being cool-headed enough to select a New York Jew and a Kansas Methodist] and last November we both voted for Ike Eisenhower."

Desi then introduced Lucy as "my favorite redhead," adding: "That's the only thing red about Lucy—and even that is not legitimate."

Spotting Lucy, the studio audience cheered wildly. She denied she was ever a communist and declared, "When you're right, you're right. I have nothing to fear."

Earlier that day, when the story appeared in the *Los Angeles Herald and Express*, Lucy had telephoned a miffed Hedda Hopper to make amends. Sobbing, she apologized for not fessing up during their previous conversation. "The reason we didn't tell you the other day was that the committee had asked us not to," Lucy explained. "If I did something wrong to you the other day, please forgive me," pleaded Desi. "When you get in a spot like this, you don't know what the hell you're doing."

Mollified by her juicy scoop, Hopper penned a sympathetic account of l'affair Lucy for the front page of the *Los Angeles Times*. "It's terrible, Hedda, that something the poor kid did in 1936 to please her grandfather can kick back in her face now," said an exasperated Desi, taking the phone when Lucy broke down in tears. "She has never in her life done wrong to anyone; has never had any sympathy for these Commies. You know, the girl has never even been connected with these pinks out here; she has never gone to meetings, never been a member of their party—this is terrible, Hedda."

On Saturday afternoon, the Desilu damage control continued at a poolside press conference at the couple's five-acre estate in the San Fernando Valley. Asked if she thought her registration as a communist in 1936 would hurt her career, Lucy replied, "I have more faith in the American people than that. I think any time you give the American people the truth, they're with you." As Lucy's eyes watered, Desi kissed her cheek and confided, "Now Lucy, I wanna tell you. I have been married to you thirteen years and in that time you have signed I don't know how may thousands of papers. And you haven't read one of them yet!" Badgered with another intrusive question—"How old were you then?"—Lucy stood on her gender rights. "I don't even know how old I am now," she snapped.

As the Lucy story careened and crescendoed, the network, the sponsor, the public—all the usual suspects, ordinarily so willing to fold under pressure and toss a controversial personality overboard—lined up behind the beleaguered star. Telegrams flooded in to CBS from fans supporting Lucy. Sponsor Philip Morris stood firm. CBS vice president Harry Ackerman publicly voiced his support. "The record is clear for anyone to read and the network is satisfied,

Damage control: a beset Lucy and Desi meet the press (September 12, 1953). (Courtesy Herald Examiner Collection/Los Angeles Public Library)

just as are Rep. Donald Jackson and [HUAC investigator] William Wheeler that Miss Ball is not and has never been a communist," declared Ackerman. "People seem to feel this thing is silly, not serious, and they all love Lucy."

The next Sunday, September 13, 1953, Winchell went on the air and recanted. "The Lucille Ball story which rocked the nation has had a very happy ending," he said, without mentioning that he had started the nation rocking. "Congressman Jackson was the very first to give Lucille Ball a clean bill. Newspapers and those who know her best were understanding and sympathetic. The explanations by Miss Ball and her husband were fully believed and accepted."

However, not all reporters were as quick as Winchell to fade out to the happy ending. "What happened during the intervening seven days," lectured Jenkins, "was a nightmare the likes of which few innocent people are called upon to face." Mike Connolly, Jenkins's blacklist-friendly colleague at the *Hollywood Reporter*, detected the handiwork of sinister forces in the whole affair. "The commies themselves had a big part in breaking the Lucille Ball story and here's why," he explained. "They feel that when Miss Ball proves she was never a Red it'll tend to discredit charges of commie membership still to be lodged against others. Fiendishly clever, these fiends."

By Monday the storm had calmed. The redhead and the blacklist proved to be a weekend story: broken on Friday morning, stanched that night, soothed and treated that Saturday, and healed over by Sunday. Desilu had contained the damage and *I Love Lucy* suffered no backlash, no consequences. CBS backed Lucy, Philip Morris backed Lucy, and an adoring public backed Lucy.

Of course, the moneyed classes had other motives in supporting their star investments. Over $10 million had been invested in the couple—$8 million on the television show, and $2 million by MGM for a just-completed motion picture, *The Long, Long Trailer* (1954). The exposure of Lucille Ball's pink roots by HUAC undermined capitalism in a way the CPUSA never could.

As a television commodity, Lucy was irreplaceable, sui generis. "It isn't the formula that makes Lucy a great show," noted the ever astute John Crosby. "It's Lucille Ball. . . . All the people who are now drawing up imitation *I Love Lucys* mustn't forget their first problem is to find another Lucille Ball and Desi Arnez." Unlike the disposable Philip Loeb, Lucy embodied the franchise.

Luckily too, Lucy's brush with the blacklist came after the Korean War and after years of bonding with the American public. Had the decade-old flirtation with communism, typeset in official government documents, been exposed just a year earlier, with combat in Korea and before viewers had embraced Lucy and Desi not just as husband and wife but as Mom and Dad, the couple may not have escaped unscathed from a congressional investigation.

As it was, Lucy's clearance was facilitated at the highest levels of the federal government. On November 23, 1953, Lucy and Desi delayed the regular Friday night filming of *I Love Lucy* for a more important gig: a command performance for a very prominent fan on the CBS special *Dinner with the President*.

Shining among a lineup of arthritic performers lobbing stale jokes and stilted rhetoric, Lucille Ball, Desi Arnez, William Frawley, and Vivian Vance stole the show. In a fulsome introduction, the quartet is recast as a kind of sitcom version of a Warner Bros. combat squad: "These four people, all with different national backgrounds, decided to make people laugh," proclaims host Rex Harrison. "These four Americans, blending the gifts of many stocks, working together, created the most successful TV show since, well, since ancient Greece. That's our kind of story—that's why we love Lucy!"

Dressed in matching pinstriped suits and doing a sprightly soft-shoe dance, Lucy and Desi cracked jokes and mock-squabbled to gales of laughter and thunderous applause. From the dias, President Eisenhower, three network presidents, four Supreme Court Justices, and FBI director J. Edgar Hoover beamed and chortled.

During the 1953–54 season that marked Lucille Ball's seven-day brush with the blacklist, *I Love Lucy* was the most watched show on television, drawing some 50,000,000 loyal viewers each week. "Everyone still loves Lucy," shrugged the bewildered liberals at the *New Republic*. From the episode of the redhead and blacklist, the lesson learned was that while the small fry were hooked and gutted, the big fish would be tossed back.

FOUR

HYPERSENSITIVITY

The Codes of Television Censorship

In the 1950s, television images traveled over the air, not via coaxial cable or fiberoptic lines. Electrons swirled out from towering transmitters, surfed on the electromagnetic spectrum, bombarded rooftop antennas, and linked up to the living room receiver, also known as the television set. The networks owned the equipment and the viewers owned the set, but the atmospheric path from station to station was a public trust, controlled by the federal government— and the highway patrol demanded tribute for using the road.

The electromagnetic spectrum, the atmospheric corridor for television signals, might be likened to prime real estate where the early settlers have seized prize acreage in a mad land grab, staked their claim, and begun hauling out cartloads of gold. The immutable fact was that the electromagnetic spectrum was limited. As Will Rogers might have said, the atmosphere wasn't generating any more of it.

To avoid chaos in what insiders quaintly called "the ether," a traffic cop, the Federal Communications Commission, allocated space in the spectral zones. Passed during the populist-minded New Deal, the Federal Communications Act of 1934 loftily decreed that the electromagnetic real estate should be utilized for the "public interest, convenience, and necessity." Like most American property, however, it was exploited to make as much money as humanly possible.

In accord with the iron rule of real estate—location, location, location—the competition for the choicest parcels was fierce. The Very High Frequency channels (numbers 2 to 13) were most coveted, but even a consolation prize among the seventy proposed channels in the Ultra High Frequency range (numbers 14 to 83) was, as the saying went, permission to print money. So fevered was the rush to obtain broadcast licenses that on September 30, 1948, the FCC ordered a peremptory "freeze" on the allocation of new television channels. Aspiring telecasters could but look at the fertile territory from the other side of the fence and dream of mining the bandwidth for profit. In major markets between the coasts, eager families had already purchased television sets that stood dormant in the living room, with nary a test pattern to receive. Premature televiewers-to-be, they waited to turn on, tune in, and drop into the tantalizing programming they could only read about—Berle, Lucy, Murrow . . .

Finally, on April 14, 1952, the freeze was lifted. After four years of "no construction" permits, over five hundred applications were pending at the FCC. Though plenty of desirable parcels still sat on the auction block, the interregnum had allowed station owners lucky enough to settle in early the chance to cultivate the property. Among the emerging television networks, NBC and CBS consolidated a broadcasting hegemony won during their radio days while their weak sisters ABC and DuMont fought less for third place than survival.

Being supplicant business enterprises subject to government oversight, networks and independent stations alike paid due fealty to the liege and kept well clear of political and cultural controversy. Whether under examination for ideological reasons (the specialty of the House Committee on Un-American Activities and the Senate Internal Security Subcommittee) or for commercial and legal reasons (the purview of the House Committee on Interstate and Foreign Commerce and the Senate Committee on Interstate and Foreign Commerce), the scrutiny of legislative bodies frazzled the nerves of network executives. The feds held the deed to the property and, in theory, could call in the marker at any time.

More stringent than the regulatory authority of the FCC, however, was the dictatorship of the customers eyeballing the goods. As an advertiser-supported medium in embryonic development, television was exquisitely sensitive to viewer protests and product boycotts. Casting the widest demographic net possible, the networks strived for "100% acceptability" and assiduously avoided offending any group of potential viewer-buyers, no matter how small in number or eccentric in outlook. Thus, in defending the blacklisting of the actress Jean Muir, a General Foods spokesman explained that "what concerned us was the fact that she had apparently become a controversial personality, whose presence seemed to alienate the goodwill of many people. If she had been a vegetarian, whose presence on the show alienated the goodwill of many meat eaters, our attitude would have been the same."

The flack for General Foods was not being entirely disingenuous. In 1950 outspoken vegetarianism might well have rendered Jean Muir unemployable. Throughout the early days of television, the lines between properly political censorship—that is, restrictions on content and personnel attributable to the pressures of McCarthyism—and a broader kind of cultural censorship—restrictions based on considerations of commerce, morality, or taste—are sometimes hard to disentangle.

"TV, in practically all areas of sensitivity, emerges as America's No. 1 problem child," *Variety* observed in 1953, meaning that the medium had already edged out film and radio as the prime target for moral guardians. That same year, Francis Cardinal Spellman, the powerful and censorious Archbishop of New York, took his eyes away from the motion picture screen long enough to caution network executives to "do their utmost to bring into the homes of America programs that are instructive and stimulating; programs that give recreation and, at the same time, strive not to offend." Strive as they might to be inoffensive, however, network executives lacked a reliable compass to navigate the gripes of politicians, private interest groups, and thin-skinned viewers. Often stumbling unawares into the crosshairs of controversy, uncertain as yet of its place in the cultural hierarchy, television erred on the side of temerity on a whole range of issues that, on the surface anyway, had nothing to do with the superpower rivalry.

The lack of a reliable index to viewer sensitivities enhanced the prevailing insecurity among broadcasters. Before the instant feedback of overnight ratings and precision demographic breakdowns by age, race, and gender, surveys of television audiences might be as fuzzy as the reception on a UHF station. "Were the shows well received by the public?" asked the trade magazine *Television Age* about the live coverage of congressional hearings during the 1953 season. "There's no way of telling, for the telecasters didn't run any careful studies of audience reaction."

A variety of research companies provided information on the television audience: the American Research Bureau, C. E. Hooper, Trendex, Telepulse, Videodex, Conlon, and, the brand name that soon became synonymous with television ratings, the A. C. Nielsen Company.[1] Results from the companies fluctuated wildly, however, and management greeted the numbers with open skepticism. According to one station manager, a ratings firm had reported that his station had won an evening time slot while telecasting dead air. "We do not believe any rating service yet devised can show the user or prospective user of the medium its full scale effectiveness," declared Ward Dorrell, a former vice president for C. E. Hooper, in *Sponsor*. Joe Ward, president of the Advertising Research Bureau concurred: "I say ratings are opinion—not fact." "Ratings services," quipped satirist Fred Allen, "are the only guys in the numbers racket the police haven't caught up with yet."

But if formal ratings were doubted or discounted, more tangible reactions from viewers were read as scripture. Letter writers, telegram senders, telephone callers, and other unscientific samplings kept the ears of station managers close

---

1. In the early 1950s, Nielsen depended upon a recording device known as an "audimeter," which was attached to the television sets of 650 very influential American families who were paid 50 cents a month for their decisive duties.

to the ground. The general rule of thumb was that for every one person who took the trouble to call or write, ten people felt the same impulse. "As a sponsor, it makes sense for you to get the most out of your viewer mail . . . as a barometer of public opinion and a measurement of program popularity," *Sponsor* advised. "Remember, veteran advertisers believe it's the most sensitive measuring tool you have—quicker than a rating, often far more revealing."

Unfortunately, everyone with command of a typewriter, pencil, or crayon seemed to nurse a grievance against television. Miffed at the cast of Italian surnames subpoenaed to testify during the Kefauver Crime Committee hearings of 1951, Italian Americans protested the depiction of Italian hoods in crime series and news shows. Japanese Americans objected to the buck-toothed yellow menaces in World War II films and the villainous Great Togo and Mr. Moto in wrestling matches. Flexing a newly acquired political muscle, African Americans condemned "stepinfetchit" stereotypes. After the outbreak of the Korean War, veterans groups called for the suspension of comedy skits lampooning the military. "Nothing is terrorized so easily as a sponsor with a large television investment to protect," editorialized *Broadcasting/Telecasting*. "It is up to telecasters to immunize themselves against the frights that a flurry of letters can induce among their customers."

But how to tell the lone cranks from the authentic vox populi? In 1951, *Sponsor* estimated that two-thirds of the roughly 30,000 letters a day sent to the four networks were written spontaneously by an irate viewer with a personal gripe. "But it's the remaining one-third that sponsors have learned to dread, for this is the portion that's usually tagged 'pressure group.' This can be an exceedingly powerful weapon, particularly if the complaining is being done by a well disciplined organization or an influential group." From this vantage, the sponsor needed to be just as leery of the Women's Christian Temperance Union complaining about alcohol use in *Studio One* as a *Counterattack* item decrying the appearance of an alleged communist on *Toast of the Town*.

Facing a deluge of vituperative letters—actually facing a trickle—television executives tended to crumble and fold. "It's getting so a man can't express an intelligently honest opinion these days without being accused of just about everything in the book, all of it bad and most of it utterly stupid," groused Dan Jenkins at the *Hollywood Reporter*, a frequent critic of the "hypersensitivity on the part of the public and the resultant overly-cautious attitude adopted with increasing apprehension on the part of radio and TV networks and stations." Given all the "sponsors, agencies, networks, pressure groups, pickets, professional blacklisters and blackmailers, witchhunters and self appointed guardians of 'our way of life,'" complained Richard Powell, president of the TV Writers of America, a comedian had trouble throwing a decent punch line. "If Will Rogers were alive today, he'd probably go back to rope twirling."

Faye Emerson's Breasts, Among Other Controversies

The brouhaha over Faye Emerson's breasts places the touchy sensitivities of early television in prominent relief. A former contract player at Warner Bros. in the early 1940s, Emerson traded subaltern status in motion pictures for star billing in television as hostess of the gossipy *The Faye Emerson Show* (1950) and *Faye Emerson's Wonderful Town* (1951–52) and guest star on a slew of quiz, chat, and dramatic shows. Game for anything, Emerson was a utility player comfortable in comedy skits with Jack Benny, dramatic roles in *The U.S. Steel Hour*, panel discussions on *Author Meets the Critics*, or charity appeals, rolling up her sleeve with Dave Garroway to donate blood for the Red Cross on *The Today Show*.

Though an eclectic entertainer and articulate hostess, Emerson was known less for her performance talents and intellectual endowments than for what one keen observer called "her snowy shoulders and well-rounded upper slopes in a plunging neckline gown." Highlighted by low-cut garb, Emerson's flashy trademarks caused no end of coy smirking. "As for that item the fans call Faye's 'TV neckline,' there wasn't much 'V' to it," noticed Jack O'Brian in a review of *Faye Emerson's Wonderful Town*. "More a gracefully feminine diagonal slide starting high on the left shoulder and scooting decorously down to a safe distance above the left side of her—oh, you know!"

Counterintuitively, not all viewers enjoyed scanning the vista. "Too many beautiful babes are personally conducting tours of viewers' eyes far above the mammary foothills, up to the heights where no St. Bernard should lug his keg," warned a station manager. Chiding the bluenoses bent out of joint by Emerson's décolletage, *Sponsor* joshed: "By the thousands, viewers griped that it might be stylish to wear clothes like that in to the Stork Club but in the front parlor—No!" No fool she, Emerson flaunted her selling points by asking on air whether she should wear low-cut or high-neck gowns.[2]

That the mammary-obsessed 1950s gave Faye Emerson's breasts a careful once-over accords with expectations, but Cold War eyes fixated on a range of items neither properly political in the McCarthyite sense nor sexual in the Emersonian sense. To steer clear of trouble areas, television asked only to be warned up front. But no matter how careful the programming and personnel were monitored, the medium could not avoid blundering into controversy.

---

2. In matters of measurement and popularity, Emerson was surpassed by a busty comedienne named Dagmar, who played a dumb blonde on the Jerry Lester episodes of NBC's late-night variety show, *Broadway Open House* (1950–51). Dagmar, however, was a slapstick conceit parading during the wee hours. Emerson was a real personality presented in stark daylight.

Censorable décolletage: the versatile television star Faye Emerson flaunts her trademark "V" on *The Faye Emerson Show* (1949). (Courtesy CBS Photo Archive)

The brushfire set off on CBS's *This Is Show Business* (1949–1956), telecast on December 21, 1952, illuminates the nonideological nonerotic hypersensitivities of early television. A regular panelist on the show, the acerbic playwright George S. Kaufman declared that he was fed up with the incessant playing of "Silent Night" on Christmas special after Christmas special. "Let's make this one show on which no one sings 'Silent Night,'" he joked.

Unamused and unsilent, viewers flooded CBS with letters accusing the network and the playwright of sonic blasphemy. An abashed Kaufman responded that his annoyance with "Silent Night" was "not wittingly an anti-religious remark. I was merely speaking out against the use and over-use of this Christmas carol in connection with the sale of commercial products." The jittery sponsor of *This Is Show Business*, the American Tobacco Company, compelled CBS to fire Kaufman for his hymnal sacrilege. "It's a shame that responsible people in the TV industry have given in to such foolish pressure," the comedian Garry Moore ventured to declare on his own CBS show, *The Garry Moore Show.* "That's the kind of business it is," responded a philosophical Kaufman. "It shouldn't surprise anyone. It's a fear ridden industry and that's the way it's ruled. When they get some letters, they're afraid not to fire somebody and then they're afraid to hire him back."

Not necessarily: the Kaufman firing was in turn protested by a second stream of letters defending the playwright and excoriating CBS, which then felt pressured to rehire Kaufman. Upon the playwright's return to *This Is Show Business,* moderator Clifton Fadiman introduced the chastened panelist as "the unpredictable George S. Kaufman." Kaufman observed only that "I have been on *This Is Show Business* continuously with the exception of one brief interval which shall be nameless." (On matters of religion, television was ecumenically skittish: the September 18, 1953, episode of *The Goldbergs,* normally a live show, was telecast on kinescope so that the Jews in the cast might avoid criticism from Orthodox Jews for working after sundown on Yom Kippur, despite the fact that Orthodox Jews should not have been watching television on Yom Kippur.)

Of all the exposed nerve endings susceptible to pressure, the most sensitive belonged to the sponsor, the entity holding the purse strings. Bonehead demands from hypersensitive sponsors have become a cherished part of the lore of early television: how General Motors refused to permit the surname Ford (as in Ford Theater) to be featured in a historical drama depicting the assassination of Abraham Lincoln; how Westinghouse insisted that a *Studio One* production of Rudyard Kipling's "The Light That Failed" be retitled "The Gathering Night"; how *I Love Lucy* and other shows sponsored by Philip Morris cigarettes avoided the word "lucky" (as in rival brand-name Lucky Strike cigarettes); and how the National Gas Association bleeped the word "gas" from a description of Nazi death chambers in the *Playhouse 90* presentation of "Judgment at Nuremberg" (1959). Ultimately, the quiz show scandals of 1959–60 helped the networks wrangle direct content control away from sponsors, but during the 1950s advertisers were the court of first resort and their decree was law.

The most devious instance of sponsor-mandated hypersensitivity concerned a health not communist menace. In November 1952, *Reader's Digest,* a periodical that did not depend on advertising, published a landmark article entitled "Cancer by the Carton," a notification that inspired a spate of "cancer scare" stories in newspapers and magazines. The next year, the American Cancer Society issued its first warnings about the causative link between smoking and lung cancer. For anyone who wanted to know, the correlation between smoking and lung cancer was already solid enough to sway the prematurely health conscious, but a collective cultural denial, abetted by the media's dependence on tobacco revenue, blacked out the bad news on what *Variety* called the "smoke-ringed manna from heaven." Estimating that 50 percent of all tobacco advertising was earmarked for television, the trade periodical *Television Age* salivated over how "burning cigarettes lighted up television screens [in 1952] with a $35 million blaze" and breathlessly anticipated "a flaming $42.7 million outlay for 1953!" No network wanted to douse that bonfire.

In addition to the commercials—the famous dancing cigarette packs and the satisfied exhalations of white-coated physicians and velvet-voiced singers—cigarette brand names got top billing on the most prestigious anthology dramas and variety shows: *Your Lucky Strike Theater, Your American Tobacco Theater, The Lucky Strike Hit Parade, The Chesterfield Supper Club*, and so on. Until 1956, the name of NBC's flagship news broadcast was *The Camel News Caravan*. "Sit back, light up a Camel, and be witness to the latest happenings," coaxed a smooth-talking announcer.

Newscasters who defied the smoking signs discovered that straight reporting could be hazardous to their career. Ironically, the blacklist-friendly journalist Walter Winchell ran into the tobacco brand of censorship on his 15-minute gossip-*cum*-news program on ABC, *The Walter Winchell Show*. On December 13, 1953, he minced no words in a commentary on the link between cigarettes and lung cancer. Usually Winchell read the news with his eyes down and his nose buried in his copy, barking into a big radio microphone, the very image of a radio-bred anachronism on the television screen. For his remarks on smoking, however, he removed his glasses and looked straight into the camera. "Never was any newspaperman's responsibility to others and his own integrity to himself a heavier burden than mine tonight when I tell you the facts as I know them for and against the cigarette now on trial for its life," he began. After a brief review of the medical evidence, Winchell closed with a firm declaration. "Now my editorial opinion is this: the scientists may be unconvinced that the cigarette is guilty, but I am fully convinced it is very far from innocent."

ABC's tobacco clients were livid. Unable to retaliate against the Winchell show, which was sponsored by a watch company, the Brown and Williamson Tobacco Company canceled its sponsorship of *Orchid Award*, the show that immediately followed Winchell's—not just guilt by association but surrogate revenge.[3]

At least the embargo on bad news about smoking fenced out a clear forbidden zone. In most other areas, the circular system of pressure groups and

---

3. Eventually, Edward R. Murrow, a four-pack-a-day man for whom cigarettes were both prop and crutch, would telecast back-to-back reports on the link between smoking and lung cancer on *See It Now*, May 31 and June 7, 1955. Murrow's sponsor was Alcoa, the aluminum company. He smoked throughout both shows.

pressure points—wherein pressure groups pressured the sponsors, sponsors pressured the advertising agencies and networks, and sponsors, advertising agencies, and networks pressured the producer of the show—incited successive waves of panic attacks as complaints ricocheted along executive corridors. Sometimes a single well-focused letter landed with the impact of a hand grenade. Resenting the depiction of a rude telephone operator on NBC's *Fireside Theater* (1949–1958), a real telephone operator complained to her local union, which took the complaint to union headquarters, which complained to AT&T, which in turn complained to Proctor and Gamble, the sponsor of *Fireside Theater*, and NBC, the network, which relayed the complaint to the ad agency involved. Apologies were hastily issued all around "all because one lone woman didn't like one scene in one half-hour film at 9:00 o'clock on Tuesday night in Connecticut," as a disbelieving Dan Jenkins reported.

The desire for uniformity, consensus, and the protective shield of written guidelines resulted in the Television Code. Negotiated and refined throughout 1951, the Television Code was modeled on the strict censorship regime of the Hollywood Production Code, whose outlook and rhetoric of high moral seriousness it imitated. The networks adopted the Television Code for precisely the same reasons the studios adopted the Production Code in 1930: to placate moral guardians, to lend respectability to a disreputable medium, and to avoid the threat of federal censorship.

Taking effect on March 1, 1952, the Television Code defined television as a "family medium" committed to "wholesome entertainment." Obscenity, blasphemy, vulgarity, illicit sex, and explicit violence were prohibited. "Television is seen and heard in every type of American home," intoned the preamble to the Television Code. "These homes include children and adults of all ages, embrace all races and all varieties of religious faith, and reach those of every educational background. It is the responsibility of television to bear constantly in mind that the audience is primarily a home audience, and consequently that television's relationship to viewers is that between guest and host." And like a polite guest, television should never say anything to make the evening unpleasant or the host uncomfortable.

Underlying the rhetoric, of course, was the legally sanctioned power of the FCC to regulate and censor what went out over the airwaves. *Sponsor* stated the obvious: "Patently, Code and accompanying statement were aimed squarely at deflating Bentonites[4] who push for outside censorship." Unlike motion pictures,

---

4. Sen. William Benton (D-Conn.) was a frequent industry critic and a proponent of FCC-supervised censorship. Bentonites caused the networks nearly as much worry as McCarthyites.

whose First Amendment rights were beginning to be affirmed in Supreme Court decisions, television was a public trust, subject to government fiat. "Controlled as it is by a government agency, the FCC, the industry has always felt an uncertain shadow over it, depending on the character of the commission and the political temper of the times," *Television Digest* noted in 1954. "One chairman actually once ordered a network hearing on renewal of its station license because Mae West used what he construed as an indecent inflection in her famous line, 'Come up and see me sometime.'"

Yet the most indecent inflection in the television industry was ignored by federal authorities. Over the blacklist, the FCC claimed no jurisdiction. In 1952 the Authors League of America requested a hearing to discuss blacklisting, but FCC chairman Wayne Coy replied that the matter was "not properly the subject of a general hearing of the commission since the judgment of talent by station operators falls into the scope of day to day operations, ceded to licensees by the Federal Communications Act." Ever jealous of their prerogatives, the networks applauded the FCC's hands-off attitude. "It is, after all, the responsibility of the broadcaster and nobody else to determine who does and does not go on the air," editorialized *Broadcasting/Telecasting*. "If Actor X can prove he has been deprived of a livelihood or has otherwise been damaged as a result of his being listed in *Red Channels*, his recourse must be to the courts, not the FCC." In other words, government and industry each agreed that the FCC served as traffic cop for the airwaves, not as a guardian of civil rights on the airwaves.

But while the FCC and the Television Code maintained a stony silence about the blacklist, the regulatory authorities stood vigilant on other ticklish matters. "The costuming of all performers should be within the bounds of propriety, and shall avoid such exposure or such emphasis on anatomical detail as would embarrass or offend home viewers," read the Code's section on "Decency and Decorum in Production." Roused to action by complaints "regarding the dress of a nationally known performer who had appeared on a program of wide distribution"—Faye Emerson—the Television Code Review Board scrutinized kinescopes for flagrant exposures of anatomy. "It was the feeling of all present," the report concluded, "that the costume might not be in the best taste and that the program producers should tighten up their controls on variety type programs as presented by the particular broadcasting service."

In 1953, in the first report to the public on the progress of the Television Code, the National Association of Radio and Television Broadcasters proudly proclaimed that "indecent costuming typified by the plunging neckline" had been exposed and rooted out. "Since the Code's implementation it must be said that what was once causing much criticism of the TV industry has been reduced to a great extent." Maybe not reduced, but—in the case of Faye Emerson's breasts—covered up.

Amos 'n' Andy: Blacks in Your Living Room

The most successful campaign to censor a television show for purely political reasons—to yank off the air a beloved and highly rated series solely because it departed from the dominant ideology of Cold War America—was waged not by the HUAC or *Red Channels* but by the NAACP and the African American press. A mirror image of the anticommunist campaigns in the tactics employed and assumptions shared, the battle by civil rights advocates against a deviationist situation comedy is another leading indicator of the rise of television as the preferred site for political shadowboxing. Even as the civil rights movement struggled to expand freedom of access to the public space of swimming pools, rest rooms, and schools, it worked to restrict freedom of expression in the public realm of the television screen.

The flashpoint for the firestorm was the video incarnation of the phenomenally successful and perennially controversial radio series *Amos 'n' Andy*, an American classic and an African American bane since its debut in 1929. The brainchild of two white entertainers, Freeman Godsen and Charles J. Correll, *Amos 'n' Andy* was the first coast-to-coast sensation in broadcasting history and a national ritual six nights a week at 7:00 P.M. EST. From the mythic precincts of the Fresh Air Taxicab Company of America, "Incorpulated" and the meeting halls of the Mystic Knights of the Sea, the humble, likable Amos, the gullible, lackadaisical Andy, and the blustering, conniving Kingfish contributed catchphrases to the language ("check and double check"; "sitchiatin") and reimprinted ripe caricatures into the Caucasian imagination. The alleged verisimilitude of the show was credited mainly to the ethnographic discernment of Virginia-bred Freeman Godsen, "who learned the Negro dialect, the mental traits of the average colored individual, and the lovable characteristics of the race by studying them as he grew to manhood," as a flattering portrait in the *New York Times* explained in 1930.

The anticommunist blacklisters targeted artists for their associations and opinions, arguing less that television purveyed communism than that the flush paychecks of television performers helped fill Communist Party coffers. Even *Red Channels* didn't pretend that *The Aldrich Family* or *The Goldbergs* injected Soviet propaganda into American households. The "reds in your living room" alarum summed up the mentality. Neither the character nor the content, but the mere sight of a known communist was sufficient affront to patriotic vigilance, an actor or a byline manifest proof of infiltration. Behold, there he is: ecce commie.

By contrast, the civil rights movement scrutinized the text not just the talent. Like literary scholars deploying the New Criticism then fashionable in university English departments, the NAACP and the African American press undertook close textual examinations of the characters portrayed and the messages sent forth. With an eye on the prize arena, they demanded that television showcase positive role models and communicate a progressive, egalitarian agenda. Just as W. E. B. Du Bois had urged the race to uplift itself on the shoulders of a well-spoken, well-dressed, and well-educated "talented tenth," the same exemplary ratio should comprise the full percentage of African Americans seen on television. "Perhaps no greater vehicle of communication in the United States today is contributing to a better understanding of the American Negro than television," asserted the *Pittsburgh Courier*, the influential African American weekly, in 1954. "Television presentation must reflect the best [because] the American Negro will get favorable publicity that he has never before enjoyed, and it will reflect credit upon the race."

From this perspective, and within the context of the time, television was a sympathetic, even breakthrough, medium for African Americans. Its salutary role in the realignment of American racial attitudes began long before Rosa Parks refused a backseat bus ride in Montgomery, Alabama, in 1955. The network news landmarks—National Guard units integrating Little Rock High School at gunpoint in 1957, demonstrators beset by snarling dogs and gushing firehoses in the early 1960s, and the March on Washington in 1963—were presaged by prime-time programming far more integrated than public facilities or private relationships offscreen. Like the rhythm and blues beckoning from the radio dial, the siren call of African American culture enticed television.

As ever, the crucible for the first tectonic shift in American racial attitudes since the Emancipation Proclamation was the Second World War. Under the guidance of the Office of War Information, the popular media had celebrated an egalitarianism that embraced every ingredient of the American melting pot. In posters, radio series, and motion pictures, a diverse range of ethnicities and regionalities worked shoulder to shoulder against the Nazi Übermensch and the Imperial Japanese. Boomeranging back, the American propaganda against the self-styled master races overseas brought homegrown racism into stark relief and fostered a neo-abolitionist credo dedicated to the death of Jim Crow. Though the Office of War Information was dissolved in 1945, the national media continued to promulgate an ethos born in wartime even without the official government monitor.

The major league debut of Jackie Robinson that made professional baseball a truly all-American pastime in 1947, the integration of the U.S. military in 1948, and the tolerant spirit of Hollywood social problem films such as *Pinky* (1949), *No Way Out* (1950), and *Bright Victory* (1951), found plenty of analogues on television. On variety shows and anthology dramas, in news reports and sports events, African Americans gained heightened visibility and higher status.

Television shattered the walls of segregated space in two decisive ways. First, it brought African American images into private homes where African American people would never cross the threshold. Second, the images moved within a free-flowing, integrationist context. Traditionally, Hollywood had relegated African American performers to separate and unequal screen space as restricted as a Jim Crow lavatory. On television, variety show hosts such as Ted Mack, Arthur Godfrey, and Ed Sullivan showcased African American dancers, singers, and actors in a casual manner that radiated good fellowship.

"Here any man or woman, regardless of creed or color or station in life, can have a chance at the entertainment goal he seeks," declared Ted Mack, host of *The Original Amateur Hour*. Watching the warm physical contact between Mack and his contestants, the *Chicago Defender* noticed that "the losers get the conventional 'better luck next time' pat on the back that seems to come naturally to Ted Mack. His words and pats of consolation are for the artist only with no thought of the color of his skin." To an age touchy about interracial touching, the simple gesture of human contact sent a powerful message.

The integrationist gestures were encouraged by the belated recognition of a lucrative market hidden behind the color wall. "The American Negro has become the most important, financially potent, and sales-and-advertising serenaded 'minority' in the land," trumpeted *Variety* in a front-page story in 1954. "The Negro market, which during the depression was despised as marginal and underprivileged, has become a 15 billion dollar market. In numbers it exceeds the total population of Canada." In America, the prospect of profit has a way of softening prejudice. "The many Negroes who are investing in television sets would love to see a free home demonstration of democracy in their living rooms," the bandleader Cab Calloway pointed out in 1950.

In many ways, television was more persistently and forcefully integrationist than Hollywood's prestigious social problem films. Motion pictures could be shut out from exhibition; network television could not be so easily turned off. For decades, southern exhibitors had simply refused to book films deemed too integrationist by community standards. "Southern states continue to fight, clip, or reject feature films in which Negro characters are shown in positions of prestige as social equals of whites, or where there is direct or implied sex potential," *Variety* reported in 1957. In a Hollywood film, the singer Lena Horne was objectionable when "singing in a plush nightclub that reflects a degree of social acceptance against which the South preponderantly still rebels." In the plush environs of the television variety show, however, Lena Horne looked right at home.

From a Confederate point of view, violations of Jim Crow custom on television were far more insidious than in motion pictures. Not only did the visible transgressions come directly into the home, they did so live, unmonitored, and at the speed of light. In 1956, state legislators in Louisiana accused the television industry of following "the communist technique of brainwashing for racial integration by bringing into private homes in this state harmful programs designed to affect the minds and attitudes of juveniles." To combat the threat, they proposed a bill prohibiting "showing or displaying interracial theatrical, drama, vaudeville, burlesque, skits, dancing entertainment or any such program in which members of the white and Negro races participate or which involve social contacts between members of both races." Yet to preview shows telecast live was impossible and to stop the network feed and not telecast shows already sold to sponsors meant bankruptcy. Trapped by technology and commerce, station managers in the Deep South telecast images of interracial amity they would never have countenanced in their hometown newspapers or at the local Bijou.

The nationwide transmission of the ethos of equality was television's most important contribution to the ongoing civil rights revolution. The lily-white image of American television in the 1950s purveyed by syndication chestnuts such as *The Donna Reed Show*, *Father Knows Best*, and *The Adventures of Ozzie and Harriet* sends back a false picture of the video color scheme. Telecast live, the integrationist variety shows and anthology dramas were seldom preserved on kinescope and never syndicated—hence the dim glow in popular memory. More multicolored than monochromatic, and more multicultural in spirit than most of the nation, television in the 1950s ran far ahead of the tolerance curve.[5]

Always too the sheer voraciousness of the medium, the relentless demand for entertainers to fill the airwaves, opened up spaces for talent long shut out. Like Ted Mack's *Original Amateur Hour*, Ed Sullivan's *Toast of the Town* practiced an open admissions policy, mixing an eclectic lineup not just of opera singers and circus acts but of races and nationalities. "Sullivan's video offering has from its beginning, back in 1948, offered opportunities without restriction to persons of talent," observed the *Pittsburgh Courier*. "It is always true that Sullivan presents Negro entertainers as an integral part of his show, knit well into the whole proceedings, with never a hint of bias." When nervous advertisers objected to Sullivan's penchant for Louis Armstrong or Pearl Bailey, he

---

5. The television historian Horace Newcomb vividly recalls the eye-opening expansion television worked on his own racial and regional consciousness. In 1951, as a young boy, Newcomb watched the Joe Louis–Ezzard Charles prize fight in a showroom of a hardware store in Sardis, Mississippi. "The gathering of white men and boys, watching two black men fight hard against each other with their fists" challenged the folkways of a "closed culture" defined by race. "Television intruded into my culture, offering me a perspective on the world at large that I rarely found in other media, other forms," he remembers.

told them to "go hang" and went about his color-blind casting. The mean-tempered Arthur Godfrey was also notably warm-hearted in matters of race. The Mariners, an interracial quartet featured on *Arthur Godfrey and His Friends* from 1949 to 1955, offered a weekly lesson in black and white harmony. Mr. Television himself expressed the televisual consensus. When signing off from *Texaco Star Theater*, Milton Berle dropped the clown face to remind viewers of all ages:

> When you're choosing up a team just before you play
>   the game,
> Never choose the player by his race or his name.
> What's the difference if he's poor?
> What's the difference if he's rich?
> The only thing to ask him is—can he pitch?

The selfsame sentiment was inscribed in the Television Code, which stated that "racial or nationality types shall not be shown on television in such a manner as to ridicule the race or nationality." The Code explicitly forbade "words (especially slang) derisive of any race, color, creed, nationality or national derivation except wherein such usage would be for the specific purpose of effective dramatization such as combating prejudice." Though the results were seen in matters small and large across all ethnic and racial lines (CBS banned "Sam, You Made the Pants Too Long" as offensive to Jews and deleted the word "chink" from "Chinatown, My Chinatown"), the main beneficiary was the subculture that had always received the harshest treatment from the national culture.

Keeping a sharp eye out for material that "might be offensive to Negroes," Bob Wood, head of NBC's continuity acceptance division, was guided by "common sense upon a public relations basis. We don't want to say slavery never existed, but we don't want to play it up." NBC and CBS banned black-face minstrel routines and "stepinfetchit" characters and changed words like "darky" and "mammy" to "children" or "brothers" in "Old Kentucky Home," "Swanee River," and "Shortnin' Bread." More open-minded, ABC retained the original lyrics to Stephen Foster's "Old Black Joe" on the grounds that Foster evoked "an era which factually existed."

The racist legacy of Hollywood cinema now filling the television airwaves challenged a credo of "100% acceptability" when 10 percent of viewers cringed at the pictures. Stereotypes from vintage Hollywood films—Farina in the old *Our Gang* series, "spook" comedy antics, and minstrel show sequences—were deleted "by the hundreds every month." Of course, given how thoroughly racist stereotyping permeated American popular culture and the blindness of

white censors to potentially offensive material, even the most determined revisionism failed to filter all racially incendiary material. Moreover, unlike the
networks, independent stations seldom censored the ripe stereotypes on view
in syndicated collections of cartoons, shorts, and films packaged and sold by
the motion picture studios.

Besides, Hollywood's most sinister racism was not the visible stereotype but
the invisible erasures: the removal of African Americans from the normal ebb
and flow of American life. Television strived to fill in some of the omission.
Fueled by color-conscious teleplays from card-carrying liberals like Reginald
Rose, Paddy Chayevsky, Rod Serling, and Ernest Kinoy, *Studio One*, *Philco
Television Playhouse*, *Playhouse 90* and other jewels from the Golden Age of
Television showcased African Americans as a natural backdrop to the Ameri-
can tapestry. "Talent has no color, no religion, no nationality," declared NBC
vice president Edward D. Madden. "We have just one yardstick—the selection
of performers without regard to racial derivation." Very much in line with
NAACP goals, the NBC policy was called "integration without identification,"
whereby African Americans were cast in roles where race was immaterial.
Madden touted a recent appearance by Sidney Poitier on *Philco Television
Playhouse* as exemplary. Poitier played a parole officer, but the teleplay "in no
way identified the role as being played by a Negro. Rather, he, like the rest of
the cast, was strictly an individual concerned with the problems that might
confront any parole officer."

Civil rights groups appreciated the gestures but kept up the pressure. In
1953 the Coordinating Council for Negro Performers challenged the networks
to cough up "some of the plums as well as the crumbs." Despite the progress
in variety shows and dramatic series, the council railed at the most conspicuous absence in television programming. Commercials ("which heretofore
have completely excluded Negroes in TV and radio") remained whiter than
white.

Nonetheless, whether as background extras, in small speaking parts, and,
more rarely but not negligibly, in prominent featured roles, African Africans
edged closer toward statistical representation. News programs were especially
vigilant about covering African American life with due respect. Reports on the
Korean War, notably on Edward R. Murrow's *See It Now*, conscientiously
picked out black GIs from the sea of faces on a troop ship, a parade ground,
or a hospital ward. Man-on-the-street surveys of the vox populi—not least
Eisenhower's landmark "Eisenhower Answers America" spots in the 1952 election—pointedly included African American faces and voices. Tallying up the
black performers showcased during a single week in 1950 on Milton Berle's
Texaco Star Theater, Ed Sullivan's *Toast of the Town*, and various other shows,
the *Pittsburgh Courier* declared that "all and all it had been a good week for

beige troupers in television. It looked very much as though there were going to be even better weeks ahead."

Into this atmosphere of relative progress and enlightenment shambled the ghosts of broadcasting's past. With radio shows of all stripes proving adaptable to television, *Amos 'n' Andy* followed the path paved by Arthur Godfrey and *The Goldbergs* and jumped media. On television, however, the once conventional characters of Amos 'n' Andy 'n' the Kingfish became controversial personalities.

The move of the radio ensemble into the video neighborhood was preceded by a massive, yearlong publicity buildup. In May 1949, realizing that age and pigmentation disqualified them from fronting the television series, Godsen and Correll sent out a nationwide casting call for African American actors. The talent scouts in the star search included President Truman, who suggested that Godsen check out the undergraduates at the all-black Texas State University, and General Eisenhower, who called on the Army to track down a former soldier he thought might fit the bill. Securing a sponsor for the show was easier than casting the parts. Blatz Beer, a product of Schenley Distillers, paid top dollar, $40,000 a week, for the filmed series and launched the premiere episode with a $250,000 promotional campaign.

Yet even as CBS fired up the publicity machine, warning signs blinked on the horizon. "Considering that this is the first major use of Negroes in commercial broadcasting, the responsibility [is] two fold: 1) not to offend the sensibilities of a large segment of the US population; 2) and to present them honestly without caricaturing weaknesses that are inherent in any human, regardless of race or color," cautioned *Variety*. Behind the ethical qualms were economic fears. "As the chief victim of racial stereotyping, the Negro market is sensitive indeed to advertisers who thoughtlessly perpetuate offensive images of the Negro as ignorant, lazy, menial, etc.," *Sponsor* advised. "Advertisers are now pretty well briefed, or they should be, as to the everyday hazards lurking in racial jokes, dialects, characterizations, and superiority-inferiority situations." For the first time in the history of American popular entertainment, show business producers worried that offending African Americans might be more costly than amusing white Americans.

To reframe the show and disarm the opposition, Blatz purchased advertising space in the African American press. "For the first time on television America can see—is privileged to see—an all-star cast . . . an all-Negro cast . . . in a sterling half hour of human drama and warm comedy," assured the copy. "This is not just another television program. This is the start of an era—an even greater era than the one Amos 'n' Andy created in the past."

On June 28, 1951, *Amos 'n' Andy* debuted on CBS. Though the series was shot on film, a surviving kinescope records the moment of revelation when Godsen and Correll first unveiled the video metamorphosis of the Amos and Andy cast to "a studio audience of 500 people, representing all walks of life, both white and colored." Anticipatory laughter and delighted giggles greet the appearance of each player. "If we had the power to meld a character to fill the shoes of Andrew H. Brown, I don't think we could do a better job than the boy that we found in Oklahoma City," enthuses Godsen. "This fella Spencer Williams actually comes to life as Andrew H. Brown and I venture to say that three or four seconds after you see him, you will always think of him when you think of Andy."

Just as in Hollywood's early sound era, when the vocal debut of silent stars shattered the pitch-perfect images beheld on the motion picture screen, radio personalities struggled with the transition to television. By common consent, however, the casting for Amos 'n' Andy met aural expectations. As the bearish figure of Spencer Williams ambles on stage, the audience gasps at the flesh-and-blood embodiment of a long-imagined radio character. Milking the moment, Williams, in character, tips his hat and gives a broad, "Hel-lo." Even more jaw-dropping was the sight of the rotund, cigar-chomping Tim Moore as the con artist Kingfish. "This really is the Kingfish," proclaims Correll. Moore obligingly recites his signature line: "Don't forget—we is all brothers in that great fraternity, the Mystic Knights of the Sea."

But if the actors fit the images, the images no longer fit the times. Like so many politically charged legacies of the 1930s seen in a postwar light, Amos 'n' Andy looked like an antique lawn ornament from another zeitgeist. The Goldbergs was inoculated from antidefamation protests by the ethnic pedigree of producer-star Gertrude Berg. Spawned by white fathers, Amos 'n' Andy appeared on television as the bastard sons of two unreconstructed Confederates.

The ill-chosen content of the first episode inflamed the situation. Mistakenly sent a draft notice, a terrified Kingfish tries to elude military service. His plight is resolved when all branches of the armed forces agree to classify him 4-F even in case of invasion. Mocking the courage of African Americans in the midst of the Korean War seemed almost calculated to enrage civil rights groups.

No less ill-timed was the premiere of show, which coincided with the annual meeting of the National Association for the Advancement of Colored People. NAACP executive director Walter White fired off a telegram to Blatz Beer branding Amos 'n' Andy a "gross libel on the Negro and a distortion of the truth." In speeches and newspaper editorials, White raged about how "the picturization of Negroes as amoral, semi-literate, lazy, stupid, scheming, and dishonest perpetuates a harmful stereotype which departed with the old minstrel show."

Though genuinely aghast at the revival of Amos 'n' Andy, the African American press, the NAACP, and other agitators for civil rights cleverly exploited the occasion to solidify past gains and advance the present cause. On television, a

Antique lawn ornaments from another zeitgeist: Andy (Spencer Williams), the Kingfish (Tim Moore), and Amos (Alvin Childress), from CBS's controversial television version of *Amos 'n' Andy* (1951–1953).

prejudice dependent on visual recognition was difficult to turn away from. "It is the miracle of television which spotlights these dangers," insisted the *Chicago Defender*. "Seeing these images in the flesh squelches the guffaws and whips up the anger."

Like the forces behind *Red Channels* and AWARE, Inc., civil rights activists knew that the most vulnerable pressure point was located in the pocketbook of the sponsor. "As long as the *Amos and Andy Show* is on the air," pledged White, he had adopted a new slogan aimed at the brew and its owners: SWALLOW BLATZ BEER AND SWALLOW YOUR PRIDE. SIP SCHENLEY AND SCUTTLE YOUR SELF-RESPECT. In pricking the conscience of Schenley's president Lewis Rosenstiel, White did not scruple from pressing a sensitive

ethnic nerve: "As a member of another minority which has suffered cruel persecution, he is no doubt sensitive to mistreatment or misrepresentation of any
group." Delighted to be part of a Popular Front again, the communist monthly *Masses and Mainstream* urged "a blast of protesting letters to CBS and its
local stations . . . to clear the nation's TV screens of this racist poison brewed
by Blatz."

A few voices within the African American community dissented from the
rush to vilification. Figuring that work was work, the Coordinating Council
for Negro Performers passed a resolution praising CBS for its "expressed willingness to increase Negro employment in this new medium" and for giving
Negro actors their "greatest opportunity" in years. Ruth Cage, an entertainment reporter for the African American press, reminded readers that "all the
Jewish families who see *The Goldbergs* [don't] identify themselves with the go-
ings on and decry the use of a dialect [and] cultural stereotypes, and the comedy that revolves around these characteristics of the show." Sometimes too the
African American press worked both sides of the street, attacking the show on
the editorial pages while puffing up the black actors on the entertainment
pages and pocketing the revenues from Blatz advertisements.

No less offensive than the ripe stereotypes, however, was the Jim Crow color
line enforced on the show. Like the segregated all-black musicals and variety
cavalcades of classical Hollywood, the televisual world of *Amos 'n' Andy* depicted an all-black bubble isolated from white America. To show the races rub-
bing shoulders was to risk the kind of friction that might scorch the comic conceit and consume the commercial property. "Even the Kingfish has to come in
contact with the non-Negro world occasionally," complained Walter White.

Unfortunately, when the Kingfish did come in contact with the white world,
the interracial tension muddied the laugh track. Take, for example, the inadvertently grim "Diner" episode, an anomaly both in its breach of racial boundaries and its choice of narrative hook. For once the Kingfish is not engaged in
a rascally scheme: Andy and he aspire to the American dream by becoming self-
sufficient businessmen through dint of honest hard work. Unbeknownst to the
pair, however, the busy diner purchased from two Caucasian hustlers will soon
become a white elephant when the new highway under construction bypasses
the site. After toiling to make the diner spic and span, Andy and the Kingfish
proudly hang out their "Open for Business" sign and eagerly await customers.
None appear. No overt racism is expressed in the text, no slurs are uttered, but
the stunted options of African Americans who come in contact with the non-
Negro world comes too close to racial reality for comic comfort.

Taken aback by the "strenuous objections" within the African American
community and finally alerted "to the seriousness of the controversy," CBS
and Blatz attempted to "smooth out some of the ill feeling inspired among

sections of the colored community by the tele series," according to *Variety*. In vain: the hamhanded attempts backfired, notably when a planned personal appearance by the cast of *Amos 'n' Andy* in a parade sponsored by the *Chicago Defender* had to be canceled when Walter White forbade their participation.

In 1953, after two years of bad press and harmful boycotts, Blatz dropped its sponsorship of the still popular, still highly rated *Amos 'n' Andy*. CBS gamely asserted that it "didn't anticipate it being shelved for long," but for once sure profit succumbed to a poor profile. The television life of the *Amos 'n' Andy* franchise, shrugged *Variety* in a postmortem, ranked as "one of the all time major casualties in the radio-to-video transition, of stellar properties."

Once taken off the national screen, however, *Amos 'n' Andy* thrived. Operating under the radar in a syndication package of 78 episodes, often playing in more than two hundred markets as "the fastest moving comedy team in the syndicated film field," the show hung on tenaciously until, in the mid-1960s, African American cultural clout had penetrated even the regional syndication circuit. Circulating in 16mm, and later on videotape (though still exiled even from the usually wide-open environs of cable television), the series survives yet as a guilty pleasure for aficionados of early television comedy—and a still-hot button to press in debates on race and American culture.

Like reds, blacks in the living room were flashpoints for controversy and occasions for ideological combat in Cold War America. Unlike the entertainers tarred by the blacklist, however, the entertainers who trafficked in racial stereotypes were banished because of their performance not their background. Hence, the controversial personalities on *Amos 'n' Andy* could not be cleared, only canceled.

FIVE

FORUMS OF THE AIR

Unlike motion picture stars, who shambled into television reluctantly, as if the smaller screen conferred a shrinkage in magnitude, politicians rushed before the cameras with lapdog enthusiasm. The popular misconception—that the marriage between television and politics was consummated only with the Kennedy-Nixon debates of 1960—is at least a decade off. From its inception, television transformed the way politicians operated, candidates for public office being as cagey as advertisers in sensing the tremendous marketing potential of a vast coast-to-coast billboard.

The first presidential election in the age of television confirms the prescience of the political class. In 1948, NBC and CBS telecast the Republican and Democratic conventions from Philadelphia, the major parties readily agreeing to hold their quadrennial confabs in the same East Coast city to save expenses for the networks and to facilitate technical hookups. Already the calculus of the electoral college was balanced against the lure of television coverage.

Watching the impact of television on American politics, Cold War commentators expressed two contrary opinions, polarized outlooks that are rehashed whenever an electorally significant advertisement, hearing, debate, speech, or act of violence highlights the symbiosis between Jeffersonian democracy and Nielsen demographics.

On the one side, critics worried about the threat of a video-fueled tyrant, a glib politician rousing the rabble via the airwaves. Remembering how Huey Long and Father Charles Coughlin had ridden radio to power during the Great Depression, print-based commentators dreaded the ascent of a sinister telegenic visage. "Up to now no greatly talented demagogue has had access to TV," noted a relieved Erwin D. Canham, editor of the *Christian Science Monitor*, in 1953, "but one can readily imagine that a person with a hypnotic voice and personality could play tricks with the whole nation." "Video is the answer to the thought controller's dream," fretted the *American Mercury* in 1954. "A nation of TV gazers is a set up for a new-style demagogue who has mastered television's unique art of folksy, sincerity-loaded talk."

Crystallizing the worst fears of the ancient regimes in both Washington and Hollywood, director Elia Kazan and screenwriter Budd Schulberg conjured a nightmare vision of the electoral future in the overheated social problem film *A Face in the Crowd* (1957). With a nation of narcotized viewers in his grip, a megalomaniacal television star slithers smoothly from Madison Avenue to Pennsylvania Avenue. In clinical close-up, the video demagogue chortles like a hyena, his cavernous yap filling the motion picture screen: George Orwell meets Arthur Godfrey.

Yet for every Cassandra who conjured the face of Big Brother scowling down from a television monitor, a Pollyanna foresaw a bright democratic vista. "The fact that 100 million Americans can sit in on their political machinery by watching their television sets at home" meant "the death of demagoguery, false prophets, and phonies," asserted ABC newsman John Daly in 1956. "Even the politician who is a good actor soon tips off his viewer that he is pulling an act." Just as starry-eyed educators envisioned a prime-time line-up of Shakespearean drama and classical music to uplift the masses, the same optimists doted on the promise of a polis energized and enlightened by television. Looking back on the 1952 convention coverage, the *New York Times* decreed that television "gives democracy an all-seeing eye" and, upping the metaphorical ante, the *Washington Post* predicted that "the gold fish bowl and not the smoke-filled room hereafter will be the proper symbol of American political conventions."

Having emerged into the video daylight from the tobacco haze, however, politicians needed to look the part. Observing that Republicans had been telecast "to distinct disadvantage due to harsh lighting" during their 1948 convention, WFIL-TV in Philadelphia recruited a makeup artist from Max Factor "to repair the ravages of time and smoke-filled rooms by prettying up the Democrats about to be telecast." Delegates obediently sat for preliminary makeup and camera tests and then walked into the convention hall for the main event, their appearance on television.

Whether with qualms or fervor, crafty politicians knew television was not just changing the face of politics but becoming the main stage for the show. At the network and local level, office seekers cultivated their video performance skills. Stylistic recalcitrants and stubborn holdovers—most notably, two-time Democratic presidential candidate Adlai Stevenson, who in 1952 refused to run television spots selling his candidacy—were relegated to also-rans and asterisks in the electoral sweepstakes. "That sunspot on Adlai's television noggin was caused by his refusal to apply make up to his pate, customary among TV baldies," snickered television critic Jack O'Brian.

By 1958, both major parties were endorsing a booklet entitled *A Guide to Your Television Appearance*, distributed to video virgins seeking elective office. "Make-up for television should not be dismissed as degrading or sissified," cautioned the guide. "When a director or makeup artist suggests covering a heavy beard, toning down the shine on a high forehead, or removing the 'bags' from beneath your eyes, don't balk." Balk? Like smitten suitors, American politicians primped for the big date and batted their eyes to make the medium come hither.

Egghead Sundays

"One of the most interesting and enlightening commentaries on present-day TV is the mental stimulation provided by the forum shows," *Variety* observed in 1953. "The fact that these represent non–show biz facets of TV programming and the fact that each week finds their audiences growing is a healthy reflection of the intellectual curiosity of the nation's video viewers." *TV Guide* tallied up fifteen news shows usually telecast during the ratings-thin time slots of "egghead Sunday." Appealing to civic responsibility and church avoidance, offering friendly chatter and fiery exchanges, the forum shows quickly grew into a chautauqua of the air, a klieg-lit clearinghouse for democratic conversation and an open audition for would-be leaders.

Like most entries on early television, radio laid out the blueprint for the forum shows. Though the practice of prominent radio newsmen guiding political guests through well-rehearsed discussions of timely issues was commonplace by 1932, the events leading up to World War II forced a quantum leap in the quality of radio-borne information. To keep pace with the blitzkrieg march of Nazism in the late 1930s, radio sent out a new kind of news, more global in outlook and incisive in tone. No longer simply a staccato recitation of facts, radio news ventured into newspaper-like commentary and interpretation. The complex geopolitics of a world on edge and soon in flames required historical background, political orientation, and critical scrutiny. Led by Edward R. Murrow and the knight templars clustered around the *CBS News Round-Up*, radio newsmen assumed the guise of intellectuals who lent meaning to events rather than stenographers transmitting information. Expert analysts astride a media power-base, they might rightly engage politicians, businessmen, and scientists as equals.

The minimal start-up costs and low overhead for the format augured for a smooth transition into television—especially since the basic ingredients were obtainable in bulk at bargain prices: unpaid guests eager for a high-profile platform, journalists accustomed to working cheap, and threadbare desks emblazoned with the name of the show and the logo of the sponsor.

More a sop to civics than commerce, the forum shows fulfilled the dour mandate of the Federal Communications Act of 1934 for programming in the "public interest, convenience, and necessity." Like live coverage of congressional hearings and news events, they served not as profit centers but as public-interest trophies, cementing friendly relations with the FCC and underscoring the mutual interests between politicians and broadcasters. Moreover, viewership was skewed to better-educated, better-informed, and hence more desirable consumers.

The forum shows also suited the only kind of news television could transmit live. Before mobile television units and videotape playback facilitated off-site coverage of remote events, news from television was verbal and stage-bound. "The special event, the elections, the hearings, the political meetings, those which are done live, are, for the most part, superbly done by skilled craftsman using the latest mobile equipment," explained See It Now producer Fred W. Friendly in 1953. "But the daily news shows which must meet deadlines not synchronized with the big live stories must depend upon film, and they are forced to use equipment designed for weekly theatrical newsreels." Unless the event were scheduled in advance (not the best description of news), early television simply couldn't deliver live pictures. Thus, radio remained the preferred medium for what was called "spot news"—fast-breaking information beamed in from remote locations. "We still turn instinctively to the radio when it comes to finding out what's going on in the world," Dan Jenkins confessed in 1952. "TV seems to be at its best with such semi-news shows as See It Now, Meet the Press, and the weekly film news reviews, but the hourly newscast just doesn't seem to be the newer medium's forte."

Low cost and low tech, the forum shows required no off-site newsreel cameras and no quick turnaround of exposed film. They allowed television to manufacture, rather than just report, news, and thereby to generate the selfsame product (news) that helped sustain the operation.

The "live-ness" of the face-offs held a unique fascination for citizens used to seeing politicians only in stage-managed settings and stiff filmed interviews. "Filmed television can offer no substitute for the quality of NOW," asserted Martin Stone, producer and creator of Author Meets the Critics. "Here is television at its best as it offers the exciting spectacle of news as news is made." What the forum shows lacked in scintillating visuals, they gained in dramatic tension, spirited exchanges, and the pleasing sight of politicians pinned under glass. Not least, the forum shows fostered a rough parity between the contestants: network journalist and government ruler, Nielsen-approved surrogate and voter-approved representative.

Though network anchors were already being chosen for looks and congeniality rather than brains and credentials, the reporters on the early forum shows tended to look like the ink-stained wretches they usually were. In training and demeanor, they personified the print-based roots of an earlier journalistic era, exuding little of the élan but most of the seediness of the fast-talking, hard-drinking, world-weary newspapermen of *The Front Page*. The suits were cheap, the attitude surly, and the eyes baggy and bloodshot from too many long nights in the precinct house, early mornings in court, and round-the-clock vigils at a teletype. Before modern dentistry set a pearly white standard for talking heads, their teeth were decayed and crooked, stained with tobacco and coffee. And these newsmen were the telegenic ones.

NBC's *Meet the Press*, an import from radio that debuted in 1947, was the prototype for the video forum show and the prize berth for politicians and journalists alike. (At $125 per appearance, it was also the most lucrative gig for newsmen.) Other vintage shows included CBS's *Man of the Week* (1951–1954) and *Face the Nation* (1954–present), NBC's *American Forum of the Air* (1947–1957), ABC's *At Issue* (1953–54), DuMont's *The Big Issue* (1953–54), and the syndicated series *Chronoscope* (1951–1955). Every major metropolis mounted a local version of same with names like *Washington Comes to California* on KTTV in Los Angeles or *Report from Washington* on WMCA in New York.

An added attraction of the forum shows was that the stringent ethos of "100% acceptability" was stretched to meet the elastic requirements of news and commentary. "Please remember that their questions do not necessarily reveal [the reporters'] point of view—it's their way of getting a story for you!" a chirpy disclaimer cautioned before each episode of *Meet the Press*.

Playing devil's advocate, reporters took open delight in challenging the goliaths and shibboleths of Cold War America, none more so than McCarthy and McCarthyism. Fittingly, since the stock in trade of the format was free expression, the forum shows returned again and again to the person as a guest, the ism as a topic. For his part, McCarthy relished the on-camera combat with surly newsmen. Though always more video-centric than video-savvy, he understood the prestige to be gained merely by entering the ring with the champions of journalism.

Soon after McCarthy burst into national consciousness in February 1950, he became a sought-after, A-list guest on the forum shows. Drawn by mutual self-interest, the newsmen and their prize catch acted out the psychodramatics of a conflicted codependent relationship. The shows eagerly booked the controversial man of the hour, but the panelists seldom treated him with deference or goodwill. McCarthy was repeatedly beset by journalists whose contempt was thinly veiled, if veiled at all. He responded in kind.

For example, on July 2, 1950, during McCarthy's second appearance on *Meet the Press*, the panel sharply quizzed the senator about the propriety of a book deal and his troubles with the IRS. "Just a minute, just a minute,"

Duelling namesakes: Sen. Joseph McCarthy (*left*) and Rep. Eugene McCarthy (D-Minn.) appear on *American Forum of the Air*, with producer-host Theodore Granik (*center*) (June 22, 1952).

blusters McCarthy, "you're not gonna ask [another question] until I finish this [reply]."

Later, Marshall McNeil, a correspondent for Scripps-Howard Newspapers, asks, "Well, Senator, after all this investigation and stuff, [do] you believe as of the moment there are communists in the State Department?"

"Communists or worse," shoots back McCarthy.

"Want to name a few?" McNeil challenges. "And by the way," he continues in a folksy drawl, referring to McCarthy's privilege of senatorial immunity, "you got that immunity cloak wrapped around you today or not?"

Afraid of legal action against NBC should McCarthy name a name, coproducer and host Martha Roundtree hastily intervenes. "Maybe so, Mr. McNeil—but I don't think *we* have [an immunity cloak]." Everyone laughs.

Likewise, on an episode of *Chronoscope* telecast on November 16, 1951, the press and the politician evince mutual hostility. McCarthy's chief interrogator was William Bradford Huie, the fearless investigative reporter then best known for his racy novel *The Revolt of Mamie Stover*. "You are," Huie begins laconically, "one of the most controversial figures we've had in the Senate in a long time and you have the distinction of having coined a new word for the dictionary—namely McCarthyism." Grinning, baiting the fish, Huie asks, "Now, how do you define 'McCarthyism?'"

"Mr. Hooey," McCarthy replies, willfully mispronouncing his surname (not "hue-ey" but "hoo-ey" as in "foolishness"), "I didn't coin the phrase. *The Daily Worker* originated the phrase. They're the first paper that used it. It's their phrase. We'll let them define it." Undaunted, Huie bores in again. "Do you think that you have been guilty of any un-Americanism yourself in your efforts to combat what you define as un-Americanism?"

Another testy exchange between journalists and McCarthy occurred on June 21, 1953, on NBC's *American Forum on the Air*. When McCarthy attacked Great Britain for trading with Red China, Paul Scott Rankine, the Washington Bureau chief for the London-based Reuters News Agency, rose to the defense of his homeland. Whereas America "was once recognized as a sanctuary for independent thinkers and rugged individuals," asserted Rankine, McCarthy "was erecting a climate of fear under which people were afraid of confessing political misjudgment or else suffer the loss of their jobs, intimidation, and social distrust." Later in the show, when McCarthy accused Albert Einstein of advising intellectuals to "conceal secrets of sabotage and espionage," moderator Frank Blair interrupted to correct him.[1]

On November 7, 1954, McCarthy, by then mortally wounded by the backlash from the Army-McCarthy hearings and a censure resolution being debated in the Senate, was the guest for the premiere episode of CBS's *Face the Nation*. Again, the reporters are confrontational, but now almost contemptuous of an opponent no longer worthy of their mettle. "Let's leave the adjectives out for a minute, Joe," cautions William Hines of the *Washington Star* when McCarthy insults Sen. Arthur Watkins (R-Utah), cochairman of the committee considering McCarthy's censure. "You have misquoted him on five or six occasions about that, Joe," Hines interjects again. Scowling at McCarthy, William Lawrence of the *New York Times* is not so polite. "Senator, I hold in my hand—which is one of your favorite expressions—,"

---

1. Earlier that year, a high school science teacher subpoenaed to testify before the Senate Internal Security Subcommittee had written Einstein to solicit his advice on the most honorable course of conduct. In a widely publicized letter written on May 16, 1953, Einstein responded that "every intellectual who is called before one of the committees ought to refuse to testify" because "it is shameful for a blameless citizen to submit to such an inquisition and that this kind of inquisition violates the spirit of the Constitution."

Lawrence smirks, to underscore the irony of McCarthy complaining about the injustice of rogue senatorial investigations.

When not personally under interrogation, McCarthy seemed to hover just out of camera range whenever the topic of domestic communist subversion was broached. Virtually every Cold War politician who appeared on a forum show during McCarthy's four-year reign was buttonholed for his or her opinion on the junior senator from Wisconsin. Unlike communism, McCarthy was controversial: Democrat or Republican, opinion on the communist menace was conventional. In contrast, opinions on McCarthy were varied, passionate, and risky. The forum shows courted McCarthy's political opponents—notably Margaret Chase Smith (R-Me.) and Ralph Flanders (R-Vt.)—for their lacerating statements on McCarthy, not their opinions on international tariffs and income tax reform.

McCarthy not only made news; as a kind of inadvertent talent recruiter, he made newsmakers. Whenever McCarthy accused an opponent by name, he thrust his target into the public eye. Obscure government functionaries and behind-the-scenes players became instant celebrities and sought-after guests for the forum shows. Once dragged into the spotlight by McCarthy, they gained a television platform to attack McCarthyism.

No target of McCarthy better exploited the ricochet effect than James Wechsler, editor of the full-throated anti-McCarthy tabloid, the *New York Post*. In September 1951, under the title "Smear Inc.: The One-Man Mob of Joe McCarthy," the paper ran a 17-part series that for sheer vitriol probably ranks as the nastiest hatchet job on any American politician during the 1950s, a blistering assault on McCarthy's personal finances, military record, and patriotism. "Three things are clear about Sen. Joe McCarthy," the series asserted in summation. "He's a bore. He's a fake. He's trouble."

Wechsler had never made a secret of his past membership in the Young Communist League from 1934 to 1937. Like many former communists since redeemed, he touted his years in the party as the catalyst for his current militant anticommunism. As a panelist on *Author Meets the Critics*, telecast on March 27, 1952, he had frankly discussed his communist past. But attacking McCarthy exacted consequences even for a known anticommunist. In 1952, having assailed McCarthy and thereby become a controversial personality, he was yanked from his regular spot as a panelist on DuMont's *Starring the Editors*. However, banning an eloquent anticommunist for his recanted communist past was too surreal even for Cold War television: Wechsler was reinstated on the show two weeks later. Unable to secure a sponsor, however, the show was soon canceled.

Where *Starring the Editors* shunned Wechsler's services, another kind of forum show, namely the McCarthy committee, demanded his guest appearance. On April 24 and May 5, 1953, in closed sessions whose transcripts were released to the public at Wechsler's insistence, McCarthy and his lieutenant Roy Cohn impugned Wechsler's patriotism as an American and his professionalism as a journalist. "You have fought every man who has ever tried to fight communism," McCarthy charged. "Your paper, in my opinion, is next to and almost paralleling the *Daily Worker*." Firing off a loaded term, Wechsler responded that he regarded the investigation "as the first in a long line of attempts to intimidate editors who do not equate McCarthyism with patriotism." The editor later observed that McCarthy seemed "rather proud to be an ism as well as a Senator."

After testifying before McCarthy's committee under duress, Wechsler testified on television with enthusiasm. On May 17, 1953, he faced a panel of his fellow journalists on *Meet the Press*. Unbowed, Wechsler derided McCarthy's "perfectly pointless inquiry" and accused him of using "a senate committee as a front for a reprisal against a newspaper in which he was engaged in a controversy." These "domestic inquisitions" and "spectacular, often irrelevant and flamboyant hearings" have "exceeded the good." It was only "an accident of history" that had made McCarthy an expert on communism, Wechsler asserted. Of McCarthy's book, *McCarthyism: The Fight for America*, which Arthur Schlesinger Jr. had reviewed scathingly in the *New York Post*, Wechsler sniffed, "We reviewed it as a curious exhibit but not as a piece of literature." Wechsler felt proud that he and his paper were fighting McCarthy "as vigorously as we ought [to fight] a man named Joe Stalin."

If Wechsler expected kid glove treatment from his fellow journalists, he was mistaken. Aware of being watched for any undue partiality to a cojournalist, the *Meet the Press* panel gave the crusading editor a rougher session than any mere politician. "Mr. Wechsler," asked Frank Waldrop of the *Washington Times-Herald*, "if you're the only brave editor and all these others are cowards, why are you appealing to the ASNE [American Society of Newspaper Editors] to bail this situation out for you?" Wechsler replied that small community newspapers in conservative regions had a harder time than he did in a liberal Democratic bastion like New York. "If the Washington reporters on this NBC-TV stanza were to try to rake over guest salons who pontificate before them as bitingly as they did their fellow journalist, they would doubtless stir up more news scoops," noted *Variety*. "The press boys seemed set to bait Wechsler."

In truth, the *Meet the Press* boys were just playing equal-opportunity interrogators. Two weeks earlier, Roy Cohn, chief counsel for the McCarthy committee, had appeared on the show and offhandedly tried to smear Wechsler. "He has been active in the communist movement," Cohn asserted. Cohost Lawrence Spivak's ears prick up at Cohn's verb choice. "[Wechsler] *was* active a long time ago—" Spivak interrupts. Ernest Lindley, the Washington bureau chief for *Newsweek*, chimes in to remind the 26-year-old Cohn that Wechsler was "definitely *anti*communist—even before *you* appeared on the scene."

Late in 1953, Wechsler published *The Age of Suspicion*, an account of his tangle with McCarthy and a rumination on McCarthyism. On January 31, 1954, DuMont's *Author Meets the Critics* selected Wechsler to meet his critic William F. Buckley, then a youthful right-wing savant due to his 1951 exposé of Ivy League elitism, *God and Man at Yale: The Superstitions of Academic Freedom*. Taking the orthodox Cold War liberal line, Wechsler argued that it was possible to be both anticommunist and anti-McCarthy. Buckley allowed that while he didn't think Wechsler was disloyal, he had "no contempt for those who question your loyalty." And, no, Buckley retorted, you could not be anti-McCarthy and anticommunist at the same time.

Actually, you could. Though never veering from the normative anticommunism of the day, the reporters on the news forum shows held fast to the principles of unfettered conversation and unbound interrogation. No matter who the guest or what the topic, the panelists were open to recalcitrant opinion and predisposed to be sharply critical of McCarthyites who would shut them, or others, up.

Direct Address

The most coveted forum of the air, unmediated by pesky journalists, unencumbered by rival claimants for face time, and unbroken by commercial interruption, was the direct address: a politician speaking straight into the camera lens, whether in a formal televised speech before a live audience or solely to the audience of greater import in the living room. The true imprimatur of authority, direct address was reserved for only the most elect of the elected.

Of course, the locus classicus for the direct address is the 30-minute tour de force delivered by the besieged Republican vice presidential candidate Richard M. Nixon on September 23, 1952. With his place on the bottom half of the Eisenhower ticket in jeopardy, Nixon took to the airwaves to defend himself against charges of campaign corruption. Audaciously betting on the galvanizing force of a first-person video plea, he exploited the confessional quality of a medium that thrived on the raw exposure of personal intimacies. At a time when tax returns and family finances were held as matters of intense privacy by Depression-scarred Americans, Nixon bared his bank account as well as his heart in a wrenching bout of exculpatory self-revelation.

As Nixon told it, the items in his psychic account books were threadbare but honestly earned: a mere $4,000 in life insurance, a common 1950 Oldsmobile, and "a respectable Republican cloth coat" worn by his wife Pat, who was Irish, born on St. Patrick's Day ("the Irish never quit"). Then, his master stroke, the canny canine reference to "a little cocker spaniel dog" given to him by a man from Texas and whom his daughter, Tricia, "the six-year-old," had named "Checkers." As if reluctant to broach the topic, Nixon put his hand to his face, ashamed not for himself but for his unscrupulous enemies, who had sunk so low as to force him to discuss so innocent a family matter and drag his little girls into this smear campaign. Cost what it may, though, he will not succumb to the mudslingers. "And you know, the kids, like all kids, love the dog—and I just want to say this right now"—an avowal begun in friendly tones and concluded with steely determination—"that regardless of what they say about it—we're gonna keep him."

Though ripe kitsch for later generations of Nixon haters, the "Checkers" speech was by all contemporary reckoning a televisual master stroke. Cued to the red light signaling which camera was "hot," Nixon makes eye contact with each of the three cameras recording the scene—two focused on him, one on Pat, who sits demurely stage left. A beat late sometimes in redirecting his gaze to the lens, he commits a more serious gaffe by mistiming the talk: when the allotted half hour of airtime runs out, his image fades out as he winds up for a big finish. No matter: Nixon and his cocker spaniel were lapped up by viewers who flooded the Republican National Committee with supportive telephone calls and telegrams. "Video-wise," observed a dry-eyed *Variety*, "it was a brilliant feat of political journalism. Translated into a commercial suds saga, it would have been a cinch to garner a renewal for at least another 52-week cycle."

Later so maladroit and anxious before the camera, a study in flop sweat and phoniness, Nixon was adjudged a television natural in his early direct address performances. On October 13, 1952, after the "Checkers" showstopper, Nixon appeared on CBS to speak about the fateful encounter he had arranged between communist agent Alger Hiss and his accuser Whittaker Chambers at the Hotel Commodore in New York in 1948, a tale that also reminded voters that Democratic presidential candidate Adlai Stevenson had been a character witness for Hiss. Again, Nixon sat behind a desk and explained a complicated case in commonsensical language. Relating the tense face-off between accused and accuser, Nixon came from behind his desk and reenacted each part. "If Senator Richard M. Nixon isn't elected Vice President, he can always get a job as a TV actor," blurbed *Variety*. "He turned in the kind of a job that should have had GOP adherents gleeful at their sets and the Demos gnashing in frustration."

Paid political addresses like Nixon's "Checkers" speech and his Hiss-Chambers monologue were simple business transactions, underwritten by the political parties and tallied up by the networks as an extended commercial. By contrast, when a network bestowed free coverage on a direct address as a news event, it risked violating the most noxious of FCC fiats, Section 315 of the Federal Communications Act, the so-called equal time provision. In 1934, to prevent one-party dominance of broadcasting, the FCC decreed that "equal time" had to be accorded all candidates in a political contest. Thus, by covering a newsworthy speech by a telegenic candidate, a network might be required to telecast a boring tirade by the nontelegenic opposition. Made only after deep deliberation at the highest levels of network authority, the decision to telecast or not to telecast a political speech was fraught with unforeseen consequences. Theoretically, under the terms of Section 315, the networks faced an endless series of cascading demands for rebuttal and counter-rebuttal.[2] Not until 1959, bowing to lobbying from the National Association of Radio and Television Broadcasters, would Congress amend the provision to exempt "bona fide" newscasts, forum shows, and news documentaries from the equal time provision. But in the 1950s—the president always excepted—uncertainty swirled around who to telecast and who not to.

However, the debate over and the resolution of two kindred incidents, each involving a direct address and a demand for equal time, served to clarify the application of Section 315. Predictably, both fracases involved McCarthy. The shift in network policy from the first case to the second case traces both the sinking career arc of the senator and the rising tide of television in American culture.

At 11:00 P.M., November 16, 1953, former president Harry Truman took to the airwaves to deliver his version of a long-simmering controversy over the case of Harry Dexter White.[3] For some fifteen minutes, Truman defended his actions, but the key paragraph submitted his acidic definition of McCarthyism. Though Truman pretended to divorce the man from the ism ("I am not referring to the senator from Wisconsin—he is only important in that his name has taken on a dictionary meaning of the word"), his linkage of McCarthyism with

---

2. In 1956, when President Eisenhower filmed a three-minute charity plea for the Community Fund and Council of America to be telecast during *The Ed Sullivan Show*, CBS felt compelled to solicit "equal time" waivers from Democrat Adlai Stevenson and thirteen other candidates for president that year.

3. Assistant Secretary of the Treasury under FDR and Truman, Harry Dexter White was also a Soviet spy. In an ill-advised outburst, Truman had initially called the accusations against White a "red herring." Though White died of a heart attack in 1948, shortly after testifying before HUAC, he served as a convenient blunt instrument for Republicans charging Democrats with lax security practices. On November 6, 1953, Eisenhower's attorney general Herbert Brownell ratcheted up the controversy by accusing Truman of appointing White as executive director of the International Monetary Fund despite FBI warnings that White was a Soviet agent.

Nazi Propaganda Minister Joseph Goebbels's tactic of "the Big Lie" was a personal insult that McCarthy took personally.

"I am notifying the Federal Communications Commission and will demand time on the air to answer Mr. Truman," McCarthy announced the next morning. At first, the networks resisted, arguing that "compensating time" for the Truman broadcast would be provided by telecasting highlights from Attorney General Herbert Brownell's testimony before the Senate Internal Security Subcommittee the next evening. Unmollified, McCarthy insisted upon "radio and television time to answer Mr. Truman's attack upon me last night."

McCarthy's threats rattled the networks not just because of the uncertain application of the equal time provision under FCC guidelines but because of an ominous changeover in FCC personnel. With the election of Eisenhower, the FCC, for the first time since its creation in 1934, became a berth for Republican patronage jobs. By late 1953, two men perceived as McCarthy allies, Robert E. Lee, a former FBI agent and administrative assistant to J. Edgar Hoover, and John Doerfer, a Republican from Wisconsin, held seats on the commission. Network executives worried that the Republican commissioners meant "a stepping up of the campaign to ferret out so-called subversive elements in radio-TV circles" under directional guidance from McCarthy.

The early actions of the Republicanized FCC seemed to confirm the worst fears of the networks. In 1953 broadcaster Edward Lamb, a prominent Democratic Party contributor, began to have routine license applications and renewals with the FCC delayed and impeded. McCarthy was presumed to be blocking the applications because of Lamb's former association with the National Lawyer's Guild, an alleged communist front organization. "The influence of McCarthy friends and henchmen on the FCC," reported Drew Pearson, made already skittish executives even more prone to kowtow.

Fearful of FCC retaliation, the networks caved in to McCarthy's demand for equal time to reply to Truman. "There was no reason—except for the corny and unworkable 'equal time' provision—for broadcasters to be put in the nasty position of risking their license renewals on a McCarthy nix," Variety complained. "For this they can thank the complicated and capricious 'equality' code on controversial subjects tagged 'public service.'" An NBC executive admitted, "McCarthy has scare value and we're scared." In fact, McCarthy got more than equal time, not the fifteen minutes allotted to Truman but a full thirty.

On November 24, 1953, from 11:00 to 11:30 P.M., McCarthy took command on all networks. In medium shot, positioned in front of a curtain and sitting at a desk with a glass of water and pages of notes before him, the senator began by insulting the former president. "Tonight I shall spend but very little time on Harry Truman—he is of no more importance than any other defeated politician," he scoffed. Just as Truman had defined McCarthyism, McCarthy attempted to define "Trumanism" as a "sordid picture" of obliviousness to "a pattern of deliberate communist infiltration." If the former president was not complicit in the communist conspiracy, he was surely a useful idiot. Drawing a distinction between the many good, patriotic Democrats and the "communists, follow travellers, and Truman-type Democrat," McCarthy listed the dangerous lapses in security and judgment during the FDR-Truman regime. He quoted Abraham Lincoln's warning that the nation will be destroyed not from without but from within. "Brutalitarian dictatorships" and the "Stygian blackness of communist night" await the complacent. Unwisely overreaching, he also contradicted President Eisenhower's opinion that communism would not be an important issue in midterm elections the next year.

In lending a direct address pulpit to a common senator, the networks had conferred upon McCarthy a near presidential status. Rather than placating the politician, television had empowered the threat to itself.

Less than four months later, a repeat of the Truman-McCarthy equal time contretemps loomed when another prominent Democratic leader attacked McCarthy on national television. On Saturday, March 6, 1954, at 10:30 P.M., Adlai Stevenson lashed out at the Republican Party in a speech before the Southeastern Democratic Conference, an address broadcast live from Miami Beach "as a public service program" over CBS television and NBC radio. Slyly using McCarthy to attack Eisenhower, Stevenson linked the below-the-belt senator with the above-the-fray president. "Why have the demagogues triumphed so often?" asked Stevenson. "The answer is inescapable: because a group of political plungers has persuaded the president that McCarthyism is the best Republican formula for political success." Also reaching back to Lincoln, Stevenson called the Republicans "a political party divided against itself, half McCarthy and half Eisenhower."

Again, as with the Truman telecast, McCarthy demanded time to respond to Stevenson's "good police court lawyer's job of attacking me." "If the radio and television networks granted free time to Stevenson last night, I intend to ask them for the same hour of the same day of the week in [exchange]," promised McCarthy. "I have no doubt but they will offer me the time." A nervous spokesman for CBS responded, "We'll decide what to do when he asks us." Already getting media-wise, the Democrats baited McCarthy and Eisenhower. "Don't get me wrong, I'm all in favor of it," said Stephen Mitchell, the Democratic National Chairman. "I'd like to have McCarthy on the air for an hour a day to let the American people have a plain look at him. It's fine with me."

In the intervening months, however, particularly after January 1954 when McCarthy turned his fire on the Army and hence the commander in chief, the high-flying hawk had become a political albatross for the Eisenhower administration. On March 10, 1954, at a tense press conference, the president departed from custom and responded directly to Stevenson's charges. "Nonsense," he snorted. More dramatically, Eisenhower finally distanced himself from the McCarthy half of the Republican Party. "With an emphasis that is rare when he discusses individuals," observed the *New York Times*, "the President's whole position today, punctuated by anger and near bluntness, was viewed as additional evidence that the President and some party leaders were toughening their attitude toward Senator McCarthy."

Registering the change in the atmosphere, the networks denied McCarthy equal time. "This time the webs won't buckle under and are planning a united stand in upholding their rights as set forth in FCC regulations," *Variety* predicted. Outmaneuvering McCarthy, CBS and NBC offered the Republicans equal time for either GOP Chairman Leonard Hall or Vice President Richard Nixon, on Saturday March 13, 10:30 P.M., the same time slot Stevenson had commanded.

Enraged, McCarthy went on the offensive. "They [the networks] will grant me time or they will learn what the law is. I will guarantee that," he threatened. "I am delegating no one to answer the attack upon me. Everyone knows the FCC rules provide they must give me time, otherwise it's completely dishonest and unfair."

Fed up with a constant annoyance who had become a major liability, Eisenhower backed CBS and NBC. "I am not going to make the decisions that, of course, the Federal Communications Commission makes, and that the networks make on their own responsibility," stated Eisenhower. "I think that the networks have certainly discharged their responsibility for being impartial when they give to the Republican National Committee the right to answer as they see fit." FCC commissioner Robert E. Lee, a putative McCarthy ally, agreed that the accommodation "seems like a square deal to me."

That Saturday, direct address star Richard Nixon responded to Stevenson on CBS television and radio and NBC radio. "Before I get to my talk tonight, I want to thank the radio and television stations for providing time for me to reply to the attack which was made by Mr. Stevenson over these same stations on President Eisenhower and his administration last week," Nixon began agreeably. "To give both sides a chance to be heard is in the fair, best American tradition." After praising the networks, he responded to the attacks on Eisenhower and ignored the attacks on McCarthy.

McCarthy was infuriated at the denial of televisual parity. He threatened to petition the FCC to change its rules to allow free airtime to anyone attacked on television, but the "consensus is that it wouldn't have the proverbial chinaman's chance," gloated *Television Digest*. Off-the-record assurances from the Eisenhower administration that the FCC would not retaliate helped fortify the networks' backbone. Stymied, McCarthy called the two networks "completely immoral," "arrogant," and "dishonest," pledged to boycott NBC and CBS, and turned his back on their cameramen and radio reporters.

"While television cameras often have been turned away from witnesses at sessions of the Senate Permanent Subcommittee on television," the *New York Times* noted drolly, "this was the first time that they have gone off Chairman McCarthy at his own request."

The Ike-onoscope

Throughout the 1950s, the reigning master of television and politics was not Estes Kefauver, not Richard Nixon, and not Joseph McCarthy, but Dwight David Eisenhower, the president. The natural affinity of the well-liked Ike for the medium he well suited was embedded in a pun favored by the television trade press: the "Ike-onoscope" liked Ike. He was the first president to permit his press conferences to be recorded and televised (though not broadcast live), the first president to telecast a live cabinet meeting, the first president to telecast special ceremonies such as the signing of bills and the lighting of Christmas trees, and the first president to inform and rally the nation through the systematic deployment of direct address. Significantly too, he was the first president to watch a lot of television, cementing his video kinship with the electorate by bringing an ultra-modern RCA 21-inch color set into the White House.

Of course, any chronicle of the romance between broadcasting and the presidency begins not with Eisenhower but with his wartime commander in chief, Franklin Delano Roosevelt, the first president to harness the means of mass communication with virtuoso skill. A magnetic figure in the sound newsreels and a spellbinding voice on radio in his legendary "fireside chats," FDR set a towering standard for political performance. In 1939, at the New York World's Fair, he became the first president to appear on television, but FDR, a natural on the newsreels and radio, never lived to exploit another fireside medium that would have perfectly fit his cool, patrician manner.

By definition, then, Harry S. Truman was the first television president, his term in office—April 12, 1945, to January 20, 1953—coinciding with the early years of the medium. Though more comfortable with the archaic epistolary format, Truman staged a number of television premieres. On January 20, 1949, his inauguration ceremonies were the first to be telecast live and, on September 4, 1950, his speech to the Japanese Peace Treaty Conference in San Francisco occasioned the first transcontinental telecast. Truman also introduced the televised direct address to the chief executive's repertoire, made film clips of the president at public events a regular feature of television news, and initiated the tradition of a televised farewell address to the nation.

However, it was an informal television performance by Truman that helped chip away at the time-honored reserve between the presidency and the electorate. On the afternoon of May 3, 1952, he escorted Frank Bourgholtzer of NBC, Walter Cronkite of CBS, Bryson Rash of ABC, and an estimated 17 million viewers through the newly refurbished White House. Playing host and master of ceremonies, Truman agreed "to guide us himself through the renovated but still history-filled rooms." Like a proud homeowner showing off his dream house, he waxes loquacious, sharing anecdotes and architectural expertise. Some of the dialogue is patently scripted ("You had a story about this wonderful picture, Mr. President?" coaxes Bryson Rash), but the number of times Truman responds to a question with a frank admission of ignorance ("I don't know." "I can't say." "I can't answer you.") indicates the relative spontaneity of the proceedings.[4] Repeatedly, almost obsessively, the Korean war-torn Truman mentions that the presidential seal, showing the eagle clutching the olive branch in one talon and the arrows of war in the other, must always have the profile of the eagle facing in the direction of peace.

Despite uneven lighting and glimpses of White House staffers scrambling out of camera range, the Truman show garnered terrific notices, especially for the good-natured musical performance by the president. When Frank Bourgholtzer asks permission to hit a note on a piano "to show people what it sounds like," Truman takes the cue. "I'll show you what it sounds like," he says eagerly and plays a few chords standing up, praising the "beautiful tone" of the instrument. Later, he sits down to give equal time to another piano with a strain from Mozart's "Night Sonata." "If Mr. Truman is wondering about a job next January," suggested *Broadcasting/Telecasting*, "he might look in to the video field—especially if he will talk instead of read or memorize his lines."[5]

However, the first true television president, the man who provided a model for each successor to follow with greater or lesser degrees of telegeniety, was Dwight D. Eisenhower. The superstar media presidents who preceded him (FDR) and immediately followed him (JFK) have obscured how deftly Eisenhower forged his public image, first via radio and the newsreels during his wartime command of the Allied forces in Europe, and later on television during his campaigns for the presidency and throughout his two terms in office.

---

4. By February 14, 1962, the next time a television tour of the White House was conducted, the precise choreography, stilted dialogue, and videotape format showed that little was being left to chance. Telecast simultaneously on CBS and NBC at 10:00 P.M. EST, and four days later at 6:30 P.M. on ABC, *A Tour of the White House with Mrs. John F. Kennedy* was a primer on interior design, with the starstruck CBS reporter Charles Collingwood playing consort to the First Lady.

5. On the morning of November 13, 1953, then former President Truman broke down official reserve still further by shaking hands with J. Fred Muggs, the popular simian mascot on NBC's *The Today Show*.

Chief executive and master of ceremonies: President Harry S. Truman tickles the ivories for NBC newsman Frank Bourgholtzer on a televised tour of the White House (May 3, 1952). (Courtesy Harry S. Truman Library)

Then and now, as in so much else, Eisenhower's media smarts and performance skills have been underestimated.

Even before Eisenhower assumed the presidency he was deemed a television natural. On February 2, 1951, from 10:45 to 11:00 P.M. on all networks, he made his direct address debut when, at the request of President Truman, then General of the Army Eisenhower reported to the nation on the status of NATO. Putting his martial authority squarely behind an internationalist foreign policy, he called for the creation of "a wall of security" that would protect the Free World "until communist imperialism dies of its own inherent evils."[6] "Professional TV men still speak admiringly of that performance," recalled

---

6. Experimenting with an exhibition strategy aimed at undercutting the competition, the Paramount Theater in Times Square interrupted its motion picture program to project Eisenhower's television address on its big screen. After Eisenhower's talk, the regularly scheduled feature was screened, Dean Martin and Jerry Lewis's service comedy *At War with the Army* (1950).

Television Age in 1955. "General Eisenhower sat behind a broad desk in a Pentagon office, his arms stretched forward, his hands palm-down on the desk top. He read from huge lettered cards held behind the cameras, but he seemed to be talking without notes. He spoke rapidly, earnestly, with utter conviction. His report made a sledgehammer impression on those who saw and heard it on television." Watching with grudging respect, a Democratic politician commented, "I knew right then if that fellow ran for President, we might as well give up."

When Eisenhower did run for president, he orchestrated his television campaign with military precision. On June 4, 1952, he announced his candidacy in a live telecast from Abilene, Kansas. Unexpectedly beset by a drenching prairie downpour, he exploited the elements. "I can assure you there is not half as much water here today as there was in the English Channel eight years ago today," quips Ike. In commanding tones, he speaks out against "senseless fear," calls for "cold logic" in fighting the Cold War, and cautions against giving way to "fear and hysteria." As if on cue, thunderclouds rumble when Eisenhower refers to the "communist menace." The wind, the rain, the date, Eisenhower's flinty visage against the elements—everything evokes the glorious memory of D-Day. Watching the video tableaux, Democrats must have sensed the landslide defeat on the horizon.

Seizing the initiative in the first true television campaign in American political history, Ike showcased himself to tremendous advantage in a famous series of forty filmed advertising spots entitled "Eisenhower Answers America." Produced under the supervision of veteran advertising executive Rooser Reeves, the spots took only one day to film. "I thought we would complete perhaps ten spots, but the General was intent on finishing the lot," recalled Reeves. "He performed so beautifully there were few retakes and we went though all our usable material in short order." Intercut with the general, a parade of average Americans, nonactors carefully chosen by ethnicity, class, and regional accent, pepper the candidate with questions. Ike responds with brusque expertise. Shelling out over $2 million for airtime, the Eisenhower campaign blitzed the airwaves with the "telespots" two weeks before the election.

Lauded, or condemned, as the first calculated use of commercial advertising techniques to sell a president on television, the Eisenhower spots portended neither a dark age of Orwellian demagoguery nor a bright dawn of Jeffersonian democracy but a round-the-clock orgy of Barnumesque hucksterism. "He was the product," Reeves admitted. Wags recited a bouncy jingle:

> Eisenhower hits the spot,
> One full General, that's a lot.
> Feeling sluggish, feeling sick?

Take a dose of Ike and Dick.
Philip Morris, Lucky Strike,
Alka Seltzer, I like Ike.

Ike's video coach was Robert Montgomery, the popular motion picture star and wartime hero. As host and sometime actor for the weekly anthology series *Robert Montgomery Presents* (1951–1957), Montgomery understood not only that television beckoned as a comfortable rest home for fading motion picture stars but that the person who tied up the package got richer than the face on the box.

To better distill the essential Eisenhower, Montgomery studied the president "in the office, at home, in public." As a "public figure not an actor," the president had "a right—and an obligation—to appear to the public as he is, not as someone else wants him to appear," said Montgomery, who aspired only to "help project Mr. Eisenhower's own personality and thoughts in as natural a manner as possible."

Montgomery personally attended to the many artificial techniques needed to project the natural Eisenhower. He counseled the president to replace his heavy horn-rim glasses for a pair with lighter rims and endeavored to keep glare from Ike's bald head. He also checked out camera angles, lighting, and studio acoustics.

Guided by White House Press Secretary James C. Hagerty, Montgomery, and his own innate leadership style, Eisenhower launched a series of television innovations during his eight years in office. In 1949 only ten hours of Truman's inauguration ceremonies had been telecast to 10,000,000 viewers. In 1953, Eisenhower's inauguration was staged as an elaborate television special to twice as many citizen-viewers. Playing the good corporate citizen, CBS distributed a ten-page booklet entitled *Guide to the Inauguration* "to enable students to follow the civic ceremonies intelligently." For an audience as yet unjaded to glacial ceremonies witnessed in real time, the inaugural pageantry made for enchanting spectacle. "The odd thing about the telecast is the fact that even though you knew it was coming and could have written the script virtually word for word, you had to watch it and you had to be thrilled by it," marveled Dan Jenkins at the *Hollywood Reporter*.

During the Cold War, when a president could command network airtime virtually by fiat, Eisenhower regularly employed direct address to rally and inform the nation. Just as FDR had spoken to the radio generation sometimes as a friendly neighbor, sometimes as a determined commander in chief, Eisenhower could be the congenial living room guest or the stern military leader. On March 15, 1954, explaining his tax and fiscal policy, complete with charts and a pointer, he assumed the teacherly mode of the former president of Co-

Eisenhower: the forgotten television pioneer on the campaign trail (1952).

lumbia University rather than the present president of the United States. Before the cameras, said an admiring critic, the president was "as at home as a southern colonel on the veranda." The United Press report hit upon a more resonant image, calling the televisual Eisenhower "as relaxed as a neighbor leaning on his lawnmower."

Perhaps Eisenhower's most memorable direct address was delivered on the evening of April 5, 1954. Later dubbed his "Multiplicity of Fears" talk, the presidential therapy session diagnosed the pervasive anxieties of a nation beset by menaces foreign and domestic. Playing calm father to a nervous nation, Eisenhower recited a grim litany of Cold War terrors—fear of Soviet expansionism, fear of the H-bomb, fear of another Great Depression, and fear of (as another president put it) fear itself. Among the multiple fears abroad in the land Eisenhower did not neglect McCarthyism, but, characteristically, he refrained from naming the name. Instead he cautioned Americans not to "fall prey to hysterical thinking" and decried the "very grave injustices" that can be "committed against an individual if he's accused falsely by someone having immunity of a Congressional membership." As he spoke, Eisenhower leaned back casually, familiarly, against his desk, arms folded, and faced the camera nonchalantly. "Whether Ike learned the lesson alone, or whether his friend and advisor, actor-producer Robert Montgomery, taught it to him one can only surmise," *Broadcasting/Telecasting* surmised. "But the relaxed unpose of the

President was more than a little like the superb ease of the experienced Mr. Montgomery."

Nonetheless, the Eisenhower television appearance desired most by television eluded it for eight years: a live telecast of a presidential press conference. Custom decreed, and custom was obeyed, that the president could not be quoted directly without formal permission, much less recorded or filmed without official sanction and vetting by the White House. At the beginning of each of Eisenhower's two terms in office, presidential press secretary James C. Hagerty tantalized broadcasters with the possibility that the president would permit live telecasts. "We are in a new era with a new medium which we will take and use," he promised. In the end, however, Ike, Hagerty, and Montgomery thought better of it. Only with JFK, who on January 25, 1961, inaugurated the tradition of live telecasts of presidential press conferences, would the high-wire act become an initiation rite for each new chief executive and a mandatory duty of democratic leadership in the age of television.

Not that Eisenhower was inaccessible. The president spoke to reporters almost every week for about thirty minutes at regularly scheduled press conferences. The conferences were recorded on audiotape, filmed by newsreel cameras, and transmitted by television cameras for recording on kinescope. Hagerty then reviewed the footage, cutting about four or five minutes from each session before releasing it to the networks. Following the practice of the newsreels, whose cameras had refrained from showing the paralyzed FDR to disadvantage and who under Truman had allowed the White House to confiscate film "on the grounds that President Truman's privacy was invaded," television abided by the editorial oversight that gave the White House final cut over presidential performances.

The warm linkage between Eisenhower and television was made cozier by the well-publicized recreational habits of the First Family. "Usually after dinner, the President changes into slacks and an old golf sweater, and he and Mamie adjourn to the second-floor hall and turn on TV," ran a typical profile of "Ike and Mamie at Home" in 1953. "Mamie likes the plays and movies—even the old ones. Ike prefers newsreels and light comedy, although he occasionally watches a panel discussion show when it features an administration official." The president's preference in television showmen seemed to mirror America's preference in presidents. "One of the president's favorite TV programs has been *The Arthur Godfrey Show*, which apparently appealed to him for its relaxed easy going quality. A friend quoted him as saying that he liked it because you don't have to give it all of your attention."

Unlike the sedative Arthur Godfrey, however, a more irritable television figure ultimately demanded Eisenhower's full attention. During the election campaign of 1952, Eisenhower had courted McCarthy, going so far as to refrain, in a notorious lapse that ever after tainted his reputation, from defending his mentor George C. Marshall against McCarthy's slanders. After the election, however, with McCarthy continuing to attack the State Department and the military as if the Democrats and not his fellow Republicans were still at the helm, Eisenhower's personal antipathy for the senator accorded with political expediency. Yet since Eisenhower seldom mentioned an individual by name, thinking personal attacks beneath the dignity of the presidency, he spoke to McCarthy and McCarthyism elliptically, in a coded but easily decipherable language.

Eisenhower's coded discourse is best showcased in the special presentation *Dinner with the President*. Telecast live on CBS on November 23, 1953, from 7:00–8:00 P.M., and rebroadcast on kinescope by the other networks later that night, the show chronicled the fortieth anniversary of the Anti-Defamation League of the B'Nai B'rith, which was honoring the president with its annual award. Hosted by newsmen Bob Gruen and Walter Cronkite and actors Lilli Palmer and Rex Harrison, the variety show-*cum*-testimonial dinner featured a star-studded, multicultural cast of entertainers. Besides the guest of honor, the dinner was also a testimonial to how thoroughly Republicans had capitulated to the tenets of FDR's New Deal, how deeply the ethos of ethnic and racial tolerance had penetrated mainstream sensibilities, and how powerful American Jewry had become in postwar American culture. In addition to Eisenhower, five Supreme Court Justices and J. Edgar Hoover sat on the dias to demonstrate their own support for the goals of the ADL.

The special opens with a close-up shot of an engraved invitation card: "you are cordially invited to a dinner with the President" held at the Mayflower Hotel in Washington, D.C. Host Rex Harrison boasts that the ceremony is "dedicated to the proposition that all men are created equal and to the conviction that, opinions from behind the Iron Curtain to the contrary, there's a lot that's *right* about being American." A newsreel paean to FDR's New Deal stops for emphasis on Executive Order 8802, which forbade discrimination in the awarding of federal contracts, and on the image of Eleanor Roosevelt, whose picture draws warm applause. Ike's own "ceaseless struggle for human rights" on the field of battle and in government is also commemorated.

The entertainment portion of the dinner served up the standard variety show smorgasbord. Comedian Thelma Ritter ambled on stage as the Statue of Liberty, Helen Hayes reprised her Broadway role as Harriet Beecher Stowe, baseball great Jackie Robinson lent his emblematic presence, African American baritone William Warfield performed an aria from *Faust*, and singer Eddie Fisher crooned a ballad in honor of an American Indian, killed in action in Korea but denied burial in his all-white hometown cemetery.

In a rare gesture of internetwork comity, the presidents of NBC, CBS, and ABC take a bow (the absence of Alfred Du Mont is a bad omen for the fourth network). The television triumvirate inspires Rex Harrison to remind viewers that the ancient Greeks believed that the size of a democratic state was limited by the range of a human voice. This "challenging definition" was answered in the twentieth century by the technology of television and radio, pioneered for American democracy by Gen. David Sarnoff of the Radio Corporation of America, Leonard Goldenson of the American Broadcasting Company, and William S. Paley of the Columbia Broadcasting System. Due to the ingenuity of these noble men and their colleagues, "a single voice can reach millions upon millions—a voice to entertain, a voice to communicate, a free voice speaking to free men." Yet the voices are not loud and angry but calm and reasoned. "We are not a mob to be led by demagogues," asserts Cronkite.

When Eisenhower is introduced to receive the ADL award "for a life devoted to the furtherance of freedom," he walks purposely to the podium. The president begins with a bit of self-deprecation and repeats to comedic effect a verb of recent coinage, "I have been briefed—and briefed—and briefed."

Earnest yet relaxed, Ike recalls his hometown of Abilene, a frontier outpost still bound by the Code of the West, where "a man can walk upright" and "you could meet anyone face to face with whom you disagree." "You could not sneak up on him from behind and do any damage to him without suffering the penalties of an outraged citizenry," says Ike. "If you met him face to face and took the same risks he did, you could get along with almost anything"—pausing a beat, repeating the line for emphasis—"you could get along with almost anything"—gesturing now, pointing to his chest—"as long as the bullet was in the front." Warming to the theme, he hammers home the point. "In this country, if someone dislikes you or accuses you, he must come up in front. He cannot hide behind the shadow. He cannot assassinate you or your character from behind without suffering the penalties of an outraged citizenry." Wild applause fills the room.

Eisenhower then segues into some light banter. "The only responsibility I have is to some individual in front of me who has [cue] cards—[to tell me] if I used up all my time. I just noticed—he says, 'Go ahead, it's all right.'" Appreciative chuckling cascades through the hall, at the notion of the chief executive deferring to the demands of a cue-card holder, when, as anyone could plainly see, he was the true master of the medium.

SIX

ROMAN CIRCUSES AND SPANISH INQUISITIONS

The quality of live—the electrifying sense of witnessing events as they happened, of sharing experience in time across space—was the decisive and unique attraction of early television. Describing the radical switch from the grammar of motion pictures to the grammar of television, the media historian Erik Barnouw observed that the "real time" codes of live television recovered "an element that had almost vanished from film—one which few viewers noticed consciously but one which undoubtedly exercised an hypnotic influence." Before television, spectators were conversant in only one moving image language, a dialect that found its most eloquent expression in the "invisible style" of classical Hollywood cinema. Not only was the designing hand of the filmmaker concealed, but a syntax of smooth dissolves, eyeline matches, and seamless editing worked to suspend the passage of time. Yet no matter how fluid the flow of celluloid, "movie time" is time filmed, always a moment from out of the past projected into the present. Live television happens in the same temporal frame: for beheld and beholder, the same existential moment, the same imaginative space.

The best-remembered exemplar of the thrill of the live is the anthology series, the flagship product of the Golden Age of Television. Typified by the earnest melodramas staged on *Studio One*, *The U.S. Steel Hour*, and *Playhouse 90*, and dating roughly from 1948 (when *Studio One* premiered under producer-auteur Worthington Miner) until 1958 (when the same show rang down the curtain on live performance for videotape recording), the genre lent a high-brow luster, or at least middlebrow respectability, to prime-time programming. "The advantages of live TV are subtle and complex: you have to deal largely in intangibles," admitted John Crosby in 1953. "Film possesses no sustained acting or mood, little of the tremendous feeling of urgency and immediacy of live TV." Hollywood filmmakers who took "a patronizing attitude toward a new medium" were fooling no one, boasted Worthington Miner in 1955, taking a patronizing attitude toward the old one. "Television is young—scarcely eight years old—yet in that time it has encouraged more original, more creative, and more courageous thought than pictures have in half a century."

Like all golden ages, the short-lived but storied epoch of live television shined more brightly as time rolled on. By the early 1960s, television pioneers were already waxing nostalgic about the halcyon days of high-quality, high-intensity televisual theater. Max Liebman, producer of the live comedy-variety hour *Your Show of Shows* (1950–1954), tried to put things in perspective. "There was no 'golden age,' of television," he explained. "Some shows were better and some were worse." Mainly, though, the recollected enchantments of the raptures of live television were immune to revisionism. "TV was invented as a live animal," Fred Coe, the esteemed producer of *Goodyear TV Playhouse*, reflected in 1965. "It produced an eyewitness account of happenings in the arts, in sports, in theater, in current events."

In fact, when telecast live, news events and political hearings exerted the same hypnotic influence as the anthology series—and, occasionally, the same improvisational delights of the variety shows. Though the production facilities were more primitive and the shows more specialized, Washington, D.C., like New York and Los Angeles, originated some of the most compelling programming on early television. "What do you get out of the McCarthy investigations on TV that you can't get in the papers?" asked television critic Marya Mannes. "The answer is: Plenty. The telephoto lens, bringing each human element close to the eye, makes it an experience probably more intense and disturbing than actual presence in the committee room." Television critic Jack Gould agreed. "The absorbing attraction is to follow the testimony as it goes first one way and then the other," he explained. "On TV it is the drama of unrehearsed actuality unfolding for everyone to see at home."

The first televised hearings from the Senate and the House of Representatives were symbolic Cold War harbingers. On November 11, 1947, WMAL-TV, the ABC affiliate in Washington, D.C., telecast testimony from Secretary of State George C. Marshall before the Senate Foreign Relations Committee, a plea for the historic plan that would bear his name. On August 25, 1948, the first telecast from the House of Representatives offered another preview of coming attractions: the inquiry by the House Committee on Un-American Activities into accusations by ex-communist Whittaker Chambers that Alger Hiss, a former State Department official and current president of the Carnegie Endowment, had operated as a Soviet agent in the 1930s.

Telecast to a mere 10,000 sets in the capital, the primal "hearingcasts" of the late 1940s were treated more as novel experiments than media landmarks. In 1948 *Variety* snickered at the prospect of "continuous coverage of the Congressional follies." But as television's penetration soared upward—from roughly a tenth of the population in 1949 to around two-thirds by the end of

Premier screening: as Alger Hiss (*far left, second row*) listens, Whittaker Chambers testifies at a televised hearing of the House Committee on Un-American Activities (August 25, 1948). (Courtesy United Press International)

1954—the live legislative programs launched two backbenchers into the ranks of political stardom. The first is a man largely forgotten to American history because his performance is not readily retrievable on kinescope; the second is a man remembered all too well because his appearances are carefully preserved and incessantly rewound. Between them, Sen. Estes T. Kefauver (D-Tenn.) and Sen. Joseph R. McCarthy (R-Wis.) showed that heretofore obscure legislators might rise to national prominence not through the traditional means of ascent—party service or public accomplishment—but exclusively through deeds performed on television.

"Kefauver Fever": The Kefauver Crime Committee Hearings of 1951

From January to March 1951, the Senate Committee to Investigate Crime and Interstate Commerce, chaired by the lanky and slow-talking Estes T. Kefauver (he preferred the adjective "Lincolnesque") barnstormed across America conducting a series of public investigations into organized crime. When tele-cast live from New York through the facilities of independent station WPIX, the Kefauver committee's crime hearings proved that political events might rival serial entertainment, variety shows, or sports events as magnetic attrac-tions. In a nation just getting hooked into television, the congressional drama made for dynamic programming.

Formed on May 10, 1950, the Kefauver committee sought to investigate the rising tide of organized crime in America, or at least its heightened visibility and perceived resurgence. In retrospect, the crime wave that washed over the nation seems but a ripple, the alarum another random outbreak of Cold War jitters. Yet postwar prosperity had given law-abiding citizens a surfeit of dis-cretionary income and, while most of the paycheck paid mortgages and pur-chased the sleek new appliances cluttering the suburban castle, more than the skimmings sustained the biblical vices of prostitution and gambling and the baksheesh that greased the palms of the police. By centralizing operations and running affairs on a solid business footing, criminal enterprises thrived. In this sense, the rise of organized crime paralleled the nationalization of all Ameri-can experience in the 1950s. No less than the interstate highway system and tel-evision itself, the business of crime had become a matter of networks, with na-tional syndicates annexing the fiefdoms of provincial racketeers.

Unlike the proliferation of television under the watchful eyes of the FCC, however, criminal networks were largely unencumbered by federal interfer-ence. For decades, FBI director J. Edgar Hoover had stubbornly refused to ac-knowledge the existence of organized crime, the Mafia, or any other national crime syndicate. It was left to Senator Kefauver to introduce a permanent con-tribution to the American vocabulary: "the Mafia." Helpfully correcting mis-pronunciations by a panel of reporters on *Meet the Press* in 1951, Kefauver de-fined the Mafia as "the most cohesive national [crime] organization" though "it is more a way of life than a particular formal organization."

Hoover's obtuseness notwithstanding, the Kefauver committee beheld an America suffused with organized crime, where "gangsters, mobsters, and gam-blers are literally getting away with murder." Deploying the rhetoric of anoth-er threat to the domestic tranquility, the committee warned that "the secret government of crimesters is a serious menace, which could, if not curbed, be-come the basis for a subversive movement which could wreck the very foun-dations of this country." The Soviet analogy also occurred to Spruille Braden of the Citizen Crime Commission, who testified before the Kefauver commit-tee in geopolitical terms. "Of one thing we can be sure," railed Braden, reeling off the names of some of the most notorious mobsters, "the Costellos, the Adonises, and the rest of this scum, and still more, the miserably corrupted law enforcement officers, are among the Kremlin's best friends."

However, compared to those other menaces to the body politic, a societal threat as venerable as crime was almost reassuring. Rather than the stark polarities of loyalty and treason, of democracy and communism locked in a twilight struggle careening headlong into nuclear oblivion, the Kefauver face-offs pitted virtue against vice, cops against robbers, crusading prosecutors against kingpins of crime. The dialectical materialism uncovered by the Kefauver hearings concerned only the good old deadly sins (lust, avarice, envy) engaged in for the most American of motives (money). If many of the culprits had names that ended in vowels and residency status that facilitated swift deportation, at least they held firm to a cracked-mirror version of the American success ethic. As long as the executive actions of Murder Inc., were intramural, the civilians didn't get too upset about the crossfire.

Besides, the criminals called to testify before the Kefauver committee might have stepped from a Warner Bros. gangster film or Damon Runyon short story. If the reality was the consolidation of nationwide crime networks overseen by devious thugs, the appearance was of colorful "deese-and-dem" hoods speaking in fractured English, criminals as character actors. Never an inhospitable home for outlaws and gangsters, America saw not the corporate criminality of the Mafia but the rugged individualism of feisty palookas hustling for the main chance. In fact, just down the street from the Kefauver hearings in New York, Damon Runyon was undergoing pop cultural revival in *Guys and Dolls*, Broadway's hottest ticket and a lighthearted musical about the very kinds of activities the Kefauver committee was crusading against.

Rolling the dice himself, Kefauver gambled on television by inviting cameras to cover the action of his permanent floating committee. Almost alone among his colleagues in 1951, he understood that television was the emerging proscenium for politicians on the make. Lauded as "one of the most TV-minded of Washington legislators," Kefauver nearly rode his video celebrity to the nomination for president on the Democratic ticket the next year (in 1956 he settled for the vice presidential spot under Adlai Stevenson). "By no means do I want to minimize the great role played by newspapers and radio in dissemination of information," Kefauver declared, "but television provides the public with a third dimension which helps in interpreting what actually goes on."

However, no one—not the senator who beckoned the cameras, not the station managers who telecast the show, and not the viewers who welcomed whatever programming was aired during daytime—anticipated the magnitude of the public response. It was spontaneous, not premeditated, and, like all the best drama, it snuck up slowly and struck suddenly.

Beginning in January 1951, the Kefauver committee lit out from Capitol Hill for the hinterlands, almost as if trying out the show on the road before hitting Broadway for the major reviews. In a tour that criss-crossed the country, the senator presided over open hearings in New Orleans, Detroit, St. Louis, Los Angeles, San Francisco, New York, and Washington, D.C. Typically, special investigators for the committee preceded Kefauver into town and held closed sessions to winnow out the small-time punks from the big-time crooks. Besides putting fear into the hearts of corrupt local officials, news reports of the closed sessions served as a warm-up for the arrival of Kefauver and the open hearings. Usually the senator performed solo as a "subcommittee of one," taking over a downtown courthouse, rousing the forces of local law enforcement, and subpoenaing suspicious characters.

Although the Kefauver committee had inaugurated its road show the previous summer (including a stopover in Chicago, the spiritual epicenter of American crime), it was in New Orleans on January 25–26, 1951, that the hearings were first simulcast on radio and television. The Crescent City boasted an exceptionally colorful and lunkheaded crew of corrupt law enforcement officials. Around the parishes adjacent to the city, bayou sheriffs were not shocked that gambling was going on under their noses—they were shocked that anyone else would be shocked. One local lawman denied knowing that slot machines were really illegal. "I know it's against the law, but they have them all over the state," he explained. Nor did prostitution strike him as forbidden by tradition and statute, though he assured Kefauver that all the brothels in his jurisdiction were segregated.

Only an hour of the hearings was telecast over WSDU-TV, the sole television station, but New Orleans set a pattern for each successive stop on the tour: the local station canceled regularly scheduled programming and the community was gripped with a video-induced spell of "Kefauver fever."

In Detroit, where the two days of hearings were telecast in their entirety without commercial interruption by both WWJ-TV and WJBK-TV, an estimated 90 percent of the television sets throughout the region tuned in. In St. Louis, KSD-TV was forced to extend its limited plans for coverage "after the station's switchboard was swamped with calls from viewers wanting to see more," reported the *St. Louis Post-Dispatch*. "Never have so many amateur television actors held the interest of so many listeners."

In Los Angeles, ABC affiliate KECA-TV, the only station to anticipate the intensity of public interest, telecast all sixteen hours of the hearings over two days. Kefauver then went north for two days in San Francisco, where live coverage was provided by two of the city's three stations, KGO-TV and KPIX.

As in the South and Midwest, the West Coast succumbed to Kefauver fever. Each set of hearings drew the largest daytime audiences yet recorded and inspired "wild bursts of public enthusiasm." Motion picture producer Stanley Kramer wired KECA-TV to praise the Kefauver telecasts as "the most intelligent coverage in public service ever rendered this community" and 2,000

"Kefauver Fever": WPIX television cameras and the newsreels capture the opening session of the Kefauver Crime Committee hearings, at the Federal Courthouse in New York City (March 12, 1951). Kefauver sits at the center table wearing a gray suit. (Courtesy AP/Worldwide Photos)

other viewers "put the KECA-TV switchboard completely out of kilter by phoning in their congratulations." The *San Francisco Chronicle* marveled at the "startling camera eavesdropping" into the sessions and predicted: "It will become the high spot in public services performed by local television."

But it was in New York that the Kefauver committee's investigations metamorphosed from a series of local news stories into a historic, near-national spectacle. From March 12 until March 21, 1951, the Kefauver committee held hearings in the United States Courthouse in Foley Square—first in a tiny room on the 28th floor, three days later in more spacious accommodations on the third floor—to investigate numbers rackets, protection payments, and graft. New York was the penultimate city on Kefauver's itinerary and thus benefited not only from the momentum built from the earlier stops but from the heightened media attention that the city claims as its birthright.

Telecast live during the day by five of New York's seven stations, and in its entirety by DuMont affiliate WABD, the hearings became a metropolitan obsession in New York and wherever viewers were hooked in to the WPIX feed. Linked via coaxial cable and microwave relay, the Kefauver show was carried in part or in full by twenty-five stations in twenty-one cities on the eastern seaboard and throughout the Midwest. Originating a total of forty-four hours of coverage, WPIX was responsible for all aspects of the production, though expenses were shared among participant stations in a pool arrangement. The bare-bones operation consisted of two cameras (four cameras after the hearings moved to the bigger room) and eight microphones, a limitation that became an advantage: the simple shot/reverse shot exchanges between interrogator and witness accentuated the mano-a-mano tension. Harry T. Brundige, formerly of the *St. Louis Post-Dispatch*, served as on-camera commentator. The cast of soon-to-be household names included Senators Kefauver, Charles H. Tobey (R-N.H.), Herbert R. O'Conor (D-Md.), Lester C. Hunt (D-Wyo.), and Alexander Wiley (R-Wis.), and chief committee counsel Rudolph Halley.

The first day of the New York hearings featured Frank Erickson, a small-time gambler who played it smart and dummied up. To whatever question was asked, Erickson parroted the same reply, a legal phrase soon turned national catchphrase: "I refuse to answer on grounds that it might tend to 'criminate me."

The star witness, the outlaw set up for a showdown with marshal Kefauver, was the notorious mobster Frank Costello. A shadowy underworld kingpin, Costello had for decades wielded control over slot machines, narcotics, and politicians in and around the New York metropolitan area. Having always kept a low profile, the camera-shy capo was a reluctant witness who refused to testify on live television. Still eager for the spotlight himself, Senator O'Conor brokered a compromise whereby the cameras would refrain from showing Costello's face. The visual amputation ultimately proved futile because newsreel cameras were filming the mobster full figure for television newscasts that same evening. However, during the day, on live television, the lucky accident of video editing transfixed some 20,000,000 viewers.

At first viewers resented the loss of Frank Costello's talking head. Gradually, though, as the camera focused in on his hands—crumpling scraps of paper and nervously fiddling with his eyeglasses, all wet palms and hairy fingers—the image became strangely hypnotic. "Somehow the camera view of the headless Mr. Costello's exquisitely tailored chest, his spotless pocket handkerchief, his manicured hands nervously picking at his faultlessly-turned lapels or toying with his eyeglasses only accentuated the impression that he is indeed a sinister figure," commented *Broadcasting/Telecasting*. Only half joking, Jack Gould dubbed Costello's gesticulations the "ballet of the hands."

Though Costello was a hard act to follow, Virginia Hill Hauser, moll of the late Benjamin "Bugsy" Siegel, topped him. Bringing sex and sizzle to the gray lineup of men in suits, she sashayed in to the committee room fashionably dressed for the black-and-white medium in a silver blue mink cape, gray suede gloves, and broad-rimmed chapeau. Arriving late, Hill snapped petulantly at the flash photographers. Kefauver excused her tardiness by remarking that "ladies from my part of the country are traditionally late."

Speaking in a whiny, magnolia accent, the auburn-haired 35-year-old told a fascinating tale: how she first came north from Alabama to "sling hash" at the Chicago World's Fair in 1933, how she met "some fellas" of remarkable generosity who showered her with money and racetrack tips, and how she knew nothing about drugs or other illegal activities. After so many dour refusals to testify on grounds of self-incrimination, Hill's colloquial backtalk was a crowd-pleasing change of pace. Asked to explain the reasons for a raucous fight between Bugsy Siegel and herself at his hotel in Las Vegas, she explained, "I hit a girl at the Flamingo and he told me I wasn't a lady." As she left the stand, she belted a female reporter, kicked a male reporter, and cursed at the flash photographers.

That weekend, Kefauver took Sunday night off to stretch his video range as the mystery guest on CBS's popular game show *What's My Line?* Even before the senator walked on stage, the panelists exhibited fluency in Kefauver-ese during opening introductions. "What do you do, Hal Block?" asked actress Arlene Francis, playing straight man for the *Variety* columnist on her left. "I refuse to answer on the grounds that it might tend to incriminate me," deadpanned Block.

The rituals of the "mystery guest" segment on *What's My Line?* required the panelists to don blindfolds, whereupon the mystery guest walked on stage and signed his name on a blackboard. Instantly recognized by the studio audience, Kefauver received sustained, fervent applause. During the role-reversal interrogation, the blurring of show business and the nation's business spawned comic confusion. "Are you in the entertainment business?" queried Miss Francis, as the audience chortled. It took less than two minutes for humorist Bennett Cerf to guess Kefauver's identity and not much longer for Hal Block to suggest that Kefauver's own television show be called *What's My Crime?* "As a matter of fact," Block quipped, "are you sure you want to be shown on television—or just your hands?" Gushed Arlene Francis: "We'd love to have your ratings!"

The second week of the Kefauver hearings began with the testimony of former New York mayor William O'Dwyer, whom the committee suspected of impeding investigations into racketeering. O'Dwyer struck back by accusing Senator Tobey of being involved with New York bookmakers. Sporting an archaic editorial eyeshade, Tobey, an eccentric 70-year-old given to bombastic

No longer the Mystery Guest: Sen. Estes Kefauver introduces himself to the *What's My Line?* panel (May 18, 1951). *From left*: Dorothy Kilgallen, Bennett Cerf, Arlene Francis, and Hal Block. (Courtesy AP/Worldwide Photos)

orations in a mellifluous baritone, launched into an emotional defense of his integrity. "That is not true! I will take the oath right here, if you will give it, Mr. Chairman. I hate a fourflusher!" Tobey stormed.

The next day O'Dwyer apologized and admitted "there is nothing to it." Tobey then delivered a mawkish soliloquy. "Hate is a terrible thing," he told the rapt gallery. "I take my inspiration from a higher source and try to forget it. . . . I have lived long years and God has been good to me. I am a poor man, and always will be. . . . But there is one thing I am. I am a free man. And I am willing that everything I ever did or said or wrote should stand in the light of day to anybody, friend or foe alike." He paused theatrically. "Let's get on with the hearing." A thunderous ovation filled the hearing room.

On March 21, the final day of testimony for Frank Costello, Senator Tobey bore into the close-mouthed mobster for a pithy exchange on the duties of American citizenship:

> *Tobey (*feigning exasperation*):* Well, you're looking back over the years now to that time when you became a citizen, and we're now standing

twenty odd years after that. You must have in your mind some thing that you've done that you can speak to to your conduct as an American citizen. If so, what are they?

Costello (pause): Paid my tax.

At that, the gallery and the senators alike erupted in laughter.

When Costello left the stand, WPIX commentator Harry Brundige took over the hearings. "Ladies and gentlemen," he said to viewers. "Mr. Costello has been a rather mysterious figure to you of the television audience because he was not photographed, but at this time Mr. Costello is willing to face the camera and let you have a good look at him."

The cameras turned on Costello, and Brundige coaxed his prize catch. "Mr. Costello, as the photographer says to the little boy, will you smile a little bit?"

Costello turned to the camera and smiled.

The nonplused committee chairman, temporarily frozen by Brundige's gall, finally took back the reins. "All right," said Kefauver testily, "that is all."

The morning after the first television marathon in American history, viewers rubbed their eyes and walked into the daylight slightly stunned and spent. During the two-week run of the hearings in New York, the city seemed to come to a full stop to watch the riveting real-time, real-life television drama. The ratings for what was hailed as "the greatest TV show television has ever aired" were unprecedented, boosting viewership to nearly twenty times the normal ratings. DuMont's WABD, the only station to telecast the entire hearings live, far outpaced the ratings of the other stations.

Watching the "spellbinding drama" of the Kefauver hearings, critics struggled to find words to describe the deep immersion compulsions of prolonged and concentrated television viewing. This was not the weekly ritual of Uncle Miltie or the Friday Night fights, but an unrehearsed and unfolding drama beheld for hours over a period of days, an intense commitment to an intimate, unrehearsed, and extended moving image spectacle. The thrill of soaking in the full force of the medium for the first time, of fronting the essential facts of life with television, was an artistic experience of a new aesthetic order. Trying to describe the urgency of the video addiction, observers resorted readily to hyperbole. "No event TV has yet covered—the United Nations, the political conventions, the presidential inauguration—presented high drama on so continuous a scale," declared *Billboard*. "These hearings are dealing with insidious factors. Watching them became equally insidious, in the sense that they relegated other duties and daily routines to the background." Tellingly, in Los Angeles, where only edited kinescopes were telecast, the Kefauver hearings ignited little of the excitement of the live telecasts on the East Coast. Likewise, *The Kefauver Crime Committee* (1951), a newsreel compilation from Fox Movietone News, languished in motion picture theaters. For congressional drama to make for gripping television, it had to be live and viewers had to know it was live.

By the time the Kefauver committee left New York for the final round of hearings in Washington, D.C., its characters and catchphrases had entered the national lexicon. Subpoenaed crime boss Jake "Greasy Thumb" Guzik, an alumni of the Al Capone school of bootlegging, proved himself an apt pupil of the New York sessions. Escorted to the witness table in handcuffs, Guzik enunciated his version of a by-now-famous response: "I'm gonna refuse to answer any questions on grounds of incrimination. It may incriminate me or tend to incriminate me or lead to incriminating me in some devious way."

Eventually, Senator Wiley asked if Guzik was a lawyer or represented by a lawyer. Guzik said no.

"Then where did to get this phrase that you've been using?" asked Wiley.

Replied Guzik: "I heard it on television."

HUAC-TV

On March 21, 1951, concurrent with the Kefauver Crime Committee hearings, the House Committee on Un-American Activities launched a long-delayed follow-up investigation into alleged communist influence in the entertainment industry. Yet unlike the Kefauver committee, and despite its publicity-hungry reputation, HUAC tended to shun the brightest spotlight. Ironically, the congressmen investigating television were almost as camera shy as the mobsters investigated by Kefauver. Farsighted politicians who sought to exploit television for access to the electorate knew that their magnified images also invited closer scrutiny. The medium might bite back, inciting voter rebellion and exposing the hidden flaws of the closed shop and exclusive club that was the United States Congress.

During the notorious Hollywood Ten hearings of October 1947, HUAC had been widely derided for conducting a "three ring circus" (the recurrent metaphor for the unruly impact of klieg lights and cameras on congressional inquiries) when newsreels showed witnesses shouting and being shouted down, ejections from the hearing room, and intemperance on all sides. The antics surrounding the Hollywood Ten sessions had been such a public relations fiasco that future HUAC hearings tended to be conducted well away from the eyes and ears of the newsreels, radio, and television. "They object to the Roman circus–Spanish inquisition incidents that have occasionally arisen in committee hearings," explained *Broadcasting/Telecasting*.[1]

In 1949, HUAC voted unanimously to ban radio, newsreel, and television coverage of future hearings, asserting that the bright lights for the cameras contributed to a "circus atmosphere" in the usually sedate chambers of Congress. More likely, the members of the committee were afraid of coming off as befuddled foils for the media-savvy witnesses in the dock. Committeemen sat dumbstruck before the theatrical flourish of character actor Ed Max, who during HUAC hearings in Los Angeles in October 1952, flung his World War II medals onto the hearing room table and shouted, "Take these back to Truman. They used to be known as 'fruit salad,' now they're known as fraud salad. I was proud of them but not any longer. You've negated their importance." Against such bravura gestures, the committee members could only play straight men—or, worse, the villains of the piece.

Aside from being upstaged, the most serious argument against television coverage of congressional hearings was constitutional. Though a ratings hit and a media milestone, the Kefauver hearings raised troubling questions about the propriety of conducting courtroom-like proceedings on live television. Kefauver committee counsel Rudolph Halley argued that "the acid glare of TV" was actually the best safeguard of a fair hearing, but many legal experts felt that the acid was eating away at due process and constitutional protections.

Opponents of live coverage fretted about compelling citizens to testify under hot lights and suspicious eyes, a gauntlet deemed self-incriminating by definition. Plagued by second thoughts after serving on the Kefauver committee, Sen. Alexander Wiley proposed legislation to curb the broadcasting and filming "of proceedings of Congress and its respective committees." Besides the sorry spectacle of "an unjust inquisition of people under klieg lights, particularly people who might not be able to testify properly under such conditions because of health reasons," Wiley envisioned the solemn deliberations

---

1. HUAC members were not averse to motion picture publicity under controlled circumstances. In the anticommunist film *Big Jim McLain* (1952), chairman John S. Wood (D-Ga.) and his colleagues perform brief cameo appearances at the beginning of the film, shot in the actual hearing room. In close-up, committee counsel Frank S. Tavenner speaks a line of dialogue he already had memorized. "Are you now or have you ever been a member of the Communist Party?" he asks an actor (playing a university economics professor not an actor) who takes the Fifth Amendment. Ready for his own close-up, Wood then recites the usual follow-up question. "Would you, if called upon, willingly bear arms on behalf of the government of the United States?"

of Congress degenerating into a "three-ring circus" or a "fourth-rate stage production with hamming and phoney theatrics." He also feared that a clever communist "could in a few minutes' time reach 10,000,000, 20,000,000, or 30,000,000 viewers with propaganda, sabotage instructions, or for some other purpose which he could not possibly achieve in any other way." Always, too, live television risked the frightful possibility of "lewd gestures being screened."

The antitelevision politicians were supported by allies in the legal profession. Unlike today, when chorus lines of camera-ready lawyers clutter the green rooms of cable television, the buttoned-down attorneys of Cold War America considered television coverage anathema to the sober work of justice, whether in Congress or the courtrooms. On February 11, 1952, the American Bar Association extended to television cameras a long-standing antipathy to newsreel cameras as devices "calculated to detract from the essential dignity of the proceedings, degrade the court, and create misconceptions." Like the ABA, the American Civil Liberties Union also elevated Fifth Amendment rights against self-incrimination over First Amendment freedoms of the press. "Until a code of fair play is adopted," declared ACLU board member Dorothy Kenyon in 1953, "we do not want extended to these [congressional hearings] the coverage of TV." Putting a politician before a television camera only intensified "the desire of a congressman, looking for publicity, to make a spectacle of the hearings" and turn the investigation "into a shambles."

For motives not purely constitutional, the print press also cast a cold eye on the coverage of Congress by rival media. "If courts find it necessary to exclude microphones and television cameras, there is even greater reason for congressional investigators to do so when individual reputations are at stake," editorialized the *Washington Post*. Of course, the other reputation at stake was that of the newspaper reporter, no longer the sole omniscient seer when television delivered the headlines.

The man who set the debate in motion was not bothered by the niceties of witnesses' rights or the threat to congressional decorum. "A public hearing is a public hearing," Senator Kefauver asserted in *Crime in America*, his personal account of the crime hearings published in 1951. "To me it makes no sense to say that certain types of information-gathering agencies may be admitted but that television may not, simply because it lifts the voices and faces of the witnesses from the hearing rooms to the living rooms of America." No strict constructionist, Kefauver felt that "the Constitution is a living, growing organism which must be kept abreast and cognizant of all new technological developments."

During the crime committee hearings, Kefauver enforced his edict on video-shy malefactors. In St. Louis, when gambling czar James J. Carroll asserted that television coverage violated his constitutional protection against self-incrimination, Kefauver recommended that the Senate cite him for contempt. Opting for the Frank Costello compromise, Carroll later agreed to testify in Washington, D.C., with the cameras turned away from him.

However, at the same sessions, a pair of hoods named Morris Kleinman and Louis Rothkopf adamantly refused to testify on camera. Cited for contempt by the Senate, they challenged the case in court. On October 6, 1952, the U.S. District Court for the District of Columbia sided with the defendants, ruling that the "close proximity" of "television cameras, newsreel cameras, news photographers with their flashbulbs, radio microphones, a large and crowded hearing room with spectators standing along the wall, etc.," might well "disturb and distract any witness to the point" where he might inadvertently blurt out an erroneous or self-incriminating remark.

Thus, on March 21, 1951, when HUAC revived its investigations into media-borne communism, two considerations constrained the proceedings: the backdrop of the circus-like 1947 HUAC hearings (a blemish on congressional dignity) and the dubious legal status of the coerced testimony of the Kefauver hearings (a threat to due process). Eager for exposure but wary of repercussions, HUAC vacillated over television coverage, first denying it, then permitting it, and then denying it again.

Though hardly idle since October 1947, HUAC had avoided sharing the stage with professional entertainers, preferring to interrogate a less charismatic cast of Communist Party apparatchiks and fellow travelers in education, labor, and government. Finally, however, on March 8, 1951, V. J. Jerome, chieftain of the cultural commission of the Communist Party, was interrogated "in order to lay the foundation for the Hollywood hearings" later that month.

Frankly admitting that "the committee has abused its publicity prerogatives in the past," HUAC chairman John S. Wood (D-Ga.) promised that the revived investigation into the entertainment industry would be no "publicity-seeking circus." Taking the high road, he banned newsreel and television cameras from the hearing room and limited access to print reporters, still photographers, and wire recorders for later radio broadcast. The decree held for the one-day hearing on March 21, but on April 10, 1951, when the committee reconvened after Easter break, Wood granted permission for film and television coverage as long as the cameras operated "with no noise, no lights, no space." The bulky television cameras and the light-dependent 35mm newsreel cameras on tripods were unable to meet the requirements, but two noiseless, high-speed 16mm sound cameras recorded the morning testimony of actor Sterling Hayden for Telenews, an outfit supplying 16mm film to television. The edited footage appeared on NBC's *Camel News Caravan* that night, without the full committee's permission.[2] Annoyed at Wood's high-handedness—and bowing to complaints of unfair treatment from the furious newsreel outfits—the full committee subsequently voted to ban all but still cameras from the hearing room.

But as HUAC persisted so did television. During seven days of hearings into communist infiltration into the motion picture industry held in Los Angeles from September 17 to 25, 1951, the committee was strong-armed into reversing itself by an enterprising station manager for KTTV named Dick Moore. Circumventing the ban on television and newsreel cameras, Moore telecast audio commentary of the hearings over still photographs of the principals. More aggressively, he hauled television cameras outside the hearing room to accost witnesses, lawyers, and HUAC members for spontaneous interviews. Confronted on camera outside the hearing room about the lack of television coverage inside the hearing room, several HUAC members admitted on air that they had no objection to television. The coverage had another calculated effect. "Both the station and the Federal Building were flooded with calls and wires from viewers demanding that the cameras be allowed to cover the actual hearing itself," noted the *Hollywood Reporter*. "Feeling at the station is that the committee will be forced to yield before the week is out."

Sure enough, HUAC bowed to viewer-voter demand and lifted the ban on television coverage. Initially, only the morning sessions were televised, leaving the afternoons for executive sessions with camera-shy witnesses, but the coverage was soon extended to the full day. Leery about the legal status of forced testimony on television, Chairman Wood ordered the cameras turned away whenever a witness balked. Dubbed the "little Kefauver" hearings and telecast on five of the seven Los Angeles stations, the investigation "scored heavily with audiences" throughout the metropolitan area.

Though far less star-studded, the September 1951 hearings in Los Angeles provided a replay of the October 1947 hearings in Washington, with cooperative witnesses reeling off dozens of names, unfriendlies baiting the committee and pleading the Fifth (no longer the First) Amendment, and the gallery applauding, hissing, and laughing on cue. Minor studio functionaries vied with the occasional better-known name, such as actor Jeff Corey, writer-producer Sidney Buchman, and screenwriter Carl Foreman. For both sides, the hearings proved mainly a mime show of thrusts and parries, but a few piercing exchanges drew real blood. However, being unpreserved on

---

2. During his testimony, Hayden called his brief membership in the Communist Party in 1946 "the stupidest, most ignorant thing I have ever done in my life." A fully cooperative witness, he also named names.

kinescope, or telecast nationally, the vignettes from the hearings have faded from popular memory.

Trying to goad assistant story editor Robert Gordon out of his Fifth Amendment drone, Rep. Donald L. Jackson (R-Calif.) asked whether Gordon had ever belonged to the Ku Klux Klan. Gordon allowed that he could respond with an "emphatic no."

"Do you belong to the Communist Party?" Jackson followed up.

"I decline to answer on the grounds of the Fifth Amendment," Gordon replied.

The gallery chortled.

The screenwriter and prodigal politico George Beck reluctantly coughed up twenty-five names already known to the committee, but feigned amnesia thereafter. "If they occur to me next week," he facetiously promised committee counsel Frank S. Tavenner, "I'll write you a letter." Beck offered laconic commentary on his reasons for joining the Communist Party in the 1930s ("Hitler and Chamberlain were playing footsie and I got a little angry"), the financial pinch of party dues ("I gave voluntarily—but with reluctance"), and the difficulty of following the party line ("I'd find myself in the middle of a sentence when the line would change").

Not all witnesses in the hot seat were as coolly jocular or warmly received. Carl Foreman, the versatile author of the integrationist combat film *Home of the Brave* (1949), the costume drama *Cyrano de Bergerac* (1950), and an anti-HUAC allegory then in production, *High Noon* (1952), tried to avoid appearing stridently unfriendly as he rebuffed the committee's demands to confess his former membership in the Communist Party and to recite the names of his ex-comrades. Foreman reminded the committee that he had signed a voluntary loyalty oath while on the board of directors of the Screen Writers Guild. "If I knew now or ever had knowledge of anyone plotting grievous damage to my government and the Constitution, I would report it," he declared. "I have always tried to be a good American." A veteran himself and an alumni of Frank Capra's famed wartime motion picture unit, the 834th Photo Signal Detachment, Foreman proudly noted that he had been awarded honorary membership in the Paraplegic Veterans for his screenplay for *The Men* (1950), a moving depiction of the struggle of paralyzed war veterans.

"The paraplegics who so honored you are disappointed in your testimony here today," shot back Rep. Francis E. Walter (D-Pa.).

Unaware that the microphones were picking up his remark, Foreman turned to his lawyer and muttered, "They really barbecue you here!"

The climax of the hearings was to be the testimony of Sidney Buchman, a former president of the Screen Writers Guild who had written Frank Capra's unimpeachably patriotic *Mr. Smith Goes to Washington* (1939). Scheduled for the last day, Buchman was expected to name a sheaf of new names. Instead, when Tavenner asked not the $64 question but the far more costly one—with whom had Buchman associated during his seven years in the Communist Party?—the writer firmly replied, "Most respectfully, I must decline." More valiantly, and unlike many of his former comrades, Buchman declined to invoke his Fifth Amendment privilege. "It is repugnant to any American to inform," he explained simply. Not only did he refuse to name names, Buchman went out of his way to *unname* names, insisting that a couple named as Communist Party members by the no-longer-unfriendly director Edward Dmytryk had merely happened to drop by his house while a Communist Party meeting was in session.

Buchman's dramatic gesture should have elicited a contempt citation, but Representative Jackson had left the hearing room, so the committee no longer mustered the necessary quorum. Open microphones caught the remaining members confusedly asking where Jackson had disappeared to.

Jackson was at his Santa Monica home watching the hearings on television. He had assumed Buchman would be a friendly witness and left the hearing early to pack for his return trip to Washington. Now his absent chair was being telecast to his constituents over five local stations. Mortified, Jackson demanded that Buchman be subpoenaed to testify again before HUAC in Washington. Pressing his advantage, Buchman again outmaneuvered Jackson in the public relations game. "I went into this out of principle," Buchman responded. "I took this risk calculatingly—and waive the lack of a quorum."

In the press, as on television, the former communist screenwriter played better than the anticommunist congressman. *Variety* juxtaposed Buchman ("the man who stood quietly on conscience") against Jackson ("the congressman who stood up his committee"). Even W. R. Wilkerson, the fervently anticommunist columnist for the *Hollywood Reporter*, condemned the congressman who went missing in action. "It was the most disgraceful bit of maneuvering we've ever seen conducted by a government body," Wilkerson stormed. (Jackson, who had been contemplating a campaign for the U.S. Senate on the strength of his HUAC performances, quickly retaliated. Buchman was subpoenaed to testify before the committee on January 28, 1952, in Washington, D.C. Buchman refused and was held in contempt of Congress. In 1953, he was convicted and fined $150. His next official screenwriting credit was in 1961, for *The Mark*.)

Shortly thereafter, the Speaker of the House, Sam Rayburn (D-Tex.), pulled the plug on television coverage of committee hearings. In Speaker Rayburn, the ABA and the ACLU found an unlikely and powerful ally. With the exception of the Republican interregnum from January 1953 until January 1955, Rayburn presided over the House of Representatives with an iron hand throughout the 1950s. A pol of the old school, he harbored a luddite suspicion of mass communications. In February 1952, he banned television cameras—along with radio, newsreels, and audiotape recordings—from committee hearing rooms. "There is no rule of the House permitting televising of House proceedings," Rayburn decreed, laying down a rule of his own. Rayburn extended the prohibition nationwide so television-friendly committees that were "not allowed to be televised under the rules of the House in the Capitol or in the House Office Buildings" wouldn't be able "to move out of town and think they could escape the rule."[3] Speaker Rayburn's decree explains why the newsworthy House investigations of the 1950s—the recurrent rounds of HUAC hearings, the quiz show scandal investigations of 1959, and the hearings into radio payola the same year—are unrecorded on kinescope or videotape.

The transfer of power from congressional Democrats to congressional Republicans in the 1952 election augured for a change in television policy. Both the new Speaker, Joseph W. Martin (R-Mass.), and the new HUAC chairman, Harold H. Velde (R-Ill.), seemed more open to television than the crusty Sam Rayburn. Martin promised that individual committee chairmen would have autonomy on the issue and Velde pledged that television coverage of HUAC would be permitted. Nonetheless, under Republican leadership too, television cameras seldom violated the House chambers in Washington. However, when HUAC went on the road, the new chairman opened the doors—a crack—to television.

In March 23–28, 1953, HUAC returned to Hollywood to conduct six days of televised hearings in the Federal Building in Los Angeles. ABC affiliate KECA-TV and KTTV pooled facilities to telecast the show and *Los Angeles Herald and Express* correspondents Tom Caton and Ed Prendergast provided on-air commentary. The staunchly anticommunist Hearst newspaper promised "startling revelations" during the questioning of nearly one hundred witnesses accused of or knowledgeable about communist activities in Hollywood. "Under the pitiless spotlight of the telecast, the souls of men are bared, falsehoods are exposed, and the deep, dangerous menace of Communism is being revealed," proclaimed an editorial.

Heeding legal precedent, the Velde committee turned off the cameras when unfriendly witnesses objected to what subpoenaed screenwriter Edward Huebsch denounced as "pillory by television." Charging that the televised hearings under Velde violated the previous rules under Democrats, and noting that the D.C. district court had upheld the right of witnesses to decline testimony on

---

3. Speaker Rayburn's decision to ban television was prompted by HUAC chairman Wood's announcement that upcoming hearings in Detroit would be televised locally. Among the members of the Wood committee was Charles Potter (R-Mich.), a candidate for the Senate that fall. Democrat Rayburn sought to deny Republican Potter the free television exposure that might bolster his campaign.

HUAC-TV: Chairman Harold H. Velde (R-Ill.) (*arrow*) opens hearings of the House Committee on Un-American Activities, held in Los Angeles and telecast locally by KECA-TV (March 23–26, 1953). (Courtesy Herald Examiner Collection/Los Angeles Public Library)

television, Huebsch and the dancer Libby Burke demanded that their subpoenas be quashed. The committee huddled to confer and told Huebsch (who had walked into the hearing room wearing a "Fire Velde" button) to return the next day, when television and radio coverage would be barred.

After Huebsch's confrontation with Velde, screen animator Philip Eastman also objected to the television coverage, so KECA-TV's cameras roamed the room avoiding his image. Though viewers flooded the stations with calls demanding that the faces of communist agents be exposed, Velde complied with the request of any witness who objected to testifying on camera.

The next week HUAC met in executive sessions, closed to the press, to interrogate the witnesses who exhibited what Representative Jackson, now conscientiously in attendance, called "a passion for anonymity." Thus, a witness subpoenaed by HUAC might choose between being pilloried on television or being pilloried for not appearing on television.

The same tangle between witnesses and investigators, television programming and constitutional prerogatives, occurred during the next session of televisable HUAC inquiries. On May 4–7, 1953, HUAC held four days of contentious hearings in the federal courthouse at Foley Square in New York City, Senator Kefauver's old soundstage. On May 6, the actor Lionel Stander forced a temporary adjournment, denouncing the hearings as an "inquisition" and objecting to the glare of the camera lights. If HUAC's courtroom drama were of the kind he had once starred in on television, said Stander, he would have no objection. "To come before the camera as a professional entertainer is one thing, but I'm not here as an entertainer," he explained. As in Los Angeles, Velde ordered the cameras to stop filming.

Whereupon, for the next eighty minutes, the raspy-voiced actor taunted and lectured the committee. "I may be here as a witness, but I am not charged with anything," snarled Stander. "I am not here as a dupe, a dope, a mope, or a schmoe." Velde threatened to have the actor removed from the hearing room unless he ceased his "insulting remarks." When Stander left the stand, the gallery applauded boisterously, forcing Velde to pound his gavel for quiet. Once outside the committee room, Stander promptly answered HUAC's $64 question. "I have never been a member of the communist party. I would not swear to this before the committee because the perjured testimony of stool pigeons and psychopathic quacks might carry more weight in a courtroom than my word. I might be convicted of perjury."

Following Stander in tactics and temperament, the songwriter Jay Gorney, composer of the Great Depression standard "Brother Can You Spare a Dime?," also defied the committee on constitutional grounds. He attempted to sing a tune he composed in honor of the First Amendment, but was ordered to desist. When Gorney protested ("Since you have allowed other singers before this committee, trained pigeons I call them ... "), Velde silenced him mid-sentence.

The Stander and Gorney appearances would have made for electrifying television, but though newsreel cameras filmed some of the testimony, television passed up the show. The Republican-controlled HUAC had granted permission to telecast the hearings, but no station exploited the opportunity.

In the end, the boisterous, raucous atmosphere of the Hollywood Ten hearings—recorded on 35mm newsreel film and ever since the archival shorthand for HUAC—has supplanted the (relatively) more placid hearings under Wood and Velde.[4] Ironically, in denying coverage to the newsreel and television cameras, the image of HUAC imprinted in memory is a melee of minor scuffling

---

4. In 1956, Francis Walter, who chaired HUAC from 1955 to 1963, staged a self-reflexive hearing into "so-called blacklisting," but, compared to previous committee chairmen, he tended to avoid the issue of communist infiltration in the popular media and subpoenaed relatively few television and motion picture performers during his tenure.

and major shouting, with a sputtering J. Parnell Thomas pounding his gavel and the cynical Hollywood Ten playing the all-American innocents before the bar of congressional injustice.

Wringing the Neck of Reed Harris: The McCarthy Committee's Voice of America Hearings (1953)

Unlike the House of Representatives, the U.S. Senate was receptive to, even so-licitous of, television coverage. In the 1950s, individual senators possessed greater autonomy and enjoyed more prerogatives than congressmen, who could be forced into line by an imperious Speaker. When the fillable air was plentiful and the novelty of congressional television was fresh, a goodly num-ber of senatorial hearings were telecast live, especially on local stations in New York and Washington. However, few were transmitted over a network hookup to a national audience, and fewer still were recorded and preserved on kinescope.

Issues of national security and law enforcement aside, perhaps the best-remembered televised hearings were conducted by the Senate Judiciary Sub-committee on Juvenile Delinquency in New York in 1954, where the menace being investigated was neither crime nor communism but comic books. "This is not a committee of blue-nosed censors," Sen. Robert C. Hendrickson (R-N.J.) solemnly assured viewers. "We want to find out what harm, if any, is being done our children." Dr. Fredric Wertham, the renowned author of the alarmist *Seduction of the Innocent* (1954) and the reigning expert on cartoon-inspired deviance, testified that "as long as these [comic] books exist, there are no safe homes. Every type of crime and delinquency is described in detail. The whole point is that evil triumphs and you can commit a perfect crime."

William Gaines, creator of *Mad* magazine and the unrepentant publisher of EC Comics, the worst offender, wasn't persuaded. "I don't think it does any harm," he testified. Gaines was then shown the cover of an EC comic book de-picting a grinning murderer standing over the torso of a woman, a bloody ax in one hand, her severed head held aloft in the other hand. Gaines responded that he considered the illustration in good taste. What, then, asked the in-credulous senators, would he consider in bad taste? Gaines pondered the ques-tion for a moment. "It would be in bad taste if the head were held a little high-er with the blood dripping out."

Of course, the ax-wielding caricature linked most vividly to the televised Sen-ate hearing is Joseph R. McCarthy. In action as a rude inquisitor, browbeating witnesses and snapping at colleagues, his brow sweaty and his tones surly, Mc-Carthy the Senatorial Scourge is a more familiar moving image than McCarthy the Master of Direct Address or McCarthy the Star of the Forum Shows. However, not until the Army-McCarthy hearings of 1954 was McCarthy's purely congressional conduct imprinted on the public mind via television.

McCarthy's debut in a televised senatorial hearing was inauspicious: as a supporting player, without a single line of dialogue, on the receiving end of a day-long denunciation by an unbowed opponent. On April 6, 1950, an investigatory subcommittee of the Foreign Relations Committee, chaired by Millard E. Tydings (D-Md.), convened to investigate McCarthy's charges that Professor Owen Lattimore, a former State Department official and Far East expert, was not only a communist but "the top Soviet agent" in the United States and the "architect" of the foreign policy that had lost China. Touted as the most widely anticipated Senate hearing in years, the appearance of Lattimore before the Tydings committee was telecast by NBC and CBS over a modest hookup limited to the eastern seaboard.

But while McCarthy's accusation had instigated the extraordinary session, the Democrats were not about to allow him to take over the show. Refused permission to cross-examine Lattimore, McCarthy was forced to sit silently as the professor lashed out at him. In a lengthy, hard-hitting opening statement, Lattimore denounced McCarthy to his face. "It is only from a diversity of views freely expressed and strongly advocated that sound policy is distilled," Lattimore lectured. "He who contributes to the destruction of this process is either a fool or an enemy of his country." Lattimore paused, raised his voice for emphasis, and, looking straight at his accuser, declared: "Let Senator McCarthy take note of that."

At that, applause rippled through the hearing room. Impressed by Lattimore's fortitude, Chairman Tydings vouched for his loyalty. McCarthy, noted an observer, "looked pale under the television lights." He did not return for the afternoon session. In *Ordeal by Slander*, a memoir of his dust-up with protean McCarthyism published in 1950, Lattimore lamented his tawdry persecution, but on television it was McCarthy who endured the ordeal.

As long as the Democrats controlled the Senate, McCarthy might command headlines and press conferences, but not subpoena power and full-scale hearings. Only after the Republican landslide in the 1952 elections did he acquire the position to stage the proceedings and star in the action. Beginning in February 1953, having ascended to the chairmanship of the Senate Permanent Subcommittee on Investigations, McCarthy launched a series of television-friendly investigations into the Voice of America, into the U.S. Army, and ultimately into his own committee. Usually in Washington or New York, occasionally further afield in locations like Albany and Boston, McCarthy chaired myriad hearings—closed hearings, open hearings, executive sessions, one-man hearings, and full committee hearings. The closed hearings and the executive sessions were conducted out of camera range, but even the open hearings were covered only intermittently by the medium they were designed to attract. Nonetheless, the first McCarthy sessions left a profound televisual as well as historical impact.

On February 16, 1953, what was now known as the McCarthy committee launched a series of headline-grabbing hearings into the Voice of America, the branch of the United States Information Service responsible for broadcasting pro-American news and information behind the Iron Curtain. A prematurely postmodern media event, the hearings showcased a politician using television to propagandize against the propaganda arm of the government for insufficient zeal in propagandizing the government.

The Voice of America hearings were not covered gavel to gavel, but WNBW, NBC's Washington, D.C., affiliate, and WMAL, the local ABC affiliate, provided intermittent coverage during a fallow period of network programming from 10:30 A.M. to noon. Some days, the committee met in executive session, closed to the cameras, and some days the committee did not meet. But over several weeks in February-March 1953, dedicated viewers might see a preview of a senatorial performance that would galvanize a broader demographic the next year.

On February 18, the first day of televised hearings, the witness was Howard Fast, a communist novelist, whose writings had somehow infiltrated the shelves of American libraries overseas. Fast invoked the Fifth Amendment when questioned about his Communist Party past and angrily affirmed his loyalty. When Fast refused to respond with yes-or-no answers and tried to explain his position, McCarthy said he would not permit the forum "to become a transmission belt for the communist party." As Senator Wiley had feared, television coverage of investigations into communism inevitably allowed the communist witness an opening to telecast a communist message.

On February 28, the McCarthy committee headed north for a session at the Foley Square Courthouse in New York that would focus on the attempted abolition of the Hebrew desk of the Voice of America. The subject and the site were calculated to appeal to New York Jews and to facilitate television coverage. NBC obliged by telecasting two hours of the hearings on a national hookup.

Back in Washington, on March 3–6, McCarthy spent four days probing the record of Reed Harris, deputy administrator for the State Department's Internal Information Administration and acting administrator of the Voice of America. In a meandering, hit-or-miss cross-examination, McCarthy excoriated Harris less for his alleged malfeasance at the VOA than for the opinions he voiced in a book he authored in 1932 entitled *King Football*. Harris tried to disassociate himself from his youthful radicalism, avowing that today he believed the American Communist Party was merely "a plainclothes auxiliary of the Soviet Red Army," but McCarthy refused to credit his political maturation. On March 3, the besieged and frustrated Harris angrily retorted that he resented "the tone of this inquiry very much, Mr. Chairman," because "it is my neck, my public neck, that you are, I think, very skillfully trying to wring."

Both NBC and ABC telecast the tense exchange between Harris and McCarthy, but, of more long-term significance, as it turned out, a CBS cameraman from Edward R. Murrow's *See It Now* was also filming Harris's wring-my-neck complaint. Reed's evocative phrase crystallized criticism of the McCarthy committee hearings as injustice summarily rendered in the public eye.[5] Highlighted in newspaper headlines and replayed on newscasts, the line and the man who uttered it would stick in the public mind.

Two days later another face-off between McCarthy and Harris exemplified the scattershot injustice of the video courtroom. The hearing opened at 10:30 and was scheduled to conclude, by prior agreement between ABC and McCarthy, at 12:30, at which time ABC affiliates were to resume local programming. Having complained of unfair treatment during his previous televised testimony, Harris was promised an opportunity to read a written statement on air. However, he was not called to testify until late in the morning and did not begin reading his statement until 12:23. At 12:30, ABC cut the feed to permit local affiliates to return to regularly scheduled programming, thus interrupting Harris mid-exculpation. (Only Washington affiliate WMAL-TV stayed with the Harris statement.)

The decision by ABC to cut off Harris's testimony incited a mini-"equal time" imbroglio. Suspecting bias, viewers demanded that Harris be given airtime to respond to McCarthy. "The episode showed more clearly than anything else how both Senator McCarthy and television are putting show business considerations above the minimum canons of fair play and responsible journalism," protested Jack Gould.

More than the Kefauver hearings, more than the HUAC investigations, the McCarthy VOA hearings raised the hue and cry of "pillory by television"— partly because well-spoken State Department officials were more sympathetic than furrow-browed gangsters or mealy-mouthed communists taking the Fifth Amendment, partly because McCarthy was more abrasive and abusive than Kefauver, Wood, or Velde. "It is indecent enough to expose the convicted before the public eye," lectured Marya Mannes during the Voice of America telecasts.

---

5. Interestingly, decades later, a similar turn of phrase would galvanize sentiment for another witness before senatorial inquisitors. In October 1991, Judge Clarence Thomas turned the tide in his favor by referring to the televised hearings of the Senate Judiciary Committee as a "high-tech lynching."

"My public neck": Voice of America official Reed Harris testifies before the McCarthy committee (March 3, 1953). (Courtesy Time-Life)

"It is even more indecent that millions, simply by turning a switch, can see these unconvicted in all of their nakedness." The *New York Times* decried "the television carnival produced, staged, and directed by Senator McCarthy," and the *Washington Post* bemoaned the plight of "the hapless witness summoned to judgment before television cameras." Wising up to the nature of television, the *New York Post* dissented. "We caught another hour of Joe McCarthy's television act yesterday and it is our considered opinion that a Voice of America official named Reed Harris stole the show," the paper editorialized, praising the beleaguered bureaucrat's "dignified and valorous performance."

Surprisingly, television itself also editorialized against the hearings—albeit allegorically. The already standard metaphor for congressional investigations into domestic subversion was the Salem Witch Trials, a trope famously deployed in Arthur Miller's connect-the-dots play *The Crucible*. Opening on January 22, 1953, at the Martin Beck Theater in New York, the attack on witch hunting was hailed as compelling drama and timely political critique. "Neither Mr. Miller nor his audiences are unaware of certain similarities between the perversions of justice then and today," noted theater critic Brooks Atkinson. At the premiere, in a gesture not purely theatrical, a wildly enthusiastic crowd called the cast back for nineteen curtain calls.

Thus inspired, CBS's popular history-driven program *You Are There* (1953–1957) reworked Salem for a veiled commentary on the ongoing courtroom spectacle. The docu-dramatic series featured real CBS reporters who covered epochal events from the past as if they were unfolding in the television present. The show was hosted—or anchored—by Walter Cronkite, who introduced mock field reports and interviews with historical figures by his CBS colleagues. The actor-journalists brought the same level of earnest professionalism to their pretend tasks as to their real assignments, categories that television was busy collapsing anyway. Not incidentally, behind the scenes of *You Are There*, writing under assumed names and dredging the historical record for germane precedent, were the blacklisted screenwriters Abraham Polansky and Walter Bernstein.

On March 29, 1953, the assignment for the *You Are There* news team was the First Salem Witch Trials on June 2, 1692. "The Massachusetts colony is in a turmoil of anger, strain, and fierce debate," reported Cronkite. As in Miller's play, the decorous rules of Anglo-Saxon jurisprudence only feed the keening hysteria of the possessed girls. Speaking directly into the camera, Cotton Mather ruminates on the "spectral evidence" of demonic subversion in the Puritan colony and accedes to the ever-widening circle of private accusations and state-sanctioned terror. "The Salem hysteria spread," reports Cronkite. "No one was safe."

In a closing commentary, Cronkite summed up the Salem precedent. "But as the madness took hold, so did a deep shame and an angry resistance in all the people high and low, forcing the authorities to order a halt and to free those remaining accused. But the wounds were deep and the tragic lessons learned were not easily forgotten." Cronkite's signature sign-off fit a dateline beyond 1692. "What sort of a day was it? A day like all days, filled with those events which alter and illuminate our times—and you were there."[6]

----

6. In 1957, *You Are There* returned to the Salem Witch Trials for a second dramatization, this time on film. When the off-camera reporter probes too deeply with his skeptical questions, the girls' eyes grow wide and suspicious. They glower into the camera, as if about to point the finger of accusation at the reporter—and the television viewer.

Despite the history lessons, Washington, Hollywood, and New York seemed condemned to repeat the past. Held virtually back-to-back, McCarthy's hearings into the Voice of America and HUAC's hearings into the entertainment industry seemed part of a coordinated bicameral assault on freedom of expression in film and broadcasting. In March 1953 television viewers in Los Angeles could watch the McCarthy hearings open the month and the HUAC hearings conclude it. "The activities of Sen. Joseph McCarthy in relation to his investigation of the Voice of America have left their imprint on Hollywood as well as other media of communication," *Variety* noted ominously. The tandem hearings sent out a single message to the motion picture and television industries: the politicians were watching.

In turn, McCarthy timed his hearings to ensure that he was the politician being watched. Usually, he scheduled the hearings for maximum television exposure between 10:30 A.M. and 12:30 P.M., taking advantage of a window when networks had no regularly scheduled programs.

Even so, ready access to the McCarthy hearings varied from market to market. Clair Worth, assistant director of news, special events, and sports at ABC, admitted that "not too many stations carry hearings, preferring to stay with locally sponsored programs." Anticipating the special interest of the entertainment industry, Los Angeles affiliate KNBH took the NBC feed for live coverage from 7:30 to 9:00 A.M., but many NBC affiliates passed up the McCarthy VOA hearings either because they couldn't clear the time or because they didn't think congressional investigations made for a "good show." Moreover, two days of the VOA hearings into the Harris case (March 4 and March 6) were not televised.

Thus, though McCarthy timed his hearings for television and rushed before the cameras to report on his hearings televised or not, the investigations were more print than television events. Tallying up the running time of congressional telecasts in the first half of 1953, *Television Age* estimated that the networks carried only about twenty-five hours of live coverage. Although McCarthy's VOA hearings attracted the most publicity, the entries included more mundane government business such as Bernard Baruch testifying before the Senate Banking Committee or the Joint Chiefs of Staff being introduced to the Senate Armed Services Committee. NBC telecast four times as much coverage as the runner-up, ABC. CBS didn't bother to enter the field.

The best evidence that McCarthy was not widely beheld on television live and unedited during 1953 is that so many viewers looked upon his demeanor and conduct as a revelation during Murrow's *See It Now* shows and the Army-McCarthy hearings in 1954—though his act had been playing for well over a year. When syndicated columnist George Sokolsky tried to tune in to McCarthy's VOA hearings, he discovered his New York affiliate was showing an old movie, thus depriving "the city with the largest Jewish population in the world" of information about the VOA's Hebrew Desk. "When will television grow up?" he wailed.

Actually, television was growing up—and away—from public service broadcasting. Once daytime entertainment programs became a profit center for the networks, the chances of unsponsored congressional hearings preempting game shows and soap operas diminished in direct proportion to the growth of advertising revenues. In July 1953 the new priorities forced the cancellation of NBC's unsponsored *Ask Washington*, a news forum show that sometimes featured congressional hearings, to make room for the sponsored series *Hawkins Falls* and *Glamour Girl*. "Full scale day-and-night television coverage of Congressional hearings such as the famous Kefauver crime probe two years ago . . . is a thing of the past and now belongs to television history," *Variety* reported after the networks chose not to telecast the 1953 HUAC hearings in New York. "TV has passed the economic point of no return. It is now basically an entertainment business . . . with its economics so geared as to make almost impossible sustaining a public service coverage on a wide scale. It would take a hot event of top importance to have the nets cancel their commercial schedules." A year later, McCarthy would instigate just such an event, a senatorial show too hot even for the profit-minded medium to cold-shoulder.

SEVEN

COUNTRY AND GOD

During the deepest chill of the Cold War, J. Edgar Hoover, director of the Federal Bureau of Investigation, reigned at the zenith of his power. Imperious, ascetic, ruthless in all things concerning the metastasizing reach of his beloved bureaucracy, he had long since federalized the face of law enforcement, reshaping the image of police authority from the town marshal to the G-man, the friendly cop on the beat to the aloof expert from Washington, D.C. Unaccountable and unassailable, Hoover occupied a unique status in the annals of unelected government officials: he towered above the law he enforced.

The FBI was born as a minor federal police agency in the Department of Justice in 1908, but it was in the leadership vacuum of the Great Depression that Hoover shaped it into a three-letter acronym for the long arm of the law. For Hoover, the 1930s began as the worst and ended as the best of times, the decade that saw him consolidate bureaucratic hegemony and secure personal prestige. Just as FDR siphoned power from state governments into the alphabet agencies of the New Deal, the canopy of Hoover's FBI spread over the outposts of small-town sheriffs and the precincts of city detectives.

But before savoring victory, Hoover endured ridicule as a bungling desk jockey presiding over Keystone Kops. While arrogant gangsters prospered during Prohibition and bold desperadoes made forced withdrawals from the banks that remained solvent during the Great Depression, the FBI flailed about hapless and ineffectual. In 1931, Hoover seethed in frustration as his fiefdom played understudy to the Treasury Department, whose agents had taken a famous scalp with the conviction for income tax evasion of Al Capone, the Chicago crime lord who eluded bootlegging and murder charges but not IRS accountants. Hoover determined never again to be upstaged as a crime fighter, a tactic that demanded he neuter the most notorious menaces to public order on his watch.

Capone's departure for the federal penitentiary caused only a momentary pause in the crime-struck headlines splashing across the tabloids of the early

1930s. A new breed of criminal—colorful, mobile, and trigger-happy—embodied an insurrectionist impulse more threatening to official authority than bootleg booze and speakeasies. With monikers like Baby Face Nelson, Pretty Boy Floyd, and Machine Gun Kelly, they outsmarted and outgunned local lawmen, leaving deputies in the dust as they sped across state lines and hid out in obscure backwaters.

To take command from the yokels, FBI agents swept into the breach—with disastrous results. On June 17, 1933, in a debacle dubbed the Kansas City Massacre, four lawmen, including one FBI agent, were killed by gangsters during a botched rescue attempt. In the long run, however, the murders had a salutary effect on FBI morale. Lobbied by Hoover and an outraged nation, the New Deal Congress passed a series of sweeping new crime bills that, for the first time in American history, gave federal police forces a uniform criminal code and greatly expanded their jurisdiction. For the first time, too, special agents of the FBI were granted the right to carry firearms.

The FBI was not long in using them. On July 22, 1934, the sidewalk execution of John Dillinger signaled a shift in the fortunes of Hoover and his agency. The most charismatic gangster of the 1930s, Dillinger had dodged the FBI's manhunt for over a year, an interval that found more Americans rooting for the larcenous fox than the baying hounds. Finally, in a made-for-Hollywood tableau on a sweltering summer night outside Chicago's Biograph Theater, Dillinger was shot dead by FBI agent Melvin Pervis.

In imprisoning Capone and killing Dillinger, federal law enforcement had neutralized the two most notorious criminals of the 1920s and 1930s. The one-two punch of bureaucratic dexterity and brute force, a potent admixture of arcane legal maneuvers and, when necessary, lethal firepower, would be the twin beams sustaining the FBI fortress. By 1935 Hoover had attained the lordly status he held until his death in 1972, even as another organization, free of FBI interference, also went national and prospered, namely the Mafia.

Before turning on him—posthumously—American popular culture adored J. Edgar Hoover and doted on the law enforcement agency built in his image. In the timely Warner Bros. crime drama G-Men (1935), the actor James Cagney, heretofore a trademark public enemy, switched allegiances and joined the feds. By the end of the 1930s, a steady stream of newsreels, radio shows, and motion pictures all served as a semiofficial publicity arm and recruitment poster for the FBI. Under constant monitoring by the FBI's Bureau of Public Affairs, the FBI-themed shows stressed the methodical procedures and calm omniscience of the agency, not screeching car chases and sizzling gunplay. Feeding ready-made scenarios ("based on actual case files!") to Hollywood studios and the radio networks, FBI bureaucrats worked as uncredited script doctors for a subgenre of police procedurals. The motion pictures and radio series flashed their subservience as a badge of honor, boasting in the credits that the narratives had been vetted by the FBI and produced with the technical advice of former agents.

With the onset of World War II, the FBI shifted its high-profile jurisdiction from crime sprees to Nazi spies. Increasingly, the bureau positioned itself not on the front lines against a criminal threat but behind the lines in a domestic war against subversion and sabotage. The tradecraft of the modern police force was surveillance, research, and infiltration. The legendary files of the bureau—"Bufiles" in the jargon of the interoffice memos—almost never recommend action; they exist for background only, to be logged, annotated, initialed, and reviewed. Committed patriots and fearless crime fighters though they were, FBI agents assumed the guise of detached professionals and collectors of data, restrained men who were clinical in their approach to criminal investigations and law enforcement. They watched, and waited, and weighed the options. When they decided to move in, the capture of the fugitive was a foregone conclusion and the culprit came along peacefully, resigned to his fate. "Don't shoot, G-men, don't shoot!" screamed a terrified Machine Gun Kelly in September 1933, abject in surrender as he christened the feds.

The Cold War against domestic subversion well suited the methodical manner and surveillance skills cultivated by the FBI: investigating a nonviolent, subterranean threat from secret cells by questioning ordinary Americans predisposed to be respectful to government officials who were businesslike and polite, not like the thuggish big-city coppers who broke down doors, threatened witnesses, and roughed up suspects. Such extralegal shenanigans as there were—wiretaps, break-ins, agents provocateurs—were hidden from public view, the bruises defacing the Constitution not the criminals.

Ever media-savvy, Hoover immediately recognized the power of television. In 1949, after ABC affiliate WMAL-TV in Washington, D.C., telecast mugshots from the FBI's Ten Most Wanted List, Hoover praised the small-screen posting. "The advent of television offers a new adjunct to law and order," he declared. "I see in this new medium an instrument of great aid and assistance in the future protection of society." In 1955, after the television-assisted capture of four criminals, Hoover issued a statement of appreciation. "The television industry has always been ready to help," he noted. "The four specific instances of arrest brought about by TV to date portend greater things to come in the alliance between the communications industry and law enforcement in coping with desperate fugitives. In addition to scheduled programming, the FBI is able to provide pictures, background, and descriptive data on wanted fugitives to every television station in the country."

Never comfortable with unscripted moments or uppity questions, Hoover characteristically avoided the risks attendant to the live forum shows: he did not meet the press, he did not face the nation. Yet he appeared regularly in the newsreels and on television news, testifying before congressional committees, speaking before civic groups, and attending public functions. Whether in documentary or fictional form, the television picture of Hoover and his FBI ranged from laudatory to worshipful. Typical was the "F.B.I." episode of CBS's popular documentary series *The Twentieth Century* (1957–1969), telecast on November 3, 1957. Based on journalist Don Whitehead's best-selling *The FBI Story*, the official history published in 1956, it chronicled the rise of the agency under the wise and courageous guidance of J. Edgar Hoover, scourge of "fascists, communists, and pseudo-liberals" alike.

At metropolitan police precincts, local cops groused about the undue prestige granted the publicity-hungry FBI ("Famous But Incompetent," snorted the men in blue), but the image of the FBI agent as the ranking warrior in the domestic fight against crime and communism remained carved in marble. "It may come as a surprise to most viewers tuning in to *Treasury Men in Action* to learn that Treasury Department agents are concerned with more than counterfeiters and other criminals violating the nation's monetary laws," *TV Guide* explained about a rival claimant to public attention. "The program, for example, has dealt with bank robbers, bootleggers, and those often believed to be FBI targets." Over the radio airwaves, on screens large and small, no threat to American culture in the 1950s—juvenile delinquency, union corruption, communist infiltration, or even straightforward crime—escaped the dragnet of federal law enforcement.

The extreme exemplar of the FBI's managed self-aggrandizement is *The FBI Story* (1959), a lavish Warner Bros. production based on the Whitehead book and directed by Mervyn LeRoy. A biopic of the bureaucracy, the film is filtered through the flashbacks of FBI everyman Chip Hardesty (Jimmy Stewart), whose career arc traces the ascent of the agency. During the Great Depression, Warner Bros. and director LeRoy had angered the FBI with the gritty gangster film *Little Caesar* (1930). In Cold War America, they now rendered tribute to the big caesar of law enforcement with a fawning institutional hagiography.

The story is not of a man but the organization, with the protagonist content to be a cog in the precision machineworks of Hoover-style law enforcement. In a brief prologue, the cameras photograph the real J. Edgar Hoover behind his desk, a crisp executive at the office, an alert sentinel always on the watch. When the narrative proper unfolds, however, his presence can only be hinted at: a shadow arresting a convict, a voice on the other end of the phone, or the back of a figure at a lectern. Like God at Paramount or FDR at Warner Bros., J. Edgar Hoover is granted a celestial status so august that the man can only be alluded to, not impersonated by a mortal actor.

Through thirty-five years of American history, the FBI rises right along with the crime rate, adapting to the shifts in social deviance, hot on the trail of the domestic terror of the moment. *The FBI Story* opens in media res with Jimmy Stewart's folksy drawl narrating a recent case history. A solicitous son buys an insurance policy for his dear mother and watches her board an airplane. In yet another Cold War vision of a blast from nowhere wiping out innocent American civilians, the plane explodes midair. The debris no sooner falls to earth than the FBI springs into action with hundreds of man hours of labor-intensive investigation: painstaking research, forensic examinations, interviews, scientific analysis, and pathology reports. Only a mammoth federal bureaucracy with an archipelago of field offices stretched coast-to-coast can solve such technologically proficient crimes.

Throughout *The FBI Story*, whether the threat to American security is from the Ku Klux Klan, John Dillinger, the Nazi Bund, or the Communist Party, the emphasis is on procedure, data, and analysis. "We don't insinuate," an agent lectures a suspect. "We collect evidence." Long shots lovingly scan the acres of bustling floor space at FBI headquarters, packed with agents, researchers, and secretaries, walking to and fro in earnest haste, pouring over papers at row upon row of file cabinets. No culprit can hope to elude the "broad research powers of the FBI—its high-speed communications, its endless flow of vital correspondence, a laboratory equipped to analyze all documents, a serology section geared to break down every known blood sample, a firearms section containing two thousand weapons—rifles, shotguns, pistols, revolvers, and machine guns—most of them collected from its clientele."

The controlling intelligence, the auteur of *The FBI Story*, is not director Mervyn LeRoy or author Don Whitehead but J. Edgar Hoover himself. The FBI's seal of approval—literally, the FBI seal—serves as a logo at the front and back of the film. Before the curtain comes down, a final genuflection to the institution and the man unscrolls on the screen:

> Our sincere thanks to the FBI and J. Edgar Hoover not only for their guidance and active participation in the making of this motion picture but also for making this world of ours a better place in which to live . . .

In *The FBI Story* and in other FBI-inspired stories told across the media, the FBI agent is an adjunct appendage of the body of the director. Unlike agent Chip Hardesty, Hoover is married only to the bureau, but his children are legion: every FBI agent is sprung from his head and cast in his mold, chips off the old block.

Father and sons alike, FBI agents personified a figure that cut across the precincts of American culture in the 1950s: the expert. Whether the task was

Uncredited auteur: FBI Director J. Edgar Hoover in his
Cold War prime.

selling detergent to housewives or diagnosing the neuroses of modern life, a
wise man in a white lab coat needed to be consulted. No longer was law enforcement a job for amateurs, the cowboy whose natural skill with a six-gun
earned him a tin star from the town fathers. Amateurs need not apply or muscle in on the territory of the experts, else they muck things up—or maybe
prove that the expert was not so infallible after all.

   Like fighting crime, deterring communism required the sober talents and
selfless dedication of the expert. In the anticommunist theater of war, however, the rankest of amateurs—ad-libbing his lines, crashing into the scenery—
was hogging the stage.

   J. Edgar Hoover eyed Joseph R. McCarthy with the wary look of a bulldog
sniffing a mongrel intruding into his turf. McCarthy was everything Hoover

was not: reckless where Hoover was deliberate, epicurean where Hoover was ascetic, gregarious where Hoover was misanthropic, cynical where Hoover was earnest. Next to the shoot-from-the-hip McCarthy, the close-to-the-vest Hoover could sound downright progressive. "In World War I, I saw abuses from well-meaning people and the development of a vigilante attitude," he declared in 1954. "In recent years I've noted a tendency toward loose name calling in matters which should be left to the hands of the FBI to prove or disprove. And this takes in the Ku Klux Klan, revolutionary movements, and fascism, as well as communism. Investigating subversives is a highly professional job. The FBI is the agency to which people who have any information should turn." So deep was Hoover's antipathy for McCarthy that he spoke out against McCarthyism.

By 1954 Hoover had held office for three decades and, like the pope, the celibate bachelor seemed assured of a lifetime tenure. No public figure—not former President Truman, not the hero of war and peace Gen. George C. Marshall, not President Dwight D. Eisenhower—was so invested with a cloak of immunity from criticism. As Hoover celebrated his thirtieth year as the FBI head, tributes poured in from editorialists and politicians pledging fealty to a man none dared cross. "Happy AnnHOOVERsary!" crowed Walter Winchell.

I Led 3 Lives: "Watch Yourself, Philbrick!"

Of all the Cold War motion pictures and television shows based on the files, real and alleged, of the FBI, none is more implicated in the crusade against communist subversion than *I Led 3 Lives* (1953–1956), the "true to life story of a patriotic young American who led three lives in the service of our country: 1. Citizen! 2. 'Communist'! 3. Counterspy for the FBI!" Shot on film and syndicated by the upstart independent production company Ziv TV Programs Inc., *I Led 3 Lives* was an instant hit, telecast in 137 cities and ranking at or near the top in ratings for most of its three-year run. "Never before has such a dramatic document appeared on TV!" shouted the ads. "Tense because it's factual! Gripping because it's real! Frightening because it's true!"

The series was based on the popular memoir *I Led 3 Lives* by Herbert A. Philbrick, published in 1952. For nine years, from 1940 to 1949, Philbrick had operated as an FBI informant in a succession of communist cells and front groups. Juggling his day job as an advertising agent for the M&P Theater Company of Boston with the duties of a loyal party hack, Philbrick did the revolutionary grunt work of distributing leaflets, soliciting funds, organizing petition drives, and attending a numbing curriculum of classes in Marxist-Leninist doctrine. His memoir chronicles the internecine struggles and ideological somersaults of the Communist Party during the Hitler-Stalin pact interregnum of 1939–1941, the U.S.-Soviet alliance during the Second World War, and the postwar purging of party members afflicted with "incurable Browderism," the tactical accommodation with bourgeois capitalism rendered obsolete after the defeat of Nazi Germany. In 1948, toward the end of Philbrick's communist career, he participated as a foot soldier in the presidential campaign of Progressive Party candidate Henry Wallace, who personified the communist notion of a useful idiot.

Appreciably less action-packed than its active-tense title implies, *I Led 3 Lives*, the book, is surprisingly moderate and level-headed. "Mr. Philbrick is no fanatic," insisted Erwin D. Canham, editor of the *Christian Science Monitor*. "There is an air of profound sanity throughout this book. There are no polemics, no lurid passages, no denunciations." Though an off-the-cuff counterspy himself, Philbrick cautions others to leave the complicated work of counterinsurgency to the experts. "Amateur Red hunters, ambitious politicians, demagogues, and rabble rousers are no match for [the dedicated Communist]," asserts Philbrick, echoing the official FBI line. "The fight against the professional Communist leader will not be won by flag waving or name calling. Patriots or would be patriots who go in for bombast and two-fisted punching find that their smashing blows against Communists too often sail through a mist of angry controversy without landing on a solid object." In another swipe at wildcat McCarthyites, Philbrick declares, "If the inexperienced Red hunter cannot distinguish between a Communist and an innocent liberal, then he is also unable to distinguish a bona-fide Communist from a government counterspy." After all, "it takes experts to fight experts. . . . No one knows that better than the FBI."

To instruct the aspiring anticommunist in the calibrations of left-wing politics, *I Led 3 Lives* includes an appendix enumerating sixteen ways to distinguish a communist from a liberal. Among the guidelines, clue #7 offers a good rule of thumb: "A Communist uses the arts—literature, painting, music—in a strictly functional sense, to further the aims of world communism." By contrast, "a liberal appreciates the arts for their own sake."

Throughout his nine-year journey through the cellular structure of American communism, Philbrick maintains a restrained tone and shows little ideological fervor. He strives to create suspense ("the sweat beaded my forehead and trickled down my back") but there is little physical danger and absolutely no violence in his tale. The threat, as Philbrick knows, is all psychological: that he will be caught in the web he has entered, that he will become the man he pretends to be.

"Wouldn't it be a fine thing," Philbrick muses, "if the evil I was trying to fight consumed me instead?" All the more danger because the effective counterspy cannot just pretend to be a communist, he must become one. Not unlike the Method acting practiced by the Group Theater in the 1930s and then-fashionable with the Actors Studio in New York, Philbrick must apply Stanislavsky to fight Stalin. "I was sinking so deep that it was no longer possible for me to 'play' the role of a spy. I could no longer simply make believe that I was a Marxist. Like an experienced actor, who must sublimate himself to his part and immerse himself in the playwright's creation, whenever I walked into the stage setting of a cell meeting, I had to *be* a young Communist. The costume alone was not enough. No disguise would have been adequate." More than a feverish template of Cold War anticommunism, *I Led 3 Lives*, book and telefilm alike, expresses the psychic turmoil of the multitasking 1950s male.

In 1953, Ziv negotiated a deal with Philbrick for the television rights to *I Led 3 Lives*. Having produced the radio series *I Was a Communist for the FBI* in 1951, based on yet another triple-threat counterspy, former FBI agent Matt Cvetic, the company had accrued experience with role-switching anticommunist serial narratives. Ziv specialized in a "beltline program operation" based on quick turnaround and no-frills production. Even by the standards of early television, however, the breakneck pace of *I Led 3 Lives* was fast and furious, sometimes shooting five episodes in ten days. "They can grind 'em out quicker and faster than anybody in the business—and sell them twice as fast and on twice as many stations," *Variety* marveled. "And if there's any doubt, take a gander at those $25,000,000 radio-TV billings." To underline its public service to public order, Ziv donated copies of the series to the armed forces "for indoctrination and enlistment purposes."

The actor tapped for the role of Philbrick was Richard Carlson, soon to become an icon of another resonant Cold War genre, the science fiction film, in *It Came from Outer Space* (1953) and *The Creature from the Black Lagoon* (1954). No anticommunist altruist, Carlson adhered to frankly capitalist motives. "It was a good financial deal. I stand to make more for this than I could ever make in pictures," he admitted. "Further still, it's paid over a period of time, which takes some of the sting out of the tax bite." Carlson expressed but one ideological qualm. "The only reaction I was afraid of," he confided in 1953, "was that we would be accused of red-baiting, the temper of the times being what it is."

Told in the clipped tones of the interior monologues of a B-caliber film noir, *I Led 3 Lives* was narrated each week by its identity-challenged protagonist, a tortured soul who juggled his citizen/"communist"/counterspy identities for the Cold War crusade. As played by Carlson, Philbrick is a classic noir antihero: hunted, wracked by guilt, involved in something unseemly, paranoid for good reason. Yet in dress and manner, Carlson-Philbrick embodies the starched uptightness of the 1950s male, who even when golfing, bowling, or tossing horseshoes wears a white shirt and tie. To really loosen up, he rolls up his shirtsleeves and unbuttons his collar.

Lacking a studio or even network-sized budget, *I Led 3 Lives* favors a minimalist visual style. Philbrick's office is housed in an ominous building that recalls the set design of the dystopic *Metropolis* (1926) more than the prosperous *The Man in the Gray Flannel Suit* (1956). "The future belongs to those who prepare for it," reads a hectoring sign in the lobby. The cheap sets, makeshift location work, and available lighting leave little room for the lush atmospherics of moody big-screen film noir: no low-key chiaroscuro or cantered camera angles enliven the telefilmic grammar. During exterior location work, sidewalk bystanders can sometimes be glimpsed gawking at the actors.

Yet as in bare-bones noirs like *Detour* (1945) and *Gun Crazy* (1949), the very sparseness of the production values enhances the truncated options and empty fatalism of the milieu. Likewise, the remedial camerawork expresses the moral gulf between the superpowers. Cozy two-shots that frame Philbrick together with his FBI handler give way to isolating shot/reverse shots when he meets with the communists: video space shields the viewer from intimate contact with the source of infection. Tight close-ups on Philbrick, beads of sweat glistening on his furrowed brow, eyes darting furtively, seem to trap him in the box of the television set and the psychic cell of his private hell. To avoid perverse identification with the villains, no recurring communist characters appear as regular players from week to week. In each episode, Philbrick encounters new cell members, new infiltrators, new American institutions under assault, an ever-expanding social canvas that makes communism seem all the more pervasive and insidious.

If the swathe of communist bad guys confirmed the worst fears about Soviet penetration, the plotlines stretched the bounds of credulity. Already, the show was "beginning to show signs of wear," opined *TV Guide* midway into the first season. "While there are many industries in this country in which Communists can infiltrate, *I Led 3 Lives* ran through the list and then bogged down into a cops-and-robbers series." Dissenting, *Variety* believed that the show "held the public interest for over two years" not simply because "the subject [of anticommunism] is popular" but because of its "tight and tingling [and] highly dramatic treatment." From a radically different quarter came a predictable reaction. "The networks have not yet offered their facilities to the Communist Party to reply to the fraud called *I Led 3 Lives*," fulminated Hollywood Ten alumnus Ring Lardner Jr., in the communist monthly *Masses and Mainstream*. "Theoretically, the Communist Party of Massachusetts could sue for gross libel, but it would have to find a court dedicated to the rare principle of equal justice for all."

Seldom, however, did the telefilmic Philbrick let loose with a hot-blooded screed against communism. Not unlike the propaganda films of World War II,

I Led 3 Lives knows that good Americans have already internalized the message. When Philbrick and his wife Eva pause to ponder the appeal of the communist ideology, they can only shrug, mystified:

> *Philbrick:* Nice boy. Clean cut. Last person on earth you'd suspect of being a communist.
> *Eva:* Why? Why do they do it?
> *Philbrick:* Why does a boy like [him] become a communist?
> *Eva:* Yes—it's so obviously a dead end.
> *Philbrick:* I think it's an illness, Eva, a mental illness.

To exploit the print-based veracity of the series, the signature montage introducing each episode telescopes in on the jacket of Philbrick's best-selling book. The subtitle red-flags the danger sign by inserting scare quotes around the trigger word ("communist"), as if, even in pretense, the label had to be kept at arm's length. Bookending each episode, the literary conceit also closes the show. Philbrick sits at a desk before his Remington typewriter, seemingly just having written a memo to the FBI describing the events just telecast. He seems a dispassionate observer, almost a journalist, perhaps even on a par with Edward R. Murrow. "Not just a script writer's fantasy—but the authentic story of the Commies' attempt to overthrow our government!" insisted advertising taglines. "You'll thrill to the actual on-the-scene photography, the factual from-the-records dialogue!"

Taglines notwithstanding, the most coveted imprimatur of authenticity— the FBI seal of approval—eluded *I Led 3 Lives.* Encouraged by a rare book-jacket blurb from J. Edgar Hoover ("Herbert A. Philbrick has performed an outstanding patriotic duty in his fearless presentation of facts in his book *I Led 3 Lives*"), Philbrick had sought the formal endorsement of the FBI for the television show. However, ever jealous of his name brand, Hoover took pains to disassociate himself and the agency, at least officially, from the series, emphasizing that Philbrick had never been a true FBI agent but only a civilian informant. "It is recommended that we tell Philbrick frankly that the Bureau has no interest at all in seeing any of the devices or investigation techniques used by the Bureau publicized on TV and that no assistance in this regard can be given," an internal memo recommended to Clyde Tolson, Hoover's aide-de-camp. Despite repeated overtures by Philbrick, Hoover denied his official blessing to the show and tersely informed all correspondents that "the FBI has no connection with the television production entitled *I Led 3 Lives*."

The show's self-presentation muted such distinctions, and viewers might have been forgiven for taking *I Led 3 Lives* as an official production of the FBI not Ziv. "This is the story—the fantastically true story—of Herbert A.

Philbrick, who for nine frightening years did lead three lives—average citizen, high-level member of the Communist Party, and counterspy for the Federal Bureau of Investigation," announced the voice-over at the top of each show. "For obvious reasons, the names, dates, and places have been changed, but the story is based on fact."

After the *Dragnet*-like synopsis, an expository teaser set up each episode. A not untypical foray into the communist netherworld, telecast in 1953, begins: "There's got to be an important reason why the communists would work for the election to Congress of a man who's rabidly *anti*communist. This week's story concerns the reasons behind the communist plan to elect this candidate." Then, an overhead shot of a bustling American city inspires an oddly pensive meditation:

> Funny thing about big cities. Most complain they're *too* big—that you can lose your identity in them. It doesn't always work that way. Sometimes you can hide your identity for a while but then sooner or later the big city closes in on you.

Closing in on Philbrick is an old friend from his precounterspy existence, who visits his advertising office to recruit him to work for an anticommunist candidate for Congress. Biting his lip, Philbrick refuses. The perplexed friend asks, "Have your political ideas changed that much?" In former days, Philbrick would have jumped at the chance to join the fight against communism.

Surveillance being the shared recreation of all sides in *I Led 3 Lives*, the ever-vigilant communists already know about the visit. As Philbrick watches himself, the communists watch Philbrick, and the FBI watches the communists watching Philbrick. Constantly under dual surveillance, Philbrick is followed by two sets of eyes: the malevolent gaze of the CPUSA and the custodial oversight of the FBI. Again and again, in episode after episode, Philbrick's clairvoyant FBI handlers materialize to rescue him from a tight fix, divining his predicament and arranging a timely extraction. No wonder his anxious voice-over is less an interior monologue than a silent prayer to an omniscient federal deity. "The FBI will know what to do!" he says more than once when at a crossroads. His faith is unbounded—and rewarded. FBI ex machina, the agents swoop in, to the rescue, guardian angels in dark suits.

Alerted to the meeting between Philbrick and his old friend, the communists summon him to an emergency meeting. Whenever called suddenly to a communist confab, Philbrick nearly comes unglued, fearful that his cover has been blown. "What have you done?" he asks himself, always in the second person, even in his own mind a creature of the imagination. "Or, more important—what do they *think* you've done?" Despite his anxiety attack, Philbrick knows "a good party member doesn't question the authority of his cell leader." He accedes to party discipline and strolls into Mrs. Dayton's Tropical Fish Store, an apt front for subsurface agitation.

Wise to the ways of counterintelligence, the communists want Philbrick to sabotage the anticommunist congressional campaign from the inside. In fact, suspicious that Philbrick missed the subversive possibilities in so tempting an offer, they quiz him about his pre-"communist" anticommunist past. What about the anticommunist rallies he attended? The anticommunist petitions he signed?

Forced to defend his communist credentials, Philbrick passionately affirms his party-line patriotism. "We *all* committed sins against the masses before we were members of the Communist Party! Every one of us!" he shouts. "We were all fools until the party became our teacher, our guide, our life!" Really getting into character, he winds up, "I refuse—I absolutely refuse—to be persecuted for sins that I committed before I became a communist!" His Stanislavsky has served him well.

Almost every episode of *I Led 3 Lives* contained a similar outburst of mock zealotry, a declaration of party-line doctrine that exploited the unholy thrill of hearing ripe communist rhetoric spouted on television, sentiments inoculated from harm because of the patriotic duty to feign treason to deceive the real communists. "I was under the toughest orders a guy could get!" boasted Matt Cvetic, the antecedent of *I Was a Communist for the FBI* (1951). "I started a riot that ran red with terror. . . . I learned every dirty rule in the their book—and had to use them—because I was a communist—*but* I was a communist for the FBI!"

To an eye trained to detect subversive implications, Philbrick's command performance mirrors exactly the plight of the blacklisted entertainer called on the carpet and forced to defend a heretical past. Like the witnesses testifying before the House Committee on Un-American Activities, Philbrick is tarnished by transgressions that predate the present. Unlike so many accused by HUAC, however, Philbrick defiantly points out the obvious ex post facto fallacy to his inquisitors and refuses to be held accountable for deeds done before he saw the Leninist light. But where the close-minded congressmen remained impervious, the open-minded communists see the logic in the argument and accept Philbrick's pledge of self-transformation.

I Led 3 Lives speaks to the blacklist with suspicious frequency: to the moral dilemma of the informer, to the problems of the prodigal politico, and to the plight of the duped liberal smeared by his past associations. As Philbrick's party comrades might put it, this is no accident. According to producer Frederick Ziv, blacklisted screenwriters wrote for the show under assumed names. Like moles burrowing from within, they commented on their own dilemma, doubtless savoring the irony of using the premiere anticommunist series on television to critique anticommunist paranoia. In another episode, when Philbrick is assigned responsibility for party security, his lesbian-coded cell leader, Comrade Jenny, orders him to hunt for subversive elements. "I needn't remind you that one of the greatest threats to communism is internal—from within the party itself. Diversionists, traitors, opportunists, social patriots, reformers—you'll make every effort to discover these enemies and report them to me." The camera holds tight on her severe face as she tells him to name names: "And should you fail to report them—I'll be forced to conclude that you are one of them yourself!"

The extension of the criss-crossing double-agentry of *I Led 3 Lives* to the writing staff may seem too symbolically perfect, but the first-person title always hinted at a double bind. If behind the mask of communist subversion lurked a patriotic American, the reverse might also hold true. "Where Communism is concerned, there is no one who can be trusted. Anyone can be a Communist. Anyone can suddenly appear in a meeting as a Communist Party member—close friend, brother, employee or even employer, leading citizen, trusted public servant," warns Philbrick in his memoir. "There is no way to distinguish a Communist from a non-Communist" (235). For the narrator, immersed in a three-way identity crisis, the stakes are higher than that: sometimes, he can barely distinguish his communist self from his noncommunist self.

This being the 1950s, the Freudian triad for the topology of the mind—superego, ego, and id—offers a convenient index to the three lives of Herbert A. Philbrick. If Philbrick's identity as all-American advertising executive is the obvious candidate for the secure, rational ego, then the locations of the superego conscience and the unbridled id fall into orthodox alignment. The voice of the FBI murmurs in Philbrick's head as the monitor of official morality, while the siren call of the CPUSA is the unspeakable desire of the subversive subconscious.

No wonder it is as his communist self that Philbrick truly comes alive—vital, alert, excited, a heroic warrior locked in a long twilight struggle with cosmic significance. Glimpsed at home, with a model 1950s housewife, Philbrick resides in another cell, and even from this domestic refuge (in both book and telefilm) he seeks private space in a secret garret to compose his FBI memoranda. Unlike the book, whose back-jacket photo shows Philbrick in a cozy family portrait, a lone male trapped among smiling wife and five blonde daughters, the telefilm gives Philbrick little discernible home life—as if to add "husband" and "father" to the identity mix would overload the already fragile circuits of his psychic equilibrium. At the beginning of one episode, he finds a note from his wife inviting him to join the kids and her at a neighborhood barbecue. "You wish you could join them, don't you, Philbrick?" he says, not quite convincingly. "You don't have much time for Eva and the children—not since you volunteered to act as an undercover agent for the FBI. Well, it's partly for them you're doing it—someday they'll understand that." Relieved, he bolts for his party meeting.

To prevent a mental breakdown, Philbrick deploys the same kind of self-willed, psychic "compartmentalization" practiced by the atomic spy Klaus Fuchs, whose sensational 1950 trial for treason laid bare the mind and motives of the communist agent. In a famous session of self-psychoanalysis explicated by the journalist Rebecca West, Fuchs described the mental gymnastics he practiced to function as an effective spy. According to Fuchs, he refined the ability to live (in his case) two separate lives, by keeping one side of his self under constant surveillance by the other side. "I could be free and happy with other people without fear of disclosing myself because I knew that the other compartment would step in if I approached the danger point. I could forget the other compartment and still rely on it," Fuchs recalled. "Looking back at it now, the best way to express it seems to be to call it a controlled schizophrenia."

For the postwar American male, controlled schizophrenia was not a mental state reserved for spies and double agents. Husband, father, student, veteran, worker, citizen: the multiplicity of roles played at the same time by the same man had never been so numerous and varied. Philbrick's plight bespeaks an entire generation juggling shifting identities and mercurial relationships, sorting through a more malleable sense of self—or selves.

"Life was becoming enormously complex for me," Philbrick writes in his memoir. "On one page I was the conservative businessman, suburban churchgoer, liberal Republican, civic enterpriser. On the next I was a deep-dyed member of the Communist Party of New England, sitting in on its multifarious conspiracy. Between the lines, I was a Federal Bureau of Investigation confidential agent, striving to perform a service." If the compartments in his head collapse or converge, he will be buried in the psychic residue. "Within these categories, there were already more subdivisions than I could keep track of," he frets. "I was burrowing so deep that I feared I might yet be trapped in the catacombs."

The queasy dislocation surfaces in the constant browbeating Philbrick aims at himself in voice-over, a litany of synaptic red alerts. "Don't push your luck, Philbrick!" he warns, or—his incessant reminder for self-surveillance— "Watch yourself, Philbrick!" In watching Philbrick watch himself, perhaps Americans identified less with his political agenda than his psychic agility, his skill in controlling the schizophrenia at a time when so many were leading three lives or more.

Controlled schizophrenia: Richard Carlson (*right*) strikes a worried pose as triple-agent Herbert A. Philbrick in Ziv's syndicated series *I Led 3 Lives* (1953–1956). (Courtesy Photofest)

Religious Broadcasting

In 1953, President Eisenhower advised Americans to turn to religion, pretty much the way they rooted for a hometown baseball team or mowed the lawn, as a useful habit to harden the glue of civic comity. "Whatever our individual church, whatever our personal creed, our common faith in God is a common bond among us," proclaimed Ike. "In our fundamental faith we are all one." Throughout the popular culture and political rhetoric of Cold War America, religion stood as a sturdy pillar in the anticommunist fortress sustaining one nation, "under God," a phrase added to the Pledge of Allegiance in 1954. Communism was godless, America was godly.

Rather than sparking a revival of born-again piety, however, the God-mongering made America less not more religious. For all the professions of faith, the faith itself was hazy and lackadaisical, undemanding and undistinguished, leavening out the devotional demands of different dogmas and creeds. Extremism in denunciation of communism may not have been a vice, but in matters of religion an undue insistence on the inerrantism of a particular doctrine was considered bad form. Increasingly, politicians referred to America not as a Christian nation but as a Judeo-Christian nation: a modifier that once meant eternal damnation now became a required prefix. Little wonder that to nonbelievers the sectarian divides in American Protestantism and Judaism came to seem more a matter of social class and housing patterns than doctrinal differences. In television's *I Led 3 Lives*, when a lifelong member of the Communist Party makes a deathbed conversion, he advises double agent Herbert A. Philbrick to turn away from communism and toward religion. "The denomination doesn't matter," he mutters, taking the Eisenhower line on theology.

Predictably, the consensus medium of television professed a consensus view of religion. Though the flood of programming tied to Christmas and Easter assumed a normative Christianity in the Nielsen congregation, the pageants were never very precise in theology or ceremony. The Jewish comedian on *The George Burns and Gracie Allen Show* and the Polish Catholic on *The Liberace Show* celebrated the holiday with the same fervent devotion to decorating the tree and gifting the kids.

Of course, for a more committed priesthood, the missionary work facilitated by broadcasting was a match made in heaven. From the earliest days of commercial radio in the 1920s, when Aimee Semple McPherson and Billy Sunday spewed fire and brimstone from the airwaves and spurred a great awakening in collection-plate profits, enterprising preachers had exploited the means of mass communications to further the work of God or, more often, man. But where radio had been a pulpit, an extension of preaching and proselytizing, television would be an altar, a site for low-definition ritual devotion.

The aura of television itself seemed to invite meditations on the mystical union of broadcasting and divinity. Invested with more celestial majesty than the typeset words of the commonplace Bible, the transmission of messages through the heavens, via the unseen waves of the electromagnetic spectrum, ranked uncomfortably near to God in source and scope. Yoking that old-time religion to an ultramodern technology, an ethereal mix of theology and broadcasting animates two of the weirdest Hollywood films of the Cold War, *The Next Voice You Hear* (1950) and *Red Planet Mars* (1952).

Produced by Dore Schary and directed by William Wellman, *The Next Voice You Hear* murmurs a liturgy of pervasive radio-borne dread. Act one finds Joe Smith (James Whitmore), Mrs. Joe Smith (Nancy Davis), and son Johnny (Gary Gray) enjoying the fruits of postwar prosperity in a pleasant, palm-lined neighborhood in Los Angeles. Joe works as a mechanic at an aircraft plant, Mrs. Smith is pregnant, and budding entrepreneur Johnny runs his own paper route.

One night, at 8:30 P.M. PST, Joe sits down to listen to the radio and regular programming is interrupted by—the voice of God. "Does He sound like Lionel Barrymore?" asks Mrs. Smith, not unreasonably. "Are the Russians behind this?" wonders Johnny, the wary Cold War baby. God's voice is never heard on-screen, nor can it be recorded on audiotape, but listeners around the world hear Him in their native tongue. Asked for an explanation, the FCC commissioner frankly admits that he is flummoxed by God's flaunting of federal regulatory oversight. For the next six nights running, at 8:30 P.M., on every network, in every nation, God speaks over the air.

The cultural historical resonance of the religious rapture is transparent enough. The apocalypse, once God's prerogative, has been usurped by man. Huddled by the radio, Mr. and Mrs. Smith long for the comfort of divine as opposed to scientific wrath. God Himself evokes His preatomic monopoly over global destruction when He reminds listeners of the forty days and forty nights of rain in the Old Testament. Only Noah's ark, an ancient bomb shelter, floated above the waves and survived the storm. *The Next Voice You Hear* transmits the jitters of a generation forever jumpy at the sound of a news bulletin, the bolt from afar that will rattle the life of the listener—not another Pearl Harbor, but nuclear attack, the worst kind of thunder from the clouds.

Typically, *The Next Voice You Hear* neglects the existence of a celestial force that Hollywood truly trembled before: television. In 1950, in Los Angeles, television penetration was not deep enough to compete with radio as the best means of mass communication, but God declines to simulcast His message. Not unlike His appearance to Moses in a burning bush, He may be heard but not seen and His face may not be transmitted even as an off-screen apparition. Still, the Smiths and God already seem out of date in their radio-centricity.

In a genre that thrived on wacko scenarios, *Red Planet Mars* may be the zaniest collage of Cold War tropes in all of Hollywood cinema: alien visitation, Nazi scientists, Soviet subversion, millennial Christianity, nuclear conflagration, and radio and television broadcasting. When a husband and wife team of scientists (Peter Graves, Andrea King) achieves radio contact with Mars, the great leap forward in mass communications wreaks economic havoc on earth. News of the 300-year lifespan of the Martians destroys the pension system; the prospect of cosmic energy ruins the oil, gas, and steel industries; and the resultant stock market crash incites a run on banks. A montage of newsreel footage from the Great Depression shows masses of men shuffling in bread lines and milling in the streets, the images of the frightful past replayed as a portent of the future.

And what hath man wrought for the future? Stricken with second thoughts about unfettered science, the wife voices the word that pervades her moment in time:

Fear—always, eating fear. The whole world's scared—why shouldn't I be? Every woman in the world—we all live in fear. It's become our natural state. Fear our sons will have to fight another war—or fear they'll face worse. We've lived on the edge of a volcano all our lives. One day it has to boil over.

As in *The Next Voice You Hear*, the news from Mars is harkened to on the older medium. Gathered around radios, Americans listen to NBC and CBS broadcasts while in the USSR Russian peasants secretly tune in to the Voice of America, still thriving despite the McCarthy committee. Television is acknowledged only when the devastated scientist, horrified at his handiwork, watches news of the economic meltdown on a futuristic flat-screen television. "Turn that blasted thing off!" he shouts. "Turn it off!"

But if the first reports from Mars sow panic among the multitudes, the messages that follow offer hope to all mankind. The Martian words are deeply spiritual, almost an echo from the Sermon on the Mount. "Is it possible that the Man of Nazarene and the man of Mars are the same?" asks the wife. It is: "God Speaks from Mars!" blare headlines.

The messages inspire a worldwide religious revival. Cathedrals overflow with worshipers and choirs sing hosannas. In the Soviet Union, Russian peasants dig up religious icons, hidden since the Bolshevik revolution. Brutal Soviet commissars cut down the devout with machine-gun fire, but the revival is unstoppable. In the first live telecast from Moscow, the newly installed leader of the former Soviet Union, the patriarch of the Russian Orthodox Church, addresses the West and proclaims the conversion of Russia.

In a devilish twist, however, the broadcasts from Mars are a cruel communist-inspired hoax. A former Nazi scientist recruited by the Soviets is beaming the messages off Mars from a transmission station located under the statue of Christ of the Andes. A nonpartisan nihilist, he seeks first to undermine world capitalism and then to destroy world communism. All of the radio messages, the economic and the biblical, are bogus, he gloats.

Ultimately, God takes matters into His own hands and begins transmitting authentic messages. Nonetheless, the scientific couple would rather perish than see the born-again faith of the earth shaken. They open a valve of hydrogen gas (it would be hydrogen), strike a match, and blow up the Nazi-Soviet scientist, the broadcasting transmitter, and themselves. The end credit reads: "The Beginning."

Released in May 1952 and set in the not-too-distant Cold War future, *Red Planet Mars* showed a certain gift for prophecy by predicting the election of Eisenhower in November 1952 and the death of Stalin in March 1953. The president is an Ike-like former army general who interprets the messages from Mars, for all their Christian cast, as a nondenominational injunction to religious faith. "All over the world, regardless of their religious beliefs, men have found a new faith . . . a faith that is universal in men of all faiths," he declares before a joint session of Congress. "For while to us the words from Mars seem the very essence of the Christian doctrine, let us not forget that they are also the essence of all other religions. Christian, Mohammadan, Jewish, Buddhist—all are heeding the call to prayer."

Like Hollywood, television meditated on destruction of biblical dimensions and the role of broadcasting in keeping the apocalypse at bay. Spooked by *See It Now*'s report on the detonation of the hydrogen bomb, a stricken Dan Jenkins ruminated that "television, whether it realizes it or not, can be an enormous influence" in helping the nation "get back to some religious base" and "think hard about our ultimate destination." Jenkins suggested that perhaps "a sobering thought could be put across by a Lucille Ball or a Sid Caesar or a Groucho Marx, either as a personal pitch or as an integrated sketch" for "the moral and spiritual well-being" of viewers. But it was not a comedian but a cleric who would preach the good word on television, and not just to a niche market of like-minded believers but to the tuned-in multitudes.

Life Is Worth Living: Starring Bishop Fulton J. Sheen

In color, His Excellency Bishop Fulton J. Sheen would have been spectacular. Bedecked in the full-dress finery of ecclesiastical formalwear—scarlet skullcap, gold crucifix, and a long, flowing red cape set off against a jet black cassock—he stood poised for action like a dashing Don Diego Zorro or a suave Count Dracula. Under a neat mane of silver fox hair, his chiseled visage beamed with warmth and vitality. The eyes could be harsh daggers piercing into the heart of a sinner or moist pools of understanding comforting the penitent. As he spun parables and waxed theological, blending gentle humor and impassioned invective, the trickle of an Irish brogue slipped into his cadences. Star of the highly rated *Life Is Worth Living* (1952–1957) and shepherd of a huge televisual flock, Bishop Sheen performed the duties of three serious vocations: cold warrior, defender of the faith, and master of the medium.

No less then Berle, Lucy, and Liberace, Bishop Sheen was a pure product of the material conditions of early television, a time when a singular face in close-up on the small screen could still lull viewers into a trance of attention. "The man has magic," gushed television critic Marya Mannes, not a woman given to swooning over just any pretty face. "He compels you to listen as if the next word were a revelation. Sometimes it is; sometimes it is simply music." Abandoning her crush on Edward R. Murrow, Mannes declared that "sometimes there is so much ease and eloquence that one wonders whether truth can be so luxuriously attired. But always there is the Bishop's face itself—a fusion of the spiritual, the intellectual, and the sensual with which few living men are endowed." Martin Stone, producer of *Author Meets the Critics*, admitted, "Bishop Sheen is the kind of television personality that fairly crosses the camera into the living room." Implying the cleric had missed his true calling, *Variety* also praised Sheen's sensual endowments: "he could probably qualify as a leading man at any studio so far as his countenance goes; he's got an almost magnetic look about him and he's possessed of a fine speaking voice."

Telecast live from the stage of DuMont's Adelphi Theater in New York, where a studio audience-*cum*-congregation laughed, applauded, and wept on cue, *Life Is Worth Living* was staged in a cozy simulation of the bishop's study. With the expensive leather chair, sturdy desk, and tasteful bookshelves stocked with real books, it might have been the prize corner office of an academically inclined corporate executive, save for the statue of the Blessed Virgin and Child positioned prominently backscreen.

Off to stage right was a blackboard on which Sheen underscored his main points, quickly scrawling at the top of each clean slate the initials "JMJ" ("Jesus, Mary, and Joseph," as parochial school kids, who wrote the same initials on each homework assignment, explained to public school pagans). When the blackboard filled with writing, Sheen moved stage left, the camera panning along with him, while an imagined off-screen "angel" he dubbed "Skippy"—presumably a trusted altar boy, actually a stagehand with a large sponge—erased the blackboard. References to the ectoplasmic Skippy were the bishop's favorite running gag. "There is as much curiosity over the Bishop's invisible helper as there is about Jimmy Durante's Mrs. Calabash," joked *TV Guide*, in an article that spilled the beans.

Besides the blackboard, Sheen's only visual aid was himself. It was all he needed. He was a commanding presence blessed not only with a priestly vocation but the theatrical instincts of a born ham. A catalogue of trademark gestures kept time with the tempo of his sermons. He waved his large hands and unclenched his elongated fingers with the grace of a prestidigitator. Outstretching his arms at his side in a gesture of supplication, he would bring them upward onto his chest, interlacing his hands onto his bosom, his fingers spread wide. To punctuate a point, he arched his index finger skyward, as if about to give a blessing. Holding the pose for a moment, he resembled a saint frozen in statuary.

Catholicism, anticommunism, and television: the multitalented Bishop Fulton J. Sheen preached to a nondenominational congregation on *Life Is Worth Living* (1952–1957).

Premiering on Tuesday nights at 8:00 P.M. on February 12, 1952, via a three-station hookup on the DuMont network, *Life Is Worth Living* was fruitful and multiplied. After a 26-week hiatus, the show returned on October 13, 1953, with a 121-station lineup. At the peak of its popularity, *Life Is Worth Living* was telecast by over 170 stations across the nation, "the largest network circuit in television history for a regularly scheduled program." The show penetrated some heretofore impregnable regions when Catholic nuns, whose convents prohibited television, were given special dispensation to watch Bishop Sheen. "Mother Superiors everywhere," he pleaded. "Please let your nuns see my program."

Beginning with the November 18, 1952, telecast, the appliance manufacturers at Admiral Corporation sponsored *Life Is Worth Living*, with the show contributing all profits to the Mission Humanity for International Charity or the

Society for the Propagation of the Faith. A few observers carped about the unholy alliance between television commerce and Catholic tenets, but the bishop shrugged off the complaints and plugged Admiral at every opportunity. Skippy the Angel had gone to sea during the hiatus and "is now bearing the great name of Admiral," he joshed. Or his angelic helper was so invisible "you can't even see him with an Admiral."

Stretching the demographic reach of his video congregation, the bishop embraced rival denominations in his prehomily warm-up, telling anecdotes about little Methodist boys, Jewish grandmothers, and Episcopalian ministers. Forty percent of his fan letters, Sheen was pleased to report, were written by non-Catholics. To American Jews, he was especially warm, referring to "those great commandments which were given to the Jews, and which have been the fabric of the world's civilization ever since." The ecumenical spirit extended to the network lineup. In 1954, when *Life Is Worth Living* went on summer hiatus, DuMont scheduled *The Goldbergs* in its 8:30 time slot. Upon Bishop Sheen's return, the Jewish family was bumped back to 8:00 P.M. to serve as his lead-in. Piggybacking on Bishop Sheen's success, the struggling ethnic sitcom was cleared for 160 of the 164 stations in his lineup, "a piece of information that could make appropriate fodder for such organizations as the National Conference of Christians and Jews," grinned *Variety*. To show her appreciation, Gertrude Berg planted a conspicuous product placement in Molly Goldberg's kitchen: an Admiral refrigerator. Whatever the tensions between Jews and Catholics in American neighborhoods, they coexisted shoulder-to-shoulder on the DuMont airwaves.

Another Judeo-Catholic televisual linkage was less congenial. In a primal experiment in counterprogramming, DuMont pitted its vigorous Catholic against NBC's vaudevillian Jew: Vatican splendor against Borscht Belt shtick, a vestment-clad bishop against a cross-dressing clown, Uncle Fultie versus Uncle Miltie. The ratings competition between Bishop Sheen and Milton Berle, whose *Texaco Star Theater* first showed signs of running out of gas when pitted against *Life Is Worth Living*, provided a deep well of religious humor. Berle cracked jokes ("We both work for the same boss—Sky Chief!"), but he steamed in private. Sheen responded with Christian charity. "I bear the deepest affection for Milton Berle, and I love his program intensely." After all, jibed the bishop gently, man is distinguished from beast by his power of laughter and, without laughter, "there could be no Milton Berle."

And no Bishop Sheen. Stylistically, Sheen claimed a closer kinship to his prime-time vaudeo rival than to his brother clerics proselytizing during the ratings wasteland of Sunday mornings. "Bishop Sheen does a great job," decreed no less an eminence than J. Edgar Hoover. "I listen to some of these hum-drum Sunday sermons on radio and television and they are enough to make children turn to another channel." With its own signature greeting ("Hello, friends"), closing benediction ("Bye now—and God love you"), and running gags, *Life Is Worth Living* followed a prime-time formula of liturgical rigidity.

A video ironist, Bishop Sheen broke the fourth wall of the small-screen frame with Brechtian verve. To keep him aware of the timing, pocket watches hung on the cameras around him. "All right, now," he would ask on air, "which watch am I to believe?"

He also possessed the knack of the quick ad-lib, a useful gift amid the glitches of live television. "My angel is getting rambunctious tonight," Sheen joked after a loud crash clattered from offscreen. Best of all, Sheen evinced a wry sense that, in the age of television, a man who is not on television is not alive, that he has no other existence save that which is telecast. "Television is purely incidental in my life," he insisted again and again, making him one of the few Americans for whom this was now true.

For the running time of each episode, Bishop Sheen spoke extemporaneously in one long take. Repudiating the earthly crutches of TelePrompTer or cue cards, he wrapped up each homily with precision timing, as if internally guided by the Holy Ghost. He quoted the parishioner who said of a preacher who read his sermons, "If he can't remember them, how can we?" Yet he never claimed that the sermons "were spoken without thought and meditation." Reaching back, characteristically, for a classical reference, Sheen confessed, "As Pytheas once said of an *ex tempore* speech of Demosthenes: 'His impromptus smell of the lamp.'"

Yet to hint at a spark of divine inspiration, Sheen made eye contact with the camera lens and preached that "the test of sincerity is somewhat lost if the speaker uses a TelePrompTer in which the message is unrolled before his eyes as he speaks." In a moment of self-reflexivity worthy of video auteur Ernie Kovacs, he confided that "one way the audience can tell whether a speaker is using a TelePrompTer is to watch his eyes." Challenging his own viewers to keep their eyes on him, Sheen mimics the video technique of lesser mortals. "[The eyes] will always move from left to right and left and back again, as if he were at a tennis match. When he reads from cards, then the eyes, instead of moving from left to right always move up and down." Sheen looks straight into the camera.

But if Sheen might josh about Skippy the Angel, Milton Berle, and TelePrompTers, he was dead serious about the rival god that was communism. Like a medieval monk battling a terrible heresy, he took to the task with Thomistic zeal, giving line-for-line refutations of the false prophets Marx and Lenin and their agent on earth, Joseph Stalin. In show after show, Sheen undertook a detailed, painstaking critique of communist ideology. He analyzed the spiritual source, or rather the spiritual vacuum, that nurtured communism in the lost soul, explained its appeal to the faithless, and depicted the superpower struggle as a cosmic drama with salvific significance.

Unlike the pessimistic wing of Cold War anticommunism, best exemplified by the manic-depressive conversion of Whittaker Chambers, who defected to the party of faith with a fatalistic suspicion that the communists were destined to win the long twilight struggle on earth, Bishop Sheen came forth as an authentic Christian optimist preaching a message of joyful deliverance. He represented a kind of normative anticommunism: not fanatical or excitable, but calm and confident. For him, the conversion of Russia was a distant but certain eschatological fact, a prerequisite to the Resurrection foretold by the revelations of the Blessed Mother at Fatima in 1917.

Sheen seldom quoted chapter and verse: he remolded the stories of the gospel to fit the times. For him, the biblical past was prologue to a crisis of faith in an economically prosperous but spiritually threatened time. It was a venerable American theme, harkening back to William Bradford's *Of Plymouth Plantation*, where the old Puritan governor ends his chronicle of the Pilgrim colony with a lament for his lost community of sanctified believers: material prosperity had spawned spiritual poverty, and the church "that had made many rich became herself poor." In the affluent 1950s, the very title of the show bespeaks an odd affirmation. "Life Is Worth Living," promised the listing in *TV Guide*, as if the opposite was being whispered, suspected. Sheen explained the title: "First, to appeal to many who are despairing because of their anxieties and frustrations, and second, to suggest the words of Our Lord: 'I have come that you may have life more abundantly.'" Anxiety amid abundance—not a bad description of Cold War America.

As if to persuade the doubting Thomases, the Bible and the headlines converged in a moment of near divine clairvoyance. On February 24, 1953, Sheen took poetic-political liberties with Shakespeare's *Julius Caesar* by rewriting Marc Antony's funeral oration to the crowd. Cheating a bit on the iambic pentameter, the bishop speculated on the death of Stalin and the struggle for supremacy among his troika of henchmen Beria, Vishinsky, and Malenkov, who were made to mouth the words of Cassias, Brutus, and Antony, respectively. "Friends, Soviets, countrymen, lend me your ears; I come to bury Stalin, not to praise him," Sheen declaimed. At the close of his extended conceit, he predicted that "the death of Stalin will also be the end of the troika or triumvirate." He concluded: "Even if this speech of Shakespeare, which we put into the mouth of Malenkov, should ever come true, it will not be the beginning of peace in the world. Stalin's evil spirit is ranging through the world crying 'Havoc' or revolution."

Nine days later Stalin died suddenly of a stroke. Chagrined, Berle later recalled, "One of my writers said, 'Why can't you do something like that?' A second writer replied, 'What for? They'll say Milton stole the bit.'"

Despite his seeming direct access to the ways of God, Sheen refused to lord his own faith over rival denominations. "The DuMont network has stressed that Bishop Sheen is not using the coaxial cable to gain converts," media critic Harriet Van Horne noted approvingly in 1952. "He never mentions the 'true Church,' nor does he refer to Catholic ritual, nor vaunt the superiority of his creed over other creeds." Nonetheless, no less than his vestments, Sheen's sermons were a uniquely Catholic expression of faith in a nation that had only lately welcomed Catholicism into the American mosaic. Less than seventy years before, the cartoonist Thomas Nast had caricatured the princes of the Roman Catholic Church as reptiles invading Anglo-Protestant America. In 1928, Al Smith, the Democratic candidate for president, was undone by anti-Catholic bigotry that cast him as a puppet of the Vatican. Now the staunchly anticommunist American Catholics were stalwart guardians of the realm, with Sheen the charismatic commander of a legion of Cold War crusaders. The two men he admired most were Abraham Lincoln and St. Thomas Aquinas. In these affinities, as in so many others, Catholicism had never been so powerfully tethered to Americanism.

Again, World War II is the deep background, the crucible that wrought the transformation of Catholics from papist invaders to all-American patriots. When the ranks of the arsenal of democracy swelled with battalions of Italian, Irish, and Polish-Catholic GIs, the tribalism that once isolated the Church of Rome from the American mainstream—the parochial schools, the Knights of Columbus, the Legion of Decency, the Lenten sacrifices, the meatless Fridays—receded with wartime mobilization and Office of War Information-mandated tolerance. Partaking as much as any group of the earthly rewards of postwar prosperity, American Catholic parishioners may have been the first of their faith to live in socioeconomic circumstances wherein the things of the world offered tangible competition to the things of heaven.

Sheen's significance as a consensus cleric comes into clearer focus when set against his obvious precursor. The last Catholic ecclesiastic to galvanize a national audience via a broadcasting medium was Father Charles A. Coughlin, the demagogic radio priest of the 1930s. Though Father Coughlin's isolationism and anti-Semitism soon alienated him from the main currents of American thought and ultimately the Church of Rome, his vituperative voice echoed as the style of Catholic broadcasting until Sheen's face appeared on the television screen. Coughlin was hot, angry, and divisive; Sheen was cool, serene, and conciliatory.

Besides, though evangelical fervor inspired his televisual missionary work, Bishop Sheen was too much the Catholic intellectual to flail around histrionically and spew hellfire like a videogenic Billy Sunday. The blackboard was a telling prop: he was as much educator as preacher, his lessons honed from hundreds of talks to wide-eyed parochial school students. Feeding off his faith, bathing in his light, the studio audience and the television viewer listened as if preparing for first communion ceremonies. Less raucous than any other public religious figure, or for that matter Uncle Miltie, Sheen was a reassuring personification of American Catholicism: the calm face of Catholic higher education in full command of the legacy of Judeo-Christian, Greco-Roman culture.

Sheen displayed a dazzling range of erudition, roaming "from Tacitus to the atomic bomb without visible signs of effect," as John Crosby marveled. Where else on prime-time television might viewers hear disquisitions on Franz Kakfa's *The Trial* and Dostoyevsky's *The Brothers Karamazov*, St. Augustine's *Confessions* and St. Thomas's *Summa Theologica*, Tennyson and Darwin, Freud and Jung, G. K. Chesterton and Dorothy Parker, and, to prove he wasn't too high-horse, an intertextual nod to Ralph Kramden on *The Honeymooners* ("One of these days, Alice—one of these days—powie!"). On the blackboard, he often broke down words into their Latin and Greek roots, tracing ideology in etymology. In 1953 the Vatican's official Latin expert returned the favor and added the word *televisio* to the third edition of the Church's dictionary, a word derived from "sight from afar."

In 1956, soon after *Life Is Worth Living* moved from the deceased DuMont network to ABC, Admiral Corporation ended its four-year sponsorship. ABC then made the mistake of programming Sheen against a Jewish comedian of cooler mien than Milton Berle. With low-key banter and Television Code–stretching wisecracks, Groucho Marx's game show *You Bet Your Life* clobbered *Life Is Worth Living* in the ratings. On Groucho's show, the only visitation from above, called down by a "secret word," was a duck.

Like the decline of Milton Berle and Gertrude Berg, whose Borscht Belt humor was deemed too Jewish for Christian America as television spread into the heartland, Sheen's fall from ratings grace was also tied to his performance style and religious affiliation. Telegenically, the appeal of a talking head in prime time shrunk as entertainment options around the dial grew more supple and seductive. Theologically, somber sermons on sacrifice and otherworldly salvation were heretical on a medium devoted to consumer indulgence and earthly pleasures.

In 1961, Bishop Sheen resumed his televisual ministry, soldiering on in color, in syndication, on videotape, until 1968. The old sermons needed little updating: as Berle joked, both he and Bishop Sheen always relied on old material. Yet *Life Is Worth Living* also transmitted a new vision of American Catholicism. Again and again, the homilies conflate Christ and country in a kind of transubstantiation of the body of the savior with the body politic. Both are incarnations of faith—one of the word of God the Father, the other the words of the Founding Fathers—and both come to bring hope to all mankind. According to the Cold War gospel preached by Bishop Sheen, the things rendered unto America and the things rendered unto God can be one and the same.

EIGHT

EDWARD R. MURROW SLAYS THE DRAGON
OF JOSEPH MCCARTHY

On Tuesday, March 9, 1954, at 10:30 P.M., CBS's *See It Now*, hosted by Edward R. Murrow, telecast "A Report on Senator Joseph R. McCarthy," a 30-minute inquiry into the methods and meaning of the man of the hour. It was network television's first unflinching assault on the senator: a video exposé that stripped McCarthy down to bare essentials, hanging him out to dry on his own words and demeanor as he browbeat witnesses, snorted snide asides, and smirked like a vulture. At the close of the show, Murrow looked into the camera and delivered the coup de grâce. "The actions of the junior senator from Wisconsin have caused alarm and dismay among our allies abroad and given considerable comfort to our enemies. And whose fault is that? Not really his. He didn't create this situation of fear; he merely manipulated it—and rather successfully."

By sign-off time at 11:00 P.M., Murrow was no longer just "the distinguished broadcaster and commentator" heralded at the top of the program. He had ascended into a pantheon of immortals as the patron saint of broadcast journalism. Celebrating the miracle of Murrow's anti-McCarthy *See It Now*, the trade press dubbed the date of telecast, without irony, "Good Tuesday."

In the years since, the epic joust between Edward R. Murrow and Joseph R. McCarthy has congealed into a kind of journalistic creation myth. Retold in awed tones, viewed through the filter of embroidered memories, the tale casts Murrow as a stalwart Lancelot going forth to rid the kingdom of a fire-breathing dragon. "One of those rare legendary figures who was as good as his myth," decreed the cultural historian David Halberstam in his otherwise irreverent history of CBS News. The illustrator Ben Shahn sketched a still-life version of the legend entitled "Edward R. Murrow slaying the dragon of Joseph McCarthy." It depicts the gallant broadcaster on a steed skewering the reptilian senator with a lance.

Since no hero escapes revisionism for long in American culture, a dissenting view of the Murrow-McCarthy duel sees Murrow's entry onto the field as a case of too little too late. Debunked and demeaned, he is recast as a glory hog who played it safe, more puffery than paladin, an elite opinion-maker smart enough to strike at the heart of a beast already hobbled by braver hearts. Once heretical, the opinion of television historian Steven Stark—that Murrow ranks "among television's most overrated" personalities—is today closer to the consensus than Halberstam's reverence. "While Murrow was a central character in several of television's defining moments, and has subsequently been canonized," argued Stark in his 1997 compendium *Glued to the Set: The 60 Television Shows and Events That Made Us Who We Are Today*, "he had a negligible impact on the overall course of the medium and its news coverage."

The gainsayers have a point. Murrow was neither the first nor did he risk the most in challenging McCarthyism. At the *Washington Post*, where McCarthy was hated on first sight, editorial cartoonist Herblock mercilessly caricatured the senator and Drew Pearson poured torrents of abuse on McCarthy in his nationally syndicated column. Elsewhere too a lengthy lineup of print journalists and radio commentators regularly ridiculed McCarthy and assailed his ism. Being hauled before the McCarthy committee only fortified the enmity of James Wechsler, editor of the *New York Post*. Both over the airwaves and in his 1954 book *But We Were Born Free*, radio broadcaster Elmer Davis decried the "climate of fear" fostered by McCarthy and HUAC. "Don't let them scare you," Davis counseled. "Now as at all times since the foundation of our government, our freedom and our safety depend on the courage of our citizens. This republic was not established by cowards nor will cowards preserve it." During the Good Tuesday broadcast itself, Murrow displayed a stack of newspapers from across the nation that had lambasted McCarthy.

But when television, the medium so leery of controversial personalities, so devoted to "100% acceptability," provided a forum for anti-McCarthyism, the gesture marked a seismic shift in the zeitgeist. Watching from the sidelines in late 1953, as the two contestants circled each other, and in early 1954, as the battle neared a climax and the champion moved in for the kill, the cheering from the crowd bespoke a pent-up enthusiasm spontaneously unleashed.

The battle between Murrow and McCarthy dramatized two central truths about American culture in the age of television, one about each corner of the ring. First, television gave reporters a rough parity with politicians. The deference that the press had once shown the people's representatives seemed suddenly akin to the custom of cringing before royalty. The two were now evenly matched—or the television journalist had a slight edge. Where the politician was elected at the ballot box in even-numbered years, the broadcaster was voted in each week by a broader American demographic, measured in Nielsen ratings.

Second, television depended upon the very freedoms of expression and access that McCarthyism sought to shut down. Ultimately, the insatiable demand for material—more thought, more talk, more tales, more personalities—would override the timidity of the medium in the presence of power. But, as legend has it, while network executives and producers still huddled in the trenches, out of sight, one brave heart rode ahead of the column to shed first blood.

TV's Number One Glamour Boy

In the postwar media matrix, Edward R. Murrow's stature was unique. As the radio broadcaster who during World War II had spoken the most vivid commentary to the most momentous story of the twentieth century, he had earned not just the trust but the affection of his listeners. Eyewitness to the Anschluss, the London blitz, the bombing raids over Germany, and, finally, at the ghastly denouement, the horrors of Buchenwald, he narrated the epic tale of the rise and fall of the Third Reich. His wartime radio backstory accrued for him a cultural capital that he spent carefully in the television era.

Murrow knew that in its own way radio was a picture medium: through sound and language, it put images in the heads of listeners. Never a detached observer, always intimately involved with the human side of the pageant before his eyes, he was a bard of the ether, a voice pitched perfectly between tenor and baritone, devoid of overt histrionics, modulating gently from rising inflections to paced sestinas. "This . . . is London," he intoned in his signature dateline from ground zero during the Battle of Britain. When he accompanied B-24 bombers on missions over Germany, he pulled crystalline metaphors out of the air as he gazed down at the firestorm below. "The small incendiaries were going down like a fistful of white rice thrown on a black piece of velvet," he reported. "They were beginning to merge and spread, just like butter does on a hot plate."

Murrow was there at the end, too, when he groped for words to conjure the sight, and smell, of the concentration camp at Buchenwald on April 15, 1945. "It will not be pleasant listening. If you are at lunch, or if you have no appetite to hear what Germans have done, now is a good time to switch off the radio," he warned Americans, who would soon see—in wirephotos, in the newsreels, in the pages of *Life* magazine—the pictures Murrow struggled to sketch in language. "If I have offended you with this rather mild account of Buchenwald," he said in closing, "I'm not in the least sorry."

Against that epochal background, the homefront story of postwar prosperity and suburban bliss made for a banal newsbeat. Prior to confronting the challenge of the new medium, Murrow seems to be spinning his wheels, looking backward not ahead. In 1948, he and his collaborator Fred W. Friendly produced the record album *I Can Hear It Now: 1933–1945*, a surprisingly popular compilation of memorable radio moments from the past. The sound bites selected—the engine roar from Lindbergh's *The Spirit of St. Louis*, the stirring tones of FDR's first inaugural address, the bulletin from Pearl Harbor, the hoofbeats and marchsteps from FDR's funeral procession—triggered powerful memories for the Great Depression/World War II radio generation. A pioneering archival achievement, *I Can Hear It Now* mined the emotional links between public history and private experience forged by the mass media. In retrospect, the record sounds like a valedictory tribute for a medium on the road to second-class status.

Unable to sidestep the next fork in the road, Murrow undertook the transition to television. As in the late 1920s, when silent screen actors struggled to adapt to sound cinema, the radio generation entered television with trepidation. Some, like Jack Benny, Bob Hope, and Arthur Godfrey, moved smoothly onto the small screen while others, entertainers and broadcast journalists alike, discovered they had faces only for radio. Instantly recognizable voices and personalities of high-voltage prestige—gossip columnist Walter Winchell, announcer Lowell Thomas, and humorist Fred Allen—were diminished or undone by television. The quality of being "telegenic" or "videogenic" (terms coined already by the late 1940s) made for prosperity or penury, a soaring career arc or a slow downward spiral. "Visually, Winchell looks like a cross between Jimmy Durante and Harry Truman," observed a cold-eyed Dan Jenkins when the famed and heretofore mighty radio reporter made the transition to television in 1952. "The familiar hat and pulled-down tie are a throwback to the old newspapering days and a far cry from the neat, personable men who make up the bulk of today's TV newscasters. The cameras keep him in constant close-up from left, right, and head-on, and he looks his years."

By contrast, Murrow and his "boys," the glittering crew of radio journalists he recruited for CBS News in the late 1930s, glided into television without missing a beat. No wonder: they were, almost to a man, singularly attractive swains—urbane, WASP, bred to a patrician coolness congenial to the medium. Whatever sixth sense allowed Murrow to pluck print journalists from behind typewriters and stand them up before microphones, his judgment was good enough not only for the rigors of radio at war but beyond. As septuagenarian éminences grises, Murrow's graying boys—Charles Collingwood, Howard K. Smith, and Eric Severeid—walked the halls of the network newsrooms for decades afterwards.[1]

---

1. As a byword for journalistic integrity, Murrow's name still remains the gold standard. In *The Insider* (1999), a behind-the-scenes look at CBS's *60 Minutes*, veteran reporter Mike Wallace (Christopher Plummer) regains his moral compass as a journalist after reading a critical editorial in the *New York Times*. "They're accusing us of betraying the legacy of Edward R. Murrow!" he gasps.

"A videogenic demeanor": Edward R. Murrow in a relaxed pose on the set of *Person to Person*. (Courtesy Washington State University Library)

On November 18, 1951, Sunday afternoon at 3:30 P.M., the most distinguished voice in radio put his face forward on *See It Now*, the linear descendent of Murrow and Friendly's *Hear It Now* radio program. A bit of video prestidigitation was arranged for the curtain opener, a tableau that has become an iconic clip from stone age television. Waving a cigarette from his left hand like a wand, Murrow instructed director Don Hewitt to call up the East and West Coasts on two different video monitors. First, a "direct pick-up" of the Golden Gate Bridge, Alcatraz, and the San Francisco skyline appeared on Monitor One, and next, views of the Brooklyn Bridge and the Manhattan skyline came into focus over Monitor Two: America from sea to shining sea seen for the first time over the monitor in the living room. Even so, the charisma of the journalist outshone the bicoastal vista. "It's a cinch that [Murrow's] the No. 1 candidate as TV's glamour boy in the realm of commentators-newscasters-analysts," enthused *Variety*. "Murrow brings to the TV cameras a sureness, naturalness, and deep understanding of what he's talking about, plus a videogenic demeanor that, in itself, gives the show a definite plus value."

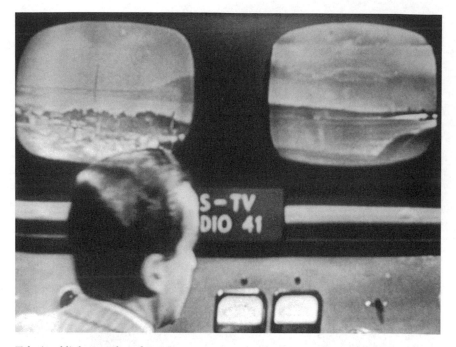

Televisual linkage: Edward R. Murrow conjures up the West and East Coasts for the premier episode of *See It Now* (November 18, 1951). (Courtesy Time-Life)

See It Now mixed live interviews, conducted by Murrow from CBS Studio 41 in New York, and filmed reports from remote locales. Murrow played anchor and center of gravity, producer Friendly functioned as managing editor, and director Don Hewitt choreographed the action. In a gesture that endeared him to his crews, Murrow always gave up-front credit to the off-camera cameramen by naming them on air. The basic template for the show was not revolutionary, but the professionalism of the presentation and the gravitas of the work grants *See It Now* a deserved reputation as the prototype for the television news magazine. "This isn't radio news with pictures, or movie newsreels which are distributed over the ether," declared Friendly in 1953. "This is television news." Unable to adapt, the print journalist Drew Pearson struggled with the syndicated television version of his popular "The Washington Merry-Go-Round" column for the *Washington Post*. On film, and hence always behind the curve of breaking news, Pearson sat at his desk, in front of the camera, and droned on and on with stiff interviews and still pictures. Better attuned to the dynamics of the new medium, Murrow and Friendly refined the art of television journalism, wherein image and montage underscored, undercut, or overpowered the words printed on the screen or spoken by a narrator.

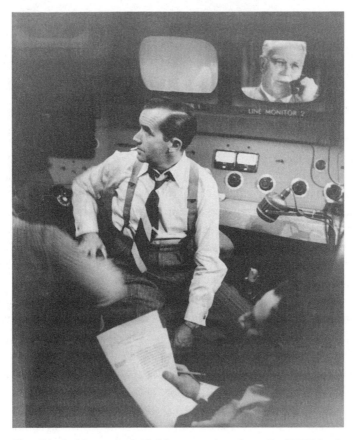

The white knight on the field: Murrow and producer Fred W. Friendly in Studio 41 during a telecast of *See It Now* (October 3, 1953). The man on the monitor is Chief Justice designate Earl Warren. (Courtesy Washington State University Library)

"We'll try never to get too big for our britches," Murrow promised viewers. Quoting verbatim from his CBS contract on the duties of a newscaster, but not the CBS loyalty oath he also signed, he pledged to "refrain, particularly with respect to all social, political and economic questions and from trying to make up the listener's mind for him." *TV Guide* took him at his word, praising Murrow's "impartial and objective reporting" and highlighting the qualities that really mattered. "Murrow has attained glamour boy status among TV's newscasters with his handsome mien, suave dress, and smooth voice."

Week in and week out, Murrow blithely violated the CBS News credo he had read so solemnly. The airdate of an early *See It Now* happened to coincide with the tenth anniversary of the Japanese attack on Pearl Harbor. After a filmed sequence on the Navy's memorial at Pearl Harbor, the last fifteen minutes of the show told the story of a single pint of blood, tracing its journey from donor to recipient, namely an American soldier wounded in Korea and medevacked via helicopter to a base hospital for emergency surgery. Visibly moved, not refraining from quite all "social, political and economic questions," Murrow raises his eyes into the camera and asks, "Spare a pint?"

On December 28, 1952, *See It Now* telecast "Christmas in Korea," a pioneering report on the first "living room war." As in his radio days, Murrow focused on the small snapshots of daily life for the common GI. "The best picture we could get would be a single GI hacking away at a single foxhole in the ice of a Korea winter or a guy on an icy road trying to change a flat tire in zero temperature," wrote Murrow in a CBS internal memo. The show began with just that sound and image. In such moments, soliciting a pint of blood for American fighting men and shivering with them in a remote outpost, Murrow embodied a tangible link from the World War II past to the Korean War present, old warrior and cold warrior.

Patriotic solicitations for the Red Cross permitted Murrow to advocate more controversial blood ties. On February 24, 1952, *See It Now* reported the case of a Chinese American, a former U.S. intelligence officer, who was barred from purchasing a home in a residential neighborhood in San Francisco because "it would hurt realty values." The report was followed by a view of the Statue of Liberty and a close-up of the Emma Lazarus poem at the pedestal ("Give me your tired, your poor, your huddled masses yearning to breathe free"), with Murrow's terse comment, "—and only last week we celebrated Brotherhood Week."

Murrow Versus McCarthy

As Murrow, Friendly, and the field producers for *See It Now* stretched their video legs, inventing a template for the television news magazine, Joseph McCarthy was also performing at the top of his form. As member and, after 1953, chairman of the Senate Permanent Subcommittee on Investigations, he commanded subpoena power. As a reliable source of good copy, he dominated newspaper headlines and radio commentary. As the ubiquitous face of anti-communism, he was an unavoidable presence in television newscasts, forum shows, and direct addresses.

Murrow too commanded a triple-threat platform: *Edward R. Murrow with the News*, a 15-minute weekday radio show at 7:45 P.M., *See It Now* on Tuesdays at 10:30 P.M., and *Person to Person* on Fridays at 10:30 P.M. Each show was a pillar in the Murrow edifice: the radio newscast linked him to the wartime past,

See It Now to the Korean War present, and *Person to Person* to the domestic sphere of the Cold War household.

Murrow and McCarthy had confronted each other on screen well before Good Tuesday. In 1953, *See It Now* had covered an emotional homecoming celebration for McCarthy in Milwaukee and as the senator mawkishly brushed a tear from his eye and thanked the crowd for their support, a dry-eyed Murrow commented "that this was the same man who had accused General Marshall of treason." Likewise, the film footage of Voice of America official Reed Harris before the McCarthy committee, which would be used to lacerating effect on the March 9, 1954, show, was first aired on March 8, 1953, on an episode that also chronicled the death of Stalin. "The juxtaposition of Stalin and McCarthy was not lost on viewers," recalled *See It Now* producer Joseph Wershba. "They wrote that it was a case of one dictator dead, another potential dictator on the way up."

Thus, from McCarthy's vantage, even paranoids have real enemies. By mid-1953, Friendly and Murrow were orchestrating a strategic campaign against the senator: reconnoitering his flank and probing for weak points before launching a full-throated attack. With intensifying force and cresting momentum, a series of five *See It Now* episodes dissected McCarthyism, the second most urgent civil rights issue of the day.

Telecast on October 20, 1953, "The Case of Milo Radulovich" was the first extensive critique of McCarthyism, though neither the term nor the senator is mentioned. The everyman moniker—Milo Radulovich? was he a character from a Preston Sturges satire or a Frank Capra film?—denoted a little guy caught in a web of forces beyond his control. As in the movies, though, the strength of character of the common man conquers his persecutors in the last act.

From the front seat of a cruising automobile, a first-person point-of-view shot frames the serene prosperity of the small town of Dexter, Michigan, home to one Milo Radulovich, an officer in the Air Force Reserve and a student of meteorology at the University of Michigan. But even remote Dexter is a front line in the domestic Cold War: a military security board has recommended Radulovich be severed from the service as a security risk because he has "maintained a close and continuing relationship" with his father and sister. Radulovich is fighting the decision, he says, because "anybody labeled with a security risk in these days—especially in physics or meteorology—simply won't be able to find employment in his field of work."

Trawling for street-corner sentiment, field producer Joseph Wershba interviews Milo's friends, an ensemble of flinty small-town types who are not afraid to speak up for one of their own: a town marshal, a dry-cleaning lady, a gas station attendant, and, lastly, the past commander of the local American Legion post, a beer truck driver who, fortified by his product, declares in a raspy voice that if Milo can be held guilty because of his family relationships, "We all better head for cover—or we better uncover what has already started."

The scene switches to Detroit for a filmed interview with Milo's father, a leathery old Serbian immigrant who speaks in halting, thickly accented English about his own loyalty and the loyalty of "my boy Milo." He reads from a letter he has written to President Eisenhower. "Mr. President, I ask nothing for myself. I ask-a-justice for my boy."

Back in Studio 41, Murrow reads from the transcript of Radulovich's loyalty board hearing, confirming that the proceeding was, as Radulovich's lawyer had charged, a "farce and a travesty of justice." Murrow's traditional end-of-show commentary is blunt. "We believe that the son shall not bear the inequity of the father—even though that inequity be proved and in this case it was not," he says. "Whatever happens in this whole arena of the relationship between the individual and the state, we will do it ourselves [*looking up, nailing the viewer with his gaze*]. It cannot be blamed upon Malenkov or Mao Tse Tung, or even our allies. And it seems to us—that is, Fred Friendly and myself—that this a subject that should be argued about endlessly."

Of course, Murrow and Friendly did not want the subject to be argued about endlessly; they wanted the case of Milo Radulovich settled immediately, in his favor.

Five weeks later, it was. In an extraordinary turnabout, Secretary of the Air Force Harold E. Talbott appeared at the top of *See It Now* to announce that it was "consistent with the interests of national security to retain Lt. Radulovich with the United States Air Force Reserve. He is not in my opinion a security risk." The surrender of the USAF to CBS was a leading indicator not just of the power of television to set the agenda, but to determine the decision. Knowing better than to gloat, Murrow gives away nothing by his expression.

Appropriately, the capitulation of the Secretary of the Air Force served as prelude to the next incursion into McCarthyism, "An Argument in Indianapolis." The argument concerned the efforts of a group of plucky Hoosiers to form a local chapter of the American Civil Liberties Union. Two patriotic groups, the American Legion and the Minute Women, opposed the chapter and pressured local businesses to deny the group space for an organizational meeting. Only when a Roman Catholic priest intervened to offer his church basement did the ACLU find a room among the inns of Indianapolis.

Crosscutting between the ACLU meeting and the American Legion meeting, the surface evenhandedness of video journalism tilts heavily toward civil liberties. The Legionnaires are stiff, constipated, and tongue-tied; the ACLU members are easygoing, good-humored, and articulate. Where the Legionnaires fumble their dialogue (including the initials "A-C-L-A-uh-U"), the civil libertarians recite their lines with practiced eloquence. "Many people mistake controversy for conspiracy," says one, but "controversy is as American as the Rocky Mountains and the Fourth of July." In covering the civil rights contretemps in a Midwest hub, Murrow puts his thumb firmly on one side of the scale. Again, the senator's name was never mentioned.

On November 3, 1953, *See It Now* devoted thirty minutes of unqualified praise to Gen. George C. Marshall, who had just won the Nobel Peace Prize. The former Army Chief of Staff during World War II and architect of the plan for European reconstruction, General Marshall was the most respected patriot and public servant of his time—except to Joseph McCarthy. On June 14, 1951, from the floor of the United States Senate, McCarthy charged Marshall, then Secretary of Defense in the Truman administration, with complicity in "a conspiracy on a scale so immense as to dwarf any previous such venture in the history of man. A conspiracy of infamy so black that, when it is finally exposed, its principals shall be forever deserving of the maledictions of all honest men." For Murrow to honor Marshall was to insult McCarthy.

Murrow usually treated politicians as, at best, his equal. Sitting with Marshall for a filmed interview at the general's home in Leesburg, Virginia, he fawns over the great man. In the second part of the show, telecast live from St. Louis, correspondent Joseph Wershba interviewed another of Marshall's friends and admirers, former President Harry S. Truman. "I think he will be considered the man of the age," Truman asserted. Wershba then delicately broached the subject of the attack on Marshall, without mentioning names and using an indefinite plural noun.

"Can you ever find it in your heart to forgive that little handful of men in public life who attack General Marshall's personal loyalty and patriotism?" asks Wershba.

"No, that's one of the dirtiest tricks that ever happened," snaps Truman. Choosing his words carefully, he finishes the thought: "The man who made that attack isn't fit to shine General Marshall's shoes." There is a long pause, the camera holding on Truman's tight-lipped visage before Wershba moves on to another topic.

After the Truman interview, Murrow made his usual closing comments. "Tonight General Marshall is recovering from an illness at Walter Reed Hospital in Washington," he says somberly, and then, brightening: "As for Mr. Truman, we have not always seen eye to eye with him, but certainly we do on the subject of George Marshall"—grinning now, savoring the punchline— "and we are also obliged to applaud Mr. Truman's selection of shoeshine boys." Though no sentient listener required a translation, *Variety* interpreted: "It was a case of 'no names,' please, but an unmistakable reference to a United States Senator. The direct way in which this was put hinted that Murrow was trying to 'smoke out' the senator for a reply, and it's no secret among a

"The man who made that attack isn't fit to shine General Marshall's shoes": a tight-lipped Harry S. Truman offers his opinion of Senator McCarthy on Edward R. Murrow's *See It Now* (November 3, 1953). (Courtesy Harry S. Truman Library)

small coterie of broadcasters, correspondents, etc. that Murrow is on the senator's 'hate' list." Fair enough: the senator was also on Murrow's hate list.

The "Good Tuesday" Homily

Heeding the Napoleonic dictate to refrain from interfering while the enemy is destroying himself, Murrow and Friendly held their fire over the next few months. *See It Now* aside, the accumulated wear of torrents of bad publicity had eroded McCarthy's power base. A widely ridiculed junket to Europe by McCarthy staffers Roy Cohn and G. David Schine to censor USIS libraries, McCarthy's sneering disrespect to former President Truman in public speeches and direct addresses, and his slander of General Marshall had cumulatively taken a toll, emboldening opponents and discouraging even his natural constituencies. Above all, the truly conservative Republican now in the White House had come to realize that a man once tolerated as a necessary evil had become a political liability.

On February 18, 1954, during hearings into Army security lapses, the senator inflicted upon himself the most serious wound to date. While interrogating Gen. Ralph W. Zwicker, commanding general of Camp Kilmer, New Jersey, McCarthy lost his temper and lashed out at the decorated war hero. General Zwicker's alleged unbecoming conduct was to coddle an Army dentist and alleged communist named Maj. Irving Peress. McCarthy derided General Zwicker as "not fit to wear the uniform," a beyond-the-pale insult that enraged the regular military ranks. With that, a sloping career arc plunged into a sharp downward trajectory.

As McCarthy's fortunes dimmed, as criticism from his fellow senators and the press intensified, Murrow and Friendly decided the time was propitious for a video assault on McCarthyism that named names, the storied *See It Now* telecast of March 9, 1954. By Saturday March 6, Friendly "had whipped the McCarthy program into shape," recalled Joseph Wershba. "In varying form, it had been ready to go almost four weeks. Each week in February, Friendly's film editors would ask, 'This week?'" Its existence was hardly a secret to industry insiders. Prior to the telecast, *Variety* reported that Murrow planned "to unwrap his long-held 'McCarthy story.' It's understood that Murrow and co-producer Fred W. Friendly had been 'waiting' for the strategic moment to spring the filmed stanza and decided 'this is it.'" Typically timorous, CBS refused to advertise the show, so Murrow and Friendly paid for an ad in the *New York Times*, deleting the CBS logo. However, the network did pay for a telegram to J. Edgar Hoover, alerting him to the upcoming show about his chief rival in anticommunist eminence.

"A Report on Senator Joseph R. McCarthy" opens with the technically true disclaimer that the report is "told mainly in [McCarthy's] own words and pictures." Actually, of course, the pictures are Murrow and Friendly's, edited and paced to inflict maximum damage on the man in their crosshairs. As McCarthy laughs nervously, unctuously, tight close-ups accentuate a sinister, sweaty visage; as McCarthy barks and blusters, the camera pans down along a mural of George Washington for unsubtle contrast. Throughout, Murrow's voice-over trails the senator like a Greek chorus: "Often operating as a one-man committee, [McCarthy] has traveled far, interviewed many, terrorized some, accused civilian and military leaders of the past administration of a great conspiracy to turn over the country to communism, investigated and substantially demoralized the present State Department, made varying charges of conspiracy at [Army Signal Corps headquarters in New Jersey at] Fort Monmouth." Another conspiracy—of words and image—subverts the senator.

Murrow describes McCarthy's two trademark techniques as "the investigation" and "the half truth" and cues up filmed examples of each. In a campaign speech on October 27, 1952, a slip of the tongue conflates a communist spy with the Democratic candidate for president: "Alger—I mean Adlai," McCarthy smirks, to knowing chuckles from the crowd. Then, Murrow reprises the testimony of Reed Harris from the Voice of America hearings on March 3, 1953. On film shot by *See It Now*'s cameras, Harris avers that he considers communists the "plain clothes auxiliary of the Red Army," but McCarthy still presses him about an obscure book he wrote in 1932. "I resent the tone of this inquiry," says Harris, "because it is my neck, my public neck, that you are, I think, very skillfully trying to wring." The sheer volume of McCarthy images already in the archival record has provided ammunition aplenty for Murrow's indictment.

The final commentary by Murrow remains the most dramatic, eloquent, and influential oration ever delivered by a television journalist, a rousing call to conscience that few news readers at an anchor desk have not fantasized about uncorking during a tense moment of national crisis and personal conscience. Murrow begins in a spirit of serene sanity. "No one familiar with the history of this country can deny that congressional committees are useful; it is necessary to investigate before legislating," he allows, before mincing no words: "But the line between investigating and persecuting is a very fine one and the junior senator from Wisconsin has stepped over it repeatedly." The use of the dismissive diminutive was calculated to rankle: the *junior* senator, as if Murrow were an adult lecturing an errant schoolboy.

"His primary achievement has been in confusing the public mind as between the internal and external threats of communism," Murrow continues, summarizing the ethos of Cold War liberalism: the threat to freedom from communism overseas should never stifle freedom at home. "We must remember always that accusation is not proof, and that conviction depends upon evidence and due process of law." Murrow looks up periodically from his written text, gazing into the camera, tobacco smoke swirling like incense in the back of the screen.

Then Murrow recites a series of lines that scan like free verse:

> We will not walk in fear one of another.
> We will not be drawn by fear into an age of unreason
> If we dig deep in our history and our doctrine.
> And remember
> That we are not descended from fearful men,
> Not from men who feared to write,
> To speak,
> To associate, and
> To defend causes
> That were for the moment unpopular.

He looks up, straight into the camera. "This is no time for men who oppose Senator McCarthy's methods to keep silent"—then, a tactical admission—"or for those who approve."

Shifting ground, Murrow takes the long view, celebrating America's pre-eminent role on the world stage and extolling the freedoms under siege.

> We cannot deny our heritage and our history,
> But we cannot escape responsibility for the result.
> There is no way
> For a citizen of a Republic
> To abdicate his responsibilities.
> As a nation we have come in to our full inheritance at
>   a tender age.
> We proclaim ourselves—as indeed we are—the de-
>   fenders of freedom where it continues to exist in
>   the world.

Again, Murrow affirms the credo of Cold War liberalism:

> But we cannot defend freedom abroad
> By deserting it at home.

Reluctantly, Murrow turns back to his main topic, the undertones as audible as the spoken language:

> The actions of the junior senator from Wisconsin
>   have caused alarm and dismay amongst our allies
>   abroad and given considerable comfort to our
>   enemies.
> And whose fault is that? [*This is not a rhetorical
>   question.*]
> Not really his. [*This man is an insect, a hustler of
>   history.*]
> He didn't create this situation of fear; he merely
>   exploited it—and rather successfully. [*His sole
>   talent is for demagoguery.*]
> Cassius was right.
> The fault, dear Brutus, is not in our stars,
> but in ourselves.

A beat, then Murrow's signature sign-off:

"The fault, dear Brutus . . . ": Murrow delivers the curtain line on *See It Now*'s famed "A Report on Senator Joseph R. McCarthy" (March 9, 1954).

> Good night
> and
> good luck.

As Murrow folds over the last page of his script, the whisper of paper rustles on the sound track. Then the CBS eye fills the screen like a period punctuating the end of the recitation.

Purely as a theatrical feat—a lone man performing without a net on live television—Murrow's talk is an act of showstopping oratory. Not once does he falter, stutter, mangle a pronunciation, or miss a cue. Reaching deep into an all-American literary tradition, Murrow draws on native sources for inspiration and argument. Shakespeare may have penned the curtain line, but the common sense of Thomas Paine and the rhetorical rhythms of Abraham Lincoln echoed through Murrow's prose.

The Shakespearean passage that serves as the leitmotiv for the commentary is taken from a play about naked ambition and the corruption of a Republic, of political betrayal and rotten friends. Perhaps not coincidentally, *Julius Caesar* was then undergoing something of a cultural revival, with Joseph L.

Mankiewicz's film of *Julius Caesar* (1953) and in the famously prophetic rewriting of Marc Antony's funeral oration by Bishop Sheen on *Life Is Worth Living*. On *See It Now*, Murrow plays Marc Antony casting yon McCarthy as Cassius with the lean and hungry look.

But where sly Antony drips sarcasm, earnest Murrow is all sincerity. Exposing the fake erudition of the nation's leading anti-intellectual, Murrow begins with a teacherly correction about McCarthy's citation of a line from Shakespeare ("if the senator had looked a little earlier in the passage . . . "), as if to say that this dolt cannot even get his Shakespeare right, that he is no more reliable with the famous text of *Julius Caesar* than with secret FBI files. By the end of the performance, Murrow has vanquished the threat to the Republic with a piercing lunge—not in the back but straight on, in the heart.

To Be Person-to-Personed

The critical and popular response to the Good Tuesday program was rhapsodic, not just because of who got skewered but because of where. Murrow's anti-McCarthy moment signaled a new courage for a cowering medium. "The Time May Come When People Can Think on TV," ran the headline over John Crosby's column, which gloated that Murrow's broadcast "left McCarthy bleeding from every orifice."

Far more important than the praise from already anti-McCarthy elites in New York, Washington, and Hollywood were the hosannas from the vox populi and the support of the sponsor. WBBM-TV in Chicago described the response as "exceeding anything in the station's history, surpassing even the reaction to the Godfrey-LaRosa incident."[2] I. W. Wilson, president of Aluminum Company of America, admitted that the controversy had generated some "uncomfortable moments," but the sponsor of *See It Now* felt that on the whole "the program was bringing us good results, both from the public relations and advertising points of view." Though several correspondents suggested that Alcoa change its name to the "Aluminum Company of Russia," letters preponderantly supported the company, and Alcoa even reported an "extremely favorable"

---

2. On the morning of October 19, 1953, in one of the best-remembered dustups from the early days of television, Arthur Godfrey peremptorily fired the popular singer Julius LaRosa during his *Talent Scouts* show. LaRosa had hired a personal agent, which Godfrey considered an act of calumny on the part of his former protégé. After LaRosa had finished crooning, Godfrey announced that "this was Julie's swan song with us." Like many early television shows, *Arthur Godfrey's Talent Scouts* was simulcast on radio. The television portion of the show had just signed off but the radio portion captured the firing live.

reaction from dealers and suppliers. "I have a wonderful contract with my sponsor," Murrow deadpanned. "They make aluminum and I make film."

See It Now did not single-handedly topple McCarthy, but it certainly upended the journalistic hierarchy. "Where the strongest conservative newspapers such as *The New York Times* and *The New York Herald Tribune* had failed to arouse any mass public indignation over the Senator's methods of investigation, a single 30-minute TV show may well go down as the lance that pricked and completely deflated the McCarthy balloon," *Billboard* sagely predicted. "What *Time* and *Life* and hundreds of newspaper editorials had failed to do, Murrow achieved by splicing some film together and adding to it his own biting commentary." A new media pattern emerged: print coverage pointed the way and television grabbed the glory at the finish line.

The Friday after Good Tuesday, on March 12 at 8:30 P.M., Murrow hosted his celebrity interview show, *Person to Person*. With his inevitable cigarette as an extra digit, Murrow sat in his studio while a remote camera crew traipsed through the home of a starlet, politician, sportsman, musician, or author. As Murrow prompted his guests with prearranged questions ("Doesn't that picture have a story behind it?"), interviewees recited favorite anecdotes with the stilted posture of folks unused as yet to the acid glare of video scrutiny. To the manor born, Murrow exuded urbane grace and good humor as he chatted with a wisecracking Groucho Marx, a brassy Sophie Tucker, a ditzy Marilyn Monroe, or a coltish Sen. John Kennedy and his beautiful wife Jacqueline.

In the 1950s, before the barricades walling off public and private realms had been shattered by the video wrecking ball, snooping about the homes of the rich and famous inspired a voyeuristic thrill. "Murrow interviews two people on the show each week, bringing viewers into their homes via an intricate system of live TV coverage," explained a wide-eyed *TV Guide*. "Aside from Murrow, the star of the show is television itself. Through no other medium would it be possible for viewers to witness this intimate tete-a-tete as it happens." Privacy, a bulwark of bourgeois culture since the eighteenth century, was being stripped bare by television.

Going person to person with Murrow was not so much the great equalizer as the supreme imprimatur. The show conferred prestige, a passport stamp of arrival at the tip-top levels of stardom and power. In the symbiotic melding of celebrity status and elite regard, Murrow bestowed certification to the lucky interview subjects; they were the guests honored to be in *his* home. In Frank Tashlin's film of George Axelrod's Broadway hit *Will Success Spoil Rock Hunter?* (1957) the seductions of the bitch goddess in Cold War America are summed up in a new verb: "Ed Murrow wants to person-to-person me!"

In Murrow historiography, *Person to Person* is set against *See It Now* as the frivolous show business side to the serious work of journalism, "low Murrow" entertainment versus "high Murrow" enlightenment as television critic John Horne of the *New York Herald Tribune* famously dubbed it, a necessary but regrettable concession to the evils of commercial television. Actually, the dialectic was less thesis/antithesis than synthesis. As a cash cow for his corporate parent, *Person to Person* accrued for Murrow a reservoir of goodwill at CBS—and earned him a higher salary than CBS President Frank Stanton. Only human, Murrow enjoyed the glow, and the profits, of celebrity, shilling coffee in magazine advertisements and going Hollywood to deliver the prologue to Michael Todd's widescreen spectacle *Around the World in Eighty Days* (1956).

Premiering on October 2, 1953, the first episode of *Person to Person* ("It's all live—there is no film!") typified the double-entry bookings wherein high culture and pop life stood side by side. A social chameleon at ease in any world, Murrow first looked in on the plush Manhattan penthouse of conductor Leopold Stokowski and his wife Gloria Vanderbilt, and then dropped in on Brooklyn Dodger catcher Roy Campanella at his more modest Long Island residence. More audaciously, the booking policy for guests violated corporate borders. At a time when networks jealously guarded the face time of their stars, Murrow "crossed network lines" by hosting NBC brand names such as Groucho Marx and Jimmy Durante.

If *See It Now* was Murrow at the office, all business and buttoned down, *Person to Person* was Murrow at home, relaxed and unguarded. Just as a testy political discussion might spoil a nice dinner party, serious talk gave way to pleasant chitchat and light anecdotes. Thus, on February 5, 1954, when Murrow's guest on *Person to Person* was Dr. Nathan M. Pusey, president of Harvard University and currently under attack by McCarthy for coddling communists on the faculty, Murrow broached the issue, but the two only got as far as an airy discussion of academic freedom. "Murrow will rarely use *Person to Person* as a controversial or solo debating medium, reserving this largely for *See It Now*," *Variety* observed. In fact, in the weeks following Good Tuesday, Murrow used *Person to Person* to cover his Nielsen flank by interviewing a greater proportion of audience-friendly celebrities.

However, the scheduled guests on *Person to Person* the week of Good Tuesday were serious characters: Gen. David Sarnoff, president of NBC, and George M. Humphrey, Secretary of the Treasury. In the wake of Murrow's attack on McCarthy, both might well have backed out of their prescheduled bookings. Neither did.

Sarnoff showed Murrow the relics of the early age of broadcasting—his Music Box memo of 1915 and the keypunch from which he monitored and transmitted news of the *Titanic* disaster in 1912. The General, who had long coveted Murrow for his own network, went out of his way to be friendly, and their first-name conviviality was like a benediction. Another name—Joe McCarthy—was never uttered.

Also showing off his "Ed" privileges, Secretary Humphrey discusses taxes, the economy, and thoroughbred horses, the last subject sparking some genuine enthusiasm from the amateur racehorse breeder. Demonstrating his own breeding, Murrow inquires after the interests of Mrs. Humphrey, who unfurls a needlepoint rendering of the Treasury Department seal. "Pretty nice of you to let us come visit you," says Murrow politely. "We feel honored," responds Mrs. Humphrey sincerely.

The joint appearance of a broadcasting titan from CBS's arch rival and a rock-ribbed Republican from Eisenhower's cabinet placed the formidable heft of the New York media and the Washington establishment squarely in Murrow's camp. It signaled that unlike so many other personalities made controversial by McCarthy, Murrow had not become damaged goods, whether to big business or big government.

"A Humble, Poverty Stricken Negress": Annie Lee Moss Before the McCarthy Committee

The *See It Now* follow-up to Good Tuesday, telecast on March 16, 1954, was a report entitled "Annie Lee Moss Before the McCarthy Committee." Both sequel and second volley, it was another crushing body blow to McCarthyism. If the civil right presently under siege was freedom of expression, the case of Annie Lee Moss highlighted another, even more urgent, civil rights issue facing Cold War America.

In McCarthy's investigation of alleged espionage within the Army ranks at the Pentagon, Mrs. Moss had emerged as a security risk because of her alleged past membership in the Communist Party and her access to secret military code rooms. Named by FBI informant Mary Marquand as a "card carrying, dues-paying member of the Communist Party," Moss had been suspended from her job pending the outcome of an internal investigation. On the afternoon of March 11, two days after Good Tuesday and the very day the Army released the incriminating documents that ignited the Army-McCarthy hearings, Moss was called to testify before the McCarthy committee.

Though not telecast, the encounter between McCarthy and Moss was filmed by a *See It Now* cameraman. By way of editing, not narration, the report contained all the elements of a high-tension courtroom drama: a sympathetic witness, righteous outbursts from the defense, overreaching from the nasty prosecutors, and surprise revelations that exonerated the accused.

"Tonight we bring you a little picture of a little woman—Annie Lee Moss and the due process of law," says Murrow, setting the scene and laying out the stakes. But though the issue is momentous, the native simplicity of the witness is taken as a matter of course. "Until three weeks ago," Murrow opines, "Mrs. Moss probably knew little about Senator McCarthy, General Zwicker, Mr. Cohn, or the other principals engaged in the argument in Washington."

Obviously out of her element and out of her depth, Moss looked to be the picture of guileless African American servility. Middle-aged, overweight, wearing functional eyeglasses and a bejeweled hat pinned in her hair, she recalled the loyal solicitude of Hollywood domestics like Louise Beavers in *Imitation of Life* (1934) or Hattie McDaniel in *Gone With the Wind* (1939). Described in the press as "a humble, poverty stricken Negress," she seemed a familiar enough stereotype.

"Is that Morse or Moss?" rasps McCarthy, as he calls the hearing to order. Assuring Mrs. Moss that she was not significant in herself ("you're not here because you're considered important in the communist apparatus"), McCarthy begins a rote cross-examination, for him a routine opening gambit before subpoenaed witnesses who usually either clammed up or shouted defiance. Contrary to expectations, however, Moss answered both McCarthy and Cohn calmly, succinctly, and emphatically. "Never at any time have I been a member of the Communist Party and I have never seen a Communist Party card," she declared. "I didn't subscribe to the *Daily Worker* and I wouldn't pay for it." The lone camera pans slowly back and forth between the aggressive men at the table and the nervous matron, leaning in to her microphone, a novice public speaker.

Confronting a witness who is neither recalcitrant nor defiant, McCarthy seems stalled. Unexpectedly, mid-cross-examination, with nothing resolved, he rises to leave. "I'm afraid I'm going to have to excuse myself," he explains, turning the chairmanship over to Sen. Karl Mundt (R-S.D.). "I have a rather important appointment to make." (The appointment is an interview with radio newsman Fulton Lewis Jr., where he will attack Murrow and accuse the Army of blackmail: March 11 is a red-letter day for Senator McCarthy.) Then, abruptly, the chairman strides out of the room, leaving the cross-examination to his lieutenant Roy Cohn.

With McCarthy off the field, Sen. Stuart Symington (D-Mo.) interjects to clear up some confusion over the identity of one Robert Hall, a white communist in the Washington, D.C., area, and another Robert Hall known to Mrs. Moss, a black man. For a moment, the two great civil rights issues confronting

Not so dumb: Annie Lee Moss on *See It Now* (March 16, 1954), shown testifying before the McCarthy committee. (Courtesy CBS Photo Archive)

Cold War America intermingle. The man named Robert Hall that she knew, says the dark-skinned Mrs. Moss, was "a man of about my complexion."

Symington coaxes her. "It's fair to say, that you didn't think he was a white man?"

"No, I didn't," chuckles Mrs. Moss, to gentle laughter from the gallery.

Symington next inquires into the details of Moss's suspension from work. For the first time since his opening exposition, Murrow's voice-over intrudes to emphasize the dumb docility of the hapless witness. His sarcastic tones italicize the implausibility of so unintelligent a woman being a Soviet intelligence agent: "This woman, under suspicion because of charges made by Senator McCarthy and Roy Cohn, *alleged* to have *examined* and *corrected* secret and encoded overseas messages, attempted to read the uncoded words of her suspension notice."

True to expectations, Moss played her part. Asked to read the official notice of her dismissal, she stumbled over the pronunciation of the bureaucratic prose. When she stalled over "adjudication," the gallery chuckled, in sympathy, in condescension, at the limited education of the poor black woman.

"Did you read that the very best you could?" asks Symington.

"Yes, I did," admits Moss, giggling.

Having exposed Mrs. Moss's level of literacy, Symington delved into her ideological sophistication.

"Did you ever hear of Karl Marx?" he inquired.

"Who's that?" she replied to gales of laughter.

A reaction shot reveals a trio of gleeful Democrats huddled together, almost cackling, unable to contain their joy at McCarthy's blunder. The camera cuts to a shot of McCarthy's empty chair and holds tight on the image.

Currently lacking a job, Mrs. Moss confesses to Senator Symington that she will soon be "going down to the welfare." A long silence follows, her fate sinking in to senators and spectators.

Whether out of Confederate chivalry or sensing the shift in the political landscape, Sen. John McClellan (D-Ark.), a staunch segregationist, rose to the defense of Annie Lee Moss. In a thick Arkansan drawl, he railed against Cohn for accusing Annie Lee Moss without evidence, in public, on television. For the first but not last time, the gallery interrupts with sustained applause. "I don't like to try people by hearsay evidence," he declaims, to more applause. From off camera, Chairman Mundt says he will rule that Cohn's comments be stricken from the record, but McClellan responds impatiently, passionately:

> You *can't* strike these statements made by counsel here as to evidence that we're having and withholding. You *cannot* strike that from the press or from the public mind. That's the—that is the—uh, *EVIL* of it. It is *not* sworn testimony. It is convicting people by rumor and hearsay and innuendo.

Again, boisterous applause fills the room.

Senator Symington then elicits the astonishing news that there are no fewer than *three* Annie Lee Mosses in the Washington, D.C., telephone book. The persecution of this Annie Lee Moss has obviously been a terrible case of mistaken identity by the reckless McCarthy staff.

Senator Symington seizes the moment. "I want to say something to you and I may be sticking my neck out and I may be wrong, but I've been listening to you testify this afternoon and I think you're telling the truth."

Applause nearly drowns out Moss's response: "I certainly am."

"And," continues Symington, "if you're not taken back in the Army, you come around and see me and I'm gonna see that you get a job."

Prolonged applause rolls over the hearing room and on the sound track, as the camera frames a silent Roy Cohn and returns again to rebuke the empty chair of Senator McCarthy.

Back in the CBS studio, Murrow breaks for an Alcoa commercial but promises "to run something else for the record" before closing. Culled from CBS's

Dinner with the President, the coda to Murrow's second direct indictment of the McCarthy committee is taken from President Eisenhower's address to the B'nai B'rith the previous November, "talking about the right of every man to look his accuser in the eye." After Eisenhower concludes, Murrow reviews the lesson: "The thirty-fourth President of the United States speaking—rather eloquently—about due process of law."

If anything, the response to the second *See It Now* show was even more appreciative: it confirmed that anti-McCarthyism was a pattern not a one-shot. "When Senator McClellan started to defend Annie Lee Moss' rights, and when Senator Symington said 'I believe you,' the sweet clean aroma of decency filled the room," observed John Crosby, who called the moment "one of the greatest experiences television has ever offered." The African American press celebrated the simple, soft-spoken witness as a folk hero. "Senator McCarthy Fails to Crack Mrs. Moss," bragged a front-page headline in the *Pittsburgh Courier*. Even in McCarthy's home state the people backed Annie Lee Moss. "Wisconsin folks saw her as a nice old colored lady who wasn't harming anyone and they didn't like their senator picking on her," reported Drew Pearson.

Moss, however, savored the last laugh. The humble, poverty-stricken Negress had donned a sambo mask to shelter herself behind the veil of white racism. As confidential FBI reports made clear several years later, Annie Lee Moss was almost certainly a Communist Party member since 1940 and thus knew the name of Karl Marx. Like so many African Americans of her day, she had simply played the fool and smiled to herself as the McCarthy committee, the gallery, Edward R. Murrow, and the television audience chuckled at the harmless mammy, shilly-shallying before the gentlemen of the big house.

McCarthy Gets Equal Time

Meanwhile McCarthy was not suffering the televisual onslaught in silence. On March 11, after scurrying from the Annie Lee Moss hearing, the senator was asked about the Good Tuesday episode by Mutual Radio's Fulton Lewis Jr. "I never listen to the extreme left-wing, bleeding-heart element of television," responded McCarthy.

The next day, Murrow responded on his radio show, *Edward R. Murrow with the News*. "I assume that most people have on their minds matters of more considerable substance than Senator McCarthy's opinion of this reporter, or mine of him," Murrow announced tightly. "However, it might serve some purpose to set part of the record straight. I may be a 'bleeding heart,' being not quite sure what it means. As for being 'extreme left wing,' that is political shorthand [for an accusation of communism]; but if the Senator means I am somewhat to the left of his position and of Louis XIV, he is correct."

The intense public interest in the back and forth between the broadcaster and senator gave the lie to Murrow's disinterested pose. No longer the objective eyewitness scrawling the first draft of history, the reporter had become a lead item in the story he was covering. Murrow strained to maintain the conceit that he was not a featured player in the unfolding drama, but the charade was unsustainable. Actually, no, most people listening to Murrow's broadcast did not have on their minds "matters of more considerable substance" than Senator McCarthy's opinion of Murrow and vice versa: nor should they have. The Murrow-McCarthy headlines belonged on the front page, above the fold.

At the opening of the Good Tuesday show, anticipating an "equal time" gambit from his target, Murrow had offered McCarthy rebuttal time on CBS. The senator suggested that the telegenic William F. Buckley appear in his stead, but Murrow insisted the equal time was not transferable to a surrogate. "Your suggestion of April 6 as a time for your reply to my recent television program is acceptable," Murrow informed McCarthy. "Transcript and kinescope of last Tuesday's program are being mailed to you. Regarding your statement that I have 'consciously served the Communist cause,' I utterly deny it. The record when it is finished will show who has served the communist cause, you or I."

Produced by the BBD&O ad agency and filmed at the Fox Movietone Studios in New York, McCarthy's response cost $6,336. The film was delivered to CBS at 10:16 P.M., a scant fourteen minutes before airtime. McCarthy stuck CBS with the bill.

Whereas Murrow's "A Report on Senator Joseph R. McCarthy" was sleek video journalism, McCarthy's report on Edward R. Murrow was a static, bare-bones direct address. In medium shot, the senator faced the camera and read a long list of transgressions committed by Murrow. "Murrow is a symbol, the leader and the cleverest of the jackal pack which is always found at the throat of anyone who dares to expose Communists or traitors," McCarthy charged. "Now Mr. Murrow said on his program, 'the actions of the junior Senator from Wisconsin have given considerable comfort to the enemy.' That is the language of our statute of treason—rather strong language. If I am giving comfort to our enemies, I ought not to be in the Senate. If, on the other hand, Mr. Murrow is giving comfort to our enemies, he ought not to be brought into the homes of millions of Americans by CBS." At the close of McCarthy's talk, Murrow wisely held his fire and ended with his usual sign-off: "Good night and good luck."

Moments later, however, at 11:00 P.M., Murrow went on radio and replied in a seven-page statement. "Senator McCarthy's reckless and unfounded at-

Equal time but not equally effective: Senator McCarthy responds to
Murrow on *See It Now* (April 6, 1954). (Courtesy AP Worldwide Photo)

tempt to impugn my loyalty is just one more example of his typical tactic of
attempting to tie up to Communism anyone who disagrees with him," said
Murrow, not displeased that he had joined a "distinguished list" of McCarthy
targets that included General Marshall. From the senator, he had expected as
much. "I went into this thing consciously."

Murrow need not have worried about the flailing counterpunch. "[Mc-
Carthy's response was] poor in quality with spotty cutting and monotonous
one-camera shots of McCarthy sitting at a desk directly facing the lens,"
judged *Billboard*'s television critic June Bundy, astutely ignoring the polemics
for the pictures. So long mute on the matter, Murrow's employer also weighed
in. "CBS subscribes fully to the integrity and responsibility of Mr. Murrow as
a broadcaster and a loyal American," said the network in a formal statement.

"Mr. Murrow's achievements during the past 19 years have brought honor and distinction to CBS."

On his April 7 radio newscast, the day after McCarthy's reply on *See It Now*, Murrow noted an exchange from the presidential news conference that day. Speaking of himself in the third person, he reported: "And today, Joseph C. Harsch of the *Christian Science Monitor* and NBC, asked the President if he would care to say anything about 'the loyalty and patriotism of Edward R. Murrow.' Mr. Eisenhower said he had known this man for many years and always thought of him as a friend." Actually, Eisenhower was more effusive, making it clear their friendship stretched back to the days of Murrow's wartime reporting in London. Again, the determined efforts to depersonalize himself, to disassociate the broadcast journalist from the news broadcast, marks Murrow as a vestige of the print-*cum*-radio age.

The next week, Friendly and Murrow continued the campaign of attrition. On April 13, CBS telecast the fourth episode of *See It Now* on McCarthyism in five weeks, "Communism: Domestic and International." At the top of the program Murrow announced that he would later take the opportunity to "correct certain misstatements of fact made on this program last week."

The show featured two interviews about communism, one a filmed report from NATO Supreme Commander Gen. Alfred Gruenther, the other a filmed statement and live interview with Bishop Bernard J. Sheil of Chicago, founder of the Catholic Youth Organization. Earlier in the week Bishop Sheil had delivered a widely reported homily on the evils not of godless communism but of reckless accusations. A prelate of the Roman Catholic Church in the Polish-Catholic stronghold of Middle America preaching against "the junior senator from Wisconsin" as a "pitifully ineffective anticommunist" was another leading indicator of McCarthy's declining public stock. The warmth between interviewer and interviewee flowed like a mutual blessing. "Good night, Ed, and thank you for the courtesy you have extended," said the one excellency to the other.

Then Murrow responded directly to McCarthy's accusations:

Last week Senator McCarthy appeared on this program to correct any errors he might have thought we made in our report on March 9th. Since he made no reference to any statements of fact that we made, we must conclude that he found no errors of fact. He proved again that any one who exposed him, any one who does not share his hysterical disregard for decency and human dignity and the rights guaranteed by the Constitution must be either a communist or a fellow traveler.

Murrow pauses, looks up from the script, and peers into the camera:

I fully expected this treatment. The senator added this reporter's name to a long list of individuals and institutions he has accused of serving the communist cause. His proposition is very simple: any one who criticizes or opposes McCarthy's methods must be a communist—and if that be true, then there are an awful lot of communists in this country.

For the record, Murrow answered McCarthy's charges. In weary tones, he said that he had never been a member of the International Workers of the World, that the British socialist Harold Laski had indeed dedicated a book to him, but so what, and that the *Daily Worker* had not praised him. Noting his own anti-Soviet background, he added, "I require no lectures from the junior senator from Wisconsin on the dangers or terrors of communism."

Murrow winds up his brief for the defense in clipped, sometimes tremulous tones:

Having searched my conscience and my files, I cannot contend that I have always been right or wise. But I have attempted to pursue the truth with some diligence and to report it even though, as in this case, I had been warned in advance that I would be subject to the attentions of Senator McCarthy.

Straining to keep his cool, Murrow stutters a bit over the closing line:

We shall hope to deal with matters of m-more vital interest to the c-country next week.

Then, his signature sign off:

Good night and good luck.

With such words and images, Edward R. Murrow may not have single-handedly slain the dragon of Joseph McCarthy, but he surely defanged the creature. If television could attack the senator with impunity, then his power to lash out and wound was waning.

For that gift, Edward R. Murrow would ever after be a journalistic byword for class, courage, and integrity. On March 29, 1954, at the annual awards dinner of the Overseas Press Club at the Waldorf Astoria Hotel in New York, Murrow accepted one of the many awards bestowed on him that year. Having just finished his nightly radio broadcast, he arrived late for the ceremony.

When he entered the room, the diners leapt to their feet, cheering and applauding wildly for the white knight of the airwaves.

NINE

THE ARMY-MCCARTHY HEARINGS
(APRIL 22–JUNE 17, 1954)

At some point during the thirty-six days of the sometimes tedious, sometimes riveting congressional inquiry known as the Army-McCarthy hearings, television emerged as the grand cathedral for the secular ritual of American democracy. The Kefauver Crime Committee hearings, the direct addresses of Truman, Nixon, and Eisenhower, the lively exchanges on the news forum shows, and the McCarthy-Murrow jousts were but warm-ups for a long-running, character-driven, political-*cum*-televisual show. After the Army-McCarthy program, the very word "hearings" sounded like a linguistic holdover: it was the pilot episode for a new series in which political events of sufficient moment and promising ratings would not only be heard and recorded by government stenographers but witnessed live by the electorate.

The Army-McCarthy hearings proved a media milestone not only because of the inherent significance of the event but because television coverage itself determined the meaning of the event. The hearings marked the first nationwide transmission of a constitutional crisis, a distinctly American ritual radiating out not in broadsheets, congressional records, newsreels, or radio, but sound and image, beheld in the privacy of the home. In time, the televised political spectacle, an unrehearsed drama played out to a constitutional script, would become a preferred format for the resolution of executive-legislative-judicial branch disputes. The great scandals and power struggles of the next decades—Watergate, Iran-Contra, Hill-Thomas, and the Clinton impeachment—would be at once constitutional and televisual, with the branches of government pleading their case before the court of viewer opinion.

Ostensibly, the most storied televisual event of the 1950s convened to investigate a convoluted crisscross of charges and countercharges leveled by the U.S. Army at Sen. Joseph R. McCarthy and vice versa, an intergovernmental brawl incited by, of all things, the daily duties and weekend furloughs of an Army private. Yet the issue before the congressional judges and the living room jury was never really the matter at hand but the means and ends of McCarthyism. What was new and surprising to senators and spectators alike was that the duel was as much televisual as political. The hearings pitted the erratic, grating Joseph R. McCarthy and the unctuous, bleary-eyed Roy M. Cohn against the serene, gentlemanly Joseph N. Welch of the Boston law firm of Hale and Dorr, whom the Army had hired as its attorney. Two contrasting televisual styles pervaded the dramaturgy: the heated bombast of McCarthy versus the calm demeanor of Welch. A decade before Marshall McLuhan coined the terms, the Army-McCarthy hearings showed how a hot personality melted under the glare of television while a cool one never broke a sweat.

Backstory and Dramatis Personae

In July 1953, the enviable existence of a consultant on McCarthy's staff named G. David Schine was interrupted by a summons that meant a steep decline in social prestige and personal freedom: a draft notice from the U.S. Army. Upon notification of the sad tidings, and throughout Schine's induction into military life in the fall of 1953, Roy M. Cohn, chief counsel for the McCarthy committee, pressured, badgered, and abused Army officials, from the Secretary of the Army on down to Schine's company commander, to provide special privileges and cushy assignments for his friend.

On March 11, 1954, the curtain was pulled back on Cohn's string-pulling when the U.S. Army, and therefore the Eisenhower administration, released what came to be known as the Adams chronology, a record of phone calls made by Cohn to Secretary of the Army Robert T. Stevens. Logged by a military stenographer and compiled by Army counselor John G. Adams, the chronology was a near-verbatim record of Cohn's efforts to mold the military to his will and Schine's convenience.

The revelations ignited a political firestorm. Cohn and McCarthy were accused of trying to blackmail the Army into making Private Schine's hitch in the military less disruptive to his social life and civilian career. McCarthy countered by claiming the Army was holding Schine "hostage" to deter his committee from exposing communists within the military's ranks. Coincidentally, even as the national media and the political classes obsessed about the duties of an Army private, two events that would shape the contours of the next decade were also unfolding. At Dien Bien Phu in Vietnam, French colonial forces prepared to surrender to the Viet Minh. Across the street from Congress, another momentous decision was being reached by the United States Supreme Court in the case of *Brown v. Board of Education*. The Vietnam War, the civil rights crusade, and the controversy over McCarthyism: the volatile spring of 1954 belies the cliché of the somnolent Eisenhower era.

As the Adams chronology proved conclusively, Cohn had indeed pressured the Army on Schine's behalf and the Army had indeed cushioned Schine's berth in the military. "The charges *on both sides* were plainly true in substance if not in every detail," the historian Telford Taylor observed at the time. "Appeasement and lack of dignity and self respect on one side and on the other arrogance, immaturity, and a wealthy young man with little stomach for basic training." All the stultifying minutiae and labyrinthine machinations that ensued never obscured the verdict that, as an inquiry into the matter at hand, the Army-McCarthy hearings presented a kangaroo courtroom with both sides guilty as charged.

Viewing the shared record of cupidity and the mutual violations of public trust, commentators right and left vented disgust at both sides of the Army-McCarthy hyphen. "Private G. David Schine was coddled, pampered, babied, and cottonwooled by the Army," charged Drew Pearson, because he had "the backing of a powerful United States Senator with broad subpoena powers. The manner in which the top brass treated him is un-American and disgraceful." Agreeing with his ideological opposite, columnist George Sokolsky stipulated "that Mr. Cohn suffers from telephonitis," but demanded "why did not Robert Stevens tell him to stop bothering him? Can anyone imagine some of Mr. Stevens's predecessors . . . arguing with a committee consul on what to do with a prospective private in the Army?"

For McCarthy's political opponents, however, outrage at the Army was offset by gratitude for the tactical blunder. In fact, the timing of the Adams chronology—released two days after Edward R. Murrow's "A Report on Senator Joseph R. McCarthy" on *See It Now*—is suspiciously coincidental. Murrow was known to be holding his anti-McCarthy show for "just the right moment" and that week, the decisive week in McCarthy's career, was surely the right moment to strike. With friends at the highest levels of government and the military, the CBS broadcaster may well have gotten a surreptitious green light about the upcoming release of the Adams chronology. Attacked from two directions, McCarthy was caught in a cultural pincer movement: a media posse, led by Murrow, and a military brigade, orchestrated offstage by the Eisenhower administration.

To sift through the charges and countercharges, the Senate Permanent Subcommittee on Investigations, which McCarthy chaired, voted to undertake a formal inquiry into the sundry claims of Cohn/Schine/McCarthy/Stevens/Adams. As a principal to the dispute, McCarthy stepped down from the committee, ceding the chairmanship to Karl Mundt (R-S.D.). The rest of the committee was comprised of three Republicans (Henry Dworshak of Idaho, Charles Potter of Michigan, and Everett Dirksen of Illinois) and three Democrats (John McClellan of Arkansas, Stuart Symington of Missouri, Henry

Jackson of Washington). To handle interrogations, the committee retained as counsel Ray H. Jenkins, a gravelly voiced criminal attorney from Tennessee. The counsel for the minority Democrats was a 28-year-old lawyer being groomed for better things, Robert F. Kennedy.

All would soon become as familiar as the actors on a daytime soap opera, but one member of the cast emerged not just as a well-known face but a full-blown star, a figure of natural and spontaneous telegeniety—Joseph N. Welch, a prominent Boston attorney and the designated defender of the U.S. Army.

The prototypical story about Joseph Welch told how, as a young attorney fresh out of law school, he found himself up against a former U.S. senator in a high-profile court case. An abashed Welch confessed to the jury that they were witnessing a David and Goliath contest, an inexperienced boy confronting a powerful giant. With his native limitations, said Welch, he could never hope to practice law "except in the minor leagues, and we are pitted now against a lawyer from the big leagues." This mismatch was especially unfortunate because his client (who, alas, was not able to afford a high-priced attorney) actually had a very good case. When the verdict came in—Welch won, naturally—a juror winked in appreciation and said, "Well, sonny, you're in the big leagues now."

Welch was never minor league. Born in Iowa, not Beacon Hill, on October 22, 1890, he took a fast track out of the cornfields: an A student in high school, Phi Beta Kappa at Grinnell College, and on to Harvard Law School, where he finished second in the class of 1919. Upon graduation, he joined the Hale and Dorr law firm, a cynosure of Boston Brahmanism, and never left. Hale and Dorr had seventeen senior partners and five junior partners, among them a young lawyer named Fred Fisher.

On television, set against a fashion wall of business suits and ramrod-straight military postures, Welch stood out in attire and body language. Sporting a bow tie, cradling his thumbs in his vest pockets, leaning back amiably in his chair, he projected polite curiosity and Zenlike serenity. "To the brawling hot tempered hearings in the Senate caucus room, the 63-year-old Welch brought an atmosphere redolent of Beacon Hill, needle point slippers, afternoon teas, and antimacassars," wrote a smitten AP reporter. Less than a week into the hearings, the *Des Moines Register* tagged Welch as a rising star "on his way to becoming a great TV favorite. The old boy, who wallows in color, seems to be the only entirely cool and unruffled man in the room. When he does strike, it has been with fine dramatic fire." Not beneath the surface rippled the affinities of class, of the establishment rallying to defend the old order. Welch was the anti-McCarthy, the anti-Cohn, the genteel WASP against the loutish Mick and the pushy Jew.

For the cameras and the gallery, Welch performed his self-deprecation routine with an impish twinkle that invited everyone in on the joke. When requesting more time to ponder a set of constitutional issues, he played the humble petitioner. "I am the world's leading amateur in this field," he claimed. Readily acceding to Welch's request, a bemused Senator Symington admits, to sympathetic chuckles all around, "Well, I am beginning to fall for Mr. Welch too." To a comment from Senator Jackson, Welch responded, "You flatter me when you imply I have ready access to the White House. I have not reached such dizzying heights."

Though not immune to Welch's charm, the gruff Ray Jenkins sometimes found the bumpkin act wearing thin. "I am a rather simple lawyer—" Welch began at one point. "Well," cut in Jenkins sardonically, "you're not under oath."[1] By the end of the hearings, with Welch basking in video-fueled fame, his trademark shtick backfired when he asked Cohn to describe the interior of the exclusive Stork Club in New York. "I bet I couldn't get in, could I, Mr. Cohn?" Welch jibed. "Well," shot back Cohn, "they cater to television celebrities, Mr. Welch."

Cohn must have savored his bon mot. Against Welch, he seldom got the better end of a punch line, and Cohn was not a man used to a verbal drubbing. In January 1953, just shy of his twenty-sixth birthday, Cohn had joined McCarthy's staff as chief counsel after a meteoric career as a ruthlessly ambitious prosecutor in the U.S. Attorney's office in New York, where he had helped obtain the conviction for espionage of Julius and Ethel Rosenberg. The son of a prominent New York judge, Cohn offered not just political connections but political protection: as a Jew, the McCarthy frontman shielded the senator from charges of anti-Semitism.

Before the cameras, Cohn was at once stiff and oily, obsequious and bullying. Oozing a false modesty, he downplayed his own authority, claiming that "wiser and more qualified heads than mine" made the real decisions, that it was absurd that he, a mere 27-year-old senate counsel, could "wreck" the Army, that anyone who knew him would confirm that he never used "vituperative language."

---

1. Inspired by Welch's mock modesty, a similar scene was reenacted in *Anatomy of a Murder* (1959), the Otto Preminger courtroom drama in which Welch made his big-screen acting debut as the presiding judge. George C. Scott, as a high-powered prosecutor from the big city, faces off against Jimmy Stewart, as a cagey local lawyer. When Stewart plays to the hometown jury with the same aw-shucks routine that Welch had patented, a reaction shot shows the city lawyer rolling his eyes at the faux rusticity.

Visible backscreen behind the main players, as if awaiting his cue to walk onto the stage of history, fidgeted the counsel for the Democrats, Robert F. Kennedy. Although friendly enough with McCarthy (who had boosted his brother's 1952 senatorial campaign by refraining from campaigning against him in Massachusetts), Kennedy despised Cohn, partly on general principles, partly because McCarthy had selected Cohn over Kennedy for the plum position of chief counsel (mainly to avoid the impolitic image of witnesses before the McCarthy committee being doubled-teamed by a pair of Irish Catholics). Kennedy sat in a row of chairs behind the Democratic senators, but the deceptive depth of field in the television lens made him appear almost shoulder-to-shoulder between Senators McClellan and Symington. With his eyeglasses resting in a tuft of hair, he could often be seen passing papers to Democratic senators and glowering at Roy Cohn. Once, the camera catches Kennedy in a moment of distraction, twirling a piece of paper around the head of a pencil, like a bored schoolboy. When he realizes the camera is on him, he slowly, sheepishly, puts the paper and pencil away.

Against the outsized personalities of the colorful combatants, the catalyst for the hearings seemed a pallid nonentity. Born in Gloversville, New York, the second of four children, G. David Schine was the scion of the wealthy hotelier and theater owner J. Meyer Schine. By all accounts, he was a pampered brat of limited talents. Even among the undergraduates at Harvard, Schine had distinguished himself as an obnoxious rich boy by hiring coeds from nearby Radcliffe College to attend his classes and take notes. In January 1953, at Cohn's invitation, he joined McCarthy's staff as the sole unpaid consultant on communism.

The senators comprised a mixed crew. The Democratic personalities ranged from the leathery southerner John McClellan, who addressed McCarthy familiarly as "Joe," to the urbane liberal Stuart Symington, who despised McCarthy as much as McCarthy despised him. Also on the Democratic side, serving his first term, was Henry "Scoop" Jackson, then and later a classic Cold War liberal, as anticommunist as he was anti-McCarthy.

The Republican side of the aisle was less telegenically astute and politically agile. Former HUAC member Charles Potter was characteristically quiet, Everett Dirksen was uncharacteristically quiet, and the nondescript Henry Dworshak was mainly missing in action. Another former member of HUAC, the steady but stolid Karl Mundt was a fair-minded bipartisan choice to chair the committee. Linked across the aisles, Potter and McClellan each had special reason to resent the McCarthy team's intervention on behalf of a fortunate son. During World War II, McClellan had lost a son, and Potter, who had enlisted as an Army private in 1942, had lost both legs in France.

Two of the most significant players in the Army-McCarthy hearings remained offstage for the entire run of the show. Both, however, took decisive action to redirect the trajectory of the drama.

From the White House, President Eisenhower (who claimed not to be watching the hearings) nevertheless eyed the proceedings with mounting anger. Barely able to speak the name of the man whose reluctance to serve in uniform sparked the investigation, he referred to Schine as "this private." At a press conference shortly after the hearings began, a reporter asked, "Mr. President, as a former commanding general of the United States Army, what do you think of the excitement at the Capitol over the privileges granted a private?" A tense silence followed. "The scene was unique in presidential press conference history. The President was flushed. His jaw was set. His eyes appeared moist. The atmosphere as he walked out was electric," reported the *Washington Post*. On May 17, 1954, after McCarthy demanded that all participants in any executive branch meeting be made available for testimony, thereby disrupting his party and defying his president, Eisenhower invoked what was then a novel notion called "executive privilege." Ten days later, McCarthy infuriated Eisenhower by calling upon federal employees to ignore the president and deliver to him, personally, any and all evidence, including classified information, of corruption and subversion in government. The administration loudly condemned the senator. Procedurally, McCarthy was stymied; politically, he was isolated.

J. Edgar Hoover also followed the hearings closely. In Hoover's mind, the subject matter—secret files, security clearances, communist subversion—was the proper, nay exclusive, province of the FBI. When McCarthy presumed to pillage and expose the contents of Hoover's sacred FBI files, the director slapped back the attempted usurpation and denied that the document in question had been cleared by him. Smarter than McCarthy, neither Welch nor Cohn presumed to provoke Hoover. When his name was uttered, nothing but awed respect flowed from their lips. Like the deus ex machina that rescued Herbert Philbrick from the clutches of the communists in *I Led 3 Lives*, Hoover injected himself into the hearings at a crucial juncture: not to save the anticommunist from disaster but to cut him off at the knees.

Gavel-to-Gavel Coverage

At 10:30 A.M., Thursday, April 22, 1954, television debuted an open-ended miniseries with the images that became the signature montage for the Army-McCarthy hearings. A camera panned the long horizontal space of Senate Caucus Room 318, usually a solemn and sparse marble chamber, now packed tight with milling and murmuring hordes of politicians, servicemen, re-porters, tourists, and what were not then called policy wonks and political junkies. The high-ceilinged room officially seated five hundred, but only some one hundred seats were allotted to ordinary citizens clamoring for the hottest ticket in town. When a vacant seat became available, Capitol Hill guards played theater usher to the crowd waiting in the exterior corridors, holding up two or three fingers to indicate the number of places available. Though men and women competed on equal terms for seating at the beginning of a session, Cold War chivalry gave women priority on empty seats when a spectator left the room.

On the first morning, a lobbyist for American Chinaware distributed com-plimentary ashtrays with the logo, "If it's American, it's worth protecting," but guards quickly removed both lobbyist and souvenirs. The ashtrays would have come in handy. In the tobacco-stained 1950s, to breathe is to smoke. Cigars, pipes, and cigarettes of all brands were lit and savored with impunity: cork-tipped Lords, mild menthol Kools, high-octane Camels, Winston Kings (with a filter "so carefully worked out it doesn't 'thin' the taste or flatten the rich, inimitable flavor"), monogrammed L&Ms ("this is it—just what the doctor ordered!"), and quite legal Cuban cigars. A gauzy tobacco haze permeated the entire atmosphere, wafting about the witnesses and settling above the caucus room, seeming to coat even the kinescopes in a filter of secondhand smoke.

Wire-service photographers roamed the room, bobbing up and down, an-gling for a shot. Whenever the huge flashbulbs from their cameras obstructed the line of sight of the television cameras, Chairman Mundt warned the shut-terbugs to duck down or assume a kneeling position, a humbling reminder of their subservient place on the media ladder. "There are a great many com-plaints from the television audience and from the television people that all the [television] cameras are getting the backs and the backs of heads of agitated photographers," Mundt lectured. "[I] had a chance to see part of the television playbacks, and I want to confirm the legitimacy of those complaints."

Sitting behind the witness table at press tables were some seventy reporters, including Walter Winchell, conspicuous in his trademark gray fedora with black hatband. The print press dutifully reported the proceedings in newspa-pers the next day, but, like the still photographers, they too were yesterday's news. Anyone with a television set could cover the beat.

The front half of the spectator section was reserved for special guests. Celebrity visitors from the arts, sports, and politics came by to see the televised hearings and be seen on television. The golfer Babe Didrikson Zaharias at-tended, as did Washington hostess Perle Mesta, who waltzed in dressed for a dinner party. Sitting in a place of privilege behind the senators, wearing a broad-rimmed black chapeau and elbow-length white gloves, and waving a

Lights, cameras, politics: Senate Caucus Room 318, transformed into a cluttered sound-stage for the Army-McCarthy hearings (1954). (Courtesy Photofest)

cigarette holder between her middle fingers, was Alice Roosevelt Longworth, daughter of President Theodore Roosevelt. Former HUAC congressman John Rankin (R-Miss.), a ghost of anticommunism past, sat next to Mrs. Joseph McCarthy. In town for their annual convention, beribbonned ladies from the Daughters of the American Revolution secured places of prominence.

The back half of the hearing room was reserved for tourists, for whom the Army-McCarthy hearings—along with the FBI Headquarters and the Bureau of Printing and Engraving—ranked as a must-see stop on the tour schedule. However, the dominant fan base in attendance was khaki-colored: the Army had packed the gallery with uniformed officers to form a visible phalanx of support for military witnesses.

Chairman Mundt began each session by cautioning spectators "to refrain from audible manifestations of approval or disapproval" at the risk of being removed from the chamber. On most days, Ray Jenkins controlled the action, cross-examining witnesses "in the dual role of Dr. Jekyll and Mr. Hyde" as he explained for the benefit of viewers, meaning that he interrogated each witness both as a prosecutor and a defense attorney. Competing with Jenkins for the

Joseph N. Welch and committee counsel Ray Jenkins in a casual moment between sessions at the Army-McCarthy hearings. (Courtesy Martin Luther King Public Library)

role of alpha male was, of course, McCarthy, who from the very first minutes of the first day of the hearings incessantly interrupted the chief counsel and his fellow senators with a parliamentary interjection that became a national catchphrase: "Point of order! Mr. Chairman, Mr. Chairman, point of order!"

Contrary to rumors, none of the participants wore makeup, nor did McCarthy wear a toupee, but all the players evinced an acute awareness of the television camera. Before each session, Jenkins recapped previous testimony "for the benefit of those who tuned in late, shall we say." Acknowledging that the testimony might get sluggish, Senator Potter reminded viewers that "we never promised that we were going to run in competition to Milton Berle; we only promised that we would ascertain the facts and let the public know the facts." When Senator Mundt ordered a statement struck from the record, Senator Jackson asked how a remark that had already been telecast could be stricken from memory. Mundt took the point and rescinded the directive. McCarthy played it both ways, making a remark for telecast, and then "striking" it from the *Congressional Record*. Thus, while accosting Secretary of the Army Stevens about the Adams chronology, he demanded, "Did you order these smear charges prepared—strike 'smear'—did you order these charges prepared?"

But if the performers in the hearing room relished the spotlight, the producers of the show were cringing at the cost of the electricity bill. In March, when the subcommittee voted unanimously to open the hearings to television, all four networks where expected to carry the proceedings live, gavel to gavel. ABC and DuMont announced commitments immediately, but a calmer look at the bottom line forced NBC and CBS to reconsider the costs of public service programming. Thus, contrary to popular memory, the Army-McCarthy hearings were not telecast on all four networks, nor were they telecast live across the nation: only ABC and DuMont telecast the full 188 hours of coverage, and only markets east of Omaha, Nebraska, received the complete live feeds.

Flush with a highly profitable daytime soap opera lineup, CBS abstained from live coverage. Calculating the cost of preempting regular programming and rebating payments to advertisers, a network executive claimed, "It's so staggering it almost floored us." CBS opted for 45-minute late-night recaps telecast from 11:30 P.M. to 12:15 A.M. The network also covered the hearings in depth on *The Morning Show* from 7:00 to 9:00 A.M., hosted by Walter Cronkite.

The withdrawal of CBS left NBC, ABC, and DuMont formally committed to cover the hearings gavel to gavel. However, on the second day (Friday, April 23), after a soporific afternoon session, NBC bailed out. The network estimated its two-day loss of revenue at $125,000. "We have a great deal to lose, including the good will of advertisers," an NBC spokesman pointed out. "After all, they pay our salaries." Henceforth NBC, like CBS, telecast nightly roundups edited from kinescopes of the daytime ABC feed, counterprogramming against CBS by scheduling its nightly recaps from 11:15 P.M. to 12:00 midnight. Commenting on NBC's decision the next Monday, Chairman Mundt declared that he had received a "deluge of telegrams" demanding that NBC continue coverage, but "any complaints that the public has to make should be directed to the broadcasting companies and not to the subcommittee."

Ambitious ABC and struggling DuMont took up the slack. Seeking to put his third-string news division on the map, ABC President Robert Kintner committed the network to complete gavel-to-gavel coverage. "As the number 3 network climbing steadily in our long-range campaign to equal or surpass the top two, we need the public's good will and we need new viewers," ABC newsman John Daly frankly admitted. "Despite the fact that ABC bore a disproportionate share of the burden of bringing the hearings to the American viewer . . . that jury was entitled to get the testimony at the moment it was being offered—not edited, not paraphrased, not summarized, and not late—but complete and instantaneous." Over thirty-six days and 188 hours, the Army-McCarthy hearings accounted for a full 42 percent of the programming time on ABC.

The decision was not a noble sacrifice for the public interest, convenience, and necessity. Unlike NBC or CBS, ABC and DuMont telecast virtually no network programming to affiliates in the 10:30 A.M.–12:30 P.M. and 2:30–4:30 P.M. time slots and therefore had none of the preemption problems that plagued the two major networks. Telecasting the hearings on a hookup of from 55 to 79 stations, ABC garnered most of the kudos for public service programming, though fading DuMont also telecast the complete hearings on ten stations.

During the two-month run, the live feed originated with WMAL-TV, the ABC affiliate in Washington, D.C. Three cameras were situated strategically about the hearing room: one at the rear of the room, facing the committee at its long table; one behind the committee table and facing the witness table and the spectators; and one at one side of the room that pivoted at various angles. Unwilling as yet to relinquish motion picture journalism to television, the newsreels also covered the hearings on film.

Forewarned by *TV Guide* that "the Mundt committee hearings may preempt regular scheduled programs," viewers heard a refrain that soon became familiar. "The ABC television network takes you now to Washington and the caucus room of the United States Senate for today's hearing of the Senate investigation of the controversy between Senator McCarthy and the Army. The complete hearings will be brought to you as a public service of the ABC network. And now here is ABC commentator Bryson Rash to set the scene."

Recapping past action and explaining the agenda for future sessions, Rash limited his off-camera commentary to exposition. ABC newsman Gunnar Back covered the hearings from the floor and wandered the caucus room freely during recesses. When the hearings adjourned for votes on the senate floor or a short break (referred to by Jenkins as a "seventh inning stretch"), Back corralled senators, witnesses, and celebrity spectators for live on-camera interviews, filling airtime, sometimes desperately, during the hiatus. Being stationed right on the floor, Back cornered the principals while their blood was still hot and sometimes got instant, snippy reactions. After Back spoke with Welch and Jenkins about G. David Schine's paltry "work product" for the McCarthy committee, Cohn berated Back on air for the "one-sided interview" and then walked off in a huff. Back shrugged and said, "that was Roy Cohn—and his opinion of the interview."

To accommodate the television coverage, the subcommittee permitted the construction of a three-tiered platform along the back wall of the hearing room for the newsreel and television cameras. The committee also juggled the seating arrangements, placing the McCarthy and Army sides right next to each other to accommodate camera coverage. (Hence Welch's angry rasp at McCarthy during a bitter face-off that "you have sat within *six feet* of me . . . ").

The two sides also alternated their seats at the table "to give each group an equal chance at full-face and profile views for the TV cameras," as *TV Guide* reported. The proximity of accused and accusers, military men and Mc-Carthyites, created a kind of video overlap, at times making it difficult to tell lawyers from clients, defendants from plaintiffs.

Also of signal importance was the superb quality of the sound recording, praised by audio technicians as "the best ever developed by TV and radio at any congressional rhubarb." For the first time in Congress, single microphones were wired to a common source, eliciting a crisp audio signal that captured the bass and treble of "Senator Joseph McCarthy's low whine, Senator Stuart Symington's growl, Senator Everett Dirksen's unctuous singsong, subcommittee Ray Jenkins's barking, and Army counsellor Joseph Welch's pixyish intonations," as *Billboard* television critic Ben Atlas heard it.

None of this came cheap: ABC estimated its production costs and lost revenue from canceled commercial programming at a then-exorbitant $500,000, the "bulk of it in renting relay facilities" to pipe the telecast to its subscribing stations. *Variety* figured that the loss of commercial revenue to NBC and CBS, had they telecast the hearings live, would have been closer to a combined total of $4,000,000.

Even so, the Army-McCarthy hearings were not a saturation television event in the modern sense. The refusal of NBC and CBS to telecast the hearings blacked out whole regions of the country from live coverage. In 1954, television was more akin to a two-lane blacktop than an information superhighway. With only a single coaxial cable stretching to the Pacific coast, and only one feed per cable, the decision by the two most powerful networks to forgo live coverage meant that the feed originating from Washington had limited space on the telecommunications highway.

With cable costs keeping ABC from relaying the hearings to Denver and points west, the coverage on the Pacific Coast was particularly sparse. In San Francisco, NBC affiliate KRON-TV broadcast the first two days of the hearings beginning at 7:30 A.M. PST, but when the network bailed so did the local station. Likewise, in Los Angeles, after the NBC blackout, viewers had to endure the technically impaired coverage on KTLA-TV, which telecast live sound from the hearings with still pictures on the screen. As the only daytime Army-McCarthy show in the city, either on television or radio, KTLA's coverage was "a smash hit" that garnered "consistently high ratings."

A few rebellious affiliate stations refused to bow to network fiat. In Houston, when NBC canceled live coverage, local NBC affiliate KPRC-TV arranged a deal with ABC for the live feed. After two weeks, however, the station announced that the "unexpected stretching out of the hearings, high coaxial cable rental costs, and disruption of regular commercial programming as well as protest from viewers over the elimination of regularly scheduled soap operas and game shows" forced a termination of coverage. "In the event the committee should subsequently find means of materially shortening the hearings, KPRC-TV will undertake efforts to reestablish coverage on a 'live' basis," the station manager promised.

By way of incentive, on May 13, Chairman Mundt announced that the subcommittee had no objection if the networks found "proper" sponsors to help defray costs. As long as the hearings were not interrupted, commercials might be inserted during the natural pauses and breaks in the inquiry. Mundt hoped, however, that "the networks will use good judgment in the types of sponsorship they secure, since these televised hearings will be going into homes and some school classrooms." The "belated permission," commented ABC newsman John Daly, "was like withholding sponsorship rights of the World Series until the third inning of the second game." Regardless, sponsors were rare, though some stations cooperated with local newspapers to underwrite the telecasts.

Despite the modest commercial subventions, a few salons worried about the majesty of Congress being sullied by the curse of commerce. (The sponsor for KTLA's coverage was the shoe polish Shinola!) "Imagine this vaudeville performance with its present considerable ham acting being used to advertise dog biscuits, mouthwash, toothpaste, refrigerators, etc.," stormed Rep. Emmanuel Celler (D-N.Y.), who introduced a bill forbidding commercial sponsorship of congressional proceedings by radio or television. *Variety* demurred: "This video show has become so bogged in detail and verbal red tape that a snappy singing beer commercial here and there would definitely raise its entertainment level."

Actually, a few commercials were sung by the committee members. McCarthy plugged the name of a Wisconsin cheese plant, but the most egregious product placement was inserted into the *Congressional Record* by Chairman Mundt, who shilled for the motion picture, *The Caine Mutiny* (1954), directed by the formerly blacklisted Hollywood Ten defendant Edward Dmytryk.[2] The not in-apt association of *The Caine Mutiny* with the Army-McCarthy hearings was engineered by Columbia Pictures, who invited the senators to a special screening of the film, based on the Herman Wouk novel about the

---

2. On April 21, 1951, Dmytryk, who had defied HUAC in 1947 and in 1950 went to jail with his Hollywood Ten comrades for contempt of Congress, testified before HUAC as a friendly witness, thus clearing himself to resume his career as a director of feature films.

court martial of a group of navel offices who relieve their paranoid captain from command. On camera, Mundt mentioned the special senatorial screening, and McCarthy himself ventured a punning reference to "the Cohn Mutiny."

Reviewing the opening acts of the Army-McCarthy hearings, critics agreed that purely in terms of dramatic punch the action paled in comparison to the well-remembered Kefauver crime hearings of 1951. Expectations that the ratings would "blow sky high every attendance record set by the Kefauver committee crime hearings" were dashed. The Army-McCarthy "speaktacular," judged *Variety*, "lacked the wallop necessary for good box office." Counseling patience, television critic Jack Gould advised senators not to worry about their comparatively modest ratings because "with any new daytime drama on TV, the first few months are always the hardest."

Gould's prediction was canny: ratings for the hearings intensified over time, sparking increases in morning television viewing 29 percent and grabbing a 68 percent share of the audience according to a Trendex survey. "Maybe Army McCarthy hearings aren't 'another Kefauver'—maybe the endless wrangling and quibbling is quite dull compared to the grilling of 'Greasy Thumb' Guzik and Frank Costello," observed *Television Digest*, "but nevertheless a substantial portion of the public is watching intently and the audience seems to be growing." In New York, the daytime television audience was 50 percent larger than normal. WMAL-TV reported a 49 percent share of the television audience in eight major cities, including Washington, D.C. Yet in terms of overall ratings, the Army-McCarthy hearings did not, and probably could not, match the numbers racked up by the Kefauver hearings. With three times as many sets in use and three hundred additional stations on the air, more video options enticed more sophisticated viewers. No longer would the blurry image of Frank Costello's hands transfix an audience.

Nonetheless, to a devout coterie of Army-McCarthy buffs, the hearings were as fiercely addictive as any soap opera. "Most noticeable in bars and restaurants in the midtown area was the silent attention which the hearings received," reported the *New York Herald Tribune*. "The normal buzz of conversation was hushed." When St. Louis station WTVI preempted coverage of the hearings to telecast a St. Louis Cardinal–Brooklyn Dodgers baseball game, 900 angry telephone calls jammed the switchboards. The Army-McCarthy hearings also beat out the ratings of another kind of horse race, the Kentucky Derby.

Cost and ratings notwithstanding, the value of the hearings as a drawing card for television offset any loss in revenue incurred from labor, equipment, airtime, and commercial buys. Though ABC and DuMont lost commercial revenue in the short run, both stations garnered prestige and public gratitude, valuable coin of the realm in the early days of television.[3] "In my memory, TV never per-formed a service which received more unsolicited evidence of appreciation of viewers," declared Ted Bergmann, managing director at DuMont. *Billboard* agreed that "the promotional value for the TV broadcasting industry is ines-timable." But of course the gavel-to-gavel coverage of the Army-McCarthy hear-ings not only promoted television but demoted the star attraction.

Climax: "Have You Left No Sense of Decency?"

The afternoon of June 9, 1954, brought the emotional climax of the Army-McCarthy hearings, the famous exchange between Welch and McCarthy over the alleged subversive background of Fred Fisher. Ignoring a prehearing agree-ment between Welch and Cohn not to broach the matter, McCarthy suggest-ed that Fisher, a lawyer at Hale and Dorr, harbored communist sympathies be-cause of his past membership in an alleged communist front group, the National Lawyers Guild.[4] Striving to control his fury while uncorking a mor-tal blow, Welch uttered an incantation that, once spoken, seemed to make the visitation that was Joseph McCarthy vanish in a puff of smoke: "Have you no sense of decency, sir, at long last? Have you left no sense of decency?" When McCarthy tried to strike back, Welch cut him off and demanded that Chair-man Mundt "call the next witness." Pausing just a beat, the hushed gallery erupted in a sustained burst of applause. The uncomprehending McCarthy, shot dead on live television, turned to Cohn and stammered, "What hap-pened?" What happened was that television, whose coverage of McCarthy's news conferences, direct addresses, and senate hearings had lent him legiti-macy and stature, had now become the stage for his downfall.

The setup for the flare-up began routinely enough. Welch had been cross-examining Roy Cohn about the McCarthy committee's visit to Army Signal Corps headquarters at Fort Monmouth, New Jersey, and the precise number of communist agents uncovered in the Department of Defense. As usual, Welch drilled in to his witness with sardonic relish and courtly élan. Cradling the

---

3. ABC was the main beneficiary. While its coverage of the Army-McCarthy hearings helped launch ABC into the network pantheon, the underfinanced and ill-managed DuMont folded in 1955.

4. Welch had agreed not to raise questions about Cohn's deferred draft status and Cohn had agreed not to bring up Fred Fisher's past membership in the Lawyers Guild. In his 1968 memoir of McCarthy, Cohn insisted, in italics, "*McCarthy approved the trade*," but "he lost his temper and blurted out the story."

Ad-libbed outburst or calculated attack?: Joseph N. Welch prepares to utter a catchphrase for the ages (June 9, 1954).

crown of his head in one hand, feigning shock at the dread prospect of so many communist agents running loose in the defense establishment, he urged Cohn "before the sun goes down" to put the FBI on the case "with extreme suddenness" and turn over the names of the alleged 130 agents to J. Edgar Hoover.

Cohn assured Welch that "Mister John Edgar Hoover" possessed the names and was better qualified than either Mr. Welch or he to assess the danger to national security.

"Then, what's all the excitement about if J. Edgar Hoover is on the job chasing down these 130 communists?" Welch asked, as a reaction shot showed Senator Symington smirking appreciatively.

The vigorous cross-examination was nothing Cohn could not handle. No novice at verbal swordplay, he seemed to enjoy honing his wits by parrying back and forth with the old pro.

McCarthy, however, was incensed by Welch's crowd-pleasing jabs at his lieutenant. He was also feeling the effects from a well-lubricated lunch break that day. Doubly off kilter, the senator then provoked Welch's withering salvo. In Mr. Welch's own law firm of Hale and Dorr, there was a "young man named Fisher . . . who has been for a number of years a member of an organization which was named, oh, years and years ago, as the legal bulwark of the Communist Party . . . "

Welch's own trivializing behavior, said McCarthy, had forced his hand. "I have hesitated bringing that up, but I have been rather bored with your phony request to Mr. Cohn here that he personally get every communist out of government before sundown." He stretched out the last phrase—"before sundown"—in a singsong nasal whine. "Therefore, we will give you the information about the young man in your own organization" whom Welch had tried to "foist" on the committee.

Chairman Mundt interjected to correct McCarthy—Welch had never named Fisher as an assistant counsel—but the senator pressed on, heedless.

Pretending to be mystified at how a lawyer so smart could be so naive about so serious a menace, McCarthy accused Welch of trying to "burlesque this hearing." Ruefully, however, McCarthy conceded that Welch was more an incorrigible ham than a fellow traveler. "While you are quite an actor, you play for a laugh, I don't think you have any conception of the danger of the Communist Party."

Welch looked down at the table for a moment before facing McCarthy. "Under the circumstances I must myself have something approaching a personal privilege," he began slowly, recalling the many points of order and personal privilege demanded by the senator. Ignoring him, McCarthy turned around to address an aide. When Welch requested his full attention, McCarthy gestured that he could talk while listening to Welch with one ear.

"No, this time, sir, I want you to listen with both [ears]," snapped Welch. Then, starting off like a kindly raconteur, finishing up like a preacher hitting the pulpit to stir a lulled congregation, the lawyer recited a morality tale for the age of suspicion.

"Until this moment, senator, I think I never really gauged your cruelty or your recklessness," Welch declared, giving a hint of what was to come. Welch recalled how he had initially invited Fred Fisher down to Washington to work on the case with his first assistant, James St. Clair.[5] At dinner on that first night together, he had asked Fisher and St. Clair if there were anything "funny in the life of either one of you that would hurt anybody in this case." Fisher admitted that he had once belonged to the Lawyers Guild, but that at present he was a member of the Young Republican's League in Newton, Massachusetts, along with the son of the governor of Massachusetts.

Anticipating that McCarthy might try to smear Fisher, Welch decided to pass over the young lawyer's services because "one of these days that [past

---

5. In a novelistic twist of televisual callback, James St. Clair was a featured player in another epochal congressional hearing, serving as President Richard Nixon's chief counsel during the House Judiciary Committee's impeachment hearings in 1974.

membership in the Lawyers Guild] will come out and go over national television and it will just hurt like the dickens."

In tones of sadness and disbelief, Welch continued his narration. "Little did I dream you could be so reckless and so cruel as to do an injury to that lad [Fisher was thirty-two years old]. It is true he is still with Hale and Dorr. It is true that he will continue to be with Hale and Dorr. It is, I regret to say, equally true that I fear he shall always bear a scar needlessly inflicted by you." As if in thought, he paused just a second. "If it were in my power to forgive you for your reckless cruelty, I would do so. I like to think I'm a gentle man. But your . . . "—he searched to find the right word—"forgiveness . . . will have to come from someone other than me."

McCarthy tried to cut in, claiming that Welch had been "baiting Mr. Cohn for hours" and repeating his charge against Fisher.

"Senator, may we not stop this?" Welch implored. "We *know* he belonged to the Lawyers Guild." Turning to Cohn, Welch addressed him point blank. "And Mr. Cohn nods his head at me. I did you, I think, no personal injury, Mr. Cohn?"

"No, sir," Cohn replied woodenly.

"I meant to do you no personal injury. And if I did I beg your pardon."

Again, McCarthy attempted to respond, but Welch would have none of it.

"Let us not assassinate this lad further, Senator. You've done enough." Then, with more anguish than anger, Welch spoke the question that, addressed to McCarthy, could only be rhetorical:

"Have you no sense of decency, sir, at long last? Have you left no sense of decency?"

"I know this hurts you, Mr. Welch," replied McCarthy.

"I'll say it hurts!" agreed Welch. "Senator, I think it hurts you too, sir."

McCarthy blustered on. "I know Mr. Cohn would rather not have me go into this—," he observed, acknowledging the discomfort of his subaltern, who throughout the exchange has been seen on camera rolling his eyes, pursing his lips, and squirming in his seat. As McCarthy rambled on, reaction shots show Welch staring straight ahead, not deigning to look at McCarthy. At one point, he catches Cohn's gaze and nods in understanding, signaling that he knows Cohn did not initiate the assault on Fisher, that Cohn had kept true to the prehearing agreement.

Mundt interrupts McCarthy again, asserting that Welch never formerly recommended Fisher as a member of the Army defense team. "Mister McCarthy," hisses Welch, dropping the senatorial honorific. "I will not discuss this further with you. You have sat within *six feet* of me and could have asked me about Fred Fisher. You have seen fit to bring it out and, if there is a god in heaven, it will do neither you nor your cause any good. I will *not* discuss it further. I will *not* ask Mr. Cohn any more witnesses.[6] You, Mr. Chairman, may, if you will, call the next witness."

There is silence for a moment, as if the dumbstruck spectators on the sidelines may now take a collective breath. A beat later, a wave of applause builds, loud and rousing, rolling through the senate caucus room. Chairman Mundt did not pound his gavel for order and did not admonish the gallery for the outburst.

Shortly after the catharsis, Welch was spotted outside the caucus room, trying to collect himself, close to tears. Surely, however, he was smiling inwardly. The actor in the lawyer must have known he had just brought the house, and the senator, down. On television, the impact of the performance was no less electric. Besides Welch's expert line readings, the sparks were generated by the dexterity of Ed Scherer, the 25-year-old ABC director helming the live feed for WMAL from a truck just outside the senate building. Three separate cameras were aimed at each of the parties to the exchange—Welch, McCarthy, and Cohn. During McCarthy's attack on Fisher and Welch's reply to McCarthy, Scherer cut away not just to the speaker and interlocutor but to Cohn, squirming in his seat, palpably pained by McCarthy's maladroit right hook, dreading the counterpunch that he knew Welch was winding up. Watching Cohn, the director sensed the imminent collision. "I kept an eye on Roy Cohn," Scherer said at the time. "Cohn has been to a lot of hearings and he usually knows who will react. When Cohn looked at someone, it was usually a good tip that the person would speak." The three-way crosscutting—from McCarthy to Welch to Cohn—typified the snap decision-making and spontaneous theatrics that made live television so nervewracking for directors and so exhilarating for viewers.

Still, if Cohn's reaction was a portrait in reflexive pain, Welch's response seemed a more calculated burst of pent-up indignation. At the time, and ever after, his soaring eloquence raised suspicions that he had somehow intuited McCarthy's upcoming misstep and rehearsed his whiplash comeback. A lawyer as crafty as he might well have anticipated that McCarthy would overreach, prepared a lethal reply, and then waited to spring the trap. Like the sermons of Bishop Sheen, Welch's lines sound too polished to be extemporaneous, the patterns of his speech scanning a bit too poetically to be unscripted. Listen again to the three-part rhythm:

> It is true he is still with Hale and Dorr.
> It is true that he will continue to be with Hale and
>   Dorr.
> It is, I regret to say, equally true that I fear he will
>   bear a scar needlessly inflicted by you.

---

6. The word "witnesses" was a rare verbal flub from Welch. He meant "questions."

But though the pacing sounds premeditated, Welch's unrehearsed remarks from earlier in the hearings confirm the perfect pitch possessed by a gifted orator-at-law. On May 28, 1954, during a break in the hearings, ABC newsman Gunnar Back conducted a live interview with Welch and Ray Jenkins. "It is clear to me that we are in something of a constitutional crisis," says Welch. "Whether or not two simple lawyers [nodding deferentially toward Jenkins]— if I may bracket you with me, sir—will have any great impact on that great crisis is more than I know." Welch then speculates in three-part harmony:

> Each of us recognizes it.
> Each of us is sure that it is a serious thing.
> And, I believe, each of us is extremely modest about
>   any ability we may have, Mr. Jenkins, in the
>   solution of that crisis.

Appreciating a master at work, Jenkins good naturedly responds, "I heartily endorse 100 percent what my learned friend Mr. Welch has said."

Rehearsed or not, even more than Edward R. Murrow's Shakespearean peroration on the "Good Tuesday" telecast of *See It Now*, the Welch riposte became audiovisual synecdoche for the slaying of the dragon of Joseph McCarthy. No sooner had the applause from the gallery died down than viewers realized an iconic moment had transpired. On ABC's *Open Hearing*, hosted by newsman John Daly and telecast on June 24, 1954, shortly after the hearings ended, commentator Bryson Rash, floor reporter Gunnar Back, and director Ed Scherer recapped the highlights of the thirty-six-day marathon. The trio offered behind-the-scenes looks at ABC's remote truck, where Scherer directed the proceedings, and discussed the technical difficulties in mounting an extended live telecast. In reviewing ABC's overview, *Variety* noted that the "topper" of the "kinescoped reprises of some of the hearings highlights" was "of course" the Welch-McCarthy exchange over Fred Fisher. Likewise, all three newsman concurred that the exchange "constituted the dramatic highlight of the series." Scherer commented that "the best shot was of Cohn. He shook his head and you could see his lips form the words 'no, no.'" Even at the time, the slashing reprimand from Welch was the indelible montage of the Army-McCarthy hearings.

Despite the third-act climax, the show sputtered on for six more days before finally closing at 6:32 P.M. on the evening of June 17, 1954. It fell to Chairman Karl Mundt to utter the curtain lines. "Now having heard more than two million words of testimony, and having heard every pertinent witness who has requested to be heard, and having heard every witness requested by any of the counsels to the entities in this dispute, the chair declares these hearings adjourned, *sine die*." Wearily, gratefully, Mundt pounded down the gavel.

Before signing off, however, ABC commentator Bryson Rash interjected, "There is one additional statistic we'd like to add to Senator Karl Mundt's statement: that the American Broadcasting Company's television network has now carried these hearings for a total of one hundred and eighty-four hours." Prophetically, television got the last word.

Denouement: Reviews and Postmortems

The Army-McCarthy hearings incited a backlash not only against Sen. Joseph R. McCarthy but against television. Opponents of televised congressional investigations dusted off the old metaphors: "circus atmosphere," "monkey show" "vaudeville act," "television carnival." Sen. Patrick McCarran (D-Nev.) called the Army-McCarthy hearings "a spectacle unparalleled in history" that brought "ridicule" and "a serious loss of prestige on the Senate." Condemning the "tawdry, tedious, and shameful hearings," Sen. Thomas C. Hennings Jr. (D-Mo.) proclaimed that senate business must not staged for "the edification of the television audience" nor "to compete with *John's Other Wife* or *Suspense* or *Dragnet*."

Appropriately, the first formal occasion for senators to express their newly camera-shy attitude was McCarthy-related. In June 1954, with McCarthy's cry of "Point of order!" still echoing from Senate Caucus Room 318, the Senate Rules Committee chaired by Sen. William Jenner (R-Ind.) conducted congressional hearings on how congressional hearings could be improved in the wake of the Army-McCarthy debacle. They were not televised.

Nor was television permitted to cover the next newsworthy round of senate business, the hearings to censure McCarthy. After the Army-McCarthy hearings, McCarthy's colleagues finally decided that he was bringing discredit upon the chamber. On September 27, 1954, a bipartisan committee chaired by Sen. Arthur V. Watkins (R-Utah) voted to recommend his censure. On December 2, 1954, by a vote of 67–22, the full senate voted to condemn, not censure him, a technical but not political victory for McCarthy.

The Watkins committee's ban on television coverage prompted CBS President Frank Stanton to deliver an editorial on behalf of the networks, an unprecedented gesture by a broadcasting executive. On August 26, 1954, Stanton appeared on *Douglas Edwards with the News* to urge Congress to give radio and television equal access with the print press in covering political hearings. The decision to shut out television "turns its back on the contributions which electronic journalism can make," Stanton argued. "It commands, 'Thou shalt not hear or see.' This is a drastic prohibition." Forgetting CBS's own refusal to telecast the Army-McCarthy hearings live, he lectured Congress that "those

A wounded demagogue: in the wake of the Army-McCarthy hearings, and after hospitalization for a sore elbow, Senator McCarthy arrives at the U.S. Senate to attend a special session to consider his censure (November 29, 1954).

who support [the ban] have a heavy burden in trying to establish the evils of radio and television coverage are so great that they justify keeping you from seeing your government in action. They have failed to establish that there are such evils."

Failed or not, Congress kept the lights out. Having proven its political power, television invited political containment. In the aftermath of the hearings, the Senate and the House alike would close their doors to the medium, fearful of a force liable to career out of control.[7] "Politicians realize that they

---

7. The next round of congressional inquiries to receive extensive live television coverage would be the Senate and House investigations into President Nixon's role in the Watergate scandal in 1973–74 and the House impeachment proceedings in 1974. However, between 1957 and 1963, the Senate Select Committee on Improper Activities in the Labor and Management Field opened up its hearings to television. Chaired by Sen. John L. McClellan and with Robert F. Kennedy serving as chief counsel from 1957 to 1959, the "rackets committee" received scattershot coverage during daytime hours when a suitably videogenic gangster or corrupt union official testified. Wary of the colorful language of some of the witnesses, the networks usually telecast these sessions on videotaped delay.

are all being scorched, some more and some less, by the bright lights in which they are caught," noted Walter Lippmann. "One thing has been definitely established by the Army McCarthy show," predicted Walter Winchell, "no other probes will get teevy coverage unless the public demand is too big to snub."

In 1956, still cut out of Congress, ABC's John Daly lambasted the selectively camera-shy politicians at a meeting of the National Association of Radio and Television Broadcasters. "It may be that Congressional leaders are penalizing us for fear their members will misbehave and disgrace them," Daly charged. "Yet they want to use us when it suits their convenience. Particularly around election time, when they want to keep their jobs, they're only too happy to preen for the cameras and persuade the folks back home that they'll do a whale of a job for them in Washington." Television had passed up many opportunities to cover congressional hearings, preferring profits to public service, but the point was prerogative: the networks wanted the right to decide *not* to cover hearings.

Of course, the most cautionary proof of the lethal rays from television was McCarthy. In January 1954, before Murrow's "Good Tuesday" telecast, before the Army-McCarthy hearings, the Gallup Poll gauged McCarthy's popularity with the American public at 50 percent favorable, 29 percent unfavorable, and 21 percent with no opinion. Immediately after the conclusion of the Army-McCarthy hearings, Gallup took another poll, utilizing a new survey method that measured not just opinion but the intensity of opinion: 45 percent voiced an unfavorable opinion of McCarthy, 34 percent expressed a favorable impression, and the same bovine 21 percent still held no opinion. American opinion on the moral stakes in the Cold War had not changed, but opinion on McCarthy had.

Attitudes about television and demagoguery had also congealed into a consensus. "Years ago, when television was in swaddling clothes," noted television critic John Crosby, "this issue was debated on purely theoretical grounds, much as Einstein arrived at his theories by pure mathematics. Television, it was argued, was God's gift to the demagogue. Or, on the other hand, television would murder the demagogue because its pitiless eye would unmask his phoniness." After the hearings, the case was settled: television had undone the demagogue McCarthy.

As if to confirm the kill, editorialists intensified their invective and former allies backed away. "My acquaintance with Senator McCarthy is not regarded by either of us as intimate," insisted FCC commissioner John Doerfer in the post-Army-McCarthy summer of 1954. "My reputation for independence of judgment is evidenced by the fact that at no time, since assuming office, has Senator McCarthy conferred with me directly or indirectly regarding any matter before this Commission." Where it had once been perilous to offend McCarthy, it was now poisonous to befriend him.

Perhaps the best barometer of McCarthy's deflated status was the rising level of ridicule heaped upon him throughout the popular media. Comedians honed impressions and worked up gags. *Mad* proved it was not just a magazine for idiots by publishing a comic-strip satire lampooning the senator. Song satirists Stan Freeberg and Dawes Butler recorded a tune called "Point of Order," a parody published in script form "so that anyone desiring to present a skit duplicating the platter will have the complete material." "Long considered too hot and too controversial, takeoffs of the junior senator from Wisconsin are now getting laughs in niteries and elsewhere," *Variety* noted midpoint in the hearings. "Satire emanates from the fact that mention of 'Point of Order!' has become funny and so has the droning 'Mr. Chairman . . . Mr. Chairman . . . Mr. Chairman . . . '" On television too, McCarthy's plunge from gargoyle to laughingstock was apparent in snide jokes and broad lampoons. CBS's *The Red Skelton Show* featured a satire of Prince Valiant with a roundtable scene that was a "perfect burlesque of the Senator."

The sharpest stab at McCarthy was a radio satire entitled *The Investigator*, aired by the Canadian Broadcasting Company on May 30, 1954, and written by the blacklisted and deported Canadian author Reuben Ship. The fanciful drama told the story of an unnamed investigator (played by John Drainie, doing a spot-on McCarthy imitation) who dies in an airplane crash and, while awaiting judgment at heaven's gate, usurps control of the tribunal. Along with other great investigators from history such as Torquemada of the Spanish Inquisition and Cotton Mather of the Salem Witch Trials, he presides over the Permanent Investigating Committee on Permanent Entry and begins ferreting out controversial personalities such as Socrates, John Milton, and Thomas Jefferson. Failing the loyalty test, all are consigned for punishment "Down There."

As on earth, the investigator overreaches by impugning the integrity of a higher authority: not Eisenhower or Hoover, but God. Banished to hell, he appears doomed until the devil refuses him entry and transports him back to earth.

Somehow an audiotape of *The Investigator* began circulating stateside and within days bootleg record versions sprang up. With no label and no credits, the records were bought under the counter and played surreptitiously. The vaguely subversive activities thrilled cliques of anti-McCarthy listeners with what Jack Gould called "the most hilarious and controversial satire ever done on the controversial Senator from Wisconsin." When the record was formally issued at the end of 1954, *The Investigator* had become more than an underground hit. A gleeful President Eisenhower reportedly played it at cabinet meetings.

More strikingly, McCarthy was insulted to his face on the stage he had once commanded, the news forum show. Appearing on *Meet the Press* on October 3, 1954, one week after a Senate subcommittee had voted unanimously to censure him, the senator looks like a wounded animal, cornered and bloody but still capable of a vicious outburst. The atmosphere reflects his demotion in status: the reporters are cautious but bemused, just this side of contemptuous.

In his heyday, McCarthy's idea of humor was the faux Freudian slip, the accidentally-on-purpose slander, as when he referred to "Alger . . . I mean Adlai" Stevenson to link one egghead to another, the Democratic candidate for the presidency with the convicted perjurer and communist spy, Alger Hiss. Murrow had played the clip to withering effect on *See It Now*.

On *Meet the Press*, the senator stammered into an authentic Freudian slip. Responding to a question, McCarthy misspeaks by referring to a "*General* Peress," upgrading the rank of the Army dentist whose controversial promotion had helped set the Army on a collision course with McCarthy. The panel is puzzled for a few seconds. "You mean *Major* Peress," they correct him, to nervous laughter all around as McCarthy hastily explains he was thinking of *General* Zwicker, the officer who had allegedly coddled Peress. In the background, off camera, a gleeful dig from the chuckling *Newsweek* reporter John Madigan is clearly audible: "You promoted him!"

TEN

PIXIES

Homosexuality, Anticommunism, and Television

On April 30, 1954, a risqué exchange provoked gales of laughter from the un-ruly spectators at the Army-McCarthy hearings. While examining a doctored photograph offered into evidence by the McCarthy staff, attorney Joseph N. Welch sardonically suggested that perhaps "pixies" were the culprits responsi-ble for the alterations. McCarthy snidely asked Welch to define "pixie" be-cause "I think [you] might be an expert on that." "A pixie," the lawyer shot back, eying McCarthy's side of the table, "is a close relative of a fairy."

The prickly banter made oblique reference to an unspoken suspicion hov-ering over the official charges and countercharges. To wit: that a homosexual liaison between Roy M. Cohn and G. David Schine spurred Cohn's obsession with Schine's welfare in uniform. Whether the attraction was consummated or platonic, neither the menace of communism nor the excesses of anticom-munism but the all-too-human thrall to eros triggered the downfall of Joseph R. McCarthy.

From the present perspective, when sexuality of every stripe is not just a fit but an incessant topic for television, when sitcoms and soap operas showcase gay characters and talk shows chatter with clinical precision about sexual ori-entations of gymnastic variety, the discretion and ignorance over matters of nonmissionary-position sexuality in America in the 1950s may be hard to credit. The very notion of homosexuality—so quick to bubble to the surface in any discussion of close male friendships today—was a thought suppressed from conscious awareness and explicit utterance on television. Forbidden by name by the Hollywood Production Code, the word *fairy* had not heretofore been heard from a screen in a context outside the never-never land of Walt Disney's *Peter Pan* (1953). In public perception and popular culture, virile commingling between adult males was more apt to be considered a normal refuge from nagging females than an aberrant desire for same-sex contact.

At the same time, however, a gender contract carved in stone was cracking around the edges. The integrity of the male and female vessels was being

The pixie picture: the controversial photograph of Pvt. G. David Schine with Secretary of the Army Robert T. Stevens is brandished by Army attorney Joseph N. Welch (*top*) and examined by Senator McCarthy (*bottom*). Roy M. Cohn sits at McCarthy's left. The young man wearing glasses and glaring at Cohn is Robert F. Kennedy. (Courtesy of the Martin Luther King Public Library)

breached by medical science (in the case of the pioneering transsexual Christine Jorgensen), social science (in the reports of the notorious sex researcher Alfred Kinsey), and, not too far under the surface, in television programming. Even without a magnifying glass, pixies, or their close relatives, seem to be flitting all over the airwaves.

The transsexual Christine Jorgensen was the most publicized personification of the upending of the divine order. The inspiration for Z-movie director Ed Wood Jr.'s cri de coeur *Glen or Glenda* (1953), Jorgensen was a 26-year-old Army veteran born George W. Jorgensen who traveled to Denmark for surgical modification to become female. In December 1952, news of the miracle of science reached stateside. "Ex-GI Becomes Blonde Beauty!" shrieked the headline in the *New York Daily News*. "Nature made a mistake," the new Miss Jorgensen explained to the folks back home, "and now I am your daughter."

On February 12, 1953, when Jorgensen returned from Copenhagen, thousands of curious onlookers packed the terminals of New York's Idlewild (now John F. Kennedy) Airport. NBC filmed the scene for *The Camel News Caravan*, but network censors vetoed the clips until newsmen concocted a journalistic peg to legitimize the story: the wild melee greeting Jorgensen was contrasted with the tepid reception accorded former presidential candidate Adlai Stevenson the previous day. Dressed in a nutria coat and draping a mink cape over one arm, Jorgensen made clear that she had defected only from gender not country. "I'm happy to be home," she bubbled. "What American woman wouldn't be?"

Across the media, whether in variety shows, nightclub acts, or gossip columns, Jorgensen's very name provoked smirks and titters. "Just count the number of ribs," suggested Walter Winchell. "That'll settle it." Yet the punch lines tickled more than the funny bone. In breaking the gender barrier, Jorgensen was a reproach not just to the immutability of sexual identity but to the hierarchy of preference. A *he* had rejected all-American manhood to become a *she*. Even at the time, the insistent, overripe jokes seemed to protest too much. Weary of the routine, *Hollywood Reporter* columnist Dan Jenkins pleaded, "Note to all radio and TV comedians, both amateur and professional: please, for everybody's sake including your own, no more gags about Christine Jorgensen. It wasn't funny to begin with and it's even less funny now."

Though Danish in derivation, Jorgensen reborn was a pure product of Cold War America in her instinct for the compensations of instant celebrity. To cash in on her notoriety, she recorded a tell-all album entitled *Christine Jorgensen Reveals* ("Unquestionably the most publicized, controversial, and interesting personality of this generation!") and put together a nightclub act. The transition from vaudeo to video was inevitable.

On April 5, 1953, Jorgensen unveiled herself on DuMont's *Arthur Murray Party* to make an appeal for the Damon Runyon Cancer Fund. Hostess Kathryn

Gender defector: pioneer transsexual and Cold War punch line Christine Jorgensen arrives in New York (February 12, 1953). (Courtesy Photofest)

Murray provided a sympathetic introduction, and a straight-faced *Variety* employed the correct pronouns. "Her voice is a bit deep, but perhaps not more so than some born-to-the-sex femmes. Her elaborate gown did not seem to fall too gracefully upon her; perhaps she needs more experience in accoutrements." That experience, however, would be acquired away from television cameras. Always a double-edged novelty for the queasy 1950s, the sensation that was Christine Jorgensen faded when further medical investigation revealed that the surgery in Denmark wrought not a genital transition but an organic elimination.

The only sexually charged name more risible than that of Christine Jorgensen belonged to Dr. Alfred C. Kinsey, the renowned sex researcher. In 1948, Kinsey's taboo-breaking *Sexual Behavior in the Human Male* gave the imprimatur of science to what had heretofore been confined to locker rooms: public discourse about private intercourse. On September 14, 1953, the publication of *Sexual Behavior in the Human Female*, the hotly desired distaff sequel, provided a windfall of semiblue material for television comics. Choosing a resonant verb, the *New Republic* observed that "forty years ago any writer who even ventured to suggest such discussion would have been instantly dismissed and permanently blacklisted."

Network censors kept a sharp ear out for incidents of Kinsey-inspired humor that crossed the lines laid down in the Television Code. Reporting on the delicate handling of the Kinsey Report, *Variety* noted that network censors "agree that they would prefer not to have the book 'gagged up' in any way even by so much as a leer accompanied by voice." The demure policy at CBS went so far as to forbid the word *sexual* in advertising and entertainment programming, though the adjective might sneak by in news reports. The preferred sex-deprived nomenclature on all networks was "Kinsey Report." No matter: to mouth "Kinsey" was to muster hilarity. As bestsellers more thumbed than read, the two Kinsey Reports and the author echo as code words for salaciousness throughout the 1950s, the very mention of the brand name a surefire laugh line and a way to permissibly probe a verboten area.

Even beyond the trip-wire surnames of Jorgensen and Kinsey, the prim consensus medium of television often seems an orgy of sexual transgression, cross-dressing, and gender confusion. In the weekly drag routines that dolled up Milton Berle in wigs, dresses, and makeup; in the hysterical whine and clinging physicality of Jerry Lewis, the girlish half of the most successful comedy duo of the 1950s; and in the loose-in-the-loafer sashay and prissy pose of Jack Benny, to look back on the closeted subtext of Cold War television is to behold a raging text.

Red Fades to Pink

In 1954, scanning the crowd at a packed concert in Madison Square Garden, a bemused music critic for *Billboard* turned rhapsodic. "There wasn't a response that didn't shake the rafters. The audience seemed to be awed rather than electrified. There was a feeling of adoration almost religious in its impact."

The object of reverence was not Frank Sinatra, who hadn't inspired that kind of excitement since World War II, nor Johnnie Ray, the "Cry" baby whose hit song the previous year presaged the rock 'n' roll explosion, nor Elvis Presley, who was still driving a truck in Memphis, Tennessee. It was Wladzu Valentino Liberace, then basking in the white-hot glow of video-fueled celebrity: Liberace, who to all appearances, then and now, was wildly, exuberantly homosexual.

The Liberace story begins not in Las Vegas but in Milwaukee, Wisconsin, where the Polish-American piano prodigy honed his craft and perfected his shtick. After an apprenticeship on local television in Los Angeles, he shot to nationwide fame on the syndicated series *The Liberace Show* (1953–1955).

The "telepianistic marvel": Liberace, the "first genuine matinee idol" of the small screen.

Flaunting flamboyant (for the time) outfits, wavy locks, and rococo cande-
labras atop his Steinway, he performed a middlebrow repertory of accessible
classical pieces and classed-up popular songs. However, it was his patter between tunes—when he lisped adoration for his mother and cooed affection-
ately at the smitten matrons who comprised his fan base—that defined the act.
Lauded as "TV's first genuine matinee idol," "currently the greatest single
draw in the entertainment world," and the "telepianistic marvel," Liberace
was the only true musical and media sensation to pulsate in the 1950s and
thereafter without a rock-and-roll heart.

    If Christine Jorgensen was a freak of nature, and Berle, Lewis, and Benny
were comedians playacting at effeminacy, Liberace was a harlequin poised at
the outer edges of sexual acceptability. Clearly he was what he was but he
could not be seen, or at least named, for what he was. Sometimes the anomaly
of a mature man, without wife and children, surfaced as an odd absence during his show. Just as popular Jewish comedians with weekly television shows
needed to shanghai the spawn of gentile friends for their Christmas shows,
Liberace needed to borrow a family from his brother George on his Christmas

show. "When Will Liberace Marry?" asked a cover story in *TV Guide*, as if this puffy mama's boy were the most eligible of bachelors.

Rather than turn a blind eye, the press winked. "Liberace's secretary buzzed him and said 'Mr. Kinsey's on the phone,'" smirked the *Hollywood Reporter*. "After turning pale, Liberace answered the phone and it was [the publicist] Freddie Kimzey." In 1954 a syndicated series entitled "Secrets of Liberace," ran on front pages of newspapers across the nation with thinly veiled references to the pianist's impaired masculinity, including the gendered flashpoint that Liberace, as a young boy, liked to—sew.

Most suspicious was Liberace's intense devotion to his mother. "The sharpshooters have often wondered aloud why Liberace has never married, figuring him to be about as eligible as it's possible for a man to be," speculated *TV Guide*, aiming a bullet of its own. "The fact of the matter is that Liberace has come very close to getting married. The other fact of the matter, according to a close associate, is that he will never marry so long as his mother is still alive." In the Freudian-filtered, Kinsey-surveyed 1950s, Americans knew what *that* meant.

"There is much discussion about Liberace's devotion to his mother," John Jacobs, Liberace's lawyer and business manager, responded in defense. "He is accused of 'Momism,' a term invented by the notorious woman-hater Philip Wylie.[1] The term is used almost as an expletive like communism or Nazism. It is given a sinister connotation."

Though Jacobs omitted McCarthyism from his list of sinister isms, his instinctive conflation of politics and gender expressed the prevalent view of homosexuality as doubly beyond the pale. In the cultural and constitutional law of the land, the link between homosexuality and communism—of perversion and subversion, red-baiting and fag-baiting—was overt. Like domestic communists, homosexuals met in secret cells, possessed a preternatural ability to detect one another, and threatened the moral fiber of the nation. "The homosexual tends to surround himself with other homosexuals, not only in his social life but in his business life," declared a *Report on Employment of Homosexuals and Other Sex Perverts in Government* issued by the Senate Permanent Subcommittee on Investigations in 1950. "Eminent psychiatrists have informed the subcommittee that the homosexual is likely to seek his own kind because the pressures of society are such that he feels uncomfortable unless he

---

1. Philip Wylie was the author of *A Generation of Vipers*, published in 1946, a widely read screed decrying, among other distressing postwar trends, the feminization of the red-blooded American male who was unmanned by doting matriarchs, a phenomenon he dubbed "Momism."

is with his own kind. . . . Under these circumstances if a homosexual attains a position in government where he can influence the hiring of personnel, it is almost inevitable that he will attempt to place other homosexuals in government jobs."

As a potential threat to national security, however, a homosexual was more likely to be considered a "security risk" than a "loyalty risk," a distinction crucial to the calculus of Cold War patriotism. A loyalty risk expressed anti-American or pro-communist beliefs or joined the Communist Party USA or an alleged "front" group. Such sentiments or affiliations justified the termination of employment from sensitive government jobs and surveillance by government agents. By contrast, a security risk was an individual who, although not anti-American or pro-communist in opinion or association, was subject to blackmail because of personal habits or affiliations. An alcoholic, an immigrant with relatives in Eastern Europe, or a homosexual might be unquestionably loyal to the United States but as a potential target of pressure from communist agents would be unfit for sensitive positions in government or private industry.

The bipolar distinction between loyalty and security, originally established under President Truman in 1947, was recalibrated by President Eisenhower with Executive Order 10450, issued on April 27, 1953. Henceforth, security rather than loyalty would be the decisive standard. "It is important to realize that many loyal Americans, by reason of instability, alcoholism, homosexuality, or previous tendency to associate with Communist-front groups are unintentional security risks," Eisenhower explained in his memoirs. "In some instances, because of moral lapses, they become subjected to the threat of blackmail by enemy agents."

Obviously, the regulations promulgated under the Truman and Eisenhower administrations conflated the essence of patriotism with the habits of personal life. Like the distinctions between loyalty and security, the differences between communist activity and homosexual practice tended to commingle. No wonder red fades to pink in so much of the ideological color scheme of Cold War America.

In critical commentary and news reports, in film and television, the rhetoric of communist aberration slips smoothly into the language of sexual deviance. "No charge can be leveled against any performer more damaging, career-wise, than the charge of being, having been, or tending to be a follower of Communist party fronts," *Variety* commented in 1954. "By contrast, it would hardly ruffle anyone's feathers to be branded a psycho, homo, or wino." In *Tea and Sympathy* (1956), Hollywood's first veiled treatment of homosexuality, a crew of manly swimmers takes a magazine test to determine their "masculinity quotient." Instinctively, a joker blurts out a congressional catchphrase: "I refuse to answer on grounds that it may tend to incriminate me."

The most famous homosexually charged, communist-affiliated Cold War couple was Alger Hiss and Whittaker Chambers. In 1948, when Chambers accused Hiss of engaging in espionage for the Soviet Union in the 1930s, Hiss and his defenders rallied by characterizing Chambers's accusations as the vengeful retaliation of a jilted homosexual cruiser. In 1954, *New York Post* editor James Wechsler referred elliptically to the tactic and contemptuously to the liberals who employed it. "The spread of a loathsome whispering campaign," wrote Wechsler, "[was] encouraged with peculiarly ill grace by men who were then engaged in decrying the phenomenon of character assassination in other areas of American life."

One legacy of the Hiss-Chambers contretemps was that Hiss's former bureaucratic berth, the State Department, was painted as a seething hotbed of homo-communist activity, an enclave of effete patricians by day doubling as perverted espionage agents by night. In Leo McCarey's anticommunist melodrama *My Son John* (1952), actor Robert Walker portrays the title subversive as a mincing mama's boy. Fresh from his homoerotic turn as the murderer in Alfred Hitchcock's *Strangers on a Train* (1951), Walker plays a treasonous State Department functionary whose inflections and gestures exude an aberrant sexuality befitting his subversive agenda. Likewise, in *I Led 3 Lives* the Communist Party cell leaders encountered on a weekly basis by triple agent Herbert A. Philbrick tend to be prissy intellectuals who wilt before the virile Americanism of actor Richard Carlson while the female comrades tend to be lesbian-coded spinsters immune to his masculine magnetism.

Naturally, the preeminent monitor of subversive activities discerned a logical correlation between sexual and ideological deviations. "One reason why sex deviates are considered security risks is that they are subject to blackmail," Sen. Joseph McCarthy declared in *McCarthyism: The Fight for America*, a thin volume published in 1952. "It is a known fact that espionage agents often have been successful in extorting information from them by threatening to expose their abnormal habits." In 1954 the cultural critic Leslie Fiedler connected the dots. "McCarthy's constant sneering references to 'State Department perverts' are not explained by his official contention that such unfortunates are subject to blackmail, but represent his sure sense of the only other unforgivable sin besides being a communist." Or better: to link the two sinners arm in arm.

Mindful of the Television Code, news shows insinuated the linkage between communism and homosexuality mainly by way of between-the-lines shadings. On *Meet the Press*, telecast on December 13, 1953, soon after President Eisenhower had fired 1,427 government employees under the authority of Executive Order 10450, a suggestive dialogue occurred between Senator McCarthy and *Newsweek* reporter John Madigan.

Choosing his words carefully, Madigan inquired of McCarthy, "Do you know how many of those [1,427 fired employees] were actually loyalty risks and how much involved human frailty?"

McCarthy shuffled somewhat. "The number who were discharged on the grounds of communist convictions is extremely high . . . it varies . . . but it's extremely high. You take those discharged for communist connections and perversion, add the two together, it runs over 90 percent."

"Ninety percent for what?" injected *Meet the Press* cohost Lawrence Spivak.

"Ninety percent of the total of 1,427."

Spivak pressed on. "Ninety percent for perversion and 90 percent for loyalty?"

"The combination of communist activities and perversion?"

"Yeh," Spivak replied patiently. "But what part of that is communist activity? Do you know?"

"I couldn't break that down for you, Larry."

Madigan interjected, "Do you think they should be made public by the administration as protection against those that maybe—were just—had bad companions?"

McCarthy: "Do you mean should the administration tell who was discharged because he had bad companions—"

Madigan completed the thought: "—and those that were loyalty risks because of treasonable potentiality?"

"I doubt that anything would be gained by that," McCarthy finally responded.

Yet on McCarthy's own subcommittee served two men, in very sensitive positions, who well fit the definition of security risks. Talk, tabloids, and television expressed the thought with an explicitness appropriate to the codes of each medium.

Airing the Cohn-Schine Affair

Like Alger Hiss and Whittaker Chambers, Roy M. Cohn and G. David Schine were an odd couple: Schine, the golden boy, laid-back and intellectually lazy, a son of privilege, content to coast on his lucky lineage; Cohn, the dark and intense overachiever, born to cutthroat politics and bent on bettering the old man. Watching Cohn during the McCarthy committee's Voice of America hearings, Marya Mannes saw "a study in corrupt precocity." If nothing else, Cohn's moondog devotion to Schine exposed a human vulnerability otherwise hidden from view. In 1952 the 24-year-old Schine bestirred himself to compose a six-page pamphlet entitled *Definition of Communism*, copies of which were placed in every room of his father's hotel chain. The pamphlet, or more likely its author, caught Cohn's eye, and on February 6, 1953, Schine began work as the sole unpaid consultant for the McCarthy committee.

Cohn and Schine were first linked in tandem in April 1953 during a highly publicized tour of European offices of the United States Information Service. For two and a half weeks, the duo descended on overseas libraries, held boisterous press conferences, and in general behaved like boorish innocents abroad. Lambasted by the media on both sides of the Atlantic, Cohn and Schine were derided as "Laurel and Hardy" and "Abbott and Costello," but the label that stuck was bestowed by Theodore Kaghan, a State Department official in Germany, who dubbed them "junketeering gumshoes." (When Cohn retaliated by accusing Kaghan of communist sympathies for a play written twenty years earlier, Kaghan was forced to resign his post.)

The shoulder-to-shoulder intimacies of the two single young men in their twenties did not go unnoticed by McCarthy's enemies. Foremost among them was investigative journalist Drew Pearson, who vented his insinuations in "The Washington Merry-Go-Round," his syndicated column for the *Washington Post*. "The two McCarthy gumshoes seemed unusually preoccupied with investigating alleged homosexuals, including one very prominent United States official," Pearson reported. "The pair also made a show of registering for separate hotel rooms, remarking loudly that they didn't work for the State Department." Smirking, Pearson described Schine as a "handsome, haughty 25-year-old kid with a dreamy look in his eye, and who sometimes slaps Cohn around as if they were dormitory roommates."

A more sympathetic reporter overcompensated by portraying Cohn and Schine as dashing and attractive ladies' men-about-town. Both in his syndicated column and on his ABC television show, Walter Winchell mentioned the pair, or Cohn singly, squiring about a beautiful socialite or would-be actress to the Stork Club. (The alleged heterosexual prowess of G. David Schine was broached on the first day of the Army-McCarthy hearings by Robert T. Stevens, the straight-laced Secretary of the Army. Stevens testified that Cohn had once phoned him to obtain a weekend pass to New York for Schine "perhaps for the purpose of taking care of Dave's girlfriend." A reaction shot to McCarthy's side of the table shows the senator cracking up, followed a beat later by Cohn and the gallery.)

On November 10, 1953, the United States Army broke up the curious partnership of Cohn and Schine—whereupon, by all accounts except his own, Roy Cohn began to act slightly unhinged. Repeatedly, obsessively, he intervened to obtain special privileges for Schine: release from KP duty, weekend passes upon demand, and the right to wear buckled shoes instead of the regulation laced military shoes. After five months of placating Cohn and cushioning Schine, the Army released its incriminating record of Cohn's flood of phone calls badgering Army officials on Schine's behalf. Immediately, and "without firing a shot in anger," G. David Schine became "America's most public private."

On March 14, 1954, Cohn faced a quartet of reporters on NBC's *Meet the Press* to address what a member of the panel referred to as Cohn's "extravagant concern for your friend Dave Schine." Prefiguring his strategy in the upcoming Army-McCarthy hearings, Cohn countercharged that the Army had offered to let him expose a homosexual ring on an Air Force base if Cohn would "get off the Army's back" about security failings at Fort Monmouth, New Jersey. Cohn alleged that "a specific proposal was made to us [by Army counselor John G. Adams] that we go after an Air Force base wherein, Mr. Adams told us, that there were a number of sex deviates and that that would make excellent hearings for us."

The *Meet the Press* panel also questioned Cohn's strangely close relationship to another member of the McCarthy committee—Senator McCarthy. After all, Cohn's recklessness had endangered McCarthy in a way McCarthy's own recklessness never had. For McCarthy, the expedient course would have been to deny prior knowledge of Cohn's interventions, condemn his hotheaded subordinate, and fire him. McCarthy could credibly claim that his own role in the whole fandango was tangential. In fact, from the moment Schine joined the subcommittee as an unpaid staffer, Cohn's doe-eyed doting had tested McCarthy's patience. "Roy thinks that Dave ought to be a general and operate from a penthouse at the Waldorf Astoria," the senator told Secretary of the Army Stevens. And later: "[Schine's induction] was one of the few things I have seen [Cohn] completely unreasonable about."

McCarthy's stubborn willingness to stand by his man raised suspicions that the relation between the senator and his chief counsel was not merely professional. On *Meet the Press*, Mrs. Mae Craig, a feisty reporter for the *Press Herald* of Portland, Maine, pointedly asked Cohn about demands by Sen. Ralph Flanders (R-Ver.) for an investigation "to find out whether you have any hold on Senator McCarthy which would induce him to keep you on." Cohn bristled and shot back, "I have no other hold on Senator McCarthy and I resent the suggestion." Cohn explained the senator's loyalty as simple reciprocity. "No chairman ever had a more loyal staff than Senator McCarthy has on that committee and I think no staff ever had a more loyal chairman than we have in Senator McCarthy."

But if television news shows needed to be circumspect, the wide-open microphone of the U.S. Senate offered protection from civil lawsuits and equal time provisions. On June 1, 1954, Senator Flanders delivered his third anti-McCarthy speech in three months. Calling for an investigation of the "personal relationship" between Cohn, Schine, and McCarthy, Flanders asked why

The odd couple: a cozy two-shot of Roy M. Cohn and G. David Schine, from the cover of *Time* magazine (March 23, 1954). (Courtesy Time-Life)

Cohn "seems to have an almost *passionate*"—he caressed the word—"anxiety to retain Schine as a staff collaborator." Flanders found McCarthy's loyalty to Cohn equally odd. "Does the assistant have some hold on the Senator?" he wondered.

The cloakroom gossip was loud enough to filter into *Rave*, a monthly scandal magazine sold for 25 cents. Billing itself, contra *Mad* magazine, as "the magazine that's not for idiots," *Rave* was a ripe version of that peculiar 1950s newsstand genre, the scandal sheet. The most notorious example is *Confidential* magazine, which specialized in innuendoes about the sex lives of the stars, such as Liberace's penchant for the companionship of husky young men and Lizbeth Scott's lesbian barhopping. Branching out in June 1954, *Rave* snubbed

Hollywood for Washington with an article entitled "The Secret Lives of Joe McCarthy" by Hank Greenspun, editor and publisher of the *Las Vegas Sun*, where the piece had originally appeared that February. Greenspun implied— actually asserted—that McCarthy was, if not a card-carrying homosexual, then at least a fellow traveler. "The plain unvarnished truth is that McCarthy, judged by the very standards by which he judges others, is a security risk on the grounds of homosexual associations," charged Greenspun.

In launching a series of charges that could only be called McCarthyite, Drew Pearson, Senator Flanders, and Hank Greenspun all took a devilish pleasure in turning the senator's modus operandi back at him. As James Wechsler noted, anti-McCarthyites felt no qualms about smearing Mc-Carthyites with a brush of a different color. Years later, Cohn pointed out that "if Senator McCarthy had said or implied something like this without any basis in fact, he would have been pilloried by the same liberals who propped up Flanders to do their below-the-belt dirty work."

Whether below the belt or under the radar, the sexual subtext hung thick in the air during the Army-McCarthy hearings. Cohn's countercharge that Adams had tried to entice him with revelations about a coven of homosexuality at an unnamed Air Force base even inspired some lighthearted byplay. In mock defense of the honor of their home states, members of the subcommittee each sought assurance from an Army witness that the alleged homosexual ring was definitely *not* located in Tennessee, or Arkansas, or South Dakota.

Yet nervous jocularity did not always keep the heavy-handed leitmotiv under wraps. After Welch unleashed his "pixie" zinger, a reaction shot shows McCarthy grinning, almost in appreciation, whereas the stricken Cohn looks as if hit in the solar plexus. Gloated the NAACP's Walter White: "If you saw [Cohn] when McCarthy made one of his worst tactical blunders—when he asked Army counsel Joseph N. Welch to define 'pixie' and received a devastating answer that 'a pixie is a close relative of a fairy'—it looked as if Cohn was either going to faint or drop from sight under the table at which he was sitting."

On May 28, 1954, another uneasy moment for Roy Cohn occurred when committee counsel Jenkins inquired into the circumstances surrounding a breakfast at Schine's suite at the Waldorf Towers.

"Had you spent the night there?" asks Jenkins.

"Had *I* spent the night there?" responds a flustered Cohn. "No, sir."

"You were there for breakfast."

"I spent the night at my own home," interjects Cohn hastily.

"Well, Mr. Cohn," drawls Jenkins, "you and this boy Dave Schine as a matter of fact now were almost constant companions as good, warm personal friends are, weren't you? Now that's the truth about it, isn't it?"

"A close relative of a fairy": Senator McCarthy smiles and Roy Cohn blanches at Joseph N. Welch's insinuation at the Army-McCarthy hearings (April 30, 1954).

Regaining his balance, Cohn replies, "I am pleased to say that the truth is we were and we are good friends. He is one of many good friends. I hope you will not ask me to scale which one is a better friend. I have a lot of good friends and I like them and I respect them all."

Later that same day, with Cohn still under direct examination, Jenkins again probed the intimate relation:

"We have friends whom we love," Jenkins admits. "I do."

"We have been on double dates," Cohn blurts out.

When Jenkins continues to pursue "your friendship for him, your fondness for him, your closeness to him," Cohn insists again that "what I did . . . was done only with relation to committee work and without regard to the fact that Dave Schine or anyone else might be a personal friend of mine."

Decades later, a sturdy branch of Cold War scholarship conducted under the banner of queer studies would highlight the homosexual subtext of the Army-McCarthy hearings, dragging into daylight what was once hidden in the shadows. But no matter how delicious, in retrospect, is the irony that sex not politics incited McCarthy's video downfall, viewing the hearings through a sexual prism obscures the other code of conduct violated by McCarthy, Cohn, and Schine: the duty to serve in the armed forces.

The obligation to perform military service was an article of faith in the democratic catechism that crossed class lines. Every able-bodied adult male was expected to serve in uniform and if not to face the terrors of combat then to endure the crucible of basic training, military discipline, and barracks life. More often than not, the sons of the wealthy did their hitch. Secretary of the Army Stevens, an urbane millionaire, had himself served in both world wars and tried, with evident sincerity, to persuade Cohn and Schine that a passage in the service was a character-builder, an experience to treasure in later life.

A poignant example of the universality of military duty sat on the McCarthy committee. In 1942 the son of Sen. John McClellan was serving quietly in the U.S. Army. When he went on sick call with an undiagnosed illness, he wrote his father and urged him to refrain from using political influence to gain him special treatment. The same day Senator McClellan unsealed the letter, he received the news that his son had died of spinal meningitis.

Another father-son relationship in the United States Senate sheds harsher light on the sexual-cultural stakes. On the morning of June 19, 1954, two days after the conclusion of the Army-McCarthy hearings, Sen. Lester C. Hunt (D-Wyo.) closed the door to his office and committed suicide by putting a rifle to his head. "I am not sure whether it had to do with the threat Senator McCarthy made yesterday that he was going to investigate a Democratic Senator who had fixed a case, or whether it was Hunt's concerns over his son's homosexual troubles," Drew Pearson ruminated in his diary. Hunt had earlier announced his retirement from the Senate for health reasons. "Personally I think he just didn't want to face the innuendo and rumors regarding his boy during the election campaign," speculated Pearson.

In Cold War America, few areas were as culturally freighted as military service, a patriotic chore that affirmed the citizen's compliance with the egalitarian ethos. In violating this contract, McCarthy, Cohn, and Schine were engaging in conduct nearly as disreputable as homosexuality. Five years later, an Army draftee whose fame far surpassed Schine's would realize—or his manager would realize—that to sidestep military service was to scuttle a career. Unlike Elvis Presley, however, G. David Schine did not possess management as coldly detached as Colonel Tom Parker, a man concerned only with protecting a meal ticket. Whatever its true source, the interest of the hot-blooded Roy Cohn in G. David Schine was never purely mercenary.

ELEVEN

THE END OF THE BLACKLIST

No ceremonial cleansing or ritual of atonement was performed to mark the end of the television blacklist. The process was mainly a series of small victories and private negotiations. Actors formerly persona non video were quietly permitted back on the air, their return unheralded; the long-absent bylines of writers and directors were discreetly restored, their names scrolling past without fanfare on the credits. The once indelible ink of the blacklist faded slowly, incrementally.

Still, the diffusion of the gestalt of the blacklist can be roughly tracked and measured. In 1954 the critic Robert Warshow had whispered about "the present atmosphere," the McCarthyite aura stifling free expression and sanitizing the popular arts. Yet even as Warshow pronounced the forecast, the atmosphere was lifting. Slowly, Hollywood, and eventually television, began to breathe more freely in the open air.

By the mid-1950s, the motion picture industry was already starting—gingerly—to defy the blacklist. Around Hollywood, the use of "fronts" and pseudonyms for blacklisted screenwriters had been an open secret almost from the day the Motion Picture Association of America issued the Waldorf Statement on November 25, 1947. Over time, the furtive practice was progressively declassified: from top secrecy, to knowing winks, and finally to outright defiance. In 1955, *Variety* columnist Frank Scully reported matter-of-factly that the Hollywood Ten and other blacklisted screenwriters had "hung around town and [gone] into bootlegging scripts, or polishing the work of less skilled professionals under the cloak of anonymity. . . . it meant to me at least that others were hiring them under the table to polish a script here and there and take money instead of screen credit."

The shadow play moved into the spotlight on March 3, 1957, when the Academy of Motion Picture Arts and Sciences awarded the Best Screenplay Oscar for *The Brave One* (1956) to Robert L. Rich, a real person whose name, as any hep insider knew, had been borrowed by Hollywood Ten stalwart Dalton Trumbo.

Ever cheeky, Trumbo appeared on Los Angeles station KNX-TV's *The Big News* and bragged that in the past decade he had been the winner of "more than one and less than four" Academy Award nominations, an interview telecast nationally on CBS's *Douglas Edwards with the News*. By 1959, Kirk Douglas, who hired Trumbo for *Spartacus* (1960), and Otto Preminger, who hired Trumbo for *Exodus* (1960), were vying for the honor of restoring his name to the screen.

Well before the proprietary credits of once untouchable artists broke the blacklist, the anticommunist zealotry behind it was being derided in film content. Conveniently enough, the motion picture industry discovered that the true hotbed of McCarthyism incubated in the television industry. Always eager to lord itself over video as an art form of greater integrity and purer impulses, Hollywood savored the twin satisfactions of attacking a repressive political force while demeaning a rival entertainment medium. According to the big screen, McCarthyism and the small screen made natural bedfellows.

In *Sweet Smell of Success* (1957), the sordid film noir directed by Alexander Mackendrick and written by Ernest Lehman and the lately controversial personality Clifford Odets, a sadistic Walter Winchell-like gossip columnist named J. J. Hunsecker (Burt Lancaster) conspires to destroy a jazz musician with a trademark technique of the blacklist, the blind item, in this case a double-barreled accusation of reefer madness and red menace. The charges are totally fabricated, the smear totally cynical, but the item gets the innocent musician fired from his nightclub gig. Like Winchell, Hunsecker not only writes a syndicated newspaper column but hosts a popular television show that serves up a sleazy mix of celebrity gossip and patriotic bombast.

Two formerly friendly witnesses before HUAC, director Elia Kazan and screenwriter Budd Schulberg, fired off a more sustained fusillade at video-borne McCarthyism in *A Face in the Crowd* (1957), a close-up dissection of a demagogic television personality whose power extends from Madison Avenue to Capitol Hill. A cross between Arthur Godfrey and Joseph McCarthy, smooth populism and crude rabble-rousing, the megalomaniacal folksinger Lonesome Rhodes (Andy Griffith) flails about as the frothing incarnation of the telegenic tyrant so feared by literary elites. Like McCarthy, Lonesome Rhodes is undone by the medium that made him. Unaware that he is speaking into a live microphone, his contempt for the viewers is telecast to his shocked fans.

By the time of *The Manchurian Candidate* (1962), the thin disguises had become heavy-handed. Based on the novel by Richard Condon and directed by John Frankenheimer, the conspiracy thriller shuffled a deck stacked with the repressed backfire of the 1950s: the Korean War, communist brainwashing, hysterical anticommunism, and even more hysterical anti-Momism. Playing a fictional senator who was a virtual McCarthy doppelganger—a

Hollywood's video nightmare: the hyena-like visage of television demagogue Lonesome Rhodes (Andy Griffith) in Elia Kazan and Budd Schulberg's *A Face in the Crowd* (1957).

boorish, television-fueled, anticommunist demagogue—actor James Gregory mimics the nasal whine and singsong cadences of the original. The former *Playhouse 90* director Frankenheimer shows how the small screen multiplies the menace, filling the motion picture frame with a house-of-mirrors lineup of sinister television screens during a simulated Senate hearing. "You just keep shouting 'point of order, point of order' into the television screens," the Svengali spouse of the senator commands while she plots a prime-time speech "rallying a nation of television viewers into hysteria." According to Hollywood, television, not the Red Chinese, performed the real work of brainwashing.

In reviewing Kazan's *A Face in the Crowd*, *Variety* noted that the inspiration for the Lonesome Rhodes character would "start a guessing game to link him up with a real life TV performer" (the hot-tempered, faux-folksy Arthur Godfrey was the best guess). The identity of the craven demagogue in *The Manchurian Candidate* required no guessing game. Most reviews of the film printed McCarthy's name as the senatorial surrogate.

Just as Hollywood's prostration before HUAC in 1947 taught television the ways of submission, Hollywood's defiance of the blacklist emboldened network television—eventually. The family medium, ever cautious, still aspiring to a close proximity to "100% acceptability," kept well back in the ranks of overt resistance. In the aftermath of the Army-McCarthy hearings in 1954, some of the pressure to purge alleged subversives from the airwaves eased, but the blacklist—both as a formal, institutionalized procedure and an informal gentleman's agreement—endured well into the 1960s. Not until September 10, 1967, on *The Smothers Brothers Comedy Hour*, was blacklisted folksinger Pete Seeger finally "cleared" for a return to network television. "He is a great artist despite his earlier political affiliations and beliefs," explained a source at CBS.

But if the movement away from the blacklist in television was glacial, two events from the mid-1950s reshaped the contours of blacklist politics and ultimately transformed implied resistance into explicit opposition. The video murmurings of the early part of the decade—the dramatic reenactment of the Salem Witch Trials on *You Are There*, the anti-McCarthy episodes of *See It Now*, and the between-the-lines message consumed during *Dinner with the President*—grew louder and more plainspoken by the end of the decade. Subtle allegory hardened into blunt argument.

In 1956, John Cogley, former executive editor of the liberal Catholic weekly *Commonweal*, released a two-volume study, the 320-page *Blacklisting in the Movies* and the 296-page *Blacklisting in Radio-TV*. Begun in November 1954 and financed with $125,000 from the Fund for the Republic, the work drew on over two hundred interviews with actors, producers, and executives, almost all of whom requested anonymity. The usual suspects were corralled and branded: *Counterattack, Red Channels*, Vincent Hartnett's AWARE, Inc., the American Legion, and the sign-posting supermarket owner Laurence A. Johnson. Cogley confirmed the obvious: that the publication of *Red Channels* in June 1950 "marked the formal beginning of blacklisting in the radio-TV industry," that AWARE, Inc. "lends position, prestige, and power to the practice" of blacklisting, that the House Committee on Un-American Activities facilitated the practice, and that an admixture of fear and greed made advertising agencies, sponsors, and networks willing accomplices.

By the time the studies were issued in June 1956, Cogley considered the practice of blacklisting to be somewhat on the wane due to widespread revulsion at the more outrageous injustices, the normalization of clearance procedures, and the paucity of new victims. Yet "the big remaining problem" was that blacklisting continued to be "institutionalized," that networks and ad agencies still retained security officers and enforced loyalty checks. "The industry set its fundamental policy after the [Jean] Muir, [Ireene] Wicker, and [Philip] Loeb cases," Cogley charged, listing the three earliest and most publicized cases of contract termination. "It has in effect agreed to accept a basic limitation upon its right to hire. While this policy is accepted and the pressure continues, there is little chance that blacklisting can be brought to an end."

Unlike Merle Miller's *The Judges and the Judged*, published in the midst of the Korean War and at the height of McCarthyism, Cogley's reports arrived three years after the truce and two years after the downfall of McCarthy. Circulated in paperback at $1.25 a copy with an initial press run of 10,000, the two reports on blacklisting were the subject of front-page notices in the *New York Times* and the trade press. Advance proofs of the report were sent to the presidents of the three networks, the Motion Picture Association of America, and the four major advertising agencies (Young and Rubicam, McCann-Erikson, J. Walter Thompson, and Batten, Barton, Durstine, and Osborn). None offered comment.

Cogley did get one quick response: a subpoena from the House Committee on Un-American Activities. In July 1956, under the chairmanship of Francis E. Walter (D-Penn.), HUAC went self-reflexive and conducted what it termed an "Investigation of So-Called 'Blacklisting' in [the] Entertainment Industry—Report of the Fund for the Republic, Inc." Called as the first witness, Cogley politely explained his survey techniques and firmly refused to name the names of his unnamed sources. He was threatened with a contempt citation, but to prosecute a Catholic editor for writing a book about a phenomenon the committee maintained did not exist ("so-called 'blacklisting'"?) was too convoluted even for HUAC.

Not that HUAC remained inactive. On June 18 and 19, 1958, still under the chairmanship of Francis E. Walter, the committee returned to New York for untelevised hearings into subversion in television. Subpoenaed witnesses Charles S. Dubin, a freelance director sometimes employed by NBC's game show *Twenty-One* and Joseph Papp, floor manager for CBS's *I've Got a Secret*, invoked the Fifth Amendment not about present Communist Party membership (which both denied) but about "past associations" (so as not to be put in the bind of naming names). Both were peremptorily fired. "NBC does not knowingly employ communists nor permit their employment on programs broadcast over its facilities," the network declared in a press statement. "Persons who refuse to testify as to their present or past affiliation with the Communist Party render themselves unacceptable as regular employees on NBC programs." CBS issued a terse statement: "The circumstances surrounding the case of Mr. Papp are such that we have decided to dismiss him."

But though HUAC and the networks still observed the old amenities—the one prosecuting suspected subversives, the other punishing them—the blacklist was no longer the unassailable, monolithic practice of a few years earlier. Not only were the committee's television victims pretty far down the food chain but the entertainment guilds and unions, so long complicit in the blacklist, began to close ranks. Several months after the hearings, Papp was ordered reinstated at CBS after an arbitration agreement brokered by the Radio and

Television Guild. For their "indefensible capitulation to the House Committee on Un-American Activities," the networks were criticized by the New York branch of the ACLU with an epithet that still stung: such actions "can only help preserve McCarthyism."

Virtually concurrent with the publication of Cogley's two-volume report, John Henry Faulk initiated the first major legal action against the blacklist, filing a $500,000 libel suit in New York Supreme Court and naming as defendants AWARE Inc., Laurence A. Johnson, and Vincent Hartnett.[1] A CBS radio show host and television personality, Faulk was vice president of the New York local of the American Federation of Television and Radio Artists, having been elected on an anti-blacklist platform, along with local president Charles Collingwood, the CBS News correspondent, and co–vice president Orson Bean, the comedian and game show personality. Soon after his election to the AFTRA board, Faulk was named in Hartnett's bulletin. Basically, his blacklistable offense was his opposition to the blacklist.

As a rallying point for anti-blacklist sentiment, Faulk was the perfect blacklist victim: a down-home Texan of liberal persuasion with no hint of fellow traveling in his background. He was also a stubborn cuss who possessed the psychic fortitude to endure six years of purgatory in the American legal system. With subvention from Edward R. Murrow and other liberal friends, he hired the high-powered attorney Louis Nizer and began the long, tortuous path of civil litigation.

Faulk alleged that the defendants "conspired to destroy his income and livelihood, as well as his reputation, by the publication of false accusations linking him with communist front organizations and communist infiltration." Vowing to "test in the courts [the] nefarious and racketeering practices which

---

1. Before Faulk's landmark lawsuit, the actor Joe Julian had brought a libel suit against *Red Channels*, alleging that his income had dropped from approximately $18,000 the year before his name had been listed in 1950 to precisely $1,524.07 in 1953. The New York State Supreme Court dismissed the case on the grounds that *Red Channels* had taken the precaution to admit that "some liberals and innocent people" might have been mentioned in the listing. "The greater proportion of those in the broadcasting industry are of sturdy mind and sound patriotism," the editors cautioned in a legally far-sighted disclaimer. "In screening personnel every safeguard must be used to protect genuine liberals from being unjustly labelled." Later, in 1954, the actor John Ireland sued the Young and Rubicam ad agency for dropping him from the lead in the syndicated television series *The Adventures of Ellery Queen*. Ireland eventually received an out-of-court settlement. *Variety* touted Ireland's case as "the first industry admission of what has for some time been an open secret—that the threat of being labeled a political nonconformist, or worse, has been used against show business personalities and that a screening system is at work determining thesp availabilities for roles."

masquerade as patriotism," he charged the defendants with "the use of intimidation and terror in order to procure the blacklisting of radio and television artists by the networks, producers, sponsors, and advertisers." Most damagingly, however, by exposing how money changed hands behind the scenes, Faulk and Nizer painted the blacklisters not as patriots, however zealous, but as profiteers engaged in "the extortion of monies in consideration for the 'clearance' . . . of radio and television artists, charged, however baselessly, with subversive or former subversive associations." Blacklist patriotism would be exposed not as the last refuge of the scoundrel but the first resort of a racketeer.

As details of the practice entered the public record, the anticommunist front so long on the offensive was obliged to play defense. Rhetorically at least, some of the enabling columnists and politicians tempered their tones and feigned condign shock at the operative reality of the blacklist. The steadfast HUAC member Donald L. Jackson expressed outrage at the "numbers of instances in which completely innocent persons have been libeled by these private sources." Though HUAC had colluded with those same private sources, Jackson condemned "a continuing problem" that was "reaching racket proportions."

The Cogley reports and the Faulk lawsuit helped drag into the sunlight a practice that thrived behind closed doors. In April 1956, a front-page story in *Variety* loudly blew the whistle on the hush-hush arrangements. Setting off the commentary quite literally in italicized parenthesis, the show business weekly reported:

> (*Officially, all phases of show business have denied the existence of "clearance lists," but it is an open secret in the trade that they exist. The lists are sold at varying prices, particularly in the television industry, and the "top secret" classifications are consulted regularly in New York. Coast casting directors, for example, in some cases are asked to submit for "clearance" the names of persons they wish to use on various shows. These names are checked against the lists, most of which are understood to be sadly incomplete in terms of clearly identifying those listed, or in spelling out any part they may have played in the probe of Communist infiltration of the industry.*)

But even as the television industry continued to enforce the blacklist, the shows were chafing against the practice. Institutional compliance coexisted with programming defiance.

In February 1956, *Omnibus*, CBS's esteemed cultural affairs forum, undertook a three-part series on the U.S. Constitution entitled "One Nation," "One Nation Indivisible," and "With Liberty and Justice for All." Each episode was a ringing endorsement of the Warren Court's notion that the Constitution was a "living document" of progressive elasticity on matters of civil rights, not least freedom of expression and freedom from self-incrimination. To alleviate any doubt about the correct mode of constitutional thinking, the host and guide for the *Omnibus* trilogy was a familiar television face, the attorney Joseph N. Welch. For playing video Virgil to "the finest visual portrayal of the main structure of the Constitution," the "kindly articulate, very much human" Welch received better reviews than the Founding Fathers.

Inevitably, the two men who together had slain the dragon of Joseph Mc-Carthy on television met via the medium. On September 14, 1956, Joseph N. Welch was person-to-personed by Edward R. Murrow. (Casting its usual wide net for complementary guests for the fourth season premiere, the low Murrow franchise booked Frank Sinatra for the first segment.) Neither Murrow nor Welch gloats or mentions the senator by name, but each exudes the blithe contentment of a victorious champion.

From his command post at CBS, Murrow smiles and smokes while Welch strolls through his home in Walpole, Massachusetts. Delighted to be face-to-face with his compatriot, Murrow praises "one of the sharpest and quietest trial lawyers they ever saw face a jury," a modest citizen who, for eight weeks, rocketed from "quiet anonymity to national prominence." Welch received Murrow's compliments with the same equanimity he endured McCarthy's insults, but he cannot conceal his pride when he shows off a cigarette box, given to him by his neighbors on July 4, 1954, a few weeks after the Army-McCarthy hearings; the inscription reads: "To the nation's acclaim we add our love." Grinning, Murrow gently mimics Welch's oft-spoken inquiry from the hearings: "May I have a simple answer—yes or no, sir?" Asked for his philosophy of life, Welch avers, "On the whole, if you look for good in people, it is my opinion, sir, you will find it in immense quantities."

Unremarked on *Person to Person* was the third member of the Murrow-Welch axis, no longer on the television A-list, no longer heeded much less feared. The man who once commanded equal time and dominated hours of daytime programming returned as the top item on television news only once more, on May 2, 1957, when the death of its incarnation marked the end of one significant, if never essential, element of McCarthyism. Shunned since his condemnation in December 1954, McCarthy had already passed from center stage in politics and television by the time he succumbed officially to "acute hepatic failure" and diagnostically to cirrhosis of the liver. "So quickly does malevolence rise and vanish in American life that the news of his death, which would have incited sensational interest two years ago, may now be noted in a paragraph, sealing as it does a verdict then returned," wrote *The Nation*, expressing the oddly muted reaction to the death of the most controversial personality of the domestic Cold War. Having disappeared from television, Mc-Carthy had receded from consciousness.

But not for long: the medium that had first empowered and then neutered McCarthy assumed a custodial, if ever more critical, interest. In 1960, keeping time with the decadal changeover, the retirement of the grandfatherly Eisenhower and the election of the vigorous John Kennedy represented a passing of the torch from generation to generation that was more than symbolic. Within days of becoming president, Kennedy ignored picketing by the American Legion and the Catholic War Veterans to attend an evening screening of *Spartacus* in Washington, D.C. A sword-and-sandals historical epic featuring Roman gladiators recast as proto-proletariate revolutionaries, the film was based on the book by Howard Fast, who had refused to cooperate with the McCarthy committee in 1953, and written by Dalton Trumbo, who had refused to cooperate with the House Committee on Un-American Activities in 1947. The atmosphere of the New Frontier would be friendlier to the unfriendlies.

It would also be less hospitable to the men who subpoenaed them. On November 26, 1962, the syndicated series *Biography*, produced by David L. Wolper and hosted by Mike Wallace, reviewed the career of the late, but still "junior," senator from Wisconsin. "Even now, years after his death, the smoke of political battle swirls around the name of Sen. Joe McCarthy," explained Wallace. "He is loved and hated, praised and damned. The debate still goes on over his significance on the American scene. Was he a dangerous demagogue or a courageous patriot?" As *Biography* chronicles "the events that made Senator McCarthy the most controversial political figure of our time," McCarthy emerges unmistakably as the former. Characteristically, though, a selective amnesia beset television's memory of the recent past. "The requirement of a loyalty oath becomes increasingly widespread in the government and throughout the nation," Wallace reports, neglecting to mention that CBS strictly enforced one of the first.

Another verdict on McCarthyism was more emphatic and influential. On June 28, 1962, after more than six years of litigation, a New York jury awarded $3,500,000—then the largest libel damage award in history—to John Henry Faulk. The huge sum was less an estimate of Faulk's years of lost income than a condemnation of his blacklisting. The depositions and court testimony had exposed and busted up the racket. Bringing star power to a Hollywood moment of courtroom drama, producer David Susskind had testified that even child actors needed to be cleared for television to cleanse any taint inherited from their parents. "We finally found a child, an American child, eight years old, female," Susskind recalled on the stand. "I put her name in [for clearance] along with some other names. That child's name came back unacceptable, politically unreliable." The jury, the judge, and the gallery all gasped. "In 1962 the blacklist had at last proven unprofitable," observed the cultural historian Stefan Kanfer in his 1973 account *A Journal of the Plague Years*, the first history of the blacklist era to truly name the names of its sources. "After a run of fifteen years, it would have to be folded. History had overtaken it."

But if court rulings and libel judgments battered the blacklist, if feature films and television documentaries undercut McCarthyism, the true turning point is marked by the convergence in time of two video texts—one direct from television, one derived from television. In January 1964, network television assailed the blacklist during an audacious hour of prime-time programming. Serendipitously, that same month, the motion picture medium raided the warehouse of its rival to attack McCarthyism with a provocative media hybrid: the first televisual documentary in cinematic history.

The Defenders: The Blacklist on Trial

Part courtroom melodrama, part New Frontier soapbox, CBS's *The Defenders* (1961–1965) reads like a legal brief for the aspirations of late-period Cold War liberalism. Week in and week out, the father-and-son law partners Lawrence Preston (E. G. Marshall) and Kenneth Preston (Robert Reed) worked pro bono to defend JFK-style progressivism before the bar of American justice. Unlike the longer-lived lawyerly melodrama *Perry Mason*, the series seldom grappled with violent criminals or engaged in courtroom theatrics where surprise witnesses broke down under cross-examination to tie up loose plot points before the final commercial break. *The Defenders* addressed Serious Issues: it was earnest, video castor oil, spiritual kindred to the postwar social problem films that decried afflictions in the otherwise healthy body of American culture. Anti-Soviet and anti-McCarthy, equally opposed to communism abroad and dedicated to civil rights at home, the Cold War liberals on *The Defenders* retained a reflexive belief that the United States of America was a force for good in the world, a conceit soon to explode in the jungles of Vietnam.

The Defenders was the creation of Reginald Rose, one of the great writers of live television drama in the 1950s, author of such teleplays-turned-feature-films as *Crime in the Streets* (1956), *12 Angry Men* (1957), and *Dino* (1957). "In a business where the blurbs are easy to bounce, Reginald Rose stands out as the conscience of television," blurbed *Variety* in 1955. Committed to both the creative possibilities and socially transforming power of the medium, Rose affected none of the disdain for television still fashionable among certain literati. "I am constantly amazed that this infant medium has managed to achieve, at least in its dramatic offerings, a maturity which, in general, surpasses the standards set by motion pictures over the past forty-odd years," he wrote in 1956. By the early 1960s, the glory days of live television were already a misty memory, but Rose retained his commitment to "expertly staged dramas with an intelligent and mature point of view" in the episodic film format. "I think controversial subjects can be handled on television if they are treated properly and done at the right time," he declared in 1961.

On January 18, 1964, Saturday at 8:30 P.M., *The Defenders* telecast an episode whose blunt title highlighted a word seldom aired outside the protective bubble of news shows: "Blacklist." It was a calculated shot across the bow, the first explicit exposure on a prime-time television series of the institutional practices of the television industry. Directed by Stuart Rosenberg and written by Ernest Kinoy, the show became the prototype for a virtual subgenre in film and television, the blacklist melodrama.

The idea for an episode on the blacklist originated when producer Rose pitched the notion to his friend Kinoy. Like Rose, Kinoy was an alumni of live television drama and, not incidentally, a playwright with a penchant for politically charged, Judeo-centric material. Though he had written some early television routines for Gertrude Berg of *The Goldbergs*, he was perhaps best known for "Walk Down the Hill," telecast on March 18, 1957, by CBS's *Studio One*. Set in a German POW camp during World War II, the play portrayed the moral quandary of a deadlier version of naming names as Nazi wardens try to separate Jewish American POWs from their fellow GIs. (In 1977, Kinoy's auteurist commitment to race, politics, and television achieved a critical and commercial zenith when he helped adapt Alex Haley's *Roots* for the landmark ABC miniseries.)

"You've got to make sure you're blacklisting the right man," Kinoy insisted to Rose, meaning that the blacklistee needed to be an alert artist-activist guilty as charged—that is, neither slandered by the shoddy research of anti-communist vigilantes nor an innocent dupe shanghaied into a Popular Front parade. "I was particularly interested in the effect of the blacklist on the ordinary working actor, not the star who could weather the storm on Broadway or in London, but the small workaday craftsman who just about got by in the best of times."

"Blacklist" begins with a cold opening depicting a brainstorming session for the casting of a film. The producer ponders for a moment and then mentions the name "Joe Larch" for a part. Eyebrows raised, the casting director demurs. "I haven't been able to get an okay on Joe Larch for ten years," she says. "Where do I find him?"

Jump-cut to a man on his knees in a shoe store. This is where to find the actor Joe Larch.

Briskly paced via match cuts to shift between scenes, "Blacklist" wastes no time, not bothering to pause for wordy exposition. Already, it seems, even in this premiere depiction of the blacklist on television, the outline of the story is too well known to belabor: unjust accusations by patriotic scoundrels, wasted years in the wilderness of retail sales for a gifted actor, and the emotional and financial costs to the victim and his family. When a stunned Joe gets the job offer, he can't believe in his deliverance from exile.

Joe's caution is well founded. Another match cut leaps to a scene of two prim women hovering over a mimeograph machine, which spits out leaf after leaf of paper into the camera lens, a smear that will disrupt, again, the professional and personal life of Joe Larch.

The backstory places Larch's original blacklisting in the year 1952, but no names are named—not *Red Channels*, not HUAC, not McCarthy. Underwritten by an anticommunist businessman modeled on the supermarket owner Laurence Johnson, the vigilante group is a composite of American Business Consultants and AWARE, Inc., named "the National Security Vanguard League." Kinoy seeks not to indict a single villain but to conjure the elusive gestalt of the blacklist, a clandestine practice whose consequences are no secret. The source of the attack is clear enough, but the agents of implementation—studio executives? Wall Street bankers? local politicians?—remain shadowy forces.

Goaded into action, Larch seeks legal advice from the Prestons. True to Kinoy's vision, Larch refuses to claim that the reds made a sucker out of him. His blacklistable offense had been to support the Republican cause during the Spanish Civil War and to align himself, at times, with communists. For this, he is unrepentant.

In setting Larch's activism during the Spanish Civil War—a cause rallied to by no less an American hero than Rick Blaine in *Casablanca* (1942)—Kinoy sidesteps the communist fellow-traveling that stained the reputation of the American left. The coziness to Stalin not Spain is the real issue, the red-letter dates not 1936 or 1938, but 1939, or 1941, or 1945. By portraying Larch as a premature antifascist and principled artist-progressive, Kinoy collapses a crucial distinction.

In the end, the producer, a good liberal making a good-faith attempt to hire Larch and break the blacklist, has no choice but to renege on his job offer. Like Gertrude Berg, compelled to jettison Philip Loeb or preside over the demise of *The Goldbergs*, the producer must choose between his actor and his show. The producer seems more anguished than Larch, who, as underplayed by Jack Klugman, walks through his ordeal with wry fatalism.

The response to the groundbreaking episode was—a shrug. No sponsor withdrew, no affiliate refused to air the show, and few commentators took note of the transgression. Far more controversial was an earlier episode of *The Defenders* entitled "The Benefactor," telecast on April 28, 1962, a sympathetic treatment of a doctor who advocates legalized abortion. Sponsors withdrew, affiliates pulled the show, and CBS earned widespread praise for not "chickening out" and telecasting the episode. As ever with television, the anti-blacklist sentiment was on the cusp of a new consensus, not the cutting edge of controversy.

Neither unwitting dupe nor prodigal politico: the unrepentant artist-activist Joe Larch (Jack Klugman, *foreground*) talks to his lawyer Kenneth Preston (Robert Reed) in the landmark "Blacklist" episode of CBS's *The Defenders*, telecast January 18, 1964. (Courtesy CBS Photo Archive)

The most noteworthy response to the "Blacklist" episode of *The Defenders* came from within the television industry. At the Sixteenth Annual Emmy Awards Show, a dual ceremony conducted in New York and Hollywood and telecast by NBC on May 25, 1964, Kinoy accepted the Emmy for Outstanding Original Writing Achievement in Drama. "I think it is very encouraging that a play on this subject should be so well received by this industry—and I thank you, and I thank E. G. [Marshall], and I thank any strangers we've collected," said Kinoy.[2] In Hollywood, when actor Jack Klugman received the Emmy for Outstanding Single Performance by an Actor in a Leading Role, a sustained ovation greeted the reading of his name. Thanking his family and friends, Klugman made no political statement, but the roar from the Hollywood crowd said

2. The "strangers" remark referred to a weird disruption that occurred during the ceremony. A tuxedoed stranger rushed to the podium with Kinoy and faced the camera momentarily before being hustled off stage by security. Kinoy wittily acknowledged the incident with the throwaway line.

enough, registering approval not only for his performance but for its representational value—almost as if Jack Klugman had been a blacklisted actor who, unlike Joe Larch, was now being welcomed back to the fold.

"A year ago," Kinoy wrote in the *New York Times* a week before the episode aired, "I would have offered odds a program called 'Blacklist' would never hit the air." No wonder: even as television programming was assailing the blacklist, the television institution continued to enforce it. Ironically, the actors on "Blacklist" needed to be cleared by CBS, so even on "Blacklist," the blacklist lived. "Politically controversial talent may no longer be completely tabu, but the risks in employing them are still measured against box office returns and rating points," *Variety* commented. "Although it's now a decade beyond the crest of the witch-hunting hysteria, this show jabbed sharply at a highly sensitized nerve in both the broadcasting and film industries."

Nonetheless, when CBS telecast a prime-time program about the injustice of the blacklist, when the Academy of Television Arts and Sciences honored the show with Emmys to writer Kinoy and actor Klugman, and when NBC telecast the ceremony to huge ratings, the practice was shifting away from business as usual and moving into beyond the pale. In condemning the blacklist and then congratulating itself for doing so, television signaled that the once house-clearing alarm of "reds in your living room!" was falling on deaf ears.

Point of Order!: The Army-McCarthy Hearings, the Movie

With a temporal synchronicity that seems conspiratorial, the very same week that the "Blacklist" episode of *The Defenders* aired on the small screen, another television landmark on McCarthyism was released on the big screen, director Emile de Antonio's synoptic collage of the Army-McCarthy hearings, *Point of Order!* (1963). The definitive record of the first great made-for-television political spectacle, *Point of Order!* extended film historian Jay Leyda's pithy dictum—"films beget films"—to a new moving image medium—"television begets films" (not to mention more television). Sifted and spliced, the history recorded and mediated by television, once deemed disposable, projected an indelible picture of the past on the motion picture screen.

A self-described "Marxist among capitalists," de Antonio was a radical artist-activist who boasted a set of eminently blacklistable credentials, having been schooled by the Young Communist League, the John Reed Society, and Harvard University. In 1961, with the encouragement and financial backing of New Yorker Theater owner Daniel Talbot, de Antonio undertook a project that was, on the whole, more aesthetically adventurous than politically provocative—the compilation of kinescopes to craft a documentary film.

De Antonio culled *Point of Order!* from the original kinescopes of the Army-McCarthy hearings warehoused by the CBS News Archives. Ironically, in accord with CBS President William S. Paley's vision of CBS News as the *New York Times* of television, the only network to forgo any gavel-to-gavel coverage was the only network to preserve the complete footage. However, such was the network's trepidation over potential backlash that CBS insisted it be a "secret partner" in its contract with de Antonio. Only after the film's warm reception did the network then brag of its midwife role.

For over two years, de Antonio screened and edited the footage, winnowing down the original 188 hours to twelve hours, then to three hours, and finally to 97 minutes. The 16mm kinescopes were then blown up to 35mm format for theatrical release prints.

Early on in the editorial process, de Antonio made two crucial decisions about the shape of the film. First, believing that voice-over narration was "inherently fascist and condescending," he relied entirely on the Army-McCarthy kinescopes, with no supplementary newsreel footage or expert testimony. Except for brief declarations at the top of the film and written "supers" introducing sequences, no narration or intertitles interrupt the flow of the footage. Rather than recapturing the quality of the original television experience, narrated by ABC reporters and interrupted by interviews with the participants, *Point of Order!* remade the hearings into one continuous current via a cinematic compression of television time.

Second, and more audaciously, de Antonio defied chronological order to structure the film dramatically. The "actual hearings were 188 formless hours ending with a whimper," he observed. "Film moves freely through all the material to make its points." Producer Talbot concurred with de Antonio's "charactological position" in the interest of "a good show." Thus, unlike the hearings, which sputtered to a close on June 17, 1954, *Point of Order!* climaxes with the Welch-McCarthy face-off on June 9, 1954. Then, as a kind of coda, the film fades to a close with the senators walking out of the hearing room as McCarthy rambles on, bellowing the schoolyard tease "Sanctimonious Stu" at his senatorial nemesis, Stuart Symington. The snippy exchanges between Symington and McCarthy actually occurred on June 14, 1954, three days before the hearings ended.

After advance screenings at the New York Film Festival, *Point of Order!* premiered on January 14, 1964, at the Beekman Theater in New York City. The original press release ballyhooed the film as the "most controversial of motion pictures," but a decade after McCarthy's on-air immolation the senator was no longer all that controversial. *Point of Order!* punctuated an emergent cultural consensus about the sinister impact of the senator and the nightmare quality of the era he lent his name to. "At the end of the film, even those with very clear memories may be confused about the specific points at issue," admitted *Motion Picture Herald*, the most conservative of the trade magazines, in a laudatory review. "But few will leave the theater without a clearer understanding of McCarthy's personality or the power he exerted in our national life."

But while opinion on McCarthy had settled into conventional wisdom, the unconventional format of *Point of Order!* was harder to classify. Befuddled by the notion of video-derived cinema, the New York Film Festival's program notes suggested that a documentary comprised entirely of unnarrated kinescopes might not, strictly speaking, even qualify as a film. *Variety* expressed confusion over proprietary credits, puzzling that "in a film of this kind, it's difficult to know where the praise should go." Was de Antonio an ingenious documentary filmmaker or merely a skillful editor? Certainly the young Ed Scherer, who directed the hearings for WMAL-TV, deserved credit for improvising the most riveting moment replayed in *Point of Order!*, the Welch-McCarthy face-off intercut with glimpses of a squirming Roy Cohn.

Back in 1954, during the original telecasts, television critic Marya Mannes had predicted that "the Army McCarthy hearings have been a picture which should obsess American memory as it has obsessed all those Americans who have seen it." Yet the crowds flocking to *Point of Order!* a decade later were not original viewers reliving a primal television memory but "large and predominantly youthful audiences" gaping at a political monster movie from another age. Not unexpectedly, one spectator dissented from the accolades garnered by the film. Calling *Point of Order!* "an obvious flop," Roy Cohn threatened to sue de Antonio, but then backed off, saying he didn't want to lend the project any undeserved publicity.

Whether as archival history or avant-garde documentary, *Point of Order!* was a timely exclamation. De Antonio could presume not only an audience well versed in television—by 1963, an entire generation had been reared at the foot of the small screen—but spectators with the bifocal vision needed to read a televisual motion picture. Fortunately, for the slower students, a mentor in media theory had recently supplied a crib sheet.

As a kinescoped flashback to American history, *Point of Order!* served as a review session for the mass communications curriculum expounded in Marshall McLuhan's enormously influential book *Understanding Media: The Extensions of Man*, released the same year. Just as Freud mapped the landscape of the mind, McLuhan devised a global positioning system for the media. A guide to the grammar of everything from smoke signals to television signals,

A Cold War monster movie: Senator McCarthy in a frame enlargement from Emile de Antonio's pioneering archival documentary *Point of Order!* (1963).

his brilliant study popularized arcane concepts like "hot media" and "cool media." "The success of any TV performer depends on his achieving a low-pressure style of presentation," decreed McLuhan. "TV is a medium that rejects the sharp personality."

Viewed through McLuhan's eyes, *Point of Order!* seemed a post hoc proof of his key insights. "TV would inevitably be a disaster for a sharp intense image like Nixon's, and a boon for the blurry, shaggy texture of Kennedy," McLuhan observed of the mismatched face-off between Richard Nixon and John Kennedy in the televised presidential debates of 1960, a judgment also suiting that other pair of names from 1954. "The American people have had a look at you for six weeks," Senator Symington snarled at McCarthy, toward the end of the hearings, at the very end of *Point of Order!*. "You are not fooling anyone." In exposing McCarthy, the medium also exposed its central truth: being uncool on television is worse than being uncool in politics.

A genuine media milestone, *Point of Order!* continues to echo through time. Just as film begets film and television begets television, archival films beget more archival films. Unlike most television moments from the 1950s, the Army-McCarthy hearings have remained alive in popular memory due to constant citation and rescreening. The film has circulated for decades on the university and repertory film circuits and is readily available on videotape and viewable on cable. Moreover, most subsequent archival documentaries on the McCarthy era cull footage not from the original kinescopes and primary research but from de Antonio's compilation. Almost by rote, with no sense of decency, snippets from Welch's comeback are lifted and replayed as audiovisual shorthand for the quietus of McCarthyism. By 1997 the Welch tagline ("Have you no sense of decency, sir, at long last? Have you left no sense of decency?") was familiar enough to be sampled by the rock group REM on a hit song entitled "Exhuming McCarthy."

TWELVE

EXHUMING MCCARTHYISM

The Paranoid Style in American Television

In writer-director Gary Ross's motion picture *Pleasantville* (1998), a lonely, fatherless teenager (Tobey Maguire) is obsessed with the serene black-and-white world of a vintage 1950s television show. Devoted to a cable channel retreading syndicated chestnuts, he stares with naked longing at a series called "Pleasantville." A hybrid of *Leave It to Beaver*, *The Adventures of Ozzie and Harriet*, and *Father Knows Best*, the show transmits the clichéd images of Cold War America as viewed through decades of monochromatic reruns, known as "evergreens" in the trade, series that just keep spiraling through time and space on an endless coaxial loop.

"Pleasantville," the television show within the motion picture, is a nuclear family sitcom whose stock characters act out the starched routines of a calcified formula: a breadwinner Dad holding down an unspecified white-collar job, a homemaker Mom larding out high-cholesterol foodstuff, and two gosh-darn all-American teenagers, son and daughter, who bubble with a clean teen perkiness unblemished by acne, rock and roll, or heavy petting.

Like Alice walking through that other looking glass, the lonesome lad and his randy sister are magically beamed into the television screen and tumble into the town of Pleasantville. Far from being frightened or disoriented, the boy is delighted by the journey into the prime-time past. Forearmed with a meticulous knowledge of the tropes of the series, he thrives in the Edenic tele-environs, a fantasy refuge removed from the tensions and confusions of late twentieth-century American culture.

But under the placid veneer of Pleasantville lurk hidden horrors: sexism, racism, lockstep conformity, blinkered perspectives, a totalitarian milieu that is truly black and white. In a sequence conjuring the newsreel footage of the book-burning bonfires of Nazi Germany, the citizens of Cold War Pleasantville unleash a virtual *kristallnacht* of terror on their nonconformist neighbors. No bucolic harbor from cruel modernity, Pleasantville is a prison camp of ranch houses and manicured front lawns, an American Reich with a dorky dress code.

Pleasantville, the motion picture, is less about the superiority of the 1990s to the 1950s than the superiority of motion pictures to television: the film heritage is in color, the television heritage is in black and white; film is a widescreen rectangle, television is a small-screen square; film is freedom of expression, television is systematic repression; film is true history, television is saccharine myth. Yet as a vision of Cold War America, the unpleasant portrait unspooled in *Pleasantville* hews to a familiar paint-by-numbers pattern. In scholarly studies, personal memoirs, and the popular arts, America in the 1950s is a land where citizens shiver in their basements, fearful of knocks on the door from Gestapo-like FBI agents. Strangers shun frank talk, decent citizens cringe before G-men in brown shoes, and the full apparatus of state terror is marshaled to suppress, intimidate, and imprison.

The Cold War Kulturkampf is not a recent construction. Throughout the 1950s, comparisons of McCarthyism to Nazism were tossed about by combative liberals with nearly as much recklessness as McCarthy's accusations of communism. Recalling his coverage of the forward march of the Third Reich for CBS radio in the 1930s, Edward R. Murrow added his voice to the image of McCarthy as a domestic Hitler. "I saw the Anschluss at Vienna, I saw the Austrians and Czechs lose their freedom," Murrow told *TV Guide* in 1955. "I saw terror and fear so strong that when I saw McCarthy's tactics, I felt obliged to speak my piece."

Looking backward, whether via scholarship, film, or television, the anticommunist crusade emerges as an irrational and inexplicable outbreak, a virus that beset a normally healthy organism, settled in the cerebellum, and deranged the body politic. Unaccountable in origin and indiscriminate in fury, McCarthyism cuts down noble progressives, well-meaning communists, and innocent bystanders alike. The language of psychosis and pathology—hysteria, witch hunt, paranoia, plague—leaps readily to the lips.

The most famous mental health diagnosis was made by the historian Richard Hofstadter in his touchstone essay "The Paranoid Style in American Politics," written in 1963. "I call it the paranoid style," Hofstadter explained, "because no other word adequately evokes the qualities of heated exaggeration, suspiciousness, and conspiratorial fantasy that I have in mind." Hofstadter emphasized that he was "not speaking in a clinical sense, but borrowing a clinical term for other purposes" and he had no desire to classify any figures as "certifiable lunatics." In turning to examples, however, Hofstadter's first case study is no surprise: "Here is Senator McCarthy . . . "

Hofstadter was careful to acknowledge not only the deep cultural roots of the paranoid style but to admit that the paranoia had, as it were, a certain validity. Its persistence rested on "certain points of contact with real problems of domestic and foreign policy and with widespread and deeply rooted American

The 1950s in black and white: William Macy and Joan Allen as the stereotypical televisual man and wife in Gary Ross's *Pleasantville* (1998). (Courtesy New Line Cinema)

ideas and impulses." After all, class resentments against aristocratic elites—what McCarthy called "that group of untouchables in the State Department" and "the Acheson-Hiss-Yalta crowd"—had warmed the patriotic blood of good Jeffersonians and bad Know Nothings since the founding of the Republic. Nevertheless, Hofstadter's diagnostic term could only engender a psychopathological framework, a sense that anticommunists in general and Senator McCarthy in particular were, well, certifiable lunatics.

After Hofstadter, the tone of the academic scholarship on what became known as the McCarthy era turned increasingly intemperate. *The Nightmare Decade*, *The American Inquisition*, *The Great Fear*—the very titles of the volumes bespeak a blighted passage in American history, conjuring images of an Irish-American Torquemada torching WASP patricians in Senate Caucus Room 318. Extremism in denunciation of McCarthyism was no scholarly vice. "More than the House Committee on Un-American Activities, or President Truman's loyalty oaths, or Russian actions, McCarthy sparked this frightening era and became the principal prophet of anti-Communism as an irrational fear consuming logical analysis and orderly process," declared media historian J. Fred MacDonald in *Television and the Red Menace: The Video Road to Vietnam* in 1985. "If one individual was responsible for the course of national life in the 1950s and 1960s it too was Senator McCarthy." From the early 1960s

onward, to utter "McCarthyism" was not only to describe virulent anticommunism but to redefine the nature of truly un-American activities.[1]

Likewise, the personal memoirs recall the agonies of martyrdom in a time
of moral cowardice and abject fear, with the narrator the sole voice of conscience amid the howls of the mob. In *Scoundrel Time*, her 1976 remembrance
of the blacklist era, the playwright Lillian Hellman tells how she wrote to
HUAC in 1952 to declare, "I cannot and will not cut my conscience to this
year's fashion." Hellman, who never scrupled to tailor her opinions to the
Communist Party line in the 1930s and 1940s, was beatified as the Joan of Arc
of civil liberties.

Motion pictures and television, the media most identified with blacklisting
and McCarthyism, memorialized the season with the same broad brush-
strokes. At once posthumous revenge and self-serving exculpation, a proliferation of solemn melodramas and McCarthy-themed documentaries depicted
a reign of terror that sucked the lifeblood from America's most precious national resource: the entertainment industry.

The cold eye cast back at Cold War America narrowed further during the
second presidential term of television pioneer Richard M. Nixon, and proceed-
ed apace after the Watergate crisis. In the retrospective Hollywood romance
The Way We Were (1973), two soft-focused lovers wilt under the anticommunist heat of the 1950s. A television writer and his fellow-traveling wife are torn
apart by HUAC testimony and loyalty oaths: he is seduced by the lure of video
success, she remains true to the good fight and is last glimpsed passing out "Ban
the Bomb" leaflets. Likewise, in the documentary *Hollywood on Trial* (1976), the
title belies the tale: as newsreel images of the 1947 Hollywood Ten hearings are
intercut with the wistful remembrances of noble blacklistees, it is the House
Committee on Un-American Activities that is tried and found guilty.

True to expectations, the motion picture industry turned to the television
industry for the most forthright exposé of the blacklist era. Directed by Martin Ritt and written by Walter Bernstein, *The Front* (1976) dramatized how
forcefully the train of history had switched tracks. Howard Prince (Woody
Allen) is a talentless restaurant cashier who, for a piece of the action, lends his
name as a front for blacklisted television writers. Getting religion and gaining
a backbone in the last reel, the apolitical nebbish acts out a liberal fantasy of
righteous courage when dragged before HUAC to name names. "Fellas, I don't
recognize the right of this committee to ask me these kind of questions," he

---

1. By 1969, even HUAC sought to muffle the Cold War echo, renaming itself the Committee on Internal Security. That committee was abolished in 1975.

instructs the congressional philistines. "And furthermore, you can all go fuck yourselves." As the end credits scroll by, a scar of shame in the 1950s has become a badge of honor in the 1970s:

Directed by
Martin Ritt
(blacklisted 1951)

Written by
Walter Bernstein
(blacklisted 1950)

Co-starring
Zero Mostel
(blacklisted 1950)

and so on.

No moment better symbolizes the cultural worm-turning than the reception accorded Lillian Hellman at the 1977 Academy Awards ceremonies. After a fawning introduction by Jane Fonda, Hellman walked to the podium to a rapturous standing ovation. It wasn't that all was forgiven of the unrepentant Stalinist; it was Hollywood that asked to be forgiven for blacklisting her.

Today, having repressed the trauma for so long, the motion picture industry returns to the McCarthy era with a frequency bordering on obsession-compulsion. Besides the above, a partial listing of feature-length depictions of the blacklist era includes *Fellow Traveler* (1989), *Guilty by Suspicion* (1991), *The Majestic* (2001), and *One of the Hollywood Ten* (2001). Few Cold War period pieces also fail to omit a hit-and-run encounter with McCarthyism. In the biopic *Chaplin* (1992), the persecuted comedian watches the untelevised 1947 Hollywood Ten hearings on television prior to being hounded out of the country. In *Class Action* (1991), a crusading lawyer recalls a politically correct "meet cute": watching the Army-McCarthy hearings on television, he notices an attractive woman in the background mouthing the words "liar" when McCarthy speaks. Smitten, he calls her for a date and true love blossoms. In *L.A. Confidential* (1997), a thick coat of sexual repression, political corruption, and cynical McCarthyism pervades the entertainment capital. (On the other hand, *My Favorite Year* [1982], a rose-colored backstage comedy set during rehearsals for a *Your Show of Shows*-like variety show, studiously avoids the blacklist or McCarthyism during its resonant dateline of 1954.)

Concurrently, as the word *sexual* came ever more to modify the word *politics*, revisions of Cold War America began to be filtered through the lens of

Held in contempt: nebbish turned champion Howard Prince (Woody Allen) defies the House Committee on Un-American Activities in Martin Ritt and Walter Bernstein's motion picture memoir of the television blacklist, *The Front* (1976).

gender. By the 1980s, the closeted sexual politics of the McCarthy era opened a doorway into a hidden history. Drawing upon FBI files obtained through the Freedom of Information Act and memoirs and biographies that saw no percentage in discretion, revisionist histories placed the homosexual shading of the Army-McCarthy hearings into boldfaced relief.

Above all, Roy Cohn's death from AIDS in 1986 served as ex post facto confirmation of the airy talk of pixies and fairies in 1954. According to popular entertainment set in the McCarthy era, such as the HBO biopic *Citizen Cohn* (1992) or Tony Kushner's Pulitzer Prize-winning play *Angels in America* (1993), the homosexual orientation of at least one of the principal McCarthyites is an established fact.

The alleged sexual orientation of another tightly wound cold warrior was more dubious as history but absolutely irresistible as myth. J. Edgar Hoover, keeper of the nation's secrets, was alleged to have hidden one of his own. In February 1993, an episode of *Frontline*, PBS's respected documentary series, lent a platform to unverified charges that the FBI director was not wed exclusively to the bureau. The truly sensational revelation was not that Hoover was a repressed homosexual, in love with his right-hand man Clyde Tolson, but that he enjoyed dressing in drag: lipsticked, nyloned, bewigged, and begowned. For American popular culture, the image of the zaftig FBI director as a Christine Jorgensen wanna-be was too delicious not to savor. In late-night monologues and sketch comedy, the repressed returned with a vengeance, trashing decades of expert image-mongering by the FBI's Bureau of Public Affairs.

Following Hollywood's lead, though this time more closely, television staged a kindred series of Cold War revivals. Though the live anthology series was long dead, its lineal descendent, the filmed Movie of the Week, served as a privileged forum for excursions into McCarthyism. The (new) consensus history congealed around two milestone television biopics dramatizing the lives of two characters at opposite ends of the moral spectrum.

On February 6, 1977, at 8:00 P.M., NBC's Big Event movie of the week telecast a three-hour chronicle of the life and times of Joe McCarthy entitled *Tail Gunner Joe*. Directed by Jud Taylor and written by Lane Slate, the drama might be dubbed a patho-biopic, a narrative of the life that despises its subject.

An unusually open-ended exculpation prefaced the program:

> This program presents a dramatized interpretation of the life and times of Senator Joe McCarthy. Some of the names have been changed, and the reporters and some of the persons interviewed have been created to serve as narrators of incidents based upon actual occurrences.

Stealing from the best, *Tail Gunner Joe* nicks the framing device from *Citizen Kane*: a guileless young television reporter researching the career of Joe McCarthy talks to former acquaintances who flashback vignettes about the late, ungreat man. However, where Charles Foster Kane is an enigma whose character shape-shifts with each eyewitness account, the picture of McCarthy comes into sharp, single-minded focus. The junior senator from Wisconsin was a duplicitous, avaricious, unscrupulous, loutish, drunken scoundrel. As actor Peter Boyle, then best known as the murderous blue-collar bigot in *Joe* (1970), mimics McCarthy's staccato vocal patterns with eerie fidelity, wizened survivors strive to communicate the remote, preenlightened epoch known as Cold War America ("Listen, it was a bad time." "It was such insanity." "In those days, if your syntax was okay, you were in trouble."). Dumbfounded, the callow broadcast journalist finds the reports hard to credit. Reassuringly, however, the third act metes out some rough karmic justice to the vile demon. Screaming and slobbering, lashing out violently as orderlies at Bethesda Naval Hospital struggle to subdue him, McCarthy ends his days in true paranoid style, racked by delirium tremens.

Tail Gunner Joe reenacts verbatim and at length several well-remembered sequences from the original Army-McCarthy telecasts as transmitted by *Point of Order!* Even in the waning days of three-network hegemony, however, censorship stifles some subtexts. Significantly, no homosexual currents pass between Roy Cohn and G. David Schine. During a reenactment of the incendiary "pixie" exchange between Welch and McCarthy, no insinuation about the nature of the Cohn-Schine axis, not even the pained reaction shot of Cohn, peeks through the veil of network standards and practices. Also, this being an NBC production, the biopic slights the role of Edward R. Murrow and CBS's *See It Now*. As always, the televisual history that seeps into the popular memory will be determined by access to the images (*Point of Order!*) and the interests of the corporate parent (NBC versus CBS).

And what has the no-longer-guileless reporter of *Tail Gunner Joe* learned from her journey through the past? "[McCarthy] more or less created a national climate of fear," she concludes.

"What you're saying is—it could happen again," says her mentor and editor.

"Hasn't it?" she responds darkly, her Watergate curtain line presuming a spiritual linkage between the paranoia of the Nixon White House and the era from which the president sprang.

Set against the demon of McCarthyism was the angelic victim and courageous fighter. CBS's *Fear on Trial*, telecast on October 2, 1975, was television's most significant look back at the underside of television's history since the "Blacklist" episode of *The Defenders*. Directed by Lamont Johnson and adapted by David W. Rintels from Faulk's memoir, the teleplay vividly captures the gestalt of the blacklist. It also names names—of the blacklisters and the victims, though not of the sponsors. "York Foods" stands in for General Foods, "White Dawn Soap" for Proctor and Gamble: the McCarthy era may be over, but the age of advertising still flourishes.

George C. Scott, who plays Faulk's attorney Louis Nizer in the docudrama, appears in a prologue to set the scene:

> In America in the 1950s, a time of McCarthyism, when an unsubstantiated charge that a man was a communist meant that a CBS broadcaster could be driven off the air, deprived of his right to earn a living, even to live, one man—John Henry Faulk—fought back against the same climate of fear which had caused teachers to be fired from schools, ministers from their churches, government workers from their jobs, against that fear, which for ten long years had turned American against American.

Fear on Trial opens in CBS's New York studios, where employees are huddled around a television monitor watching Edward R. Murrow's "A Report on Senator Joseph R. McCarthy" on *See It Now*. The telecast within the telecast

Television indicts itself: lawyer Louis Nizer (George C. Scott, *left*) and blacklist victim John Henry Faulk (William Devane) in CBS's *Fear on Trial* (1975). (Courtesy CBS Photo Archive)

replays an extended section from Murrow's soliloquy. "Good old Ed," declares Faulk (William Devane, doing a down-home Texas accent). "Good for CBS for letting him do it."

But if the dragon of Joseph McCarthy seems under siege, the blacklist still singes the television industry. "Phil Loeb killed himself tonight," a grim coworker informs Faulk, referring to the blacklisted actor who was once paterfamilias on *The Goldbergs*. Ominously, that night, the death of Philip Loeb goes unreported on the network news. More ominously, the next morning, Faulk hears that his name has tolled in the bulletin of AWARE, Inc.[2]

In short order, CBS fires Faulk from his radio show, fair-weather friends shun him, and cowering producers withdraw job offers. His wife counsels accommodation, but a noble mentor, an unrepentant communist played by the avuncular John Houseman, steers him on the path of defiance. Faulk resolves to fight Vincent Hartnett of AWARE, Inc. and the blacklisting grocer Laurence

---

2. *Fear on Trial* telescopes the timeline of blacklist history. *See It Now* (telecast on March 9, 1954), the death of Philip Loeb (September 1, 1955), and the listing of Faulk in the AWARE, Inc. bulletin (February 12, 1956) all happen within a 24-hour period.

A. Johnson not just for himself but for "Phil Loeb, Mady Christians, and Don Hollenbeck and the others who have been killed by this thing."[3]

During the courtroom scenes depicting Faulk's civil case, television convicts itself. "The networks each had a clearance board—ABC, NBC, CBS—all of them," the testimony confirms. Two witnesses are especially eloquent and effective: producers David Susskind and Mark Goodson, both playing themselves, reenacting their roles in Faulk's trial. Susskind repeats his devastating testimony about an eight-year-old actress being deemed "politically unacceptable" by AWARE, Inc. However, the most famous witness to testify for Faulk, the actress Kim Hunter, is given the pseudonym "Nan Clayburn," her brush with the blacklist still leaving the actress leery of association with controversial personalities (Hunter did appear with Faulk and Nizer to discuss the made-for-TV movie on WCBS's *Pat Collins Show* in New York the morning after the telecast).

After the verdict is returned, Scott breaks character to deliver a postmortem:

So the blacklist ended finally. Some of the worst fears of the '50s had been overcome. John Henry Faulk returned to Texas and eventually found employment on a Dallas radio station.

Scrolling by on the end credits appears a name familiar only to the cognoscenti: the blacklisted actress Madeline Lee, whose name, and looks, had once caused three other actresses to be blacklisted.

In tandem with *Fear on Trial* and *Tail Gunner Joe*, the post-Watergate era witnessed the unreeling of the McCarthy era in myriad television documentaries and news reports. Almost all hewed to the revisionist template. Typical was an *ABC News Close Up* telecast on June 23, 1983. Entitled "The American Inquisition," the program reviewed the story of two victims of McCarthyism. Correspondent Marshall Frady set the scene with a capsule history lesson in

---

3. After a short illness, the actress Mady Christians died of a cerebral hemorrhage on October 28, 1951. CBS newscaster Don Hollenback committed suicide on June 22, 1954. He had been attacked by television critic Jack O'Brian for being a faithful comrade at CBS, "the Communist Broadcasting Station." Retrospective accounts of the blacklist era tend to up the ante and portray blacklist victims as more than metaphoric, to rack up a literal body count. Similarly, the hard-living actor John Garfield, who died of a heart attack on May 21, 1952, at the age of 39, is also often counted as a victim of a lethal encounter with HUAC, not nicotine and alcohol. On the other hand, as writer Elmer Rice commented to the *New York Post* at the time of the death of Mady Christians, "Nobody could prove what mental anguish can do to a woman with high blood pressure."

Cold War America, a time when dread of Soviet Communism "set loose a national season of fear—Congressional hearings, spy trials, loyalty checks in companies (including the broadcast networks), purges in Hollywood and on campuses. Before it was all over with, it had left over America a wake of ruined lives." Frady pauses dramatically. "Tonight we'll return into that time through the personal stories of private citizens among the thousands of ordinary Americans also caught up in the McCarthy terror across this country. People very much like you. Their stories hardly embrace the whole era but they do show what was so frightening about the time."

By far the most extensive and expensive entry arrived in timely fashion at the end of the twentieth century. CNN's 24-part documentary series *Cold War* (1998) sought to sum up the political and cultural consensus on the superpower confrontation. Conceived as being to the Cold War what Thames Television's magisterial *World at War* (1972–1974) series was to World War II, *Cold War* was scrupulously nonpartisan and nonjudgmental, determined (at the personal directive of CNN President Ted Turner) to avoid any unsportsman-like "triumphalism." The main concession to the dynamics of the bipolar struggle was to film witnesses from the West facing screen left and witnesses from the East facing screen right.

Episode six, entitled "Reds: 1947–1953," is an impartial survey of the crimes of two Cold War Josephs: McCarthy, the reckless junior senator from Wisconsin, and Stalin, the genocidal maniac from Georgia. The hour-long show equitably divides the two tales of domestic oppression into two evenly parceled segments of screen time, where the hundreds dragged before congressional committees are paired with the millions shipped off to the Gulag. In the war over the memory and the meaning of the Cold War, McCarthy was granted equal time not merely with Harry Truman or Adlai Stevenson but with Joseph Stalin.

Of course, by any measured calculus, when set against the spectacular horrors of the twentieth century, McCarthyism was a blip on the cultural radar, the man himself a rank amateur as a tyrant, undisciplined, ineffectual, in the end, pathetic. He lacked the single-minded determination and predatory intelligence to orchestrate the apparatus of state terror—imprisonment, torture, murder—even if his fellow Americans had been willing accomplices. He left behind no legislation, no death camps, no mass graves. Contra Shakespeare and Edward R. Murrow, most of the evil McCarthy did was interred with his bones.

But if McCarthy sank into the dustbin of history with whirlwind speed, McCarthyism persisted as the dominant referent for the atmosphere of Cold War America and, over time, an infinitely malleable epithet in offshoots such as reverse McCarthyism, sexual McCarthyism, racial McCarthyism, and online McCarthyism. Ultimately, however, all positions on the political spectrum no longer insisted on the once essential ingredient: communism.

The other essential ingredient is never overlooked. Whether as coconspira-
tors or sworn enemies, paired in symbiosis or antagonism, television and Mc-
Carthyism are fellow travelers in American history, the rising arc of the medium and the falling arc of the man intersecting at a pivotal moment for each.
Milton Berle may have been the first superstar made by television, but Joseph
McCarthy was the first superstar undone by television. No wonder the medium has so faithfully preserved and enhanced the memory of McCarthyism.

A television critic, no less than a network executive, should be wary about
predicting the kinds of programming that will prove popular in future sea-
sons. Yet as long as the dominant medium of the last century retains dominance in the next (and with high-definition imagery, widescreen framing, and
computer hybridity, the latest video mutations are models of evolutionary
adaptation), the persistence of the television vision of Cold War America and
the screen immortality of its featured villain seems assured. For some time
now, Benjamin Franklin's dictum, *litera scripta manet*, "the written word remains," has been overdue for update: *televisio scripta manet*, "the television
text remains"—and the television texts transmitted most incessantly, most
lovingly, will always concern television itself.

1. Video Rising

Page 2: **The conventional wisdom:** A notable dissent, and a work that has shaped my own thinking on television, is David Marc, *Demographic Vistas: Television and American Culture* (Philadelphia: University of Pennsylvania Press, 1984).

Page 3: **Beset from birth:** Erik Barnouw, *Tube of Plenty: The Evolution of American Television* (New York: Oxford University Press, 1990), 112.

Page 4: **"In my frayed estimation:** Fred Allen, "In Defense of Radio?" *Variety*, September 1, 1948: 2.

Page 4: **Allen's jaundiced perspective:** Fred Allen "showed only a slight resemblance to the satiric comedian regarded by many as one of the sharpest wits in show business," judged a critic of the quiz show *Judge for Yourself* (1953–54), one of Allen's many unsuccessful attempts to jump media. *Broadcasting/Telecasting*, August 23, 1953: 18.

Page 4: **As early as 1951:** "TV Promises No More Claims Child Is an Outcast Without It," *New York Herald Tribune*, March 8, 1951: 2.

Page 5: **More necessary:** "Prized Possession," *Television Age*, December 12, 1960: 32–33, 63.

Page 5: **In 1954, NBC President:** Sylvester L. (Pat) Weaver, "Credo in Broadcasting's Tomorrow," *Variety*, January 6, 1954: 91.

Page 5: **If Weaver's forecast:** Nineteen fifty-four is the linchpin year for television penetration. By the end of that year, declared Erik Barnouw, "few people now dared to be without a television set." The cultural historian Eric F. Goldman concurred: "By 1954–55, it had gone so far that for many Americans home was close to meaning the place where the TV set was located." Barnouw, *Tube of Plenty*, 182; Goldman in *The Crucial Decade: America, 1945–1955* (New York: Knopf, 1956), 265.

Page 6: **"TV Audience Now Equals:** "TV Audience Now Equals Films," *Hollywood Reporter*, June 19, 1950: 1, 6.

Page 6: **Television "tossed Joe Louis:** Dan Jenkins, "On the Air," *Hollywood Reporter*, October 29, 1951: 14.

Page 6: **Alarmed motion picture executives:** W. R. Wilkerson, "Tradeviews," *Hollywood Reporter*, September 29, 1950: 1, 2.

Page 7: **Korea would later:** The number of combat deaths in the Korean War has long been in dispute. On June 25, 2000, an Associated Press report on the fiftieth anniversary of the conflict noted that for years after the war, the Pentagon issued a figure of 54,260, comprised of 33,643 battle deaths and 20,617 deaths from other causes. In 1989, however, the Pentagon began revising the figure because the "other causes" included U.S. military deaths worldwide between 1950–1953, rather than deaths on the Korean Peninsula. The figure given here combines the latest estimates for 33,651 battle deaths and 3,262 deaths from other causes on the Korean Peninsula.

Page 8: **By printing so many:** John Cogley, *Report on Blacklisting II: Radio-Television* (New York: Fund for the Republic, 1956), 2. Note that even before the publication of *Red Channels*, the television industry had signaled a willingness to fold under pressure from anticommunist activists. "Communist scare, which set Hollywood back on its heels two years ago, has grabbed a stranglehold on television," *Variety* reported in 1949. "Pervading fear of being tainted with any shade of red has reached such a point among TV networks and ad agencies that any actor, writer, or producer who has been even remotely identified with leftist tendencies is shunned." However, without a comprehensive list of controversial personalities or a bureaucratic process for clearance, the blacklist could not coalesce into a true racket. *Red Channels* marks the official, as it were, beginning of the television blacklist not only because of the heightened level of pressure applied but because of the systematic enumeration of targets and the clear course of action to be taken against them. "Red Scare Numbing Video," *Variety*, August 17, 1949: 33, 40.

Page 8: **It was one playbill:** *Red Channels: The Report of Communist Influence in Radio and Television* (New York: American Business Consultants, 1950).

Page 8: **Positioned atop Mount Wilson:** "Atom Test 'Goes TV,'" *Variety*, February 7, 1951: 1.

Pages 9–10: **With characteristic glibness:** "In Review," *Broadcasting/Telecasting*, April 28, 1952: 28; Jack Gould, "Radio and Television," *New York Times*, April 23, 1952: 35; "A-Bomb in TV Fluff Fizzles Fission Vision," *Variety*, April 23, 1952: 1, 55.

Page 10: **The special show:** Sonia Stein, "A-Blast to Be Sponsored by Public Service Ad Group," *Washington Post*, March 16, 1953: 21.

Page 10: **Imagine, warned civil defense:** "Atomic Bomb Telecasts," *Broadcasting/Telecasting*, May 23, 1953: 14–15; "TV View of Atomic Blast Declared Good," *Los Angeles Herald and Express*, March 17, 1953: A4.

Page 11: **Murrow failed to reckon:** "Newsreels Criticize Poor Quality of Government Footage on H-Bomb," *Variety*, April 7, 1954: 1, 56.

Page 11: **"First Films:** Universal-International Newsreel, April 1, 1952, viewed at the National Archives, College Park, Md. (hereinafter, NA-CPM).

Page 12: **Sold commercially at $28:** "CBS-TV Claims 'First' Showing of H-Films," *Broadcasting/Television*, April 5, 1954: 32.

Page 13: **"A frightening reminder:** "Tele Follow-Up," *Variety*, May 26, 1954: 39, 52.

Page 13: **No other surname:** In 1994 McCarthy's preeminence as a specter haunting American history was confirmed when the National Center of History in the Schools published a guidebook entitled *National Standards for United States History: Exploring the American Experience*. The center found that a significant portion of the American experience revolved around Joseph McCarthy. While such lesser lights in American history as Robert E. Lee, Thomas Edison, and the Wright Brothers garnered not a single mention, McCarthyism warranted nineteen separate references. According to one professor who helped set the new standards for teaching the fundamentals of American history to grades five through twelve, the scholarly consensus now held that "the 1950s were characterized as much by racism and McCarthyist repression as by suburban bliss." Lynne V. Cheney, "The End of History," *Wall Street Journal*, October 20, 1994: A22; James Atlas, "Ways to Look at the Past (Or Did It Really Happen?)," *New York Times*, November 13, 1994: D3; John Elson, "History, the Sequel," *Time*, November 7, 1994: 64.

Page 13: **If he made the:** Scholarship on McCarthy and his "-ism" has ballooned into an academic growth industry. See especially Thomas C. Reeves, *The Life and Times of Joe McCarthy* (New York: Stein and Day, 1982); David M. Oshinsky, *A Conspiracy So Immense: The World of Joseph McCarthy* (New York: Free Press, 1983); and William Bragg Ewald Jr., *Who Killed Joe McCarthy?* (New York: Simon and Schuster, 1984). A revisionist view is provided by Arthur Herman, *Joseph McCarthy: Re-examining the Life of America's Most Hated Senator* (New York: Free Press, 1999). On McCarthy as a creature of video, see Edwin R. Bayley, *Joe McCarthy and the Press* (New York: Pantheon, 1981), 176–213.

Page 14: **Unfortunately, McCarthy's career-making talk:** A taped recording of McCarthy's Wheeling, West Virginia, speech was broadcast on local radio station WWVA that evening, but the tape, as was common practice at the time, was erased afterwards. Reeves, *Life and Times*, 225–26.

Page 14: **The coinage caught on:** A sampling of contemporaneous definitions: "McCarthyism after 1950 came to mean 'character assassination'" (Jack Anderson and Ronald W. May, *McCarthy: The Man, the Senator, the "Ism,"* [Boston: Beacon Press, 1952], 351); McCarthyism means "smearing the innocent, the big lie, and 'shoot first, ask later'" (*The Progressive* [April 1954]: 51); "Whatever is illiberal, repressive, reactionary, obscurantist, anti-intellectual, totalitarian, or merely swinish" (Richard Rovere, *Senator Joe McCarthy* [New York: Harcourt, Brace, 1959], 7).

Page 15: **Also on television:** *American Forum of the Air* (NBC), December 6, 1953, screened at the Motion Picture Division of the Library of Congress, Washington, D.C. (hereinafter, MPD-LOC).

Page 16 (note 3): **The muddling of:** Lisa Nesselson, "Survival Instincts," *Variety*, June 9–15, 1997: 7, 12.

Page 16: **"Completely phoney:** "Senator McCarthy Reported Planning Weekly TV Show," *Sponsor*, September 14, 1953: 67; "Inside Stuff—Television," *Variety*, June 24, 1953: 44.

Page 16: **Whether through negligence:** Letter from Ben Custer to Edward R. Murrow, March 19, 1954, on file at the Murrow Center, Tufts University, Medford, Mass.

Page 18: **"[Truman] meant that:** *American Forum of the Air*, December 6, 1953 (MPD-LOC).

2. The Gestalt of the Blacklist

Page 19: "**Television's top detective:** Mike Connolly, "Rambling Reporter," *Hollywood Reporter*, September 9, 1953: 2.

Page 20: **The entertainment industry:** The blacklist in film and television has inspired an ever proliferating body of scholarship. The indispensable source is Stefan Kanfer, *A Journal of the Plague Years* (New York: Atheneum, 1973), the first work to name names. Robert Vaughn, *Only Victims: A Study of Show Business Blacklisting* (New York: Limelight Editions, 1996 [1972]) benefits from the actor-author's insider access to Hollywood personalities. See also Larry Ceplair and Steven Englund, *The Inquisition in Hollywood: Politics in the Film Community* (Garden City, N.J.: Anchor Press, 1980). A thriving subgenre of oral histories has also probed the memory of the blacklist era, but the personal accounts often swoon before the romance of American communism. See, for example, Patrick McGilligan and Paul Buhle, *Tender Comrades: A Backstory of the Hollywood Blacklist* (New York: St. Martin's, 1997).

Page 22: "**We are not going:** "Film Industry's Policy Defined," *Variety*, November 26, 1947: 3.

Page 23: *Motion Picture Daily*: Mandel Herbstman, "*I Was a Communist for the FBI*," *Motion Picture Daily*, August 19, 1951.

Page 23: **Although the sops:** "Johnson Cites Anti-Red Films," *Hollywood Reporter*, August 29, 1950: 6. See also "Exhibs' Tepid Reaction Cools Prod. of Commie Pic," *Variety*, August 4, 1948: 2, and "People Want Solace and Escape, Not Realistic Films Against Reds—Johnson," *Variety*, June 9, 1954: 1, 53.

Page 23: "**The feeling is strong:** "Un-Am Activities Group Under Way with Red Probe into Radio, TV, Legit," *Variety*, May 30, 1951: 2, 20.

Page 23: **Jack O'Brian:** Jack O'Brian, "Radio and TV," *New York Journal-American*, August 25, 1951: 18.

Page 23: **Conjuring a dire scenario:** "Wrong Channels," *Broadcasting/Telecasting*, April 14, 1952: 52.

Page 23: "**Those who are responsible:** Earl B. Abrams, "'Red' Probings," *Broadcasting/Telecasting*, September 1, 1952: 27, 88.

Page 23: "**Communists will endeavor:** "Warning TV Networks," *Television Digest*, February 23, 1952: 7.

Page 24: **The exemplar was:** Oliver Pilat, "Blacklist: The Veto Power in TV-Radio," *New York Post*, January 27, 1953: 4, 36.

Page 27: "**When TV came along:** Myron C. Fagan, *Red Treason in Hollywood!* (Hollywood: Cinema Educational Guild, 1949): 7; and Myron C. Fagan, *Red Treason on Broadway* (Cinema Educational Guild, 1954): 84. The front cover of *Red Treason in Hollywood!* identifies Fagan as "one of the great producers, writers, and directors of Hollywood and Broadway. Because of the facts revealed in this volume, Mr. Fagan was blacklisted by Hollywood moguls who loved profit more than patriotism."

Page 28: "**Everyone—ad agencies and networks:** John Crosby, "The 'Faceless Accusation' Is Still Plaguing Actors," *Washington Post*, July 25, 1953: 25.

Page 28: **Recruited from a class:** The phrase is from Colin Schindler, *Hollywood in Crisis: Cinema and American Society, 1929–1939* (New York: Routledge, 1996): 52–72.

Page 29: **"At that time:** "A Statement by Elia Kazan," *New York Times*, April 12, 1952: 7.

Page 30: **"I was an innocent dupe:** Marvin Sleeper, "Shaw Swears He Was Never a Red," *New York Journal-American*, May 4, 1953: 1, 2.

Page 30: **The title of actor:** Edward G. Robinson, "How the Reds Made a Sucker Out of Me," *American Legion* (October 1952): 62–70.

Page 30: **A fourth hapless actress:** Oliver Pilat, "Blacklist: The Panic in TV-Radio," *New York Post*, January 26, 1953: 4, 14. This is the first in a six-part series on the blacklist in television and radio.

Page 30: **"In the radio and television:** "Sokolsky Blasts 'Hatriots,'" *Variety*, November 11, 1953: 1, 20.

Page 31: **In 1953 *TV Guide*:** Bob Stahl, "TV Teletype," *TV Guide*, April 3, 1953: 3.

Page 31: **Yet Stander's phone:** "Stander's Stand as Anti-Commie," *Variety*, April 11, 1951: 4, 12.

Page 31: **Two years later:** "Lionel Stander Hits House Red Probe as an 'Inquisition,'" *Hollywood Reporter*, May 7, 1953: 2.

Page 31: **"You should see:** "The Truth About Red Channels," *Sponsor*, October 22, 1951: 83.

Page 32: **Gypsy Rose Lee:** "Anti-Red Protests," *Broadcasting/Telecasting*, September 18, 1950: 23, 38–39.

Page 32: **In the aftermath:** Dan Jenkins, "On the Air," *Hollywood Reporter*, January 10, 1952: 11.

Page 32: **Satirist Abe Burrows:** "Morley Testimony Charges 'Blacklisting,'" *Broadcasting/Telecasting*, November 24, 1952: 60.

Page 32: **"Individual [HUAC] members:** "Witnesses Who Aid Probers Get House Job Help," *Variety*, January 30, 1952: 1, 17.

Page 33: **At the *Hollywood Reporter*:** "Dan Jenkins, "On the Air," *Hollywood Reporter*, January 19, 1952: 11.

Page 33: **The blacklist, John Crosby:** John Crosby, "The 'Faceless Accusation' Is Still Plaguing Actors," *Washington Post*, July 25, 1953: 25.

Page 33: **The most concentrated counterattack:** Merle Miller, *The Judges and the Judged* (New York: Doubleday, 1952): 34, 209, 212.

Page 33: **"Exactly as though:** Walter Kerr, "An Exhaustive Study of *Red Channels*, Its Methods and Effects," *New York Herald Tribune Book Review*, April 20, 1952: 5.

Page 33: **On April 10, 1952:** "Tele Follow-up Comment," *Variety*, April 16, 1952: 26.

Page 34: **The most comprehensive critique:** "The Truth About Red Channels," *Sponsor*, October 8, 1951: 27–29, 75–81; "The Truth About Red Channels," *Sponsor*, October 22, 1951: 30–31, 76–85; "How to Keep Reds Off—Sanely," *Sponsor*, November 5, 1951: 32–33; 84–86.

Page 34: **Even performers fired:** "The Blacklist 'Hot Potato,'" *Variety*, March 4, 1953: 29.

Page 34: **In December 1950:** Jack Gould, "CBS Demanding Loyalty Oaths from Its 2,500 Regular Employees," *New York Times*, December 21, 1950: 1, 17; "Unions May Gang Up on CBS Loyalty Pledge; Await Authors League Stand," *Variety*, December 27, 1950: 19, 29.

Page 35: **On August 27, 1950:** "Red Issue Snags 'Aldrich' TV Bow," *Hollywood Reporter*, August 29, 1950: 7.

Page 35: **Pleading that she:** "Ousting of Jean Muir from 'Aldrich' Seen Setting Widespread Precedent," *Variety*, August 30, 1950: 1, 54.

Page 35: **The normally dulcet singer:** "Vallee Whips It Up," *Variety*, September 20, 1950: 22.

Page 35: **The ACLU lectured:** "Red Problem Mounts," *Broadcasting/Telecasting*, September 25, 1950: 27, 93.

3. Controversial Personalities

Page 37: ***The Goldbergs*** (1949–1955): *The Goldbergs* has inspired a good deal of interest from television historians. See George Lipschitz, *Time Passages: Collective Memory and Popular Culture* (Minneapolis: University of Minnesota Press, 1990): 39–76; David Weber, "Memory and Repression in Early Ethnic Television: The Example of Gertrude Berg and *The Goldbergs*," in Joel Foreman, ed., *The Other Fifties: Interrogating Midcentury American Icons* (Urbana: University of Illinois Press, 1997): 144–167; Vincent Brook, "The Americanization of Molly: How Mid-Fifties TV Homogenized *The Goldbergs* (and Got 'Berg-larized' in the Process," *Cinema Journal* (Summer 1999): 45–67.

Page 38: **Due to "radio's fear:** "Yid Comedy Gets Over," *Variety*, November 27, 1929: 65.

Page 38: **Even as Hitler:** "The Goldbergs' Rise to Fame," *New York Times*, May 4, 1930: sec. 12, p. 16; John K. Hutchins, "And Going Strong," *New York Times*, April 30, 1944: B5.

Page 39: **Reportedly, she would walk:** "*The Goldbergs*," *TV Guide*, July 24, 1953: 17.

Page 39: **"It is hard, darling:** "Again, Molly," *Newsweek*, April 11, 1949: 58.

Page 39: **"Imagine *Awake and Sing*:** Brooks Atkinson, "*Me and Molly*," *New York Times*, February 27, 1948: 27.

Page 39: **"Television called for no:** Gertrude Berg, "TV and Molly," *Variety*, July 27, 1949: 46.

Page 40: **"Despite a 17-year reign:** "*The Goldbergs*," *Variety*, January 19, 1949: 26.

Page 40: **"While *The Goldbergs* does:** "*The Goldbergs*," *Hollywood Reporter*, November 24, 1950: 3.

Page 40: **Despite the seemingly narrow:** "The Goldbergs March On," *Life*, April 25, 1949: 59.

Page 40: **It was also the first:** Dan Jenkins, "On the Air," *Hollywood Reporter*, September 7, 1950: 9.

Page 40: **"No doubt the picture:** Mandel Herbstman, "*Molly*," *Motion Picture Daily*, November 24, 1950.

Page 41: **Berg loved to tell:** "Life with Molly," *Time*, September 26, 1949: 40.

Page 41: **"You see, darling:** Morris Freedman, "The Real Molly Goldberg," *Commentary*, (April 1956): 360.

Page 42: **"When Molly Goldberg:** "Tele Follow-up Comment," *Variety*, March 8, 1950: 34.

Page 43: **Berg denied that:** "Blacklisting: Loeb's Dismissal Draws Fire," *Broadcasting/Telecasting*, January 14, 1952: 60.

Page 43: **Loeb refused:** This account is based on Loeb's public statement to the membership of Actors' Equity, confirmed by Brownstein. Minutes of the meeting of January 11, 1951: 55–56, on file at Actors' Equity Association, New York, New York (*see* Actors' Equity Minutes).

Page 43: **Thus far, the intrigue:** Jack O'Brian, "Radio and TV," *New York Journal-American*, August 25, 1951: 18.

Page 43: **Never discreet about naming:** Jack O'Brian, "Denis Bark Is Worse Than His Fight," *New York Journal-American*, June 1, 1951: 28.

Page 43: **Suspecting a "silent conspiracy":** "Sponsor Standoff Bewilders NBC in 'Goldbergs' Bid," *Variety*, October 31, 1951: 21.

Page 43: **"Since Sanka's cancellation:** "The Truth About *Red Channels*," *Sponsor*, October 8, 1951: 79.

Page 44: **Like the meeting at:** Mike Connolly, "Rambling Reporter," *Hollywood Reporter*, February 1, 1952: 2.

Page 44: **To back Loeb:** On the TvA and Loeb, see Rita Morley Harvey, *Those Wonderful Horrible Years: George Heller and the American Federation of Television and Radio Artists* (Carbondale: Southern Illinois University Press, 1996): 105–113.

Page 44: **"Either of two things:** "'Blacklist' Action in Loeb Case," *Variety*, January 16, 1952: 27, 36.

Page 45: **The writer Rex Stout:** "ACLU Asks FCC Action on 'Blacklisting,'" *Broadcasting/Telecasting*, April 14, 1952: 25.

Page 45: **"This may sound stupid:** "Loeb Hearing," *Broadcasting/Telecasting*, January 21, 1952: 70.

Page 45: **"Who is the culprit?:** Actors' Equity Minutes, 57–58.

Page 45: **TvA released a statement:** "Loeb Case," *Broadcasting/Telecasting*, January 28, 1952: 80.

Page 46: **"Isn't it possible:** "*The Goldbergs*," *Variety*, September 28, 1955: 38.

Page 47: **Like Milton Berle:** The media historian Arthur Frank Wertheim has chronicled how Berle's "technique of often playing to his large New York audience" and "citified comic style was not really suited to the new small-town and rural audiences"—meaning Berle was too Jewish. "The Rise and Fall of Milton Berle," in John E. O'Connor, ed., *American History/American Television* (New York: Unger, 1983): 55–78.

Page 47: **"There is some hinterland:** Abel Green, "Too Much Borscht?" *Variety*, February 28, 1951: 28.

Page 47: **"A certain segment:** "*The Goldbergs*," *TV Guide*, July 24, 1953: 17.

Page 47: **On April 25, 1952:** "Not Communists Performers Tell Probers," *Broadcasting/Telecasting*, September 29, 1952: 116.

Page 48: **Though the FBI:** "Communist Infiltration in the Entertainment Industry," Microfilm Reel 6, June 2, 1951 (Headquarters, Federal Bureau of Investigation, Washington, D.C.).

Page 48: **Eventually, Loeb's FBI watcher:** Philip Loeb's FBI file (#65–19839) is available from the FBI under the Freedom of Information Act.

Page 48: **He left no note:** The melancholy circumstances of Loeb's final hours are chronicled in Stefan Kanfer, *A Journal of the Plague Years* (New York: Atheneum, 1973): 3–7; Jeff Kisseloff, *The Box: An Oral History of Television* (New York: Penguin, 1995): 423–27; and Rita Morley Harvey, *Those Wonderful Horrible Years*, 178–79. For contemporary accounts, see "Loeb's Death Caused by Congestion," *New York Journal-American*, September 2, 1955: 22; and "Philip Loeb Dies; Actor, Unionist," *Variety*, September 7, 1955: 65, 67.

Page 49: **"She is a consummate artist:** Dan Jenkins, "*I Love Lucy*," *Hollywood Reporter*, October 16, 1951: 10.

Page 49: **Reaching back for:** Jack Gould, "Why Millions Love Lucy," *New York Times Magazine*, March 1, 1953: 16.

Page 50: **Company president O. Parker McComas:** "Love Lucy More Efficient Than 'Life' or Papers," *Broadcasting/Telecasting*, March 9, 1953: 11.

Page 51: **"We made no attempt:** "Lucille Ball Adheres to Television Script; Comedienne Gives Birth to 8 1/2 Pound Boy," *New York Times*, January 20, 1953: 27.

Page 51: **Fortunately, Lucy's obstetrical:** "*I Love Lucy*," *Broadcasting/Telecasting*, January 26, 1953: 14; "Lucille Ball Baby Shatters Ratings," *Variety*, January 21, 1953: 1.

Page 52: **On April 3, 1953:** "Lucy's $50,000,000 Baby," *TV Guide*, April 3, 1953: 5–7.

Page 52: **On September 6, 1953:** Selected transcripts of Winchell's telecasts are included in his voluminous FBI file, available through the Freedom of Information Act and now on the FBI's official Web site.

Page 52: **"Lucille Ball announces:** Jack O'Brian, "Television and Radio," *New York Journal-American*, September 9, 1953: 32.

Page 52: **Hot on the scent:** Hedda Hopper, "Happy Rumors Cleared, Lucy Tells Columnist," *Los Angeles Times*, September 12, 1953: 1.

Page 53: **Speaking out in defense:** "Lucille Ball Solon Plans New Checks," *Los Angeles Herald and Express*, September 14, 1953: 1, 8.

Page 53: **Two days before Winchell's:** "Transcript of Testimony," *Los Angeles Herald and Express*, September 12, 1953: 1, 2.

Page 54: **On Friday, September 11, 1953:** "—Voted for Ike," *Los Angeles Herald and Express*, September 11, 1953: 1.

Page 54: **To refute the "conjecture:** "Lucy's Commie Affiliation Causes National Sensation," *Hollywood Reporter*, September 14, 1953: 3; "Data in Star Quiz Revealed," *Los Angeles Examiner*, September 12, 1953.

Page 55: **The emotionally charged atmosphere:** Dan Jenkins, "The Lucille Ball–Communist Probe Story," *TV Guide*, October 2, 1953: 13–14; "Audience Loves Lucy," *Los Angeles Herald and Express*, September 12, 1953: 4.

Page 56: **Mollified by her juicy scoop:** Hedda Hopper, "Happy Rumors Cleared, Lucy Tells Columnist," *Los Angeles Times*, September 12, 1953: 1.

Page 56: **On Saturday afternoon:** "Lucille Ball Explains 1939 Communist Link," *Los Angeles Times*, September 13, 1953: 1, 3.

Page 56: **CBS vice president Harry Ackerman:** "Fans Love Lucy; Take Her Side in Red Affair," *Variety*, September 16, 1953: 1, 40.

Page 57: **Mike Connolly, Jenkins's:** Mike Connolly, "Rambling Reporter," *Hollywood Reporter*, September 14, 1953: 2.

Page 58: **CBS backed Lucy:** "Lucille Ball Is Cleared of Communist Association," *Broadcasting/Telecasting*, September 21, 1953: 52.

Page 58: **"It isn't the formula:** John Crosby, "The Unborn Celebrity," *New York Herald Tribune*, December 21, 1952: sec. 4, p. 1.

Page 58: **On November 23, 1953:** Leo Guild, "On the Air," *Hollywood Reporter*, November 23, 1953: 10.

Page 59: **During the 1953–54 season:** Bob Stahl, "TV Teletype," *TV Guide*, July 9, 1954: 13.

Page 59: **"Everyone still loves Lucy:** "Lucille Ball," *New Republic*, September 28, 1953: 4.

4. Hypersensitivity: The Codes of Television Censorship

Page 61: **Finally, on April 14, 1952:** On the lifting of the FCC freeze, see "Final TV Report," a special supplement published by *Broadcasting/Telecasting*, April 14, 1952.

Page 61: **Thus, in defending:** "The Truth About *Red Channels*," *Sponsor*, October 8, 1951: 76.

Page 61: **Throughout the early days:** For a nuanced study of the many pressures weighing on the emerging medium, see William Boddy, *Fifties Television: The Industry and Its Critics* (Urbana: University of Illinois Press, 1990).

Page 61: **"TV, in practically all areas:** George Rosen, "Television's Merry-Go-Round," *Variety*, January 21, 1953: 1, 22.

Page 62: **That same year:** "Personal Notes," *Television Digest*, February 28, 1953: 8.

Page 62: **"Were the shows:** "TV Cameras on Congress," *Television Age* (August 1953): 57–59.

Page 62: **"We do not believe:** Ward Dorrell, "How the Different Ratings Services Differ in the Same Market," *Sponsor*, January 25, 1954: 34–35; Joe Ward, "I Say Ratings Are Opinion—Not Fact," *Sponsor*, May 31, 1954: 40–41, 58–59. Billed as "the magazine radio and television advertisers use," *Sponsor* naturally took an intense interest in the reliability of ratings techniques. Throughout the early 1950s, it reported regularly on the troubles with ratings in determining precisely the popularity of programs and the demographic profile of viewers. See also "TV Ratings: Fact or Fraud?" *TV Guide*, April 17, 1953: 10–11, and William Dignam, "Suicide by Research," *Television Age* (August 1953): 36–37, 61.

Page 62: **"Ratings services:** "Allen's Sallies," *Variety*, April 30, 1952: 1.

Page 63: **"As a sponsor:** "Viewer Gripes Are Your Tip Off to Better Programs," *Sponsor*, August 13, 1951: 30.

Page 63: **Japanese Americans objected:** "Minority Groups Hit TV Revival of 'Hate Films,'" *Variety*, April 16, 1952: 20.

Page 63: **"Nothing is terrorized:** "George Did It," *Broadcasting/Telecasting*, January 12, 1953: 48.

Page 63: **In 1951, *Sponsor* estimated:** "Viewer Gripes Are Your Tip Off to Better Programs," *Sponsor*, August 13, 1951: 71, 72.

Page 63: **"It's getting so:** Dan Jenkins, "On the Air," *Hollywood Reporter*, January 6, 1953: 8.

Page 63: **Given all the "sponsors:** Richard Powell, "Who's Killing TV Comedy?" *TV Guide*, May 29, 1953: 10–11; "Low State of TV Comedy Blamed on Censorship, Pressure Groups," *Variety*, February 25, 1953: 1, 54.

Page 64: **"As for that item:** Jack O'Brian, "Faye's Neckline 'Slides' Where Once It Plunged," *New York Journal-American*, June 19, 1951: 28.

Page 64: **"Too many beautiful babes:** Harry Bannister, "TV's Headache—Censorship," *Variety*, January 2, 1952: 106.

Page 64: **Chiding the bluenoses:** "Viewer Gripes Are Your Tip Off to Better Programs," *Sponsor*, August 13, 1951: 71.

Page 64: **No fool she:** Val Adams, "Glamour Girl of the Television Screen," *New York Times*, February 19, 1950: B11.

Page 65: **The brushfire set off:** The Kaufman contretemps is recounted in: John Crosby, "Silent Kaufman," *New York Herald Tribune*, January 4, 1953: sec. 4, pp. 1, 4; "Top Churchman Defends Kaufman in 'Showbiz' Row, Blasts CBS' Move," *Variety*, January 7, 1953: 106; "George Did It," *Broadcasting/Telecasting*, January 12, 1953: 48; "Inside Stuff—Television," *Variety*, January 14, 1953: 34; "This Is Show Business," *Variety*, January 28, 1953: 31; and "Telecasting Notes," *Television Digest*, January 1, 1953: 6.

Page 66: **(On matters of religion:** "'Fast' Kinnie," *Variety*, September 9, 1953: 27.

Page 66: **Of all the exposed nerve endings:** "TV Script Taboos Increasing," *Hollywood Reporter*, June 11, 1954: 7.

Page 66: **Bonehead demands:** These and other sponsor demands are recounted in Ira Skutch, ed., *The Days of Live: Television's Golden Age as Seen by 21 Directors Guild of America Members* (Los Angeles: Directors Guild of America, 1998); Jeff Kisseloff, *The Box: An Oral History of Television* (New York: Penguin, 1995); and "TV Taboos: What You Can't See on TV," *TV Guide*, February 26, 1954: 7–9.

Page 66: **In November 1952:** Robert J. Landry, "It's the Smog, Not the Smoke," *Variety*, November 11, 1953: 27, 43.

Page 66: **For anyone who wanted:** "Ciggie Duel Fattens Radio, TV," *Variety*, June 22, 1949: 1, 24.

Page 67: **Estimating that 50 percent:** "The Big Smoke," *Television Age* (August 1953): 31–33, 52, 54.

Page 67: **Unable to retaliate:** "WW Ciggy Rap Loses Sponsor," *Billboard*, January 2, 1954: 1. In 1955, reviewing Edward R. Murrow's two-part investigation into the link between smoking and lung cancer on *See It Now*, *Variety* noted the cultural lag but forgot Walter Winchell's pioneering reporting and accusation. "Television finally caught up with the lung cancer story. It took a long time and brought back memories of the day the first big story on the lung cancer–cigarette link broke and the network tv news wanted no part of it." "Tele Follow-up Comment," *Variety*, June 15, 1955: 21.

Page 68: **Resenting the depiction:** Dan Jenkins, "On the Air," *Hollywood Reporter*, February 2, 1953: 10.

Page 68: **Negotiated and refined:** See, for example, Harry Bannister, "TV's Headache—Censorship," *Variety*, January 2, 1952: 106; "NARTB [National Association of Radio and Television Broadcasters] Warned of Censorship if TV Code Fails," *Hollywood Reporter*, May 1, 1953: 1, 7.

Page 68: **Taking effect on March 1, 1952:** "The Television Code," reprinted in Charles S. Aaronson, ed., *The 1956 International Television Almanac* (New York: Quigley, 1956), 676–79. All citations are from this text of the 1954 revised Television Code.

Page 68: *Sponsor* **stated the obvious:** "Report to Sponsors," *Sponsor*, December 17, 1951: 1. See also "TV Code Should Reassure Public on Industry Aims to Reform, Sez Swezey," *Variety*, December 12, 1951: 25, 41.

Page 69: **"Controlled as it is:** "More Editorializing: McCarthy Reply a Dud," *Television Digest*, March 13, 1954: 2.

Page 69: **In 1952 the Authors League:** "FCC on Blacklisting," *Broadcasting/Telecasting*, February 2, 1952: 106.

Page 69: **"It is, after all:** "Wrong Channels," *Broadcasting/Telecasting*, April 14, 1952: 52.

Page 69: **Roused to action:** "TV Seen Rid of Plunging Neckline, Off Color Gab in 1st Code Report," *Variety*, November 18, 1953: 2, 43.

Page 70: **The flashpoint for:** Melvin Patrick Ely, *The Adventures of Amos 'n' Andy: A Social History of an American Phenomenon* (New York: Free Press, 1991). See also Thomas Cripps, *"Amos 'n' Andy* and the Debate Over American Racial Integration," in John E. O'Connor, ed., *American History/American Television* (New York: Unger, 1983), 33–54.

Page 70: **The alleged verisimilitude:** "Antics of Amos 'n' Andy Win National Applause," *New York Times*, February 2, 1930, sec. 8, p. 16.

Page 71: **"Perhaps no greater vehicle:** "Television Broadens Racial Understanding," *Pittsburgh Courier*, March 13, 1954: 18.

Page 72: **"Here any man:** "Original Amateur Hour Another Case of Democracy on the Beam," *Chicago Defender*, July 4, 1953: 19.

Page 72: **Watching the warm physical:** Rob Roy, "The True Story of the Original Amateur TV Show with Plugs for Mack, Sponsor," *Chicago Defender*, March 13, 1954: 18.

Page 72: **"The American Negro:** Robert J. Landry, "Sensational 10-Year Upsurge of Negro Market; Worth 15 Billion $ Yearly," *Variety*, January 27, 1954: 1, 69.

Page 72: **In America, the prospect:** Billy Rowe, "NAACP Blasts Myth of Video 'Fair Play,'" *Pittsburgh Courier*, May 27, 1950: 21.

Page 72: **"Southern states continue:** "Global Appeal of U.S. Negro Market," *Variety*, May 9, 1957: 3.

Page 73: **In 1956, state legislators:** "State Senators' Credo: Don't Want White Kids Seeing Negro Acts Mixing," *Variety*, June 13, 1956: 1, 20.

Page 73 (note 5): **The television historian:** Horace Newcomb, "The Opening of America: Meaningful Difference in 1950s Television," in Joel Foreman, ed., *The Other*

Fifties: Interrogating Midcentury American Icons (Urbana: University of Illinois Press, 1997), 103.

Page 73: **"Sullivan's video offering:** "Ed Sullivan's TV Opus Observes Third Year as Democratic Showcase," *Pittsburgh Courier*, January 9, 1951: 17.

Page 73: **When nervous advertisers:** "Pressure on TV Talent," *Variety*, June 20, 1956: 17.

Page 74: **Though the results:** "TV Webs Switch Racial and Facial Lyrics, Ban Some," *Variety*, May 9, 1956: 1, 54.

Page 74: **Stereotypes from vintage:** "NBC's 'Talent Has No Color' Projects Negro Contribs to New High in 1952," *Variety*, March 18, 1953: 1, 34.

Page 75: **"Talent has no color:** Ibid. Entitled "Parole," the *Philco Television Playhouse* teleplay in question was telecast November 16, 1952.

Page 75: **In 1953 the Coordinating Council:** "Negro Acts Appeal to Webs for 'Plums with the Crumbs,'" *Variety*, January 28, 1953: 1, 63.

Page 75: **Despite the progress:** "Inside Stuff—Television," *Variety*, February 25, 1953: 34.

Page 75: **Tallying up the black:** "Campaign Paying Off; TV Field Opening Up," *Pittsburgh Courier*, November 18, 1950: 14.

Page 76: **The talent scouts:** "Truman's a Talent Scout," *New York Times*, June 21, 1950: 29; Val Adams, "The Hunt for Kingfish on TV," *New York Times*, June 18, 1950: B19.

Page 76: **"Considering that this:** "*Amos 'n' Andy Show*," *Variety*, July 4, 1951: 37.

Page 76: **"As the chief victim:** "Be Careful on the Air," *Sponsor*, September 24, 1951: 36–37; 76–80.

Page 77: **By common consent:** See Dan Jenkins, "*Amos 'n' Andy*," *Hollywood Reporter*, June 29, 1951: 9; and "*Amos 'n' Andy Show*," *Variety*, July 4, 1951: 37.

Page 77: **NAACP executive director Walter White:** "Radio-TV Notes," *New York Times*, July 10, 1951: 35.

Page 77: **In speeches and newspaper:** Joseph D. Bibb, "Flays Amos 'n' Andy," *Pittsburgh Courier*, August 4, 1951: 7.

Page 78: **"It is the miracle:** L. F. Palmer, "Amos 'n' Andy Bow (Even Longer) on Video So Your Scribe Spends a Dull Half Hour," *Chicago Defender*, July 7, 1951: 23.

Page 78: **In pricking the conscience:** Walter White, "Amos 'n' Andy Inspire Walter White to Fight for Their Extinction," *Chicago Defender*, July 21, 1951: 7.

Page 79: **Delighted to be part:** John Hudson Jones, "TV's *Amos 'n' Andy*: Ballyhoo vs Boycott," *Masses and Mainstream* (September 1951): 59–61.

Page 79: **Figuring that work:** "Negro Thesps Score NAACP on 'A&A' Stand; Set 'Positive Action' Council,' *Variety*, August 8, 1951: 1, 6; "Actors Enter *Amos 'n' Andy* Television Controversy," *Chicago Defender*, August 18, 1951: 23.

Page 79: **Ruth Cage, an entertainment reporter:** Ruth Cage, "Billy Rowe's Notebook," *Pittsburgh Courier*, July 7, 1951: 17.

Page 79: **"Even the Kingfish:** Walter White, "Amos 'n' Andy Inspire Walter White to Fight for their Extinction," *Chicago Defender*, July 21, 1951: 7.

Page 79: **Taken aback by:** "Blatz's Goodwill Bid in A&A Snarl Backfires in Chi," *Variety*, August 8, 1951: 25, 40.

Page 80: **In 1953, after two years:** "Blatz Beer Cancels TV's Amos-Andy, Also Drops Time," *Variety*, March 11, 1953: 25.

Page 80: **The television life:** "Blatz Cancellation May Cue A&A's TV Demise; Alive and Kicking in Radio," *Variety*, April 1, 1953: 57. The article also notes that the show hadn't "figured in the bigtime ratings payoff" on television, but that assessment gauges the optimistic expectations, given the enormous success of the radio show.

Page 80: **Circulating in 16mm:** "Amos 'n' Andy Sales," *Broadcasting/Telecasting*, May 11, 1953: 34; *Variety*, May 16, 1956: 37.

5. Forums of the Air

Page 81: **"Up to now:** "Telecasting Notes," *Television Digest*, June 12, 1953: 14.

Page 81: **"Video is the answer:** Harold Lord Varney, "How TV Molds Your Minds," *American Mercury* (April 1954): 51–52.

Page 82: **"The fact that:** John Daly, "Television Spells Doom for the Demagogue and False Prophet," *Variety*, July 21, 1956: 39.

Page 82: **Looking back on:** "Press Praise Accorded GOP Coverage," *Broadcasting/Telecasting*, July 21, 1952: 61.

Page 82: **Observing that Republicans:** "H'wood Makeup Pretties Politicos," *Variety*, July 14, 1948: 31.

Page 82: **"That sunspot:** Jack O'Brian, "Television and Radio," *New York Journal-American*, September 23, 1953: 38.

Page 83: **"Makeup for television:** Robert C. Diefenbach, *A Guide to Your Television Appearance* (1958).

Page 83: **"One of the most:** "The TV Forum Shows," *Variety*, April 9, 1952: 42.

Page 83: *TV Guide* **tallied:** "Television on Sunday," *TV Guide*, March 12, 1955: 18–20.

Page 83: **"Led by Edward R. Murrow:** Edward Bliss Jr., *Now the News: The Story of Broadcast Journalism* (New York: Columbia University Press, 1991), 81–90.

Page 83: **"The special event:** Fred W. Friendly, "Lots of Barriers Must Come Down to Develop TV News," *Variety*, January 7, 1953: 103, 182.

Page 84: **"We still turn:** Dan Jenkins, "On the Air," *Hollywood Reporter*, March 17, 1952: 7. Five years later, the static and untimely quality of television news was still a journalistic embarrassment. "Television is not an ideal medium for purveying spot news," lamented *Variety*, "—and it may never be." Leonard Traube, "News on TV: Tiger by Tail," *Variety*, December 4, 1957: 39, 50.

Page 84: **"Filmed television can:** Martin Stone, "The Case for Live Television," *Broadcasting/Telecasting*, January 19, 1953: 77–78.

Page 85: **(At $125 per appearance:** "Newsman Covering D.C. Beat Reap Bonanza on AM-TV Panel Shows," *Variety*, November 18, 1953: 2.

Page 85: **For example, on July 2, 1950:** *Meet the Press*, July 2, 1950 (Motion Picture Division of the Library of Congress, Washington, D.C.; hereinafter, MPD-LOC).

Page 86: **Likewise, on an episode:** *Chronoscope*, September 29, 1952 (National Archives, College Park, Md.; hereinafter, NA-CPM).

Page 87: **Another testy exchange:** "Tele Follow-up Comment," *Variety*, June 24, 1953: 31.

Page 88: **In September 1951:** Oliver Pilat and William V. Shannon, "One-Man Mob, Concluded," *New York Post*, September 23, 1951: 4.

Page 88: **In 1952, having assailed:** "Tele Follow-Up," *Variety*, April 2, 1952: 37; "Wechsler Ban," *Broadcasting/Telecasting*, August 8, 1952: 60; "Tele Follow-up Comment," *Variety*, September 3, 1952: 25.

Page 89: **On April 24 and May 5, 1953:** James Wechsler, *The Age of Suspicion* (New York: Random House, 1953), 269, 284.

Page 89: **On May 17, 1953:** *Meet the Press*, May 17, 1953 (MPD-LOC).

Page 89: **"If the Washington reporters:** "Tele Follow-up Comment," *Variety*, May 20, 1953: 26.

Page 89: **Two weeks earlier:** *Meet the Press*, May 3, 1953 (MPD-LOC).

Page 90: **On January 31, 1954:** "Tele Follow-Up," *Variety*, February 3, 1954: 32.

Page 91: **"Video-wise," observed:** "Just Plain Dick," *Variety*, October 1, 1952: 101.

Page 91: **"If Senator Richard M. Nixon:** "Tele Follow-up Comment," *Variety*, October 15, 1952: 26.

Page 92 (note 2): **In 1956, when President Eisenhower:** "'Equal Time' a Major Rhubarb," *Variety*, October 3, 1956: 47.

Page 92: **Not until 1959:** "Victory at Last," *Television Age* (September 1959): 53; "'315' Only Awaits Ike's Signature," *Variety*, September 9, 1959: 39.

Page 93: **"I am notifying:** Robert K. Walsh, "Talk Response Pleases Truman," *Washington Evening Star*, November 17, 1953: 1, 4.

Page 93: **By late 1953:** "Rob't E. Lee Seen FCC-FBI Link in Ferreting Out AM-TV 'Subversives,'" *Variety*, October 14, 1953: 2. See also "Closed Circuit," *Broadcasting/Telecasting*, April 13, 1953: 5; "Closed Circuit," *Broadcasting/Telecasting*, April 20, 1953: 5.

Page 93: **McCarthy was presumed:** "Doerfer-McCarthy Gangup on Lamb Seen Motivated by Political Factors; Expansion of TV Empire Stalemated," *Variety*, November 4, 1953: 23.

Page 93: **"The influence of McCarthy:** Drew Pearson, "The Washington Merry-Go-Round," *Washington Post*, May 15, 1954: 39. See also "McCarthy, Hunt, and Facts Forum," *The Reporter*, February 16, 1954: 24.

Page 93: **"There was no reason:** "How Equal Is Equal Time," *Variety* December 2, 1953: 33.

Page 94: **On Saturday, March 6, 1954:** "Text of Stevenson Address to the Southeastern Democrats," *New York Times*, March 7, 1954: 62.

Page 94: **Again, as with the Truman:** "McCarthy Seeking Air Time to Reply," *New York Times*, March 8, 1954: 1, 9.

Page 95: **"With an emphasis:** "President Implies McCarthy Is Peril to Unity of GOP," *New York Times*, March 11, 1954: 1, 14.

Page 95: **"This time the webs:** "McCarthy and the Networks," *Variety*, March 10, 1954: 27.

Page 95: **Fed up with a constant**: "D.C. Lawyers Say Webs 'In Clear' on McCarthy Nix," *Variety*, March 10, 1954: 1, 71.

Page 95: **That Saturday**: Adding insult to the injury done McCarthy, the transcript of Nixon's March 13, 1954, talk was released as a booklet by the Republican National Committee.

Page 95: **He threatened to petition**: "Senator McCarthy Threatens," *Television Digest*, March 13, 1954: 2.

Page 95: **Off-the-record assurances**: Jack Gould, "Television in Review: Rebuttal," *New York Times*, March 10, 1954: 34.

Page 96: **"While television cameras**: William R. Conlin, "M'Carthy to Push Air Time Demand," *New York Times*, March 10, 1954: 14.

Page 96: **On January 20, 1949**: Rex Lardner, "Coast to Coast Without a Hitch," *New York Post*, September 5, 1950: 68.

Page 97: **"If Mr. Truman**: "In Review," *Broadcasting/Telecasting*, May 12, 1952: 84–85.

Page 97: **However, the first true**: For an overview, see Craig Allen, *Eisenhower and the Mass Media: Peace, Prosperity, and Prime-Time TV* (Chapel Hill: University of North Carolina Press, 1993).

Page 98: **"Professional TV men**: "Eisenhower, TV President," *Television Age* (May 1955): 46–48, 84, 86–88.

Page 99: **On June 4, 1952**: Viewed at the Museum of Television and Radio, New York City.

Page 99: **Shelling out over $2 million**: Gordon Cotler, "The Plague of Spots from Madison Avenue," *The Reporter*, November 25, 1952: 7–8. See also Edwin Diamond and Stephen Bates, *The Spot: The Rise of Political Advertising on Television* (Cambridge: MIT Press, 1984): 45–65.

Page 100: **Wags recited**: Sec, "Sales Campaign," *The Reporter*, November 25, 1952: 2.

Page 100: **To better distill**: "The Producer and the President," *TV Guide*, October 30, 1954: 5–7.

Page 100: **In 1953, Eisenhower's inauguration**: "TV Fluffs Its Big Opportunity of Television of D.C. Inaugural Parade," *Variety*, January 26, 1949: 35, 42.

Page 100: **Playing the good corporate**: Bert Briller, "Iconoscopes Invade Ike Inaugural, Capturing Color, Capers, Camera-derie" *Variety*, January 21, 1953: 33.

Page 100: **"The odd thing**: Dan Jenkins, "On the Air," *Hollywood Reporter*, January 21, 1953: 12.

Page 101: **Before the cameras**: "In Review," *Broadcasting/Telecasting*, April 12, 1954: 14.

Page 101: **The United Press report**: "Telecasting Notes," *Television Digest*, April 10, 1954: 8.

Page 101: **Perhaps Eisenhower's most memorable**: "Text of the Address by President Eisenhower on 'Multiplicity of Fears,'" *New York Times*, April 6, 1954: 16.

Page 101: **"Whether Ike learned**: "In Review," *Broadcasting/Telecasting*, April 12, 1954: 14.

Page 102: **"We are in a new era**: "Telecasting Notes," *Television Digest*, January 24, 1953: 5.

Page 102: **Following the practice:** "Newsreelers in Middle of Censorship Snarl Involving President," *Variety*, March 23, 1949: 2, 14; "Ike Bows to Tape," *Hollywood Reporter*, April 30, 1953: 1.

Page 102: **"Usually after dinner:** Andrew F. Tully, "Ike and Mamie at Home," *Colliers*, June 20, 1953: 15–17.

6. Roman Circuses and Spanish Inquisitions

Page 105: **Describing the radical:** Erik Barnouw, *Tube of Plenty: the Evolution of American Television* (New York: Oxford University Press, 1990), 160–61.

Page 105: **"The advantages of live:** John Crosby, "The Arguments for Live TV," *New York Herald Tribune*, March 16, 1953: 17.

Page 105: **Hollywood filmmakers who:** "Pulitzer Prize for TV Writers Sought," *Variety*, September 7, 1955: 1, 18.

Page 106: **By the early 1960s:** "Notes from TV's Underground," *Television Age*, December 23, 1963: 22, 102–108.

Page 106: **"What do you get:** Marya Mannes, "Channels: Comments on TV," *The Reporter*, March 31, 1953: 34.

Page 106: **Television critic Jack Gould:** Jack Gould, "Television in Review," *New York Times*, April 23, 1954: 34.

Page 106: **On November 11, 1947:** "First Live Telecast of Hearing Is Presented by WMAL-TV," *Washington Star*, November 11, 1947: A1, A5.

Page 106: **In 1948 *Variety*:** "Congressional Follies on TV?" *Variety*, March 3, 1948: 27.

Page 108: **Helpfully correcting:** During exchanges with Sen. Charles H. Tobey (R-N.H.) on *Meet the Press*, March 25, 1951, and Kefauver on *Meet the Press*, April 1, 1951, the panel of reporters struggled with the pronunciation of what was to them a new coinage ("may-fia," "ma-fei," "mah-fia," or "whatever you call it") (MPD-LOC).

Page 108: **Deploying the rhetoric:** "Inquiry Names 2 National Crime Rings," *San Francisco Chronicle*, March 1, 1951: 3.

Page 108: **The Soviet analogy:** Universal International Newsreel, March 23, 1951 (NA-CPM).

Page 109: **"By no means:** "TV Kefauver's Truth Window," *Billboard*, March 10, 1951: 1, 6.

Page 109: **In a tour:** For an overview, see William Howard Moore, *The Kefauver Committee and the Politics of Crime* (Columbia: University of Missouri Press, 1974). See also Ron Garay, "Television and the 1951 Senate Crime Committee Hearings," *Journal of Broadcasting* (Fall 1978): 469–90. On the nexus between crime and communism, see Lee Bernstein, *The Greatest Menace: Organized Crime in Cold War America* (Amherst: University of Massachusetts Press, 2002).

Page 110: **In Detroit:** "Crime Hearings: Commercial Shows Canceled," *Broadcasting/Telecasting*, February 26, 1951: 80.

Page 110: **In St. Louis:** "TV Gives Front Seat View of Crime Inquiry," *St. Louis Post-Dispatch*, February 24, 1951: 2.

Page 110: **In Los Angeles:** "Southland Gambling Ties Traced at Crime Inquiry," *Los Angeles Times*, March 1, 1951: 1, 2.

Page 110: **As in the South:** "Senate Crime Probe," *Broadcasting/Telecasting*, March 12, 1951: 73.

Page 110: **Motion picture producer:** Dan Jenkins, "On the Air," *Hollywood Reporter*, March 1, 1951: 14.

Page 111: **The *San Francisco Chronicle*:** Terrence O'Flaherty, "Radio and Television," *San Francisco Chronicle*, March 3, 1951: 20.

Page 112: **Linked via coaxial:** "Crime Hearing Is TV Smash in District, 20 Other Cities," *Washington Post*, March 20, 1951: 1.

Page 112: **Harry T. Brundige:** "DuMont Pulls Most Kefauver Viewers," *Billboard*, March 31, 1951: 1.

Page 112: **"Somehow the camera view:** "In Review," *Broadcasting/Telecasting*, March 19, 1951: 28.

Page 112: **Only half joking:** Jack Gould, "Costello's TV's First Headless Star; Only His Hands Entertain Audience," *New York Times*, March 14, 1951: 1, 29.

Page 113: **Speaking in a whiny:** There is no verbatim transcript of Hill's ripe barbs away from the committee's microphone. Her language was cleaned up in contemporaneous press reports, but even less restrictive accounts vary on the placement and frequency of certain adjectives. See Andy Edmunds, *Bugsy's Baby: The Secret Life of Mob Queen Virginia Hill* (New York: Birch Lane Press, 1993), vii, 182.

Page 113: **That weekend, Kefauver:** *What's My Line?*, March 18, 1951 (Museum of Television and Radio, New York City).

Page 115: **When Costello left:** Fendeall Yerxa, "Costello, His Testimony Over, Flashes a Smile for Television," *New York Herald Tribune*, March 22, 1951: 16.

Page 115: **During the two-week run:** "Crime Probe's TV Audience Figured at 20 Times Normal," *Los Angeles Times*, March 20, 1951: 12.

Page 115: **"No event TV:** Jerry Franken, "Costello Stars in Kefauver's Strong Next-to-Closing Act," *Billboard*, March 24, 1951: 3.

Page 116: **"They object to:** "Let Voters Decide," *Broadcasting/Telecasting*, March 10, 1952: 50.

Page 117: **Committeemen sat dumbstruck:** "L.A. Red Hearings Recess to Nov. 17; Probers Assailed," *Variety*, October 8, 1952: 1, 54.

Page 117: **Kefauver committee counsel Rudolph Halley:** "Merciless Spotlight of TV Safeguard of Fair Trial, Sez Halley Re Hearings," *Variety*, June 20, 1951: 30.

Page 117: **Plagued by second thoughts:** "Sen. Wiley Proposes Curbing of Telecasts of Public Hearings," *Hollywood Reporter*, March 26, 1951: 1.

Page 118: **He also feared:** *Congressional Record*, 82d Cong., 1st sess., 1951, Appendix: A1679–A1680.

Page 118: **On February 11, 1952:** *Congressional Record*, 82d Cong., 2d sess., 1952, Vol. 98, pt. 2: 1690–1691.

Page 118: **Like the ABA:** "'Fair Play Code' by Congress Seen Way Out on Televising Hearings," *Variety*, April 22, 1953: 39.

Page 118: **"If courts find:** "Inquisition by TV," *Washington Post*, March 8, 1953: B4.

Page 118: **Senator Kefauver asserted:** Estes Kefauver, *Crime in America* (New York: Doubleday, 1951), 314.

Page 119: **On October 6, 1952:** "Gambling Duo Cleared of Contempt Due to AM-TV 'Distraction,'" *Variety*, October 8, 1952: 46.

Page 119: **Finally, however:** "Jerome Refuses to Divulge Hollywood Commie Names," *Hollywood Reporter*, March 9, 1951: 1, 15.

Page 119: **Frankly admitting that:** "Radio, Tele, Newsreels Gang Up Vs Ban by House Red Probers," *Variety*, February 9, 1949: 2; "TV Turndown on Red Hearing," *Hollywood Reporter*, March 21, 1951: 1, 5.

Page 119: **The bulky television cameras:** "TV Turndown on Red Hearing," *Hollywood Reporter*, March 21, 1951: 1, 5; "Silent TV Camera Shoots Hayden As Newsreels Get Nix," *Variety*, April 11, 1951: 1, 22; "Telecasting Notes," *Television Digest*, April 14, 1951: 12; "Only Still Cameras Permitted at Hearing," *Hollywood Reporter*, April 12, 1951: 2.

Page 120: **But as HUAC persisted:** "KTTV Forcing TV Issue on Hearing," *Hollywood Reporter*, September 18, 1951: 1, 11; "House Committee Gives in As TV Cameras Take Over," *Hollywood Reporter*, September 19, 1951: 8; Dan Jenkins, "On the Air," *Hollywood Reporter*, September 19, 1951: 12.

Page 120: **Leery about the legal:** "Telecasting Notes," *Television Digest*, September 29, 1951: 7.

Page 120: **Though far less star-studded:** "Foreman, Koenig, and Gordon Refuse Replies in Red Quiz," *Hollywood Reporter*, September 25, 1951: 8–9; text quotation from Jim Henaghan, "Rambling Reporter," *Hollywood Reporter*, September 25, 1951: 2.

Page 122: **In the press:** Mike Kaplan, "Buchman's Conscience, Jackson's Exit Give Red Probe Dramatic Climax," *Variety*, October 3, 1951: 4, 20.

Page 122: **Even W. R. Wilkerson:** W. R. Wilkerson, "Tradeviews," *Hollywood Reporter*, September 27, 1951: 1.

Page 122: **Shortly thereafter:** Robert Bendiner, "Should Congress Be Televised?" *Colliers*, January 17, 1953: 62–65, reprinted in Herbert L. Marx Jr., ed., *Television and Radio in American Life* (New York: H. W. Wilson, 1953).

Page 123: **Rayburn extended:** *Congressional Record*, 82d Cong., 2d sess., 1952, Vol. 98, pt. 1: 1334–1334.

Page 123: **Both the new Speaker:** "House Red Probers Okay Tele for Some Hearings; Less Stress on H'Wood," *Variety*, November 26, 1952: 1.

Page 123: **In March 23–28, 1953:** Owen Callin, "Herald Men Cover Red Quiz Via TV," *Los Angeles Herald and Express*, March 24, 1953: C3; "The Red Probe," ibid., C2.

Page 123: **Heeding legal precedent:** "Ask Subpoenas Nix," *Variety*, March 18, 1953: 15; "May Have Been Some Commie Slants in Pix, Scripter Tells House Panel," *Variety*, March 25, 1953: 20.

Page 124: **After Huebsch's confrontation:** "Dare Comes Clean, Hecht Talks, 2 Witnesses Defy Red Probers," *Hollywood Reporter*, March 24, 1953: 1, 11.

Page 124: **Though viewers flooded:** Owen Callin, "Flood of Protests on Blackout," *Los Angeles Herald and Express*, March 26, 1953: D4.

Page 124: **The next week HUAC:** "Commie Hearing Extended; Closed Sessions Next Week," *Hollywood Reporter*, March 30, 1953: 7.

Page 125: **On May 6, the actor Lionel Stander:** George Gilbert, "Commie Probers Studying Testimony at N.Y. Quiz for 'Contempt' Charges," *Variety*, May 13, 1953: 2, 24.

Page 125: **Once outside the committee room:** "Lionel Stander Hits House Red Probe As an 'Inquisition,'" *Hollywood Reporter*, May 7, 1953: 2.

Page 125: **Following Stander:** Ibid.

Page 125: **The Stander and Gorney:** "No Telecasts So Far of N.Y. Proceedings," *Variety*, May 6, 1953: 2.

Page 126: **William Gaines:** "Comic Books' Views Varied," *Milwaukee Journal*, April 22, 1954: 28.

Page 127: **McCarthy's debut:** "Lattimore Denies He Was Ever a Red; Tydings Clears Him," *New York Times*, April 7, 1950: 1, 6; "Lattimore Heard by a Tense Crowd," *New York Times*, April 7, 1950: 7; "Radio and Television," *New York Times*, April 6, 1950: 54.

Page 127: **In *Ordeal by Slander*:** See Edwin R. Bayley, *Joe McCarthy and the Press* (New York: Pantheon, 1981), especially his "Four Crises in Television" chapter, 176–213.

Page 128: **The Voice of America hearings:** "Hearing Coverage," *Broadcasting/Telecasting*, February 23, 1953: 52.

Page 129: **The decision by ABC:** "Fair Play Responsibility," *Variety*, March 4, 1953: 28.

Page 129: **"The episode showed:** Jack Gould, "Cutting Reed Harris Off in Middle of Rebuttal to Charges in 'Voice' Inquiry Called Disgraceful," *New York Times*, March 6, 1953: 34.

Page 129: **"It is indecent enough:** Marya Mannes, "Comments on TV," *The Reporter*, March 31, 1953: 34.

Page 130: **The *New York Times* decried:** "America's Voice," *New York Times*, March 5, 1953: 26; "Inquisition by TV," *Washington Post*, March 8, 1953: B4.

Page 130: **Wising up to:** "The Brain-Washing," *New York Post*, March 4, 1953: 41.

Page 131: **"Neither Mr. Miller:** Brooks Atkinson, "At the Theater," *New York Times*, January 23, 1953: 15.

Page 132: **The activities of:** "Hollywood Nix on 'Message' Pix," *Variety*, April 22, 1953: 5.

Page 132: **Clair Worth:** "'Kefauver Era' Gone, Say Webs; Can't See Lopping Off Sponsors," *Variety*, May 13, 1953: 33, 44.

Page 132: **Anticipating the special:** Dan Jenkins, "On the Air," *Hollywood Reporter*, February 23, 1953: 6; text quotation from "Field Day Seen for Legalities as Industry Fights Ban on Hearings," *Variety*, March 4, 1953: 27, 38.

Page 132: **Tallying up the running time:** "TV Cameras on Congress," *Television Age* (August 1953): 57–59.

Page 132: **When syndicated columnist:** George Sokolsky, "Ancient Film," *Los Angeles Herald and Express*, March 5, 1953: D3.

Page 133: **"Full scale day-and-night:** "'Kefauver Era' Gone, Say Webs; Can't See Lopping Off Sponsors," *Variety*, May 13, 1953: 33, 44.

7. Country and God

Page 135: **In the long run:** As historian Stanford Ungar noted, the 1934 federal crime bills are "one of the most important if least recognized New Deal reforms." Quoted in Curt Gentry, *J. Edgar Hoover: The Man and the Secrets* (New York: Norton, 1991), 169.

Page 136: **Ever media-savvy, Hoover:** "Hoover Hails Video as FBI Adjunct," *Variety*, February 9, 1949: 1, 61.

Page 136: **"The television industry:** Herman Lowe, "How TV Lengthens the Arm of the Law," *TV Guide*, April 2, 1955: 10–11.

Page 137: **Typical was the "F.B.I." episode:** "Tele Follow-up Comment," *Variety*, November 6, 1957: 34.

Page 137: **"It may come:** *"Treasury Men in Action," TV Guide*, May 1, 1953: 19.

Page 138: **Father and sons alike:** The touchstone essay on the trope is "The Rise of the Expert," in Richard Hofstadter, *Anti-Intellectualism in American Life* (New York: Vintage, 1963), 197–229.

Page 140: **"In World War I:** Don Whitehead, "'Pros' Should Hunt Reds, Hoover Says," *Washington Post*, May 11, 1954: 46.

Page 140: **"Happy AnnHOOVERsary!":** Walter Winchell, "Happy AnnHOOVERsary," *Washington Post*, May 12, 1954: 43.

Page 140: **Shot on film:** "Ziv's 'Three Lives' Tops Film Videodex," *Broadcasting/Telecasting*, April 12, 1954: 56.

Page 141: **"Mr. Philbrick is:** Edwin D. Cohnheim, "Invaluable Personal Report on Communism," *New York Herald Tribune Book Review*, February 3, 1952: 1.

Page 141: **"Amateur Red hunters:** Herbert Philbrick, *I Led 3 Lives: Citizen, "Communist," Counterspy* (New York: McGraw-Hill, 1952), 299–300. Subsequent references are to pages 307–308, 92, and 184–185.

Page 142: **"They can grind 'em out:** *"I Led 3 Lives," Variety*, September 30, 1953: 34. The dollar figure is for the total product line from Ziv, not just *I Led 3 Lives*.

Page 142: **To underline its public:** "Ziv Makes 'Three Lives' Available to Military," *Broadcasting/Telecasting*, April 12, 1954: 33.

Page 142: **"It was a good financial:** "Actor, Writer, Traveller: Now He's a TV Hero Who Fights Communism," *TV Guide*, December 4, 1953: 5–7.

Page 143: **Already, the show:** *"I Led Three Lives," TV Guide*, January 7, 1954: 14.

Page 143: **Dissenting, *Variety* believed:** *"I Led 3 Lives," Daily Variety*, September 26, 1955:

Page 143: **"The networks have not:** Ring Lardner Jr., "Public Beware," *Masses and Mainstream* (December 1956): 55.

Page 144: **"It is recommended:** Herbert A. Philbrick FBI file.

Page 146: **According to producer:** Shortly before his death on October 13, 2001, Frederick Ziv confirmed the long-rumored infiltration of blacklisted writers on *I Led 3 Lives* in an interview conducted at the author's request with Sofia McAllister on October 25, 2000, in Cincinnati, Ohio.

Page 147: **At the beginning of:** "Army Infiltration," *I Led 3 Lives*, 1953, viewed at the Museum of Broadcast Communications in Chicago, Illinois.

Page 148: **In a famous session:** Rebecca West, *The New Meaning of Treason* (New York: Viking, 1964), 187. A touchstone Cold War commentary on the psychology of the traitor, West's essay on Fuchs originally appeared as "The Terrifying Import of the Fuchs Case," *New York Times Magazine*, March 4, 1951: 29, 31–32, 34.

Page 153: **Spooked by *See It Now*'s report:** Dan Jenkins, "On the Air," *Hollywood Reporter*, November 18, 1952: 13.

Page 153: **Star of the highly:** Long neglected by media scholars, Sheen has lately undergone a renaissance of regard. See Mary Ann Watson, "And They Said 'Uncle Fultie' Didn't Have a Prayer," *Television Quarterly* (Winter 1993): 16–21; Christopher Owen Lynch, *Selling Catholicism: Bishop Sheen and the Power of Television* (Lexington: University Press of Kentucky, 1998); and Thomas C. Reeves, *America's Bishop: The Life and Times of Fulton J. Sheen* (San Francisco: Encounter, 2001).

Page 153: **"The man has magic:** Marya Mannes, "Channels: Comments on TV," *The Reporter*, January 20, 1953: 38.

Page 154: **Martin Stone, producer:** Martin Stone, "The Case for Live Television," *Broadcasting/Telecasting*, January 19, 1953: 77–78.

Page 154: **Implying the cleric:** *"Life Is Worth Living,"* *Variety*, October 19, 1955: 27.

Page 154: **"There is as much:** "Bishop Sheen's Angels," *TV Guide*, May 29, 1953: 9.

Page 155: **At the peak:** "Dateline," *TV Guide*, December 25, 1953: A1.

Page 155: **"Mother Superiors everywhere:** "Bishop Sheen Influence Eases TV Ban for Nuns in Catholic Convents," *Variety*, September 3, 1952: 1.

Page 156: **Piggybacking on Bishop:** *"The Goldbergs,"* *Variety*, April 21, 1954: 39, 44.

Page 156: **Another Judeo-Catholic:** "Berle Faces Tough Tues. Competition," *Variety*, October 1, 1952: 99.

Page 156: **Sheen responded with:** "Bishop Sheen's New Book," *TV Guide*, October 9, 1953: 7.

Page 156: **"Bishop Sheen does:** Vincent X. Flaherty, "Hoover Hits Crime Trend in Movies," *Los Angeles Herald and Express*, October 23, 1956.

Page 157: **"Television is purely incidental:** "Sheen on TV Screen," *Life*, March 24, 1952: 92.

Page 157: **He quoted the parishioner:** *"Life Is Worth Living,"* *Variety*, February 20, 1952: 31.

Page 157: **Reaching back:** Fulton J. Sheen, *Life Is Worth Living, Second Series* (New York: McGraw-Hill, 1954), x. Subsequent reference is to page 2.

Page 158: **Sheen explained the title:** Howard Cohn, "Bishop Sheen Answers His Fan Mail," *Colliers*, January 24, 1953: 22–24.

Page 158: **On February 24, 1953:** Sheen, *Life Is Worth Living*, 149–58. Unfortunately, as far as I can determine, the February 24, 1953, show has not survived on kinescope.

Page 158: **Chagrinned, Berle later:** Lynch, *Selling Catholicism*, 176–77.

Page 159: **"The DuMont network:** Harriet Van Horne, "The Bishop Versus Berle," *Theatre Arts* (December 1952): 65, 95.

Page 160: **Sheen displayed a dazzling:** John Crosby, "Bishop Sheen's Second Year," *New York Herald Tribune*, December 22, 1952: 21.

Page 160: **In 1953 the Vatican's:** "TV in the News," *TV Guide*, July 24, 1953: 21.

Page 160: **With low-key banter:** "Admiral, Sheen Calling It Quits?" *Variety*, March 21, 1956: 19.

8. Edward R. Murrow Slays the Dragon of Joseph McCarthy

Page 161: **Celebrating the miracle:** "Murrow & 'Good Tuesday,'" *Variety*, March 17, 1954: 27.

Page 161: **"One of those rare:** David Halberstam, *The Powers That Be* (New York: Knopf, 1979), 38.

Page 162: **Once heretical:** Steven Stark, *Glued to the Set: The 60 Television Shows and Events That Made Us What We Are Today* (New York: Delta, 1997), 406, 57–58.

Page 162: **The gainsayers:** Among the full-length biographies are Alexander Kendrick, *Prime Time: The Life of Edward R. Murrow* (Boston: Little Brown, 1969), A. M. Sperber, *Murrow: His Life and Times* (New York: Freundlich, 1986), and Joseph E. Persico, *Edward R. Murrow, An American Original* (New York: McGraw-Hill, 1988). For a survey of the literature on *See It Now*, see Daniel Leab, "*See It Now*: A Legend Reassessed," in John E. O'Connor, ed., *American History/American Television* (New York: Unger, 1983), 1–33.

Page 162: **Both over the airwaves:** "Elmer Davis Foresees Rebound by McCarthy," *New York Herald Tribune*, May 17, 1954: 19. Davis also spoke out against McCarthyism on his short-lived, self-titled Sunday afternoon commentary show on ABC-TV in 1954, but, being on ABC, it was little seen or noted. "Television Reviews: *Elmer Davis*," *Variety*, February 24, 1954: 31.

Page 163: **"This . . . is London:** Edward Bliss Jr., ed., *In Search of Light: The Broadcasts of Edward R. Murrow, 1938–1961* (1967) (Rpt., New York: Da Capo, 1997), 73–74.

Page 164: **"Visually, Winchell:** Dan Jenkins, "Walter Winchell," *Hollywood Reporter*, October 7, 1952: 7.

Page 164: **By contrast, Murrow:** Stanley Cloud and Lynne Olson, *The Murrow Boys: Pioneers on the Front Lines of Broadcast Journalism* (Boston: Houghton Mifflin, 1996).

Page 165: **"It's a cinch:** "Tele Follow-up Comment," *Variety*, November 21, 1951: 29.

Page 166: **"This isn't radio news:** Fred Friendly, "Lots of Barriers Must Come Down to Develop TV News," *Variety*, January 7, 1953: 182.

Page 167: **"We'll try never:** "Credo for Newscasters," *Variety*, December 5, 1951: 33.

Page 167: *TV Guide* **took:** "*See It Now*," *TV Guide*, April 17: 14.

Page 168: **"The best picture:** John Crosby, "The Little Picture," *New York Herald Tribune*, December 28, 1952: D1, D8.

Page 168: **Murrow too commanded:** "Murrow's 3-Way Spread as Amoco Signs New TVer," *Variety*, May 20, 1953: 25.

Page 169: **In 1953,** *See It Now*: Joseph Wershba, "The Senator and the Broadcaster: An Intimate History of the Most Famous Program in Television History: Edward R. Murrow's 'See It Now' Documentary on Joe McCarthy" (November 1953–March 1954), 10, 65. Unpublished manuscript on file at the Murrow Center, Tufts University, Medford, Mass.

Page 169: "The juxtaposition of Stalin: Ibid., 10.

Page 169: With intensifying force: For an extensive analysis of four of the pivotal *See It Now* episodes, see Thomas Rosteck, *"See It Now" Confronts McCarthyism: Television Documentary and the Politics of Representation* (Tuscaloosa: University of Alabama Press, 1994).

Page 171: On June 14, 1951: Quoted in Thomas C. Reeves, *The Life and Times of Joe McCarthy* (New York: Stein and Day, 1982), 372.

Page 173: Though no sentient listener: "'Shoeshine Boy,'" *Variety*, November 11, 1953: 33.

Page 173: By Saturday March 6: Wershba, "The Senator and the Broadcaster," 49.

Page 173: Prior to the telecast: "DC Lawyers Say Webs 'In Clear' on McCarthy Nix," *Variety*, March 10, 1954: 71.

Page 177: The critical and popular response: John Crosby, "The Time May Come When People Can Think On TV," *Washington Post*, May 26, 1954: 51. See also Leonard Traube, "'Reality' Show Comes into Own," *Variety*, March 17, 1954: 25; John Crosby, "Salute to a Brave Man," *New York Herald Tribune*, March 12, 1954: 19.

Page 177: WBBM-TV in Chicago: "Chi's 85% for Murrow," *Variety*, March 17, 1954: 35.

Page 177: Though several correspondents: Kathy Pedell, "This Is Murrow," *TV Guide*, February 5, 1955: 4–7. *Variety* singled out the sponsor for praise in "Special Citations: Ed Murrow's *See It Now*," *Variety*, April 21, 1954: 29.

Page 178: "Where the strongest conservative: "Where Others Failed," *Billboard*, March 20, 1954: 2.

Page 178: "Murrow interviews two people: *"Person to Person*," *TV Guide*, November 20, 1953: 14.

Page 179: At a time when: Bob Stahl, "TV Teletype," *TV Guide*, November 13, 1953: 13.

Page 179: "Murrow will rarely: "Television Reviews," *Variety*, February 10, 1954: 36.

Page 179: In fact, in the weeks: "Murrow to 'Person' Mary Martin; [Bill] Corum," *Variety*, April 14, 1954: 2. The article noted a "sharp upbeat of showbiz personalities on the CBS TV show." Bill Corum was the "voice" (announcer) of the Kentucky Derby.

Page 181: Described in the press: "Tele Follow-up Comment," *Variety*, March 24, 1954: 29.

Page 184: "When Senator McClellan: John Crosby, "The Aroma of Decency," *New York Herald Tribune*, March 19, 1954: 19.

Page 184: "Senator McCarthy Fails: "Sen. McCarthy Fails to Crack Mrs. Moss," *Pittsburgh Courier*, March 20, 1954: 1, 4.

Page 184: "Wisconsin folks saw: Drew Pearson, "The Washington Merry-Go-Round," *Washington Post*, April 28, 1954: 59.

Page 184: The next day: "Ed Murrow Paces 'Seven Days That Shook McCarthy,'" *Variety*, March 17, 1954: 25.

Page 185: Produced by the BBD&O: "Who Owns McCarthy 'See It Now' Pic?" *Variety*, April 7, 1954: 27; "McCarthy Wins 6G Point of Order from CBS; Has April Pic in Pocket," *Variety*, May 19, 1954: 26; "Murrow Gets Impressive Support in McCarthy Feud," *Broadcasting/Telecasting*, April 21, 1954: 88.

Page 185: **Moments later, however:** "'Strange Silence' from NBC on McCarthy Imbroglio Riles CBS," *Variety*, April 14, 1954: 24, 32.

Page 186: **"[McCarthy's response was]:** June Bundy, "*See It Now,*" *Billboard*, April 17, 1954: 12.

Page 186: **So long mute:** "More EDitorializing? McCarthy Reply a Dud," *Television Digest*, April 10, 1954: 1–2.

Page 187: **On his April 7 radio newscast:** "Transcript of the President's Press Conference," *New York Times*, April 8, 1954: 18.

Page 188: **When he entered:** "Murrow's 'Show Stopper' As Overseas Press Club Marks Annual Awards," *Variety*, March 31, 1954: 1.

9. The Army-McCarthy Hearings (April 22–June 17, 1954)

Page 189: **Ostensibly, the most storied:** The backstage maneuvering of the Eisenhower administration in the Army-McCarthy story is lucidly chronicled in William Bragg Ewald Jr., *Who Killed Joe McCarthy?* (New York: Simon and Schuster, 1984). The most extensive contemporaneous analysis of the television coverage is Michael Straight, *Trial by Television* (Boston: Beacon Press, 1954).

Page 191: **"The charges on both sides:** Telford Taylor, *Grand Inquest: The Story of Congressional Investigations* (1955) (Rpt., Ballantine, New York, 1961), 146.

Page 191: **"Private G. David Schine:** Drew Pearson, "Hearings May Curb Favoritism," *Washington Post*, June 22, 1954: 39.

Page 191: **Agreeing with his ideological:** George Sokolsky, "Mr. Cohn and the Telephone," *Washington Post*, April 29, 1954: 54.

Page 192: **The prototypical story:** Belman Morin, "Army's Atty Welch Deceptively Modest," *Houston Post*, May 16, 1954: C1.

Page 192: **"To the brawling:** Paul Cotton, "On Television," *Des Moines Register*, April 30, 1954: 10.

Page 193: **When requesting more time:** Army-McCarthy hearings, May 14, 1954. All quotes from the televised hearings are taken not from the *Congressional Record* but from the kinescopes, screened at the Motion Picture Division of the Library of Congress (hereinafter, MPD-LOC).

Page 193: **To a comment:** Army McCarthy hearings, May 24, 1954 (MPD-LOC).

Page 193: **Though not immune:** Army McCarthy hearings, May 4, 1954 (MPD-LOC).

Page 195: **At a press conference:** "Army McCarthy Hearing Stirs Scorn of President," *Washington Post*, April 30, 1954: 34.

Page 195: **At 10:30 A.M.:** Backstage atmospherics for the hearings are culled from "Special Dateline: Behind the Scenes at the Army McCarthy Hearings," *TV Guide*, April 30, 1954: A1, A2; "Preparations Feverish for McCarthy Hearings," *Milwaukee Journal*, April 22, 1954: 1; Estelle Jackson, "Army-McCarthy Hearings Still Pack Them In," *Washington Post*, May 30, 1954: 35.

Page 196: **Wire-service photographers:** "Photographers Blocking View," *New York Herald Tribune*, April 29, 1954: 13; "Get Your Backs Down, Mundt Tells Cameramen," *New York Times*, April 29, 1954: 19.

Page 198: **Before each session:** Army-McCarthy Hearings, May 28, 1954 (MPD-LOC).

Page 198: **Acknowledging that:** Army-McCarthy Hearings, May 11, 1954 (MPD-LOC).

Page 199: **"Did you order:** Army McCarthy Hearings, May 24, 1954 (MPD-LOC).

Page 199: **ABC and DuMont:** "Senate Okays TV on McCarthy VS Army," *Variety*, March 24, 1954: 1.

Page 199: **Calculating the cost:** "NBC and CBS in Tizzy over Preemption Costs of Pickup of McCarthy-Army," *Variety*, April 14, 1954: 1.

Page 199: **CBS opted for:** "Network Accounts," *Television Digest*, April 17, 1954: 7.

Page 199: **The withdrawal of CBS:** "NBC to Drop Live Hearings," *Milwaukee Journal*, April 25, 1954: A4.

Page 199: **Commenting on NBC's decision:** "'Deluge' of Protests on McCarthy 'Blackout' Smacks NBC Affiliates," *Variety*, April 28, 1954: 26.

Page 199: **"As the number 3 network:** John Daly, "'Was It Worth It?' Some Post-Mortems on the DC Hearings," *Variety*, July 28, 1954: 36.

Page 199: **Over thirty-six days:** "ABC's McCarthy Score," *Hollywood Reporter*, June 18, 1954: 11.

Page 200: **Unlike NBC or CBS:** "Telecasting Notes," *Television Digest*, April 24, 1954: 16.

Page 200: **Telecasting the hearings:** John Daly, "'Was It Worth It?' Some Post-Mortems on the DC Hearings," *Variety*, July 28, 1954: 36.

Page 200: **During the two-month run:** Florence Lowe, "Behind-Scenes-and-Necks View Wins Respect for McCarthy Video Experts," *Variety*, June 9, 1954: 1, 13.

Page 200: **"The ABC television network:** Army-McCarthy Hearings, May 13, 1954 (MPD-LOC).

Page 200: **ABC newsman Gunnar Back:** Army McCarthy Hearings, May 28, 1954 (MPD-LOC).

Page 201: **The two sides also:** The camera setups for the Army-McCarthy hearings are described in "Army-McCarthy Speaktacular," *Variety*, April 28, 1954: 1, 26; and "Special Dateline: Behind the Scenes at the Army McCarthy Hearings," *TV Guide*, April 30, 1954: A1, A2.

Page 201: **Also of signal importance:** Ben Atlas, "Washington Once Over," *Billboard*, June 19, 1954: 5.

Page 201: **None of this came cheap:** "Special Dateline: Behind the Scenes at the Army-McCarthy Hearings," *TV Guide*, April 30, 1954: A-1.

Page 201: ***Variety* figured:** "Telecasting Notes," *Television Digest*, June 19, 1954: 12.

Page 201: **Likewise, in Los Angeles:** "T-Viewers Demand Quiz Csar," *Hollywood Reporter*, April 27, 1954: 8; Leo Guild, "On the Air," *Hollywood Reporter*, April 30, 1954: 8.

Page 201: **As the only daytime:** "Station Accounts," *Television Digest*, June 19, 1954: 13.

Page 201: **In Houston:** "KPRC-TV Drops 'Live' Coverage," *Houston Post*, May 5, 1954: 1. See also "Army Hearings Resume on Fewer Stations; 5 Sponsors Lined Up," *Variety*, May 26, 1954: 35.

Page 202: **By way of incentive:** "Radio-TV Ads Cleared for McCarthy-Army," *Broadcasting/Telecasting*, May 17, 1954: 67.

Page 202: **"The "belated permission:** John Daly, "'Was It Worth It?': Some Post-Mortems on the D.C. Hearings," *Variety*, July 28, 1954: 36.

Page 202: **Regardless, sponsors:** "Network Accounts," *Television Digest*, May 15, 1954: 7.

Page 202: **"Imagine this vaudeville:** "Two Bills Vs. Com'l Hearings Hit 'Absurdity,'" *Variety*, May 19, 1954: 29.

Page 202: *Variety* **demurred:** "D.C. Hearings TV's Biggest Soaper; GOP Tries Scalpel on Hottest Show," *Variety*, May 5, 1954: 23.

Page 202: **Actually, a few commercials:** "Call Senate's Dignity (Remember?) Hurt By 'Caine' & Cheese Plugs," *Variety*, June 23, 1954: 1, 68.

Page 203: **Expectations that the ratings:** Army-McCarthy Speaktacular," *Variety*, April 28, 1954: 1, 26; "Telecasting Notes," *Television Digest*, May 1, 1954: 7.

Page 203: **Gould's prediction:** "Two Bills Vs. Com'l Hearings Hit 'Absurdity,'" *Variety*, May 19, 1954: 35.

Page 203: **In New York:** "Telecasting Notes," *Television Digest*, May 8, 1954: 5.

Page 203: **WMAL-TV reported:** "Army Hearings Resume on Fewer Stations; 5 Sponsors Lined Up," *Variety*, May 26, 1954: 35.

Page 203: **"Most noticeable in bars:** "Inquiry's Audience on TV Is Believed One of the Largest," *New York Herald Tribune*, April 23, 1954: 9.

Page 203: **When St. Louis station WTVI:** "No Show Gets Best Results," *Billboard*, May 29, 1954: 3.

Page 203: **The Army-McCarthy hearings:** "Army-McCarthy Hearing Polls 35.7 ARB Rating," *Hollywood Reporter*, June 1, 1954: 1; Leo Guild, "On the Air," *Hollywood Reporter*, May 27, 1954: 38.

Page 204: **"In my memory:** "Telecasting Notes," *Television Digest*, June 19, 1954: 12.

Page 204: *Billboard* **agreed:** "Prestige to TV in McCarthy-Army Tiff," *Billboard*, May 1, 1954: 1, 44.

Page 204 (note 4): **Welch had agreed:** Roy Cohn, *McCarthy* (New York: New American Library, 1968), 200–203.

Page 208: **"I kept an eye:** Lawrence Laurent, "U.S. Watched As He Worked," *Washington Post*, June 27, 1954: 9.

Page 209: **In reviewing ABC's:** "Tele Follow-up Comment," *Variety*, June 30, 1954: 28.

Page 209: **Scherer commented:** Lawrence Laurent, "U.S. Watched As He Worked," *Washington Post*, June 27, 1954: 9.

Page 209: **Even at the time:** See also "Welch Blisters McCarthy," *Washington Post*, June 10, 1954: 1, 18: "There were immediate indications that the McCarthy-Welch exchange, carried to millions of viewers by television, would have a major effect on the pubic reaction to the Army-McCarthy investigations, even though it had no direct bearing on the charges and counter-charges at issue."

Page 210: **Opponents of televised:** "'The Spectacle,'" *Wall Street Journal*, June 2, 1954: 10.

Page 210: **Sen. Patrick McCarran:** "Quiz Hurt Senate, Says McCarran," *Washington Post*, June 23, 1954: 23.

Page 210: **Condemning the "tawdry:** "Blackout for Television?" *Television Age* (October 1954): 36–37, 71.

Page 210: **The Watkins committee's ban:** "Year End Report on the Major Radio and TV Topics of 1954," *Sponsor*, December 27, 1954: 29.

Page 210: **On August 26, 1954:** "Blackout for Television?" *Television Age* (October 1954): 36–37, 71.

Page 211: **"Politicians realize:** Walter Lippmann, "The Big Brawl," *Washington Post*, May 17, 1954: 9.

Page 212: **"One thing has been:** Walter Winchell, "The Show," *Washington Post*, May 23, 1954: 5.

Page 212: **In 1956, still cut out:** "John Daly Raps Congress Nix on Video Coverage," *Variety*, April 18, 1956: 1, 91.

Page 212: **In January 1954:** George Gallup, "McCarthy Popularity Fall Tapers Off to a Standstill," *Washington Post*, June 9, 1954: 11; George Gallup, "McCarthy's Foes Exceed Supporters," *Washington Post*, June 23, 1954: 23.

Page 212: **"Years ago:** John Crosby, "Too Much Television May Wreck McCarthy's Act Too," *Washington Post*, June 4, 1954: 53.

Page 212: **"My acquaintance:** "John Doerfer Looks Ahead," *Television Age* (September 1954): 43.

Page 213: **Song satirist Stan Freeberg:** "'Point of Order' Song Carries Skit Cues," *Variety*, June 16, 1954: 1. See also "He Ribs the Stars," *TV Guide*, October 2, 1954: 20–21.

Page 213: **"Long considered too hot:** "Army-McCarthy Hassle Ends Personality Famine for Comics and Mimics," *Variety*, May 12, 1954: 1.

Page 213: **On television too:** Leo Guild, "On the Air," *Hollywood Reporter*, May 20, 1954: 8.

Page 213: **The sharpest stab:** Jack Gould, "'Bootleg Record of Canadian Program Parodying McCarthy on Sale Here," *New York Times*, December 31, 1954: 20.

Page 213: **A gleeful President Eisenhower:** Marya Mannes, "Channels," *The Reporter*, February 10, 1955: 10.

10. Pixies: Homosexuality, Anticommunism, and Television

Page 217: **"Ex-GI Becomes Blonde:** "The Great Transformation," *Time*, December 15, 1952: 57.

Page 217: **NBC filmed the scene:** "Camel News Finds Christine 'Format,'" *Variety*, February 25, 1953: 25.

Page 217: **Dressed in a nutria coat:** "Miss Jorgensen Returns," *New York Times*, February 13, 1953: 38.

Page 217: **Across the media:** Walter Winchell, "Of New York," *Washington Post*, March 5, 1953: 39.

Page 217: **Weary of the routine:** Dan Jenkins, "On the Air," *Hollywood Reporter*, June 2, 1953: 7.

Page 217: **Hostess Kathryn Murray:** "Christine on TV," *Variety*, April 1, 1953: 1; "Television Follow-up Comment," *Variety*, April 8, 1953: 28. Jorgensen had earlier been introduced from the audience on *The Walter Winchell Show*.

Page 218: **Choosing a resonant verb:** Bruce Bliven, "Hullabaloo on K-Day," *New Republic*, November 9, 1953: 17–18.

Page 218: **Reporting on the delicate:** "Radio-TV Behavior on Kinsey," *Variety*, August 26, 1953: 31.

Page 218: **In 1954, scanning:** Gene Plotnik, "Liberace Keys Pack Madison Square Garden," *Billboard*, June 5, 1954: 1, 10.

Page 219: **Lauded as "TV's first:** Mike Connolly, "Rambling Reporter," *Hollywood Reporter*, November 10, 1953: 2.

Page 221: **"When Will Liberace Marry?":** "Liberace: I Am Not Getting Married," *TV Guide*, October 16, 1954: 13.

Page 221: **"Liberace's secretary:** Leo Guild, "On the Air," *Hollywood Reporter*, October 14, 1953: 8.

Page 221: **"The sharpshooters have:** "The Liberace Legend," *TV Guide*, September 18, 1954: 5–7.

Page 221: **"There is much discussion:** The *Los Angeles Mirror* refused to print the Jacobs rebuttal. It was published by Leo Guild, "On the Air," *Hollywood Reporter*, March 17, 1954: 10

Page 221: **"The homosexual tends:** Joe McCarthy, *McCarthyism: The Fight for America* (New York: Devin-Adair, 1952), 14–15.

Page 222: **"It is important:** Dwight D. Eisenhower, *Mandate for Change, 1953–1956* (New York: New American Library, 1963), 376.

Page 222: **"No charge can:** "What's More Hurtful than 'Red' Slur," *Variety*, June 2, 1954: 2.

Page 223: **In 1948, when Chambers:** Alan Weinstein, *Perjury: The Hiss-Chambers Case* (New York: Random House, 1979), 67–68, 304.

Page 223: **In 1954, New York Post editor:** James Wechsler, *The Age of Suspicion* (New York: Random House, 1953), 235.

Page 223: **"One reason why sex:** McCarthy, *McCarthyism*, 15.

Page 223: **In 1954 the cultural critic:** Leslie A. Fielder, "McCarthy and the Intellectuals," in *An End to Innocence: Essays on Culture and Politics* (Boston: Beacon Press, 1955), 77.

Page 223: **On Meet the Press:** *Meet the Press*, December 13, 1953 (Motion Picture Division of the Library of Congress, hereinafter MPD-LOC).

Page 224: **Watching Cohn:** Marya Mannes, "Comments on TV," *The Reporter*, March 31, 1953: 34.

Page 224: **In 1952 the 24-year-old Schine:** "G. David Schine—Authority on Communism," in James Rorty and Moshe Decter, *McCarthy and the Communists* (Boston: Beacon Press, 1954), 154.

Page 225: **"The two McCarthy gumshoes:** Drew Pearson, "Cohn, Schine Also Disturb Sedate GOP," *Washington Post*, July 17, 1953: 51. Pearson's persistent inquiries into

Schine's draft status were probably responsible for his reclassification in 1953 from 4-F to 1-A.

Page 225: **Both in his syndicated column:** Neal Gabler, *Winchell: Gossip, Power, and the Culture of Celebrity* (New York: Knopf, 1994), 455–59.

Page 225: **(The alleged heterosexual:** Army-McCarthy hearings, April 22, 1954 (MPD-LOC).

Page 226: **Immediately, and "without:** Saul Pett, "Army's Best Known Private Wanted to Be Someone Special," *Washington Post*, May 3, 1954: 3; Drew Pearson, "Schine 'Studied' Via Secretary," *Washington Post*, May 4, 1954: 39.

Page 226: **Cohn alleged that:** *Meet the Press*, March 14, 1954 (MPD-LOC).

Page 226: **"Roy thinks that Dave:** Thomas C. Reeves, *The Life and Times of Joe Mc-Carthy* (New York: Stein and Day, 1982), 598.

Page 226: **On June 1, 1954:** Robert C. Albright, "M'Carthy Is Hit As Menace by Flanders," *Washington Post*, June 2, 1954: 1, 2.

Page 228: **"The plain unvarnished truth:** Hank Greenspun, "The Secret Lives of Joe McCarthy," *Rave* (June 1954): 58–72. The article is available in Robert F. Kennedy's papers devoted to the Army-McCarthy hearings, on file at the John F. Kennedy Presidential Library in Boston, Mass.

Page 228: **Years later, Cohn:** Roy Cohn, *McCarthy* (New York: New American Library, 1968), 244.

Page 228: **Gloated the NAACP's Walter White:** Walter White, "Walter White Says McCarthy-Army Feud on TV, 'One for the Books,'" *Chicago Defender*, May 22, 1954: 11.

Page 228: **On May 28, 1954:** Army-McCarthy Hearings, May 28, 1954 (MPD-LOC).

Page 230: **In 1942 the son:** Drew Pearson, "The Washington Merry-Go-Round," *Washington Post*, June 10, 1954: 59.

Page 230: **"I am not sure:** Drew Pearson, *Diaries*, edited by Tyler Abell (New York: Holt, Rhinehart, and Winston), 323.

11. The End of the Blacklist

Page 231: **In 1955, *Variety*:** Frank Scully, "Scully's Scrapbook," *Variety*, October, 21, 1955: 55.

Page 232: **Ever cheeky, Trumbo:** Tipped off to the charade, the FBI interviewed the real Robert L. Rich two days after the 1957 Academy Awards ceremonies. A nonwriter, Rich admitted to the FBI that he served as a front for Trumbo. "Communist Infiltration in the Entertainment Industry," microfilm, May 14, 1957; Dalton Trumbo, "Blacklist–Black Market," *The Nation*, May 4, 1957: 383–87.

Page 233: **In reviewing Kazan's:** For example: "a thinly disguised take-off of the late Sen. Joseph McCarthy played with farcical and devastating gusto by James Gregory" (*"The Manchurian Candidate,"* *Variety*, October 17, 1962: 6); Gregory's character "might just as well have been named McCarthy" (*The New Yorker*, November 3, 1962: 116); "the satire of a Joe McCarthy-like senator, for instance, is funny and vitriolic" (Richard Gertner, *Motion Picture Daily*, November 16, 1962).

Page 234: **Not until September 10, 1967:** "Pete Seeger Gets New Chance on TV," *New York Times*, August 25, 1967: 72. As a member of the fellow-traveling folk group the Weavers, Seeger had been blacklisted from television since 1950 and probably holds the record for the longest blacklist sentence in either film or television.

Page 234: **The video murmurings:** In 1959 a bellwether article in *Variety* called the television blacklist "a diminishing force" and reported that "relaxation of the 'black-list' began about a year ago [in 1958] and has continued steadily." Dave Kaufman, "Telepix Producers Say Blacklist Virtually Gone—& They're Glad," *Variety*, January 28, 1959: 25, 38.

Page 234: **In 1956, John Cogley:** Cogley, *Report on Blacklisting: Radio and Television*, 2, 134.

Page 234: **Yet "the big:** "ABC's of Radio-TV Blacklisting Bared in Fund for Republic Study," *Variety*, June 27, 1956: 22, 37.

Page 234: **"The industry set:** Cogley, *Report on Blacklisting in Radio-TV*, 67.

Page 235: **Circulated in paperback:** Will Lissner, "Actor Blacklist Found Powerful," *New York Times*, June 25, 1956: 1, 19.

Page 235: **In July 1956:** "Investigation of So-Called 'Blacklisting' in Entertainment Industry—Report of the Fund for the Republic, Inc.—Part I," Hearings before the Committee on Un-American Activities, House of Representatives, 84th Cong., 2d sess. (Washington, D.C.: Government Printing Office, 1956).

Page 235: **On June 18 and 19, 1958:** "Red Hunt Hits Again," *Television Digest*, June 21, 1958: 8.

Page 235: **Several months after:** "Red Probe Aftermath," *Television Digest*, November 15, 1958: 11.

Page 236 (note 1): **Before Faulk's landmark lawsuit:** "Ireland's $1,756,00 Vidpix Suit Bringing Blacklist into Open?" *Variety*, March 10, 1954: 43, 46.

Page 236: **Faulk alleged that:** "John Henry Faulk Files $500,000 Libel Suit Against AWARE in Blacklist Test," *Variety*, June 20, 1956: 21, 44.

Page 237: **In April 1956:** "Sneaky 'Secret Files' on Talent a Money Racket, Sez Rep. Jackson," *Variety*, April 25, 1956: 1, 18.

Page 237: **In February 1956:** "Tele Follow-up Comment," *Variety*, March 7, 1956: 27; "Bernstein & Welch," *Variety*, April 18, 1956: 28.

Page 238: **Shunned since his condemnation:** Thomas C. Reeves, *The Life and Times of Joe McCarthy* (New York: Stein and Day, 1982), 671–72.

Page 238: **"So quickly does malevolence:** "Senator McCarthy," *The Nation*, May 11, 1957: 401.

Page 238: **Having disappeared from:** Atypically reticent, the entertainment trade press mainly kept silent. Still loyal, entertainment reporter Mike Connolly ventured a single line: "There's probably dancing in Red Square today. Joe McCarthy was a great American and his death is a loss to all Americans." "Rambling Reporter," *Hollywood Reporter*, May 3, 1957: 2.

Page 239: **On June 28, 1962:** John Henry Faulk, *Fear on Trial* (New York: Simon and Schuster, 1964): 179. See also "Post-Faulk Talk: How Many Will Be the Wiser for Nizer Victory? And Will It Deter Future 'Witch Hunts'?" *Variety*, July 4, 1962: 65, 82.

Page 239: "In 1962 the blacklist: Stefan Kanfer, *A Journal of the Plague Years* (New York: Atheneum, 1973), 283.

Page 240: "In a business where: "Reginald Rose—Top Writer," *Variety*, April 13, 1955: 32. Also quoted in Frank Sturcken, *Live Television: The Golden Age of 1946–1958 in New York* (Jefferson, N.C.: McFarland, 1990), 90–93.

Page 240: "I am constantly amazed: Reginald Rose, *Six Television Plays* (New York: Simon and Schuster, 1956), x–xi. Text quotation from John P. Shanley, "An Original By Rose," *New York Times*, January 15, 1961: B13.

Page 241: "You've got to make sure: Ernest Kinoy, "Television's 'Blacklist' and Social Conscience," *New York Times*, January 12, 1964: B19.

Page 242: Far more controversial: "That CBS Abortion Program," *Variety*, May 2, 1962: 151.

Page 244: "Politically controversial talent: "Tele Follow-up Comment," *Variety*, January 22, 1964: 52.

Page 244: The definitive record: Jay Leyda, *Films Beget Films: A Study of the Compilation Film* (New York: Hill and Wang, 1964).

Page 244: A self-described "Marxist: Joseph McBride, "Documaker de Antonio Dead at 70; Attacked the System," *Variety*, December 27, 1989: 14.

Page 245: However, such was: Bill Greely, "CBS Alone Save McCarthy Films; Now Screen Hit, Web Accepts Bow," *Variety*, February 12, 1964: 38.

Page 245: The "actual hearings: Emile de Antonio, "The Point of View in *Point of Order*," *Film Comment* (Winter 1964): 35–36.

Page 245: Producer Talbot concurred: Daniel Talbot, "On Historic Hearings from TV to the Screen," *New York Times*, January 12, 1964: B7.

Page 246: "At the end of: Ronald Gold, "*Point of Order!*," *Motion Picture Herald*, February 19, 1964: 995.

Page 246: Befuddled by the notion: "*Point of Order!*" *Variety*, September 18, 1963: 6. The film premiered at the first New York Film Festival on September 14, 1963.

Page 246: Back in 1954: Marya Mannes, "Channels: 'Did or Not . . . ,'" *The Reporter*, June 8, 1954: 40.

Page 246: Yet the crowds flocking: Eugene Archer, "Point of Order a Surprise Hit; Belatedly Gets a Distributor," *New York Times*, February 11, 1964: 43.

Page 246: Calling *Point of Order!* "an obvious flop: "Roy Cohn Calls Reprise of McCarthy Hearings Unsalable, 'Obvious Flop,'" *Variety*, September 25, 1963: 1, 56.

Page 246: Just as Freud mapped: Marshall McLuhan, *Understanding Media: The Extensions of Man* (New York; McGraw Hill, 1964), 310, 309, 329.

12. Exhuming McCarthyism: The Paranoid Style in American Television

Page 250: "I saw the Anschluss: Kathy Pedell, "This Is Murrow . . . , " *TV Guide*, February 5, 1955: 4–7.

Page 250: The most famous mental: Richard Hofstadter, *The Paranoid Style in American Politics and Other Essays* (New York: Knopf, 1965), 3, 4, 5.

Page 251: **After all, class resentments:** *Meet the Press*, July 2, 1950; *Meet the Press*, June 3, 1951 (MPD-LOC).

Page 251: **After Hofstadter:** Fred J. Cook, *The Nightmare Decade: The Life and Times of Senator Joe McCarthy* (New York: Random House, 1971); Cedric Belfrage, *The American Inquisition, 1945–1960* (Indianapolis: Bobbs-Merrill, 1973); David Caute, *The Great Fear: The Anti-Communist Purge Under Truman and Eisenhower* (New York: Simon and Schuster, 1978).

Page 251: **"More than the House Committee:** J. Fred MacDonald, *Television and the Red Menace: The Video Road to Vietnam* (New York: Praeger, 1985), 49.

Page 252: **In *Scoundrel Time*:** Stephen J. Whitfield, *The Culture of the Cold War* (Baltimore: Johns Hopkins University Press, 1991), 104–106.

Page 253: **No moment better:** Addison Berrill, "Friedkin Classes Up Oscars But Feldman, Mailer Hit New Lows in Bad Taste; Hellman a Hit," *Variety*, March 30, 1977: 4, 7.

Page 254: **In February 1993:** The sensational charges by *Frontline* were drawn from Anthony Summers, *Official and Confidential: The Secret Life of J. Edgar Hoover* (New York: Putnam's, 1993), whose publication coincided with the telecast. The cross-dressing accusation is persuasively debunked in Athan Theoharis, *J. Edgar Hoover, Sex, and Crime: An Historical Antidote* (Chicago: Ivan R. Dee, 1995).

Page 256: **"Hasn't it?" she responds:** *Tail Gunner Joe* opens with a lie; three hours later it closes with a lie," fumed Roy Cohn, who reissued his 1968 memoir of McCarthy in paperback under the title *McCarthy: The Answer to "Tail Gunner Joe."* Roy Cohn, *McCarthy: The Answer to "Tail Gunner Joe"* (New York: Manor Books, 1977).

Page 258 (note 3): **On the other hand:** Oliver Pilat, "Blacklist," *New York Post*, January 30, 1953: 20.

Page 258 **However, the most famous:** "Some Fissures in 'Fear on Trial,' 2 Decades after L'Affaire Faulk," *Variety*, October 8, 1975: 56.

Page 258: **Typical was an *ABC News Close Up*:** *ABC News Close Up*, June 23, 1983, viewed at the Vanderbilt Television News Archive, Vanderbilt University, Nashville, Tennessee.

INDEX

Note: Page numbers in **bold** indicate an illustration. Initial articles (e.g., *An, The*) are ignored in sorting.